Praise for

Wake

"Powerful . . . *Wake* is operating in the wake of slavery, and in a state of being awake to the past, a process Hall frames as both devastating and grounding."
—*New York Times Book Review*

"Hall's eloquence and frank emotionalism are transcendently realized in [Martínez's] art, beckoning the reader inexorably into this story—even the parts that only take place inside Hall's mind. With its remarkable blend of passion and fact, action and reflection, *Wake* sets a new standard for illustrating history."
—NPR

"In this beautiful and moving graphic novel, historian Rebecca Hall unearths a history so often overlooked: the significant role Black women played in leading slave revolts. Through Hugo Martínez's vivid graphics, combined with Hall's brilliant insights and powerful storytelling, *Wake* transports the reader to a moment in time when a group of Black women set out to overturn the institution of slavery in British North America. Their courageous story, told with remarkable skill and elegance, offers hope and inspiration for us all."
—Keisha N. Blain, coeditor of the #1 *New York Times* bestseller *Four Hundred Souls* and award-winning author of *Set the World on Fire: Black Nationalist Women and the Global Struggle for Freedom*

"Some things that are nearly impossible to prove still need to be known. To this problem, the creativity of Black Studies provides an often urgent, elegant solution. And to this solution, with Rebecca Hall's graphic novel, *Wake: The Hidden History of Women-Led Slave Revolts*, adds comics. . . . *Wake* accomplishes what the best work in Black Studies aims to do: not just to teach us something new, but to teach us how the very shape of our knowledge could be different."
—*Los Angeles Review of Books*

"Not only a riveting tale of Black women's leadership of slave revolts but an equally dramatic story of the engaged scholarship that enabled its discovery."

—Angela Y. Davis, political activist and professor emerita,
History of Consciousness and Feminist Studies
Departments, UC Santa Cruz

"A vividly illustrated account of Black women rebels that combines elements of memoir, archival research, and informed imaginings of its subjects' lives . . . An urgent, brilliant work of historical excavation."

—*Kirkus Reviews* (starred review)

"*Wake* is a revelation. Rebecca Hall's prose intersects with Hugo Martínez's beautiful woodcut-styled illustrations to show the power of visual narratives and hearkens back to graphic masters like Lynd Ward and Frans Masereel. The stark play of light and dark in Martínez's work is a powerful index for the spiritually surreal and transcendent energy in every panel. Hall's writing cleverly flows between the reality of her research on Black women–led slave revolts and speculative imaginings that uncover the spectrum of human experience and resilience."

—John Jennings, Eisner Award–winning illustrator of
Octavia Butler's *Kindred* and
Parable of the Sower graphic novels

"Heartbreaking yet triumphant, Hall's vivid reconstructions bore laser-like into a history long hidden. Her engaged scholarship adds back facts that have been stricken from many histories, and it empowers current lives and activism. Highly recommended for educators and for all adults and teens concerned about the United States' promise, past, and future for its diverse peoples."

—*Library Journal* (starred review)

"Hall's nuanced and affecting debut graphic narrative uncovers history that has either been assumed non-existent or rendered violently so by its almost complete erasure from official record. . . . The story follows Hall as she strives to write her dissertation on women-led slave revolts. . . . Hall's singular look at these women, along with her own experiences and resilience, [highlights] how entwined the past and present really are. Martínez's resonant black-and-white art cleverly integrates historical scenes into the present-day narrative."

—*Publishers Weekly* (starred review)

"Martínez's dramatic woodcut-style illustrations are the perfect complement to Hall's clear-eyed, impactful storytelling. . . . A necessary corrective to violent erasure and a tribute to untold strength, this awe-inspiring collaboration should find a wide audience."

—*Booklist* (starred review)

"Hall and Martínez connect the past and the present in a moving and exciting narrative that brings to light the history of slavery in the United States. Showing how enslaved women resisted slavery, even though their participation in rebellions remains largely absent from written records, *Wake* will be a crucial tool to introduce students to the problematic nature of slavery primary sources."

—Ana Lucia Araujo, professor of history, Howard University

"Hall and Martínez deserve tremendous credit for their work in making this research accessible. *Wake* is a superb accomplishment on every level, and a book that every American needs to read."

—POPMATTERS

"In *Wake*, Rebecca Hall and Hugo Martínez use the graphic medium to stunning effect. More than just a history, *Wake* is a meaningful engagement with a living past. Read this book slowly. Savor the visual metaphors. Let them take you back in time while Hall's narration pins you to the uncomfortable present. Make your reading a shared journey with friends or classmates who can help you uncover the deep meanings and cope with the emotions it raises. This book will haunt you the way that the legacies of slavery haunt this country."

—Trevor Getz, professor of African and world history
and author of *Abina and the Important Men:
A Graphic History*

"*Wake*'s text is spare, informed, tuned to vibrating feeling and thought about historical and contemporary Black women's agency and actions in resistance and rebellion. As powerful as the text are the astonishing graphics. Reading, I was drawn into frame after frame of graphic action and evocative description. These drawings brought me to tears, recognition, fury, gratitude, solidarity. In both pain and joy in struggle, Hall gives her readers 'ancestry in progress.' Consequences flow from living in the wake, admitting the haunting power of histories."

—Donna Haraway, professor emerita, History of Consciousness
and Feminist Studies Departments, UC Santa Cruz

"A lot of Black history is uncelebrated narratives, but even within that history there are narratives that are especially overlooked; these tend to be the stories of Black women. Rebecca Hall's diligent research and intelligent storytelling has flipped that script to celebrate the brave enslaved Black women who fought and died for their freedom with dignity. Hugo Martínez's expressive art brings these women to vivid life on the page."

—Joel Christian Gill, author of *Strange Fruit*
and *Fights: One Boy's Triumph over Violence*

"We that live in the wake of centuries of white supremacy feel the hidden history of our ancestors' struggle to survive uncovered in this book. In its pages we not only feel their sorrow in bondage, but also their elation when they finally broke free."

—Ben Passmore, author of *Your Black Friend*

"Rebecca Hall has done something quite important in *Wake: The Hidden History of Women-Led Slave Revolts*. She makes accessible the historians' craft in the service of telling the powerful stories of women-led slave revolts. With the moving illustrations of Hugo Martínez and the impressive storytelling of Hall, we are transported into 1712, 1708, and the four-hundred-year history of the Black Atlantic, gaining a deeper sense of women-led uprisings. Mincing no words, Hall captures the fierceness of Black women's resistance. Infusing the text with her personal story and a sharp historical imagination, Hall never waivers in giving life to this history. She lifts the veil on enslaved women's leadership in the relentless pursuit of freedom. She brings into the present stories that must be read and passed on."

—Rose M. Brewer, professor, University of Minnesota Twin Cities

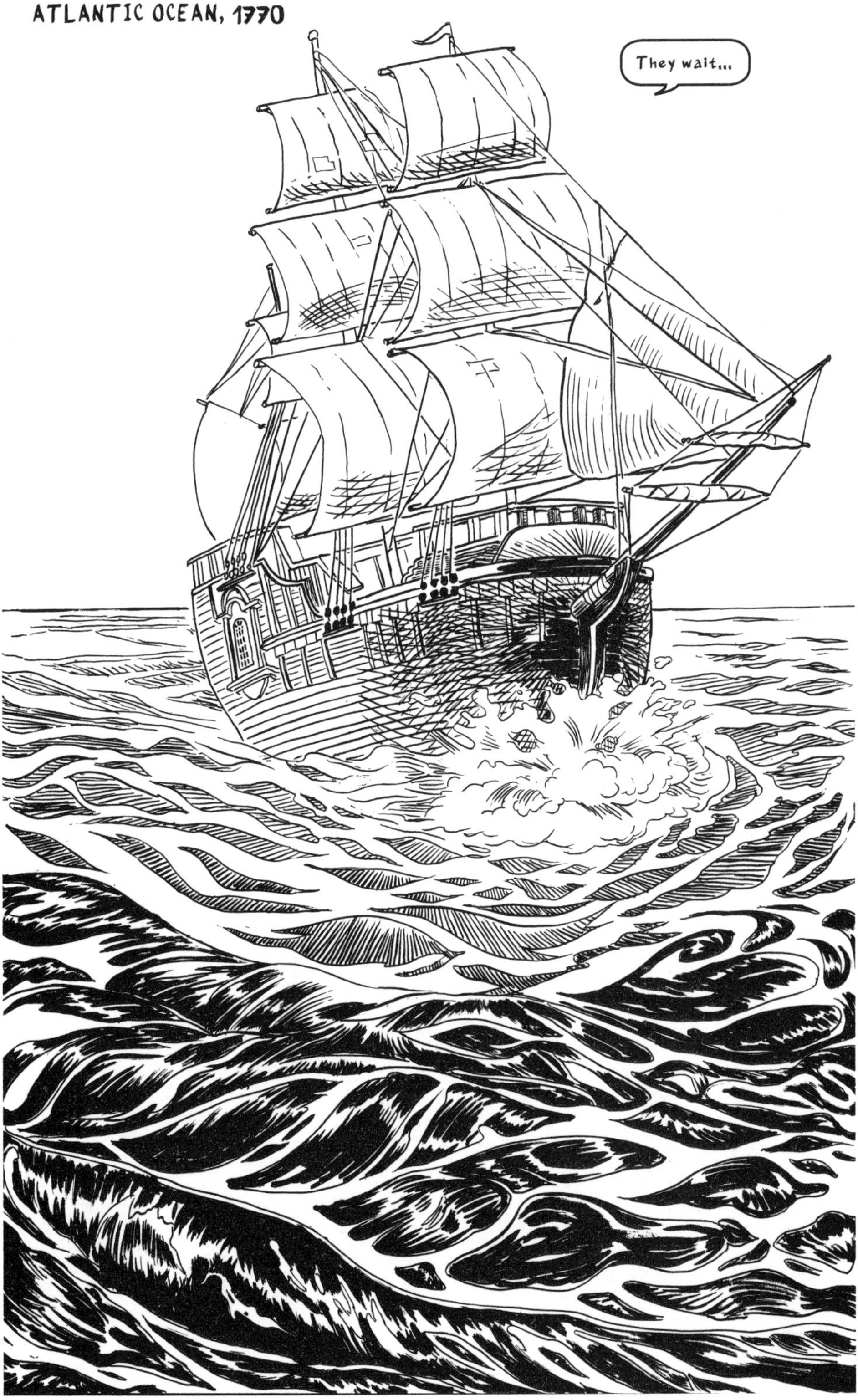
ATLANTIC OCEAN, 1770
They wait...

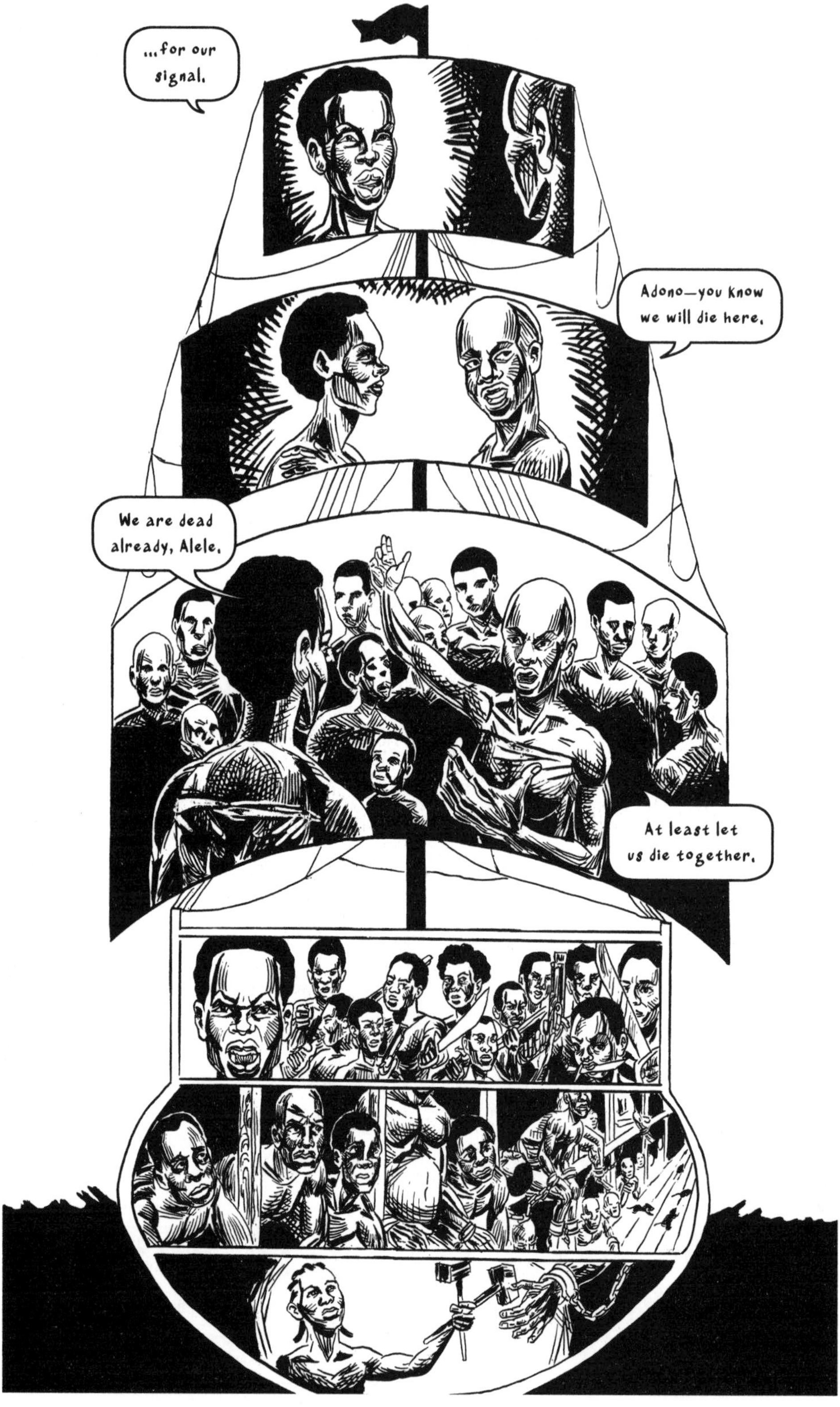
...for our signal.
Adono—you know we will die here.
We are dead already, Alele.
At least let us die together.

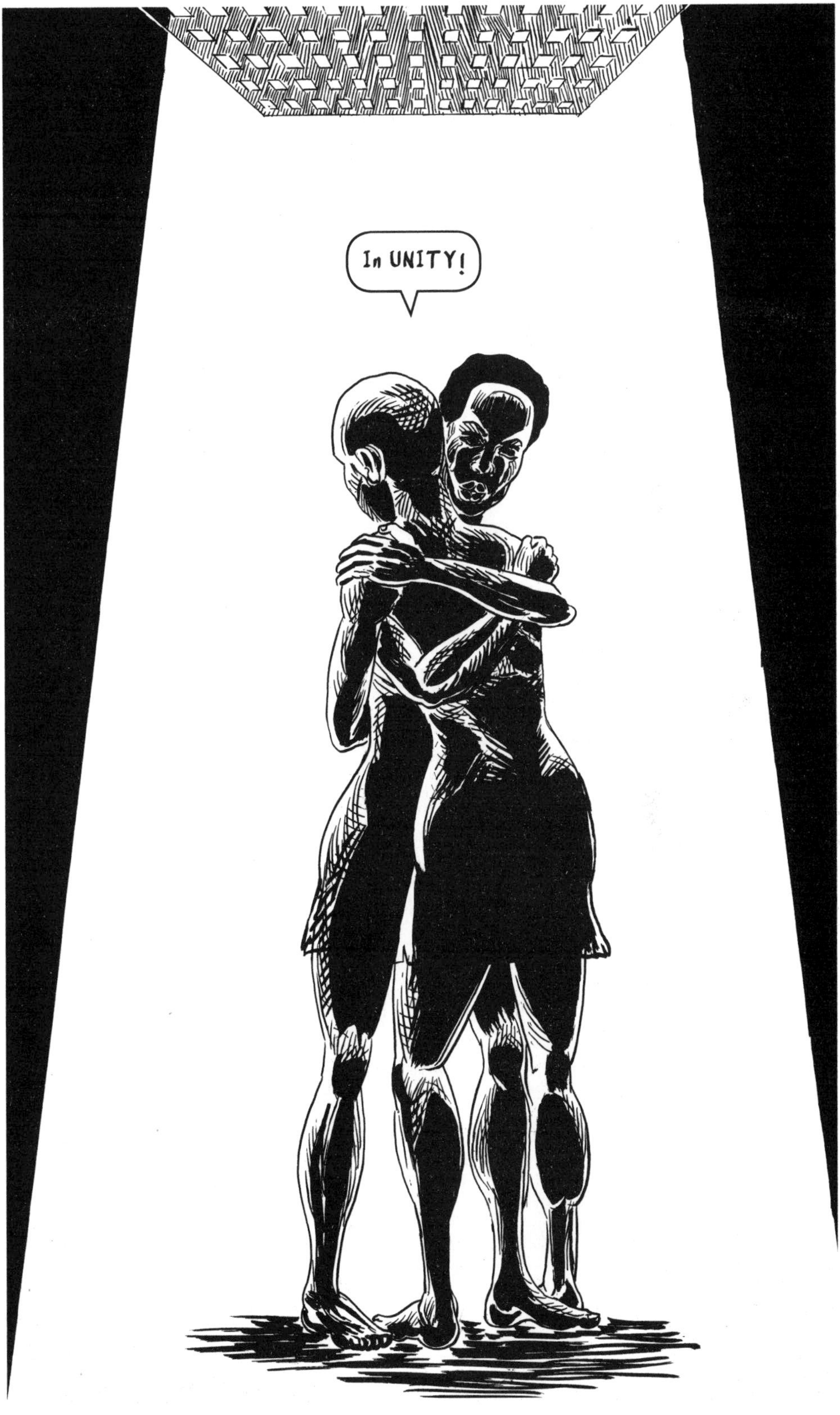
In UNITY!

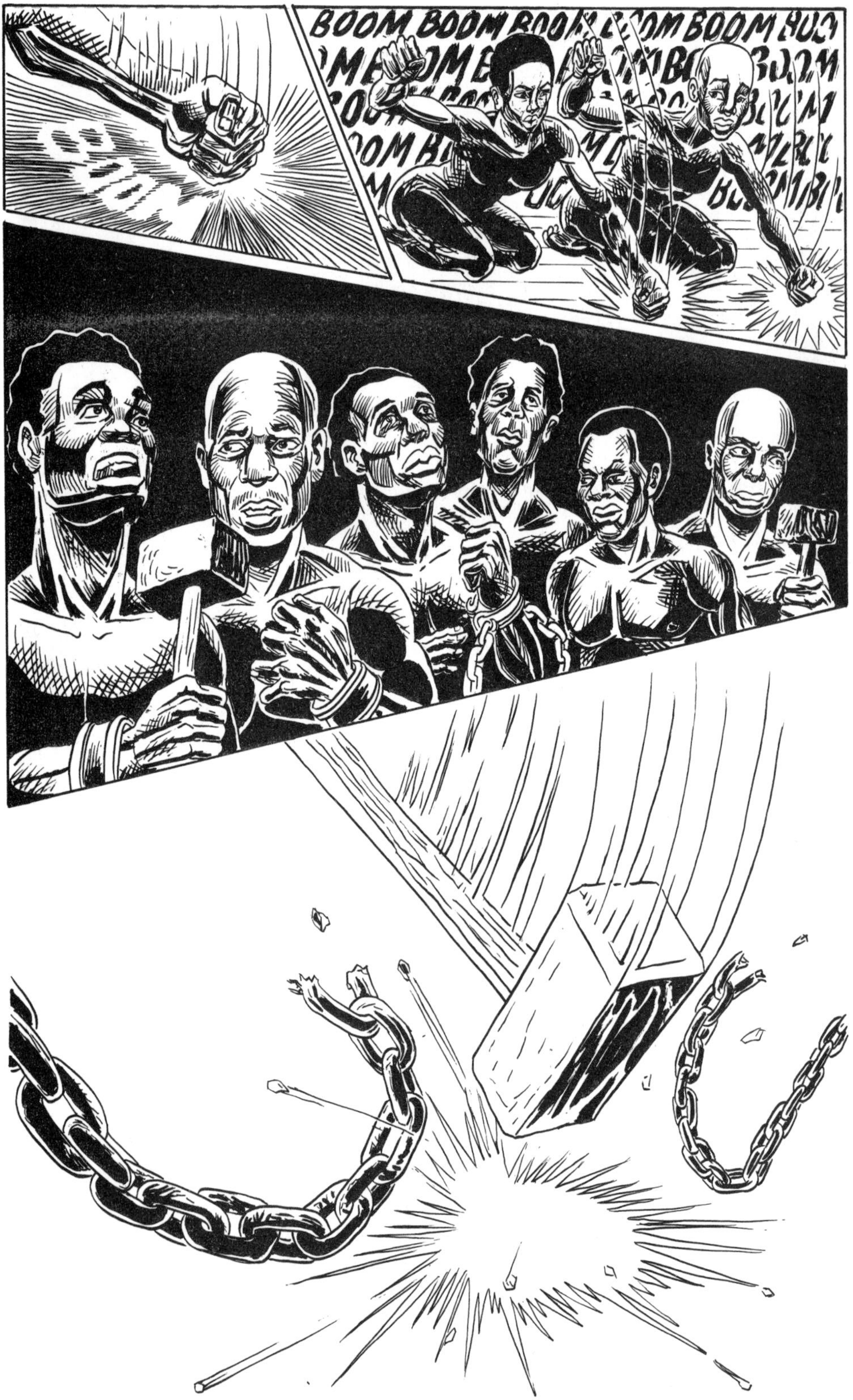
BOOM BOOM BOOM BOOM BOOM

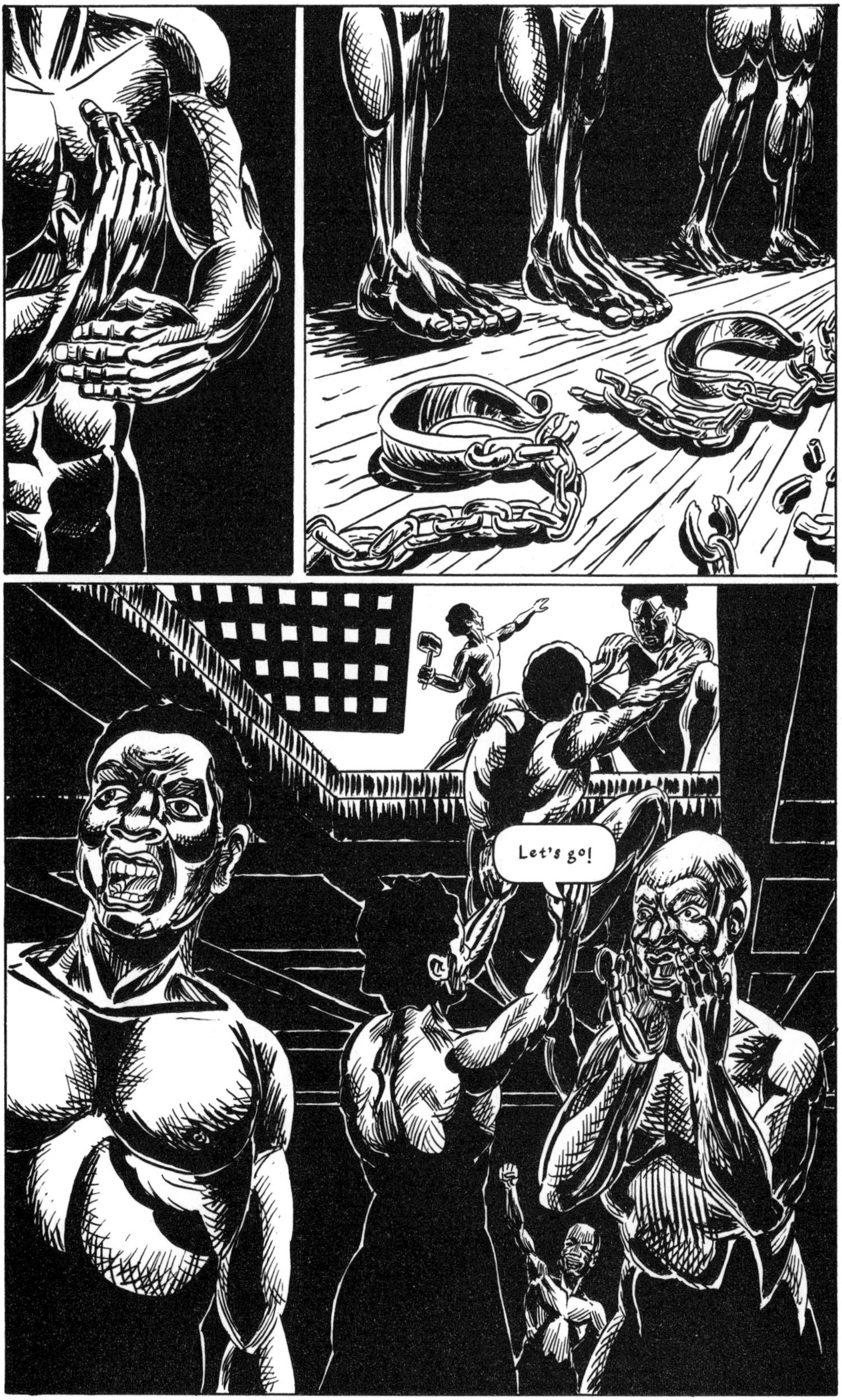
Let's go!

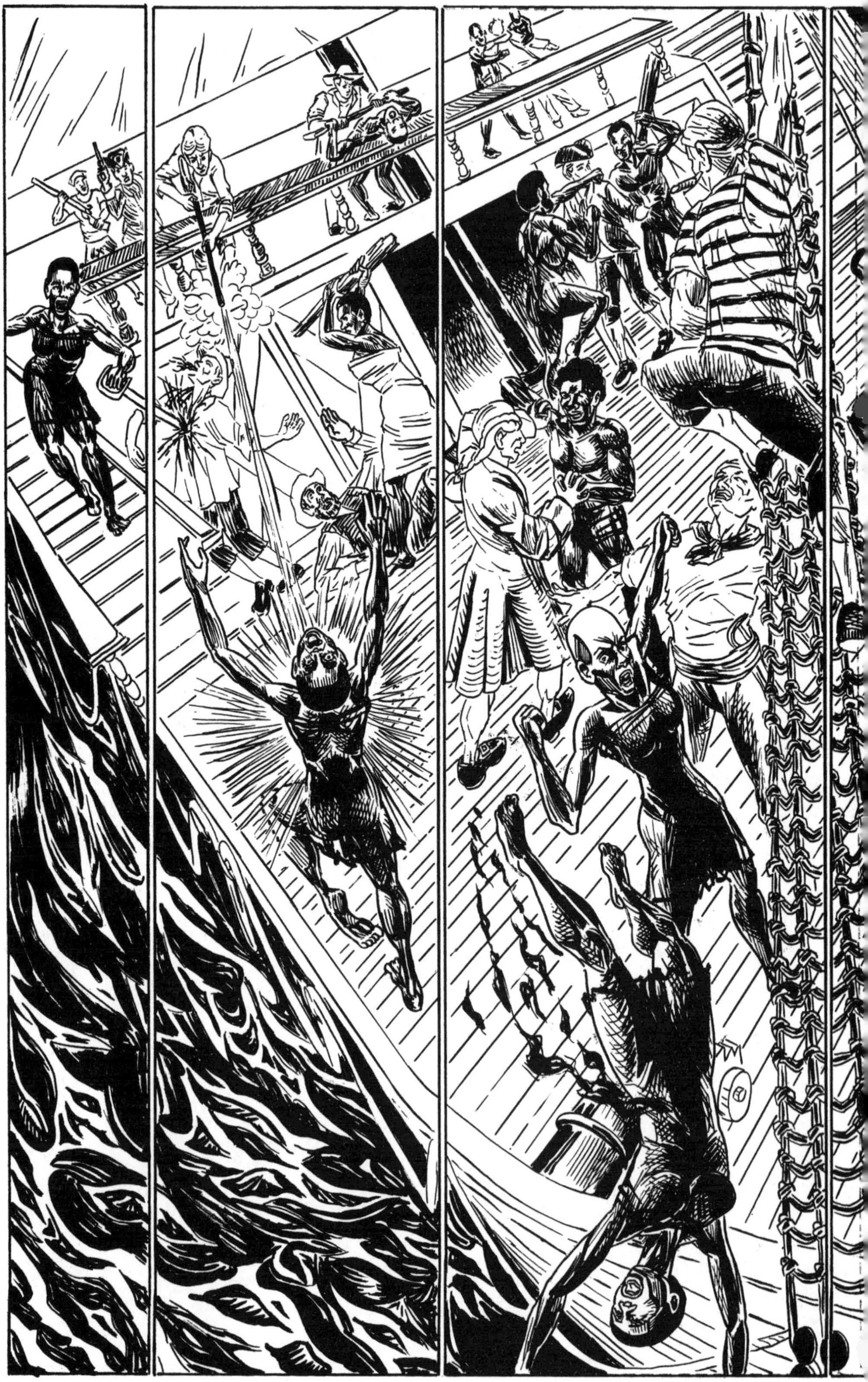

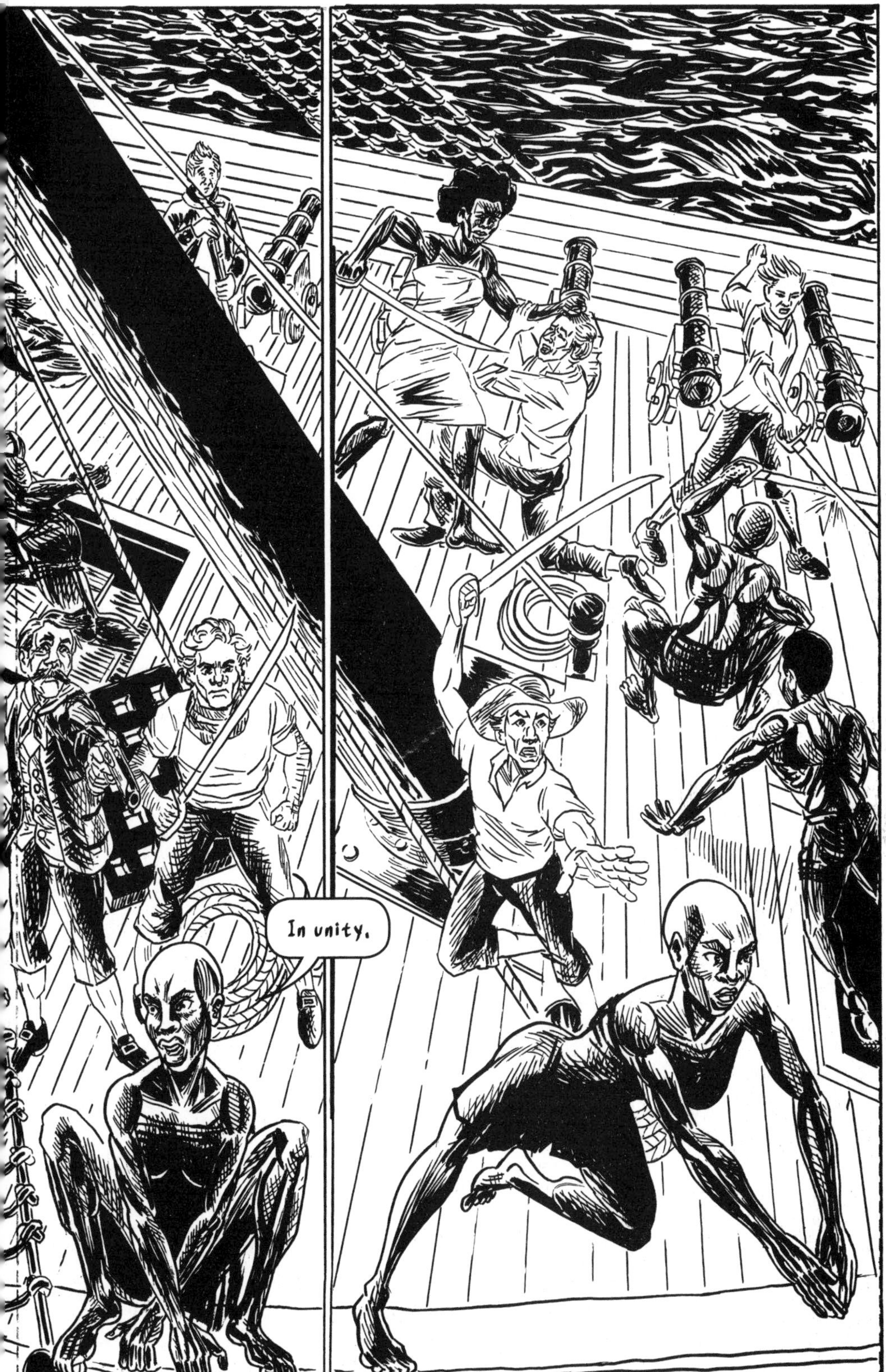
In unity.

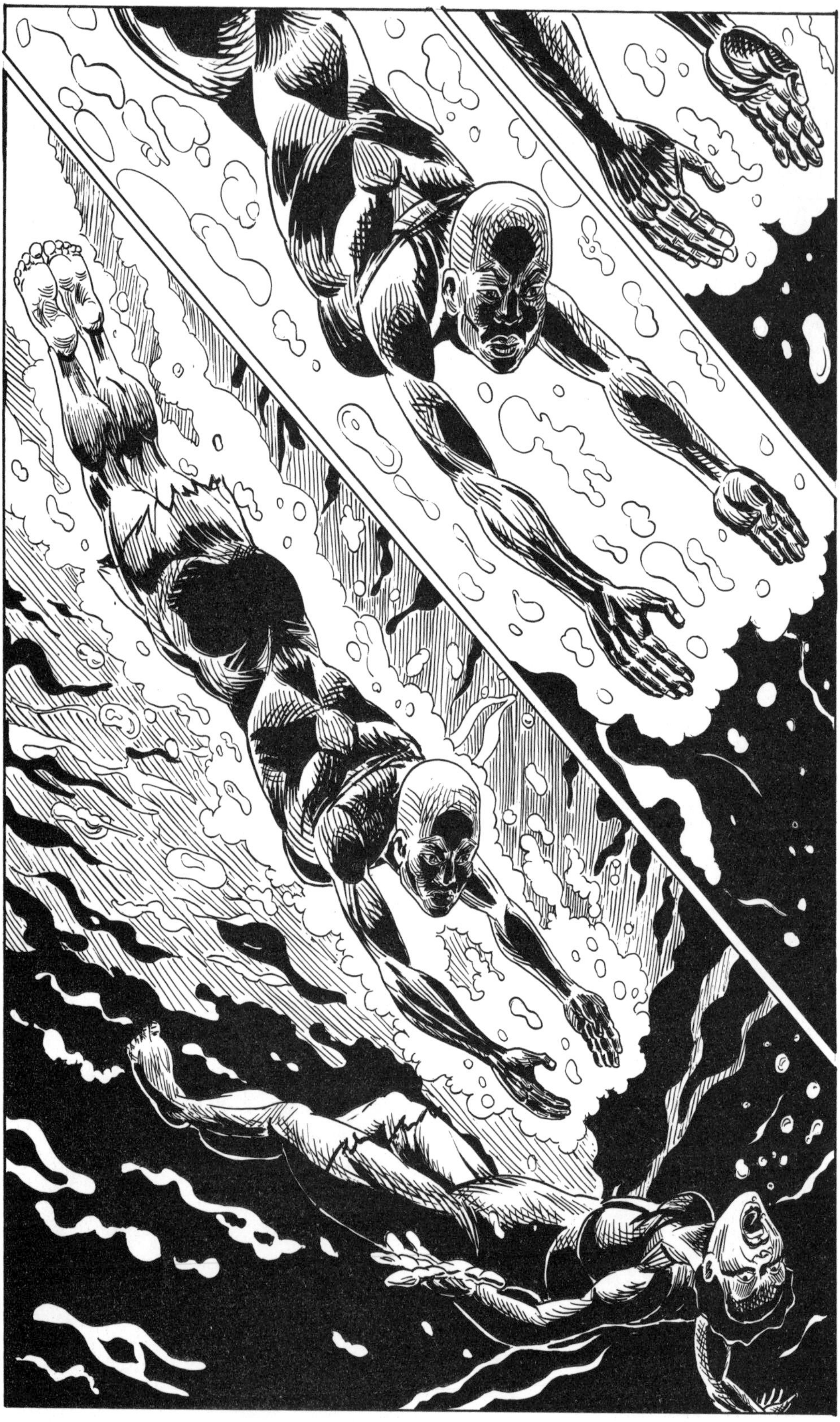

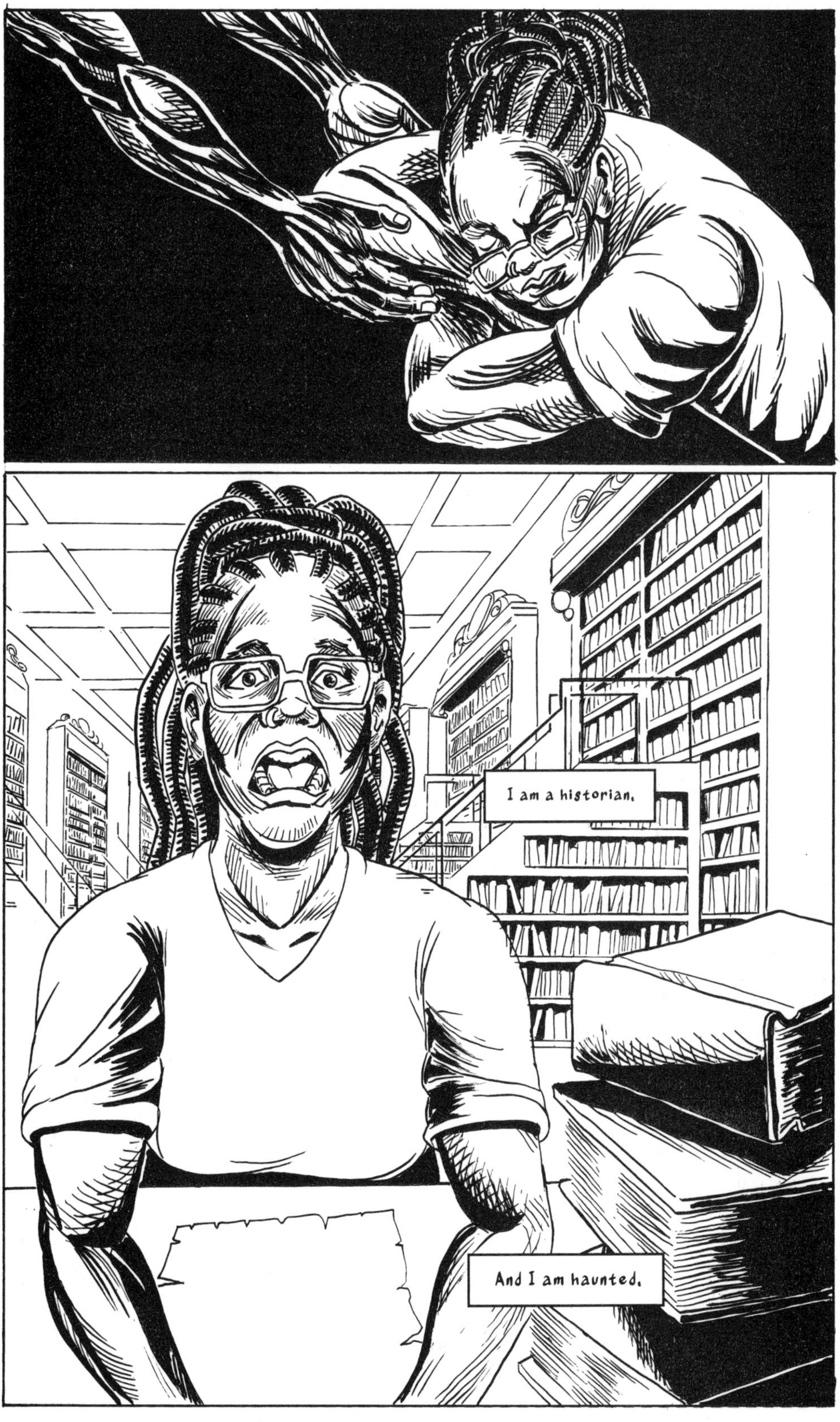
I am a historian.
And I am haunted.

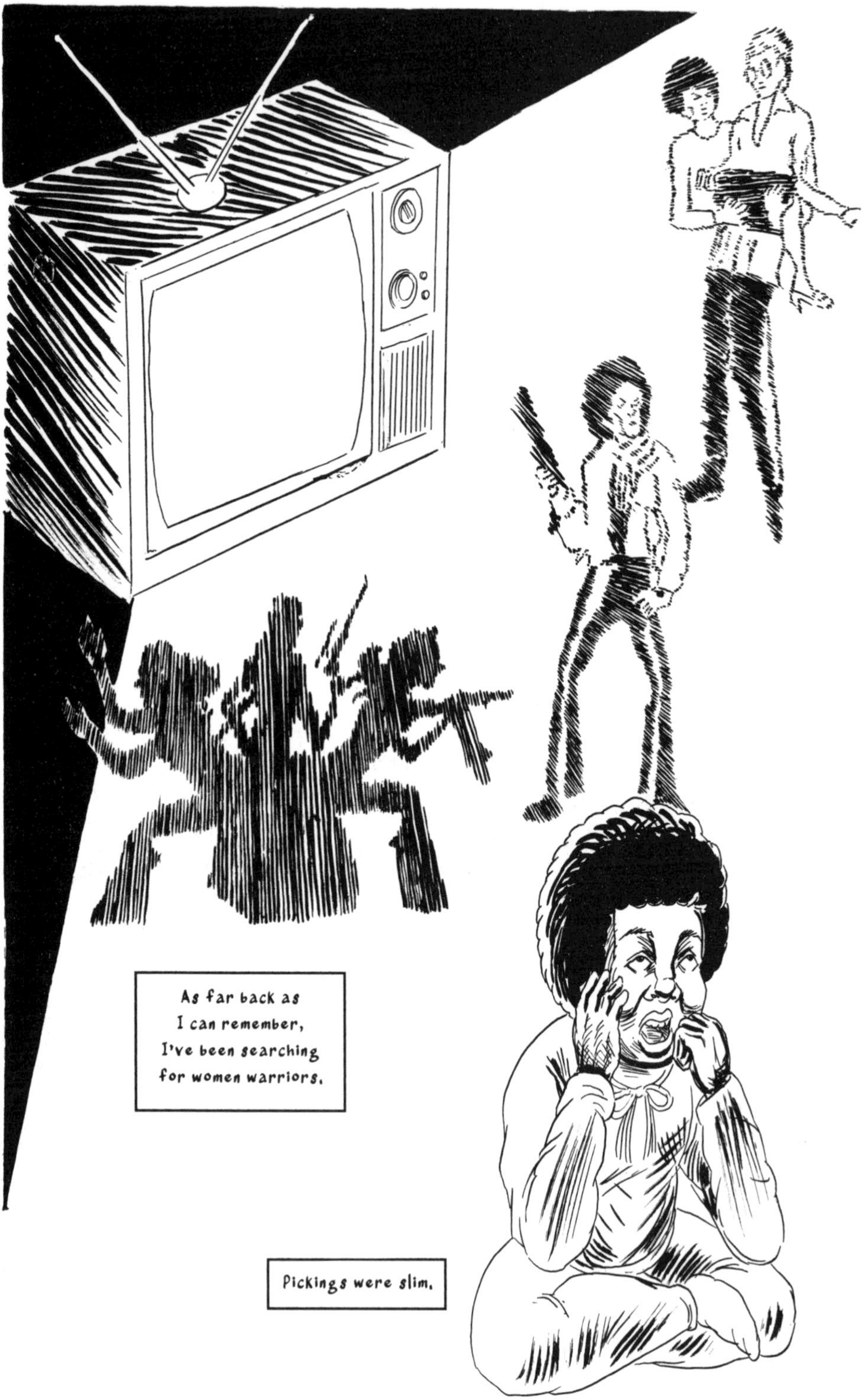
As far back as
I can remember,
I've been searching
for women warriors.
Pickings were slim.

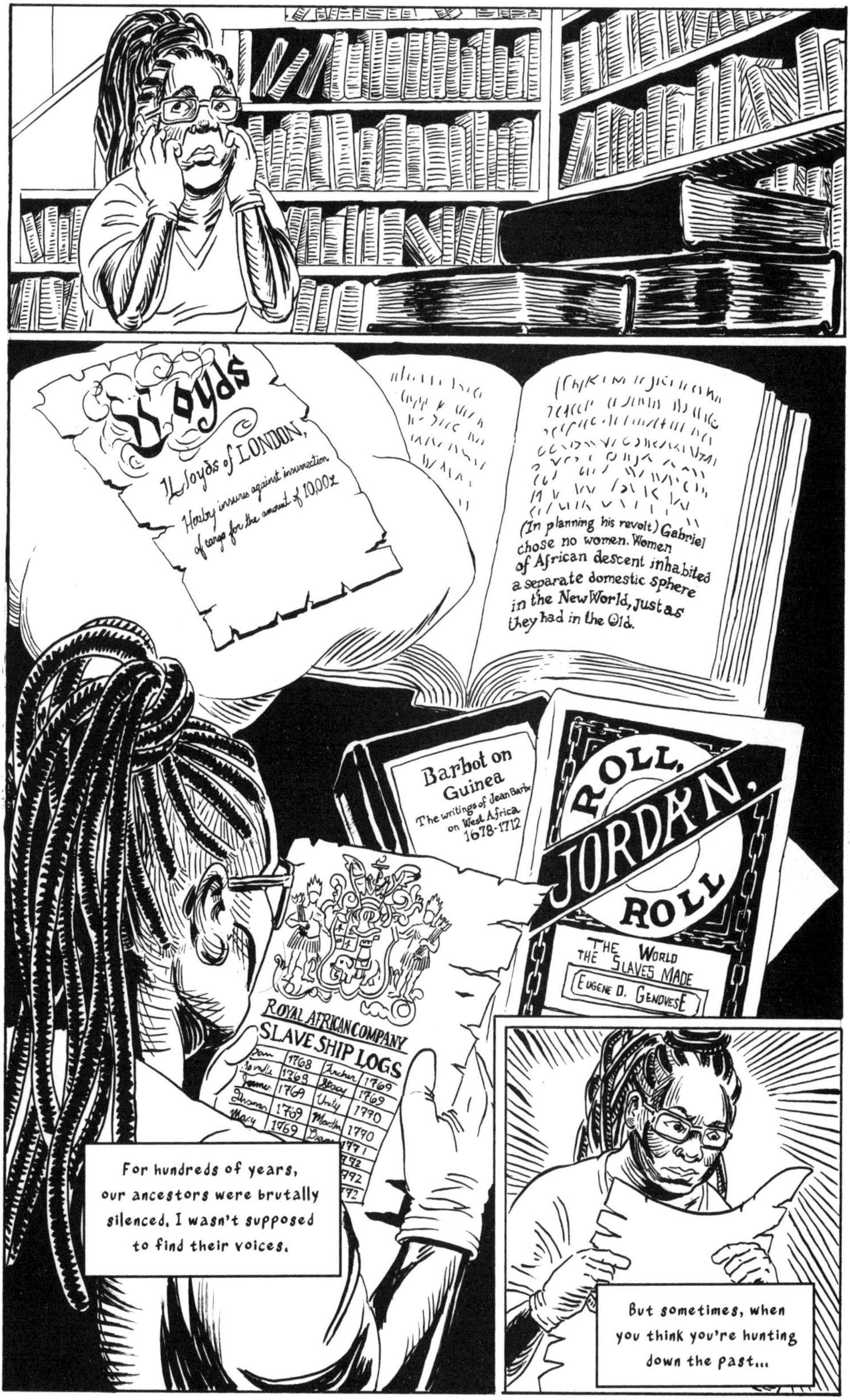
Lloyds
Lloyds of LONDON,
Hereby insures against insurrection of cargo for the amount of 10,00£
(In planning his revolt) Gabriel chose no women. Women of African descent inhabited a separate domestic sphere in the New World, just as they had in the Old.
Barbot on Guinea
The writings of Jean Barbo on West Africa 1678-1712
ROLL, JORDAN, ROLL
THE WORLD THE SLAVES MADE
EUGENE D. GENOVESE
ROYAL AFRICAN COMPANY
SLAVE SHIP LOGS
For hundreds of years, our ancestors were brutally silenced. I wasn't supposed to find their voices.
But sometimes, when you think you're hunting down the past...

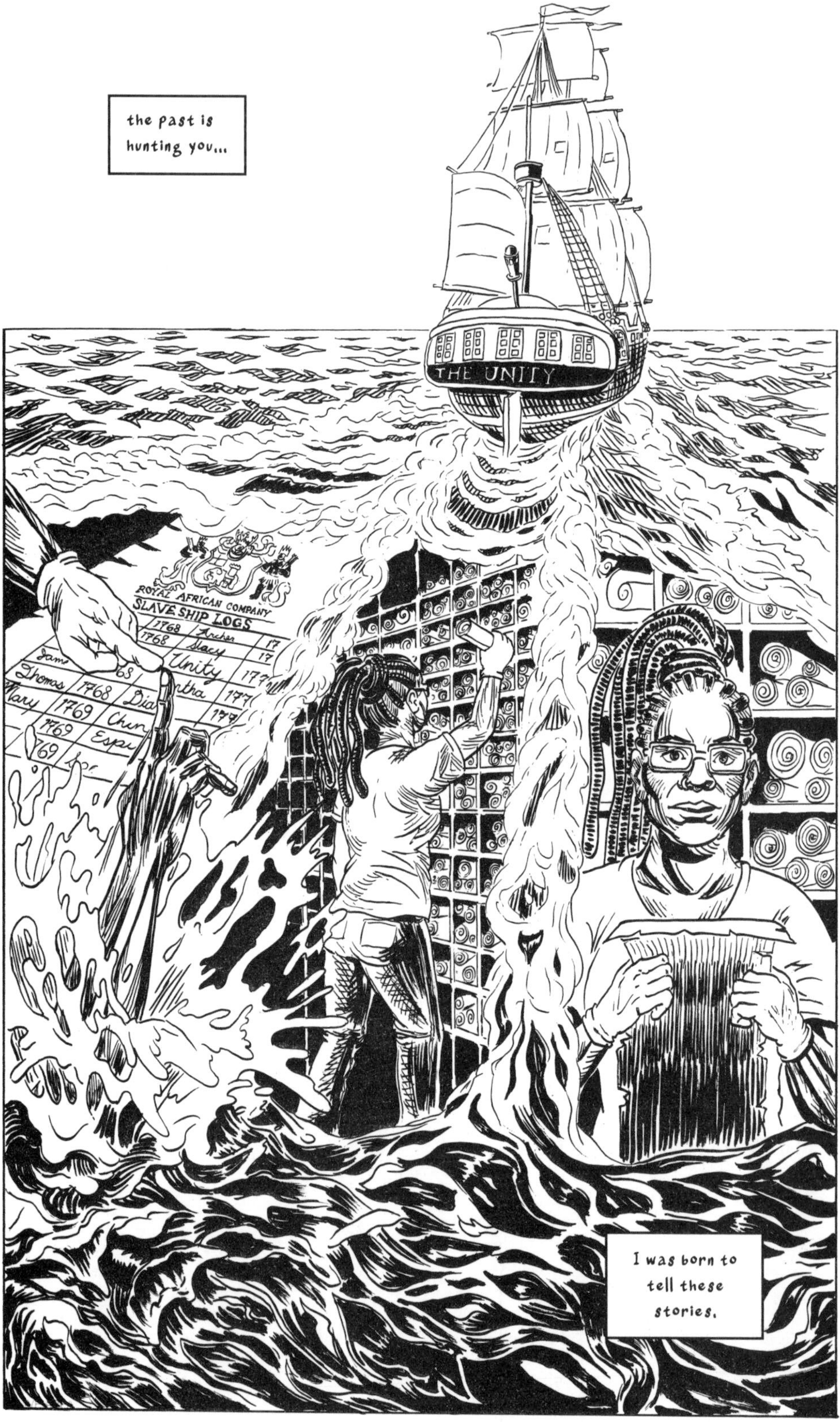
the past is hunting you...
THE UNITY
ROYAL AFRICAN COMPANY
SLAVE SHIP LOGS
1768 Archer
1768 Stacy
Unity
Thomas 1768
Mary 1769
I was born to tell these stories.

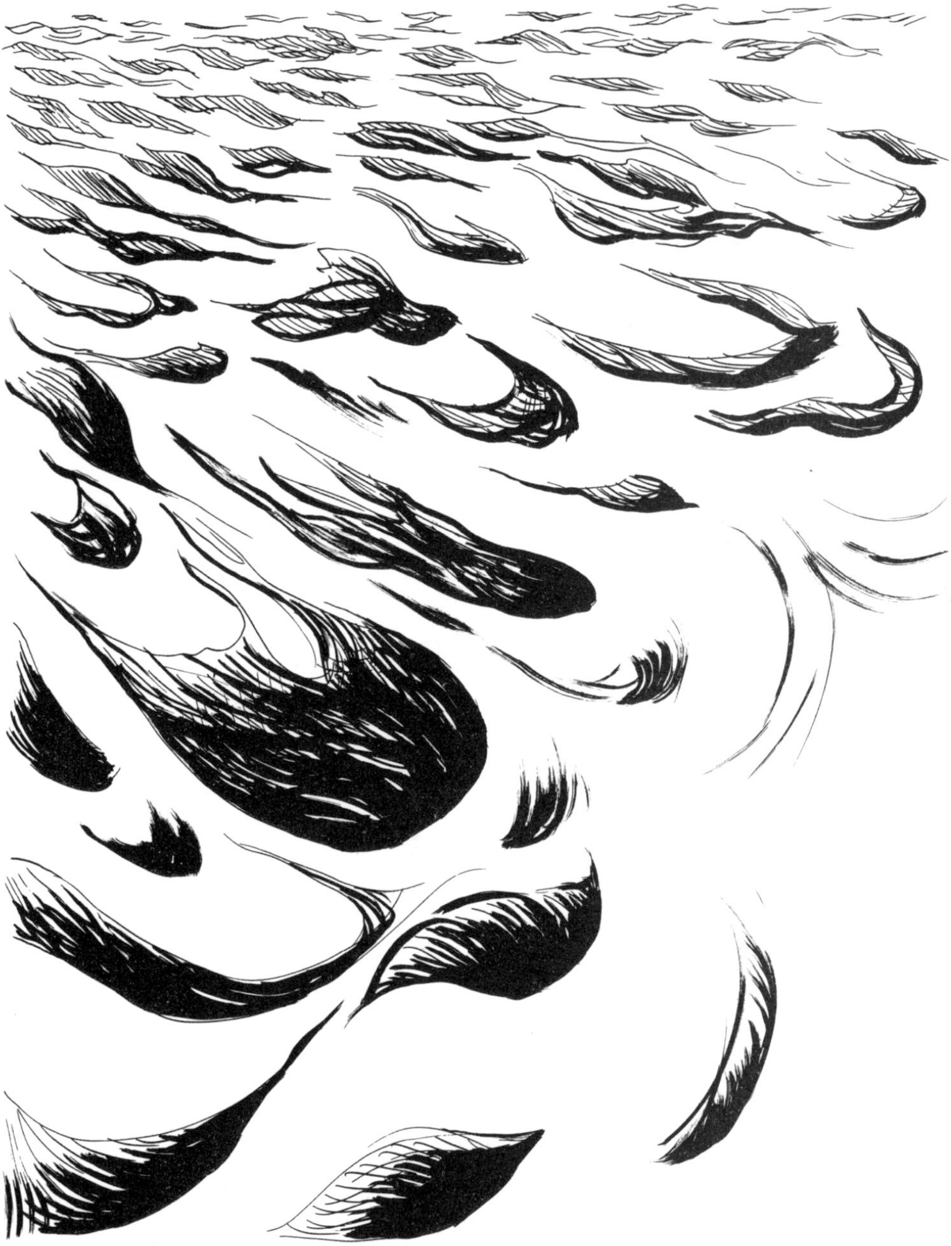

WAKE

The Hidden History of Women-Led Slave Revolts

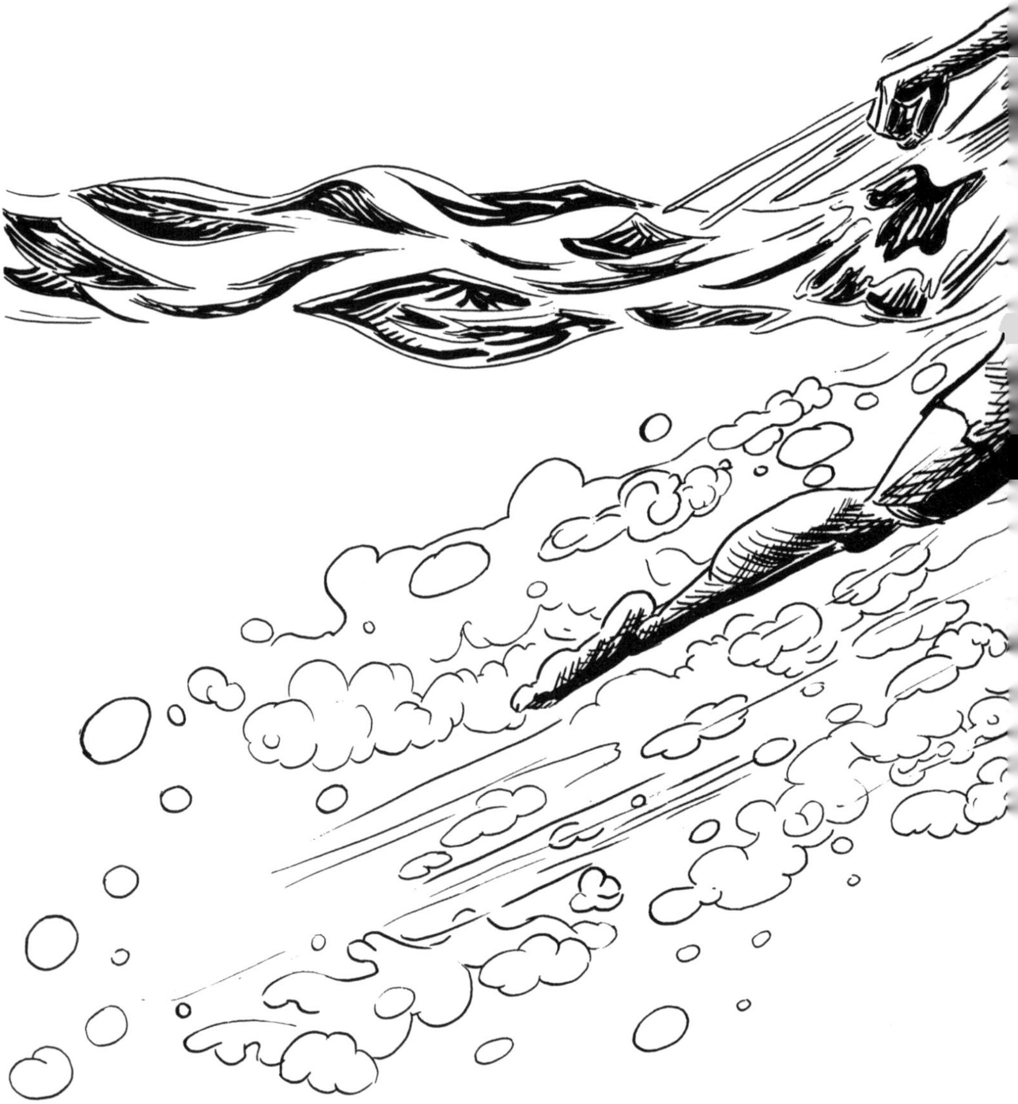

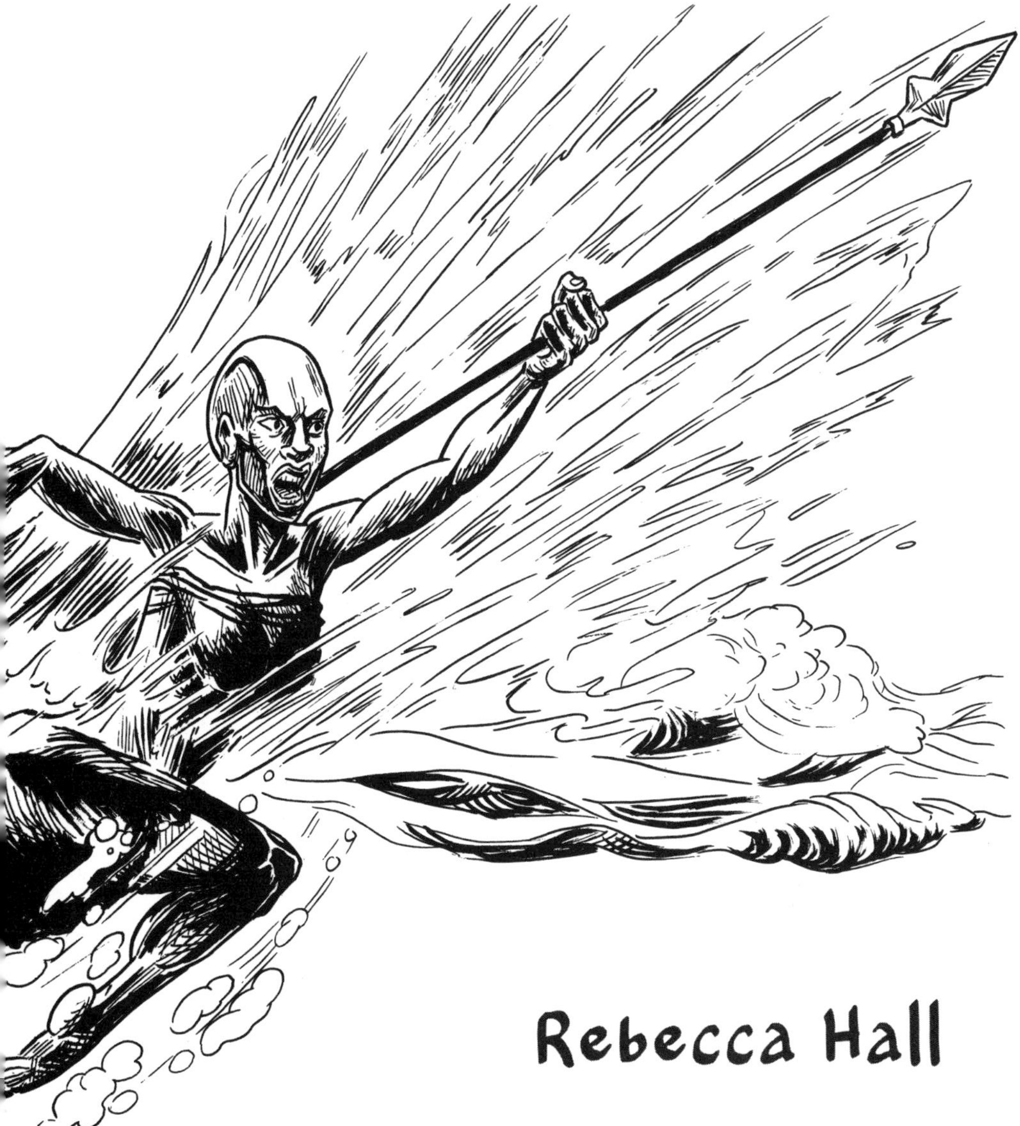

Rebecca Hall

Illustrated by
Hugo Martinez

Lettered by Sarula Bao

Simon & Schuster Paperbacks
NEW YORK LONDON TORONTO SYDNEY NEW DELHI

Simon & Schuster Paperbacks
An Imprint of Simon & Schuster, Inc.
1230 Avenue of the Americas
New York, NY 10020

This Simon & Schuster trade paperback edition June 2022

SIMON & SCHUSTER and colophon are trademarks
of Simon & Schuster, Inc.

For information about special discounts for bulk purchases,
please contact Simon & Schuster Special Sales at 1-866-506-1949
or business@simonandschuster.com.

The Simon & Schuster Speakers Bureau can bring authors to your
live event. For more information or to book an event, contact the
Simon & Schuster Speakers Bureau at 1-866-248-3049
or visit our website at www.simonspeakers.com.

Manufactured in the United States of America

10 9 8 7 6 5 4 3 2 1

Library of Congress Cataloging-in-Publication Data has been applied for.

ISBN 978-1-9821-1518-0
ISBN 978-1-9821-1519-7 (pbk)
ISBN 978-1-9821-1520-3 (ebook)

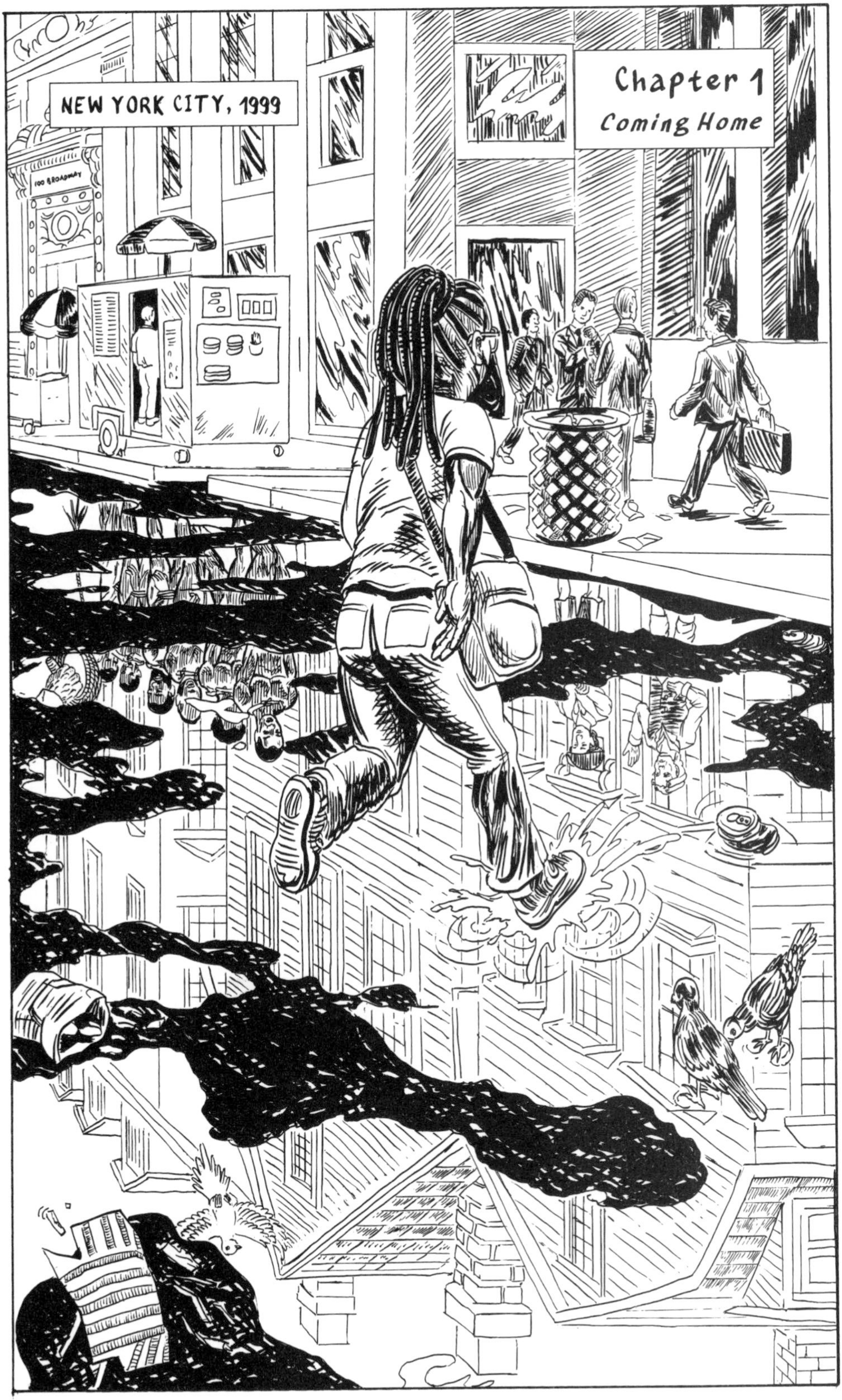
NEW YORK CITY, 1999
Chapter 1
Coming Home
100 BROADWAY

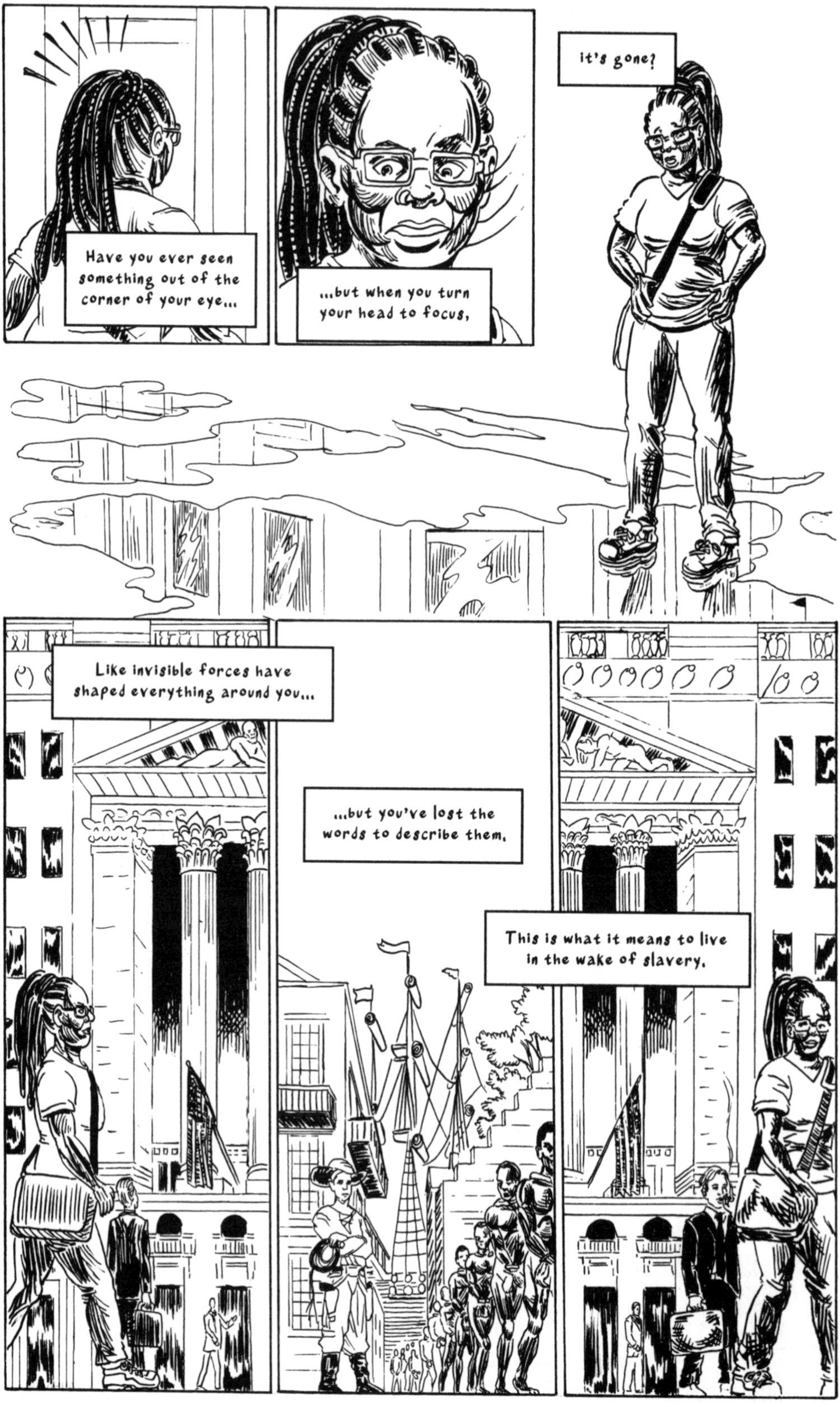
Have you ever seen something out of the corner of your eye...
...but when you turn your head to focus,
it's gone?
Like invisible forces have shaped everything around you...
...but you've lost the words to describe them.
This is what it means to live in the wake of slavery.

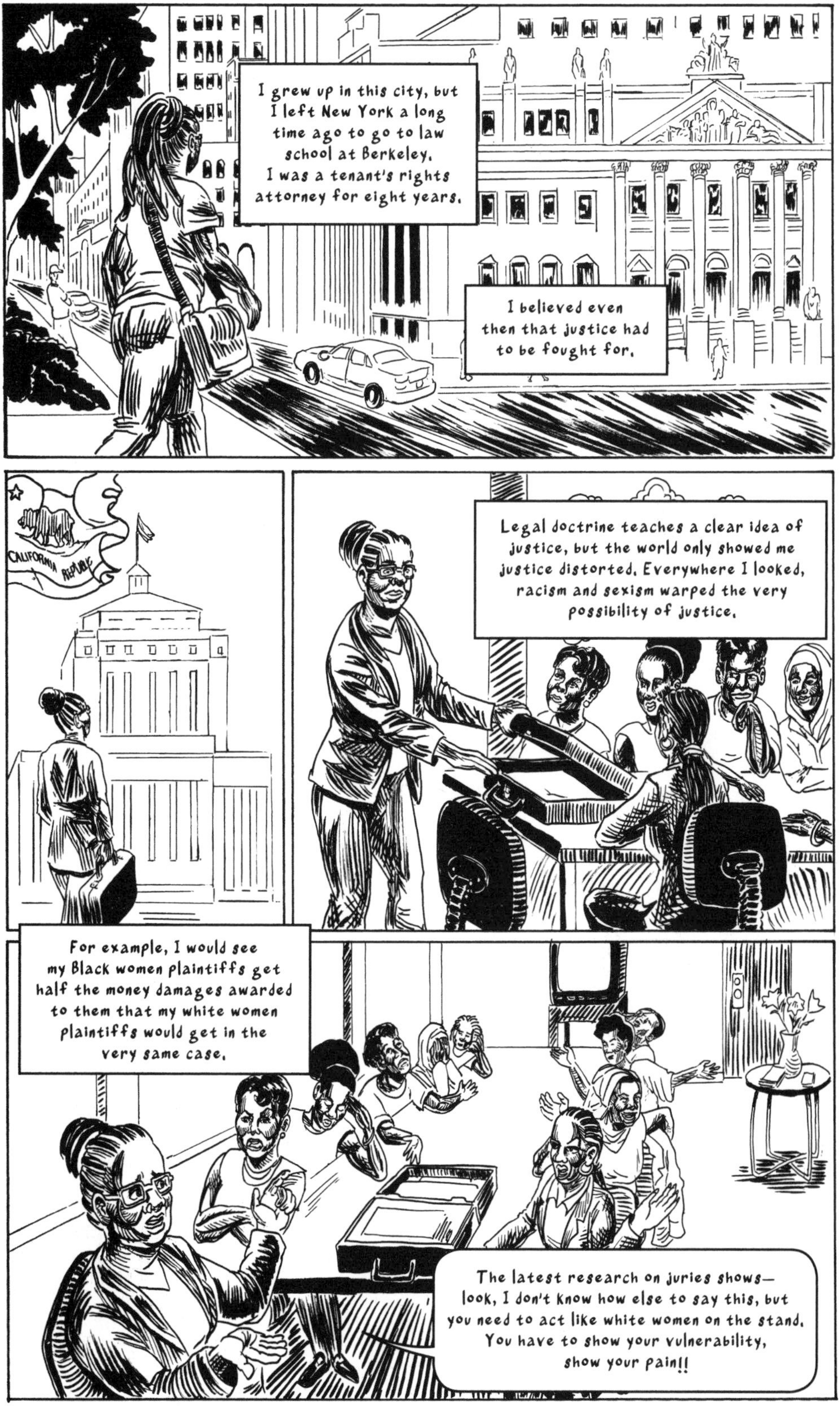
I grew up in this city, but I left New York a long time ago to go to law school at Berkeley. I was a tenant's rights attorney for eight years.
I believed even then that justice had to be fought for.
CALIFORNIA REPUBLIC
Legal doctrine teaches a clear idea of justice, but the world only showed me justice distorted. Everywhere I looked, racism and sexism warped the very possibility of justice.
For example, I would see my Black women plaintiffs get half the money damages awarded to them that my white women plaintiffs would get in the very same case.
The latest research on juries shows—look, I don't know how else to say this, but you need to act like white women on the stand. You have to show your vulnerability, show your pain!!

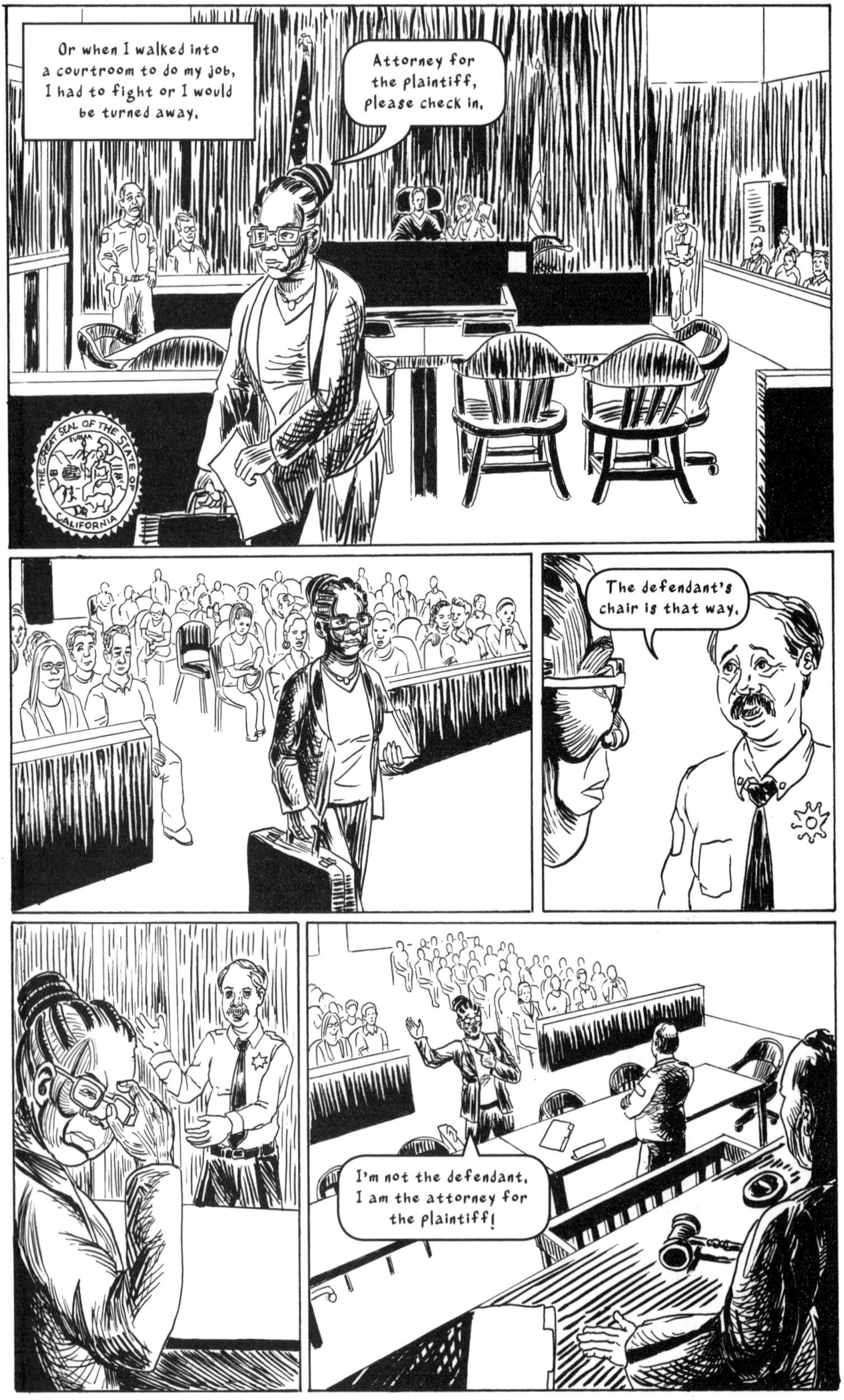
Or when I walked into a courtroom to do my job, I had to fight or I would be turned away.
Attorney for the plaintiff, please check in.
THE GREAT SEAL OF THE STATE OF CALIFORNIA
The defendant's chair is that way.
I'm not the defendant. I am the attorney for the plaintiff!

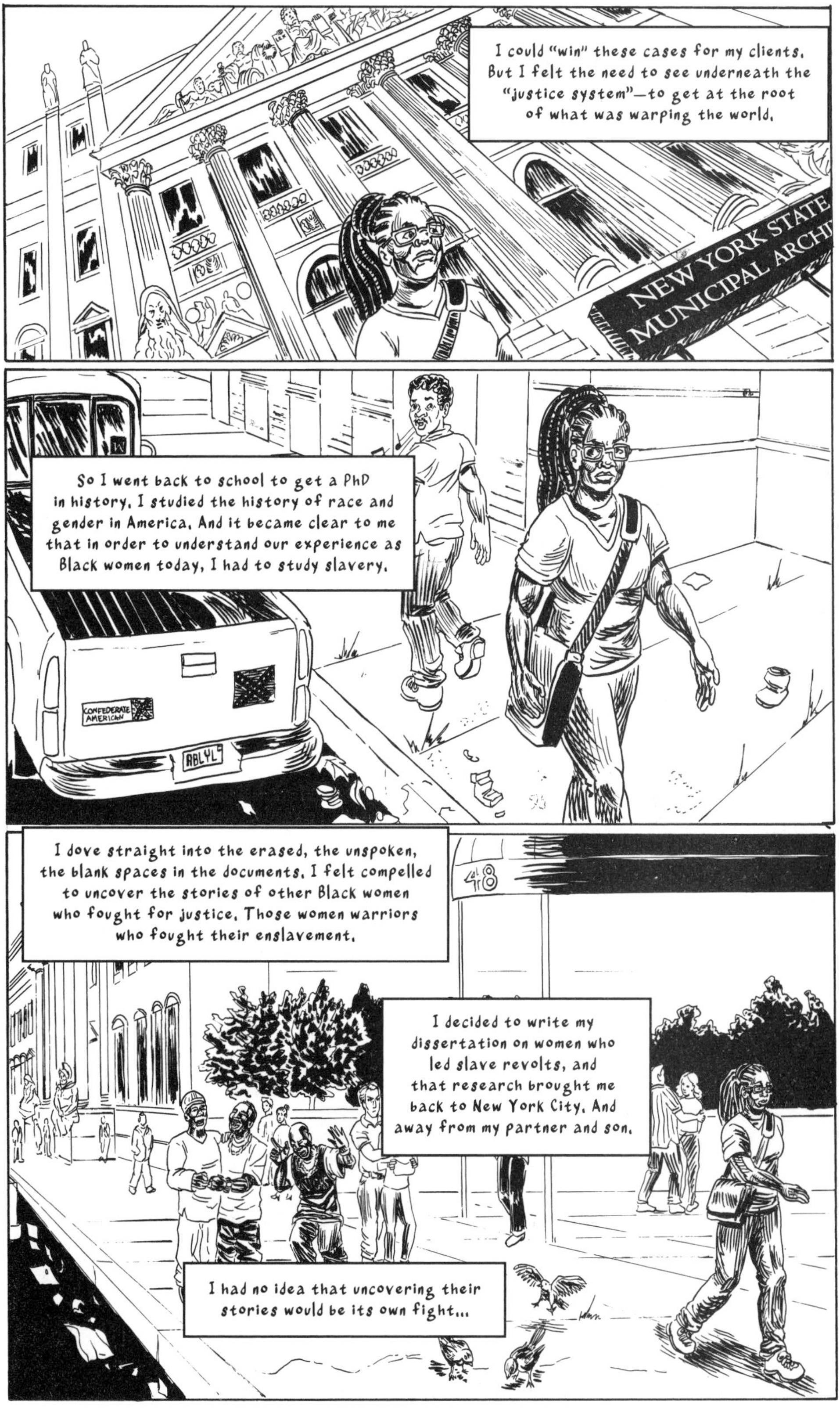
I could "win" these cases for my clients. But I felt the need to see underneath the "justice system"—to get at the root of what was warping the world.
NEW YORK STATE MUNICIPAL ARCHI
So I went back to school to get a PhD in history. I studied the history of race and gender in America. And it became clear to me that in order to understand our experience as Black women today, I had to study slavery.
CONFEDERATE AMERICAN
I dove straight into the erased, the unspoken, the blank spaces in the documents. I felt compelled to uncover the stories of other Black women who fought for justice. Those women warriors who fought their enslavement.
I decided to write my dissertation on women who led slave revolts, and that research brought me back to New York City. And away from my partner and son.
I had no idea that uncovering their stories would be its own fight...

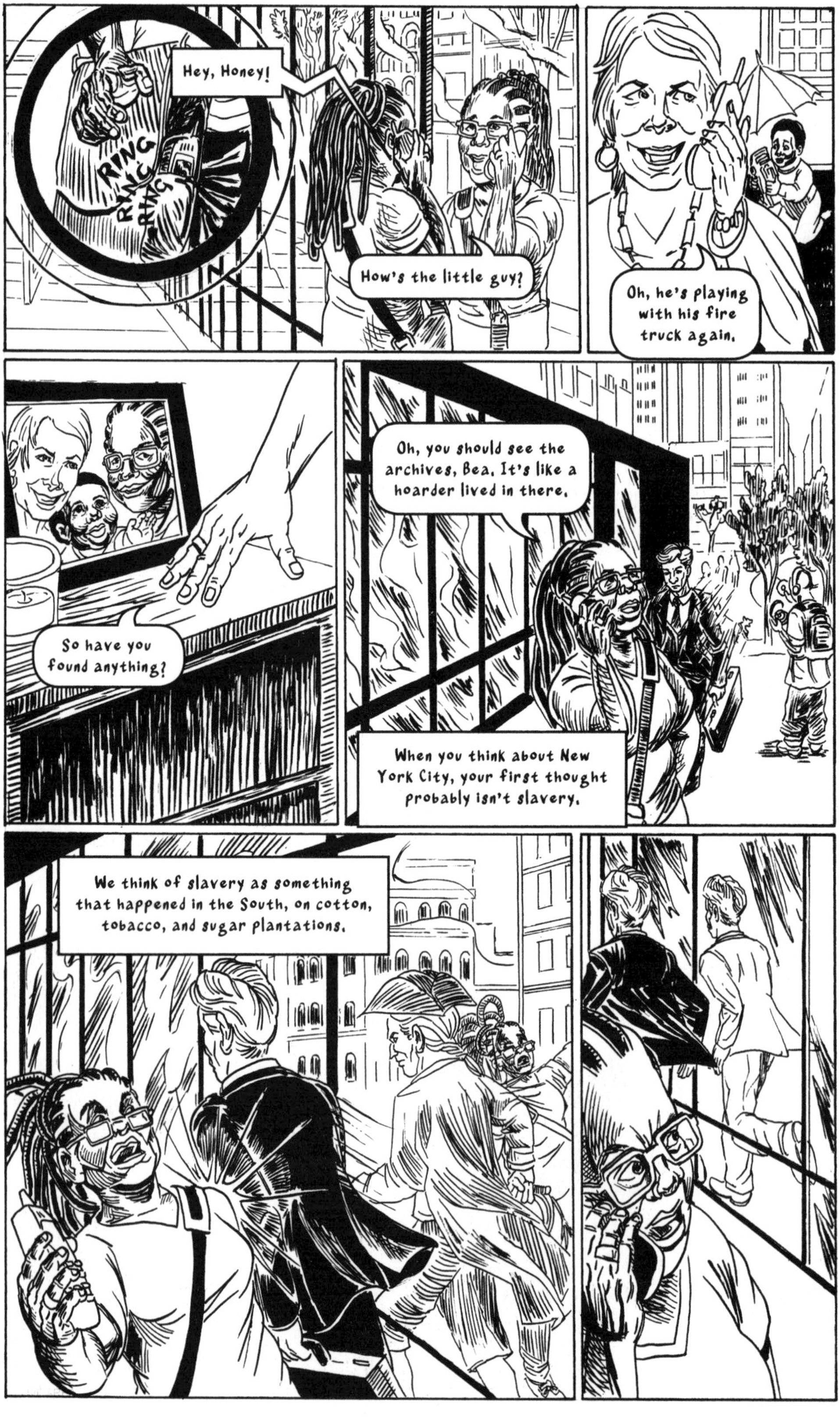
RING RING RING
Hey, Honey!
How's the little guy?
Oh, he's playing with his fire truck again.
So have you found anything?
Oh, you should see the archives, Bea. It's like a hoarder lived in there.
When you think about New York City, your first thought probably isn't slavery.
We think of slavery as something that happened in the South, on cotton, tobacco, and sugar plantations.

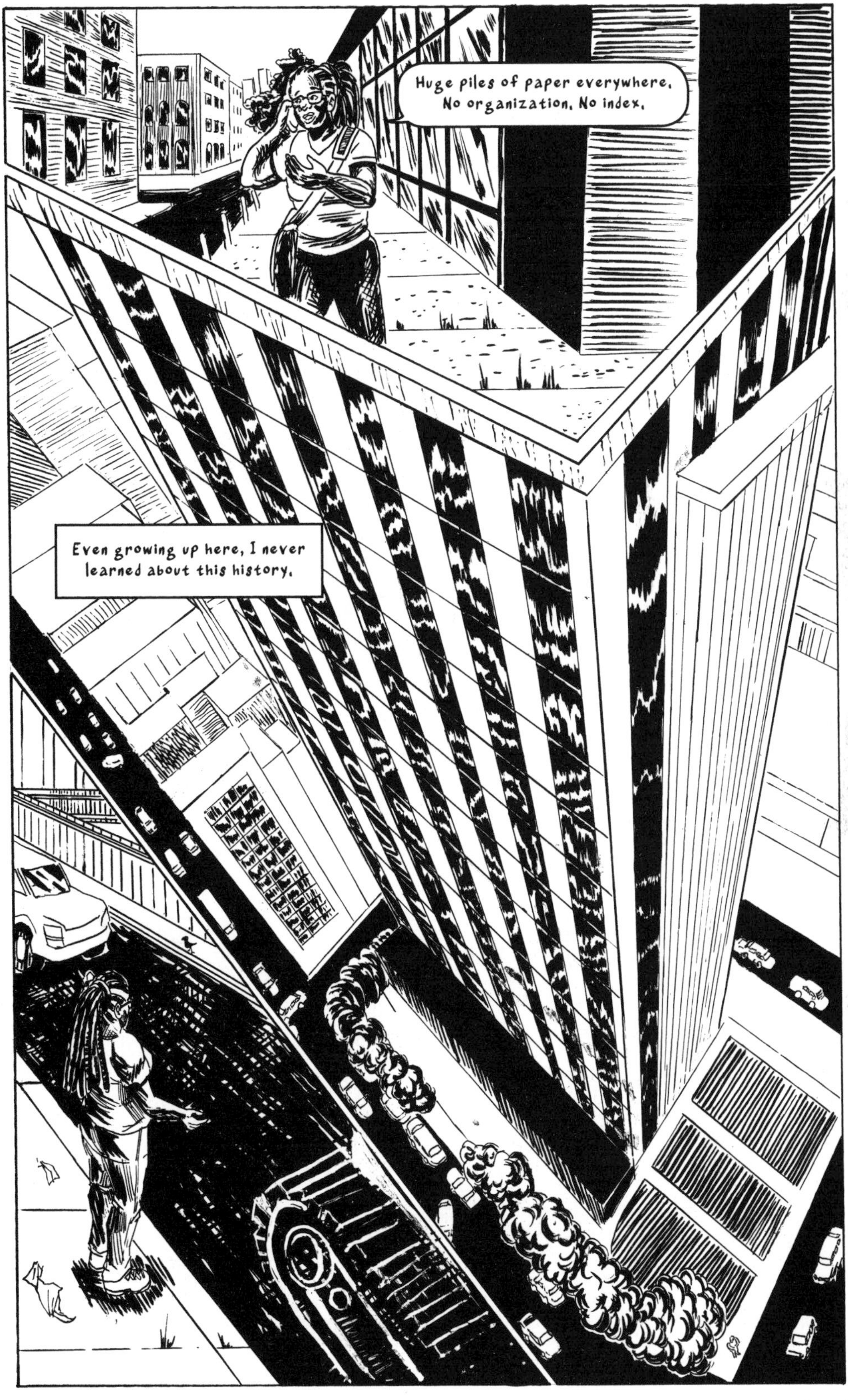
Huge piles of paper everywhere. No organization. No index.
Even growing up here, I never learned about this history.

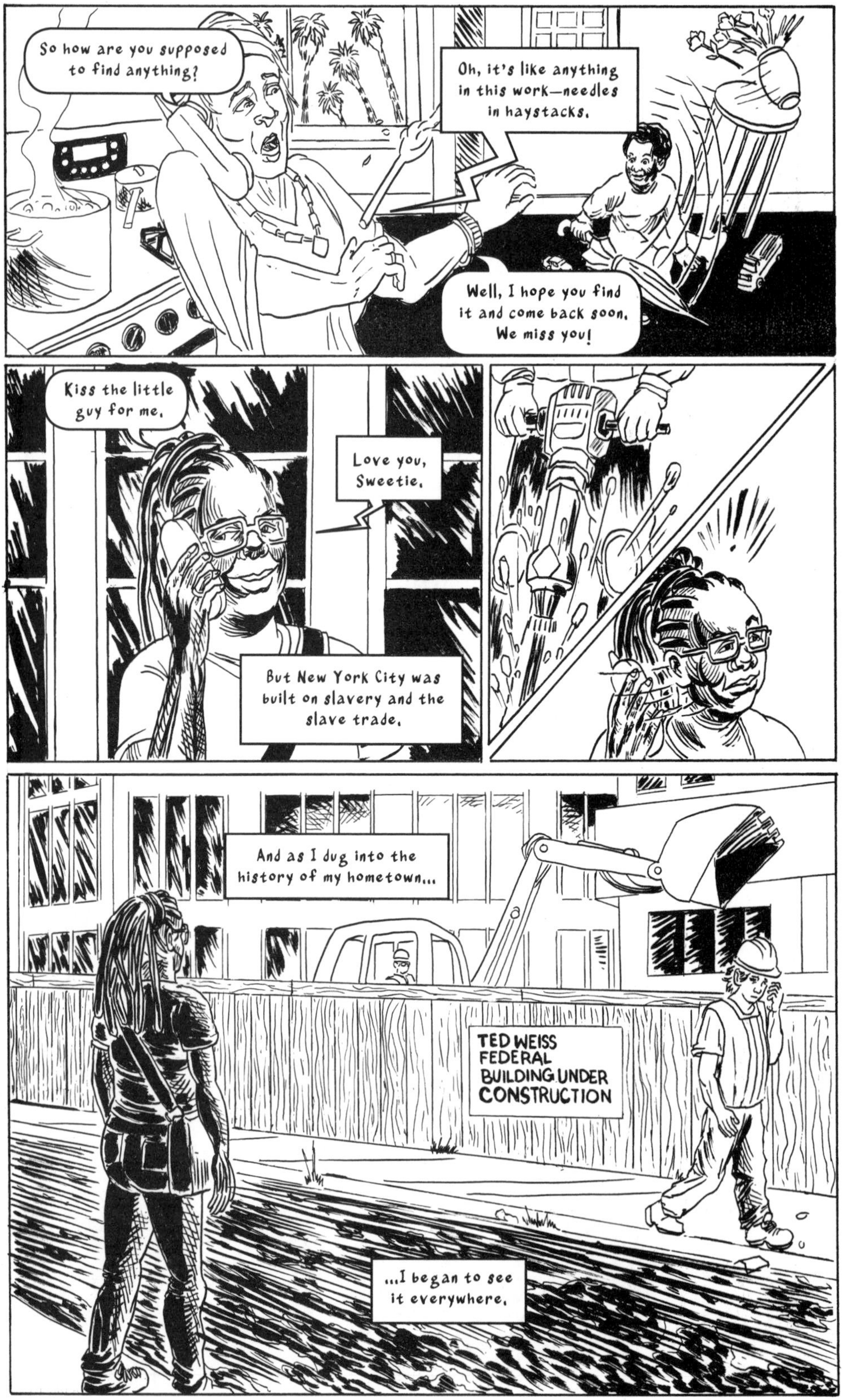
So how are you supposed to find anything?
Oh, it's like anything in this work—needles in haystacks.
Well, I hope you find it and come back soon. We miss you!
Kiss the little guy for me.
Love you, Sweetie.
But New York City was built on slavery and the slave trade.
And as I dug into the history of my hometown...
TED WEISS FEDERAL BUILDING UNDER CONSTRUCTION
...I began to see it everywhere.

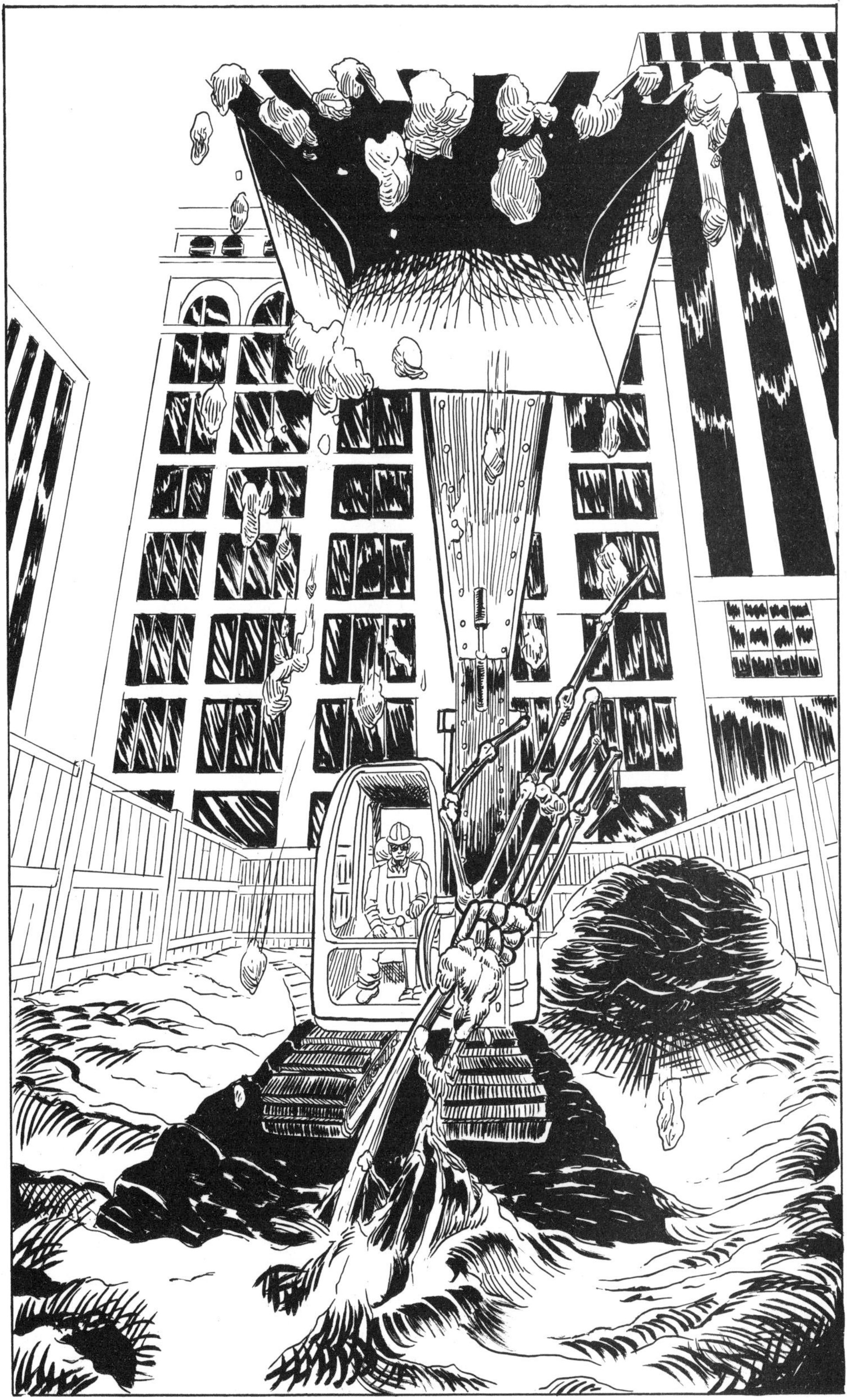

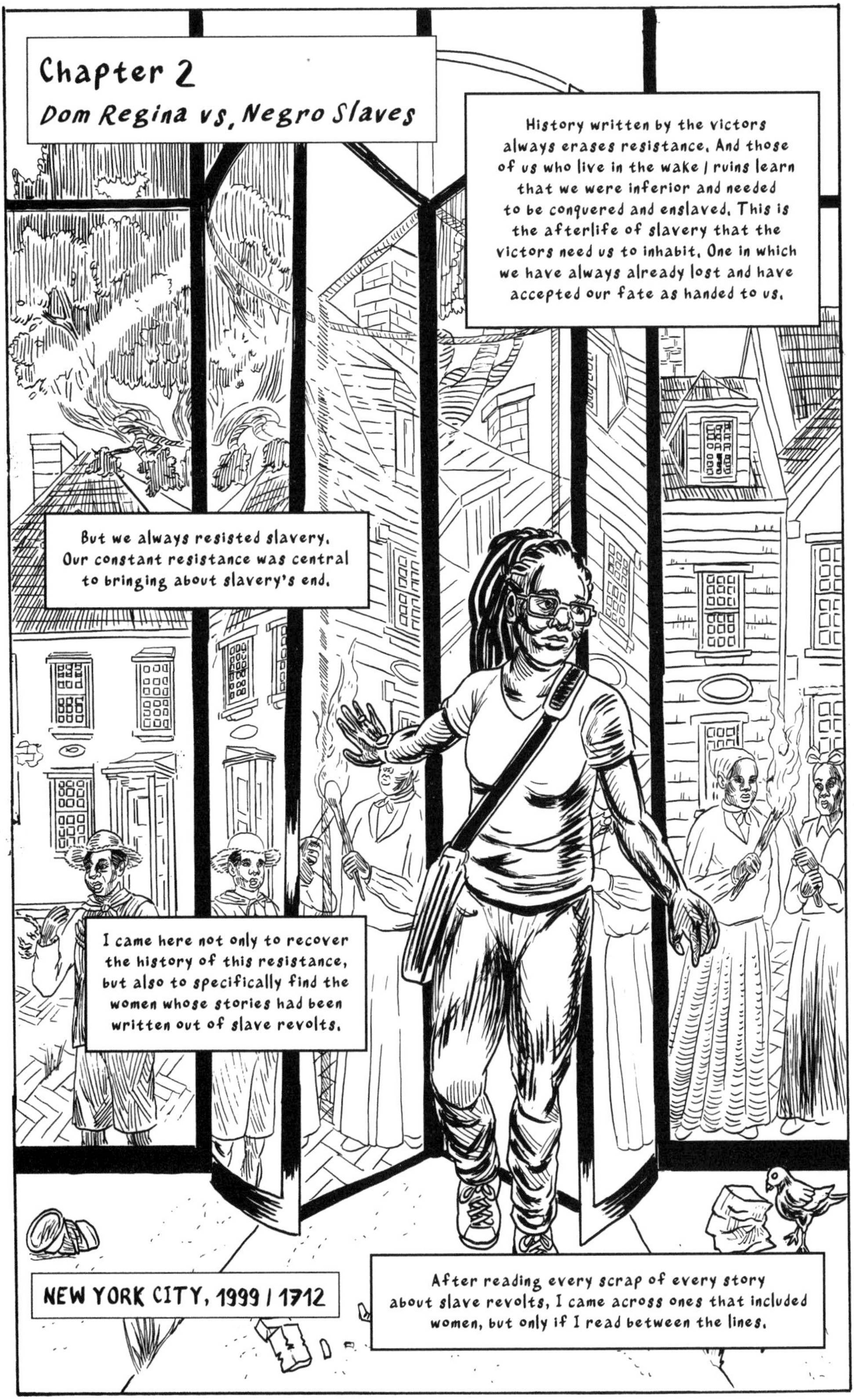
Chapter 2
Dom Regina vs. Negro Slaves
History written by the victors always erases resistance. And those of us who live in the wake / ruins learn that we were inferior and needed to be conquered and enslaved. This is the afterlife of slavery that the victors need us to inhabit. One in which we have always already lost and have accepted our fate as handed to us.
But we always resisted slavery. Our constant resistance was central to bringing about slavery's end.
I came here not only to recover the history of this resistance, but also to specifically find the women whose stories had been written out of slave revolts.
NEW YORK CITY, 1999 / 1712
After reading every scrap of every story about slave revolts, I came across ones that included women, but only if I read between the lines.

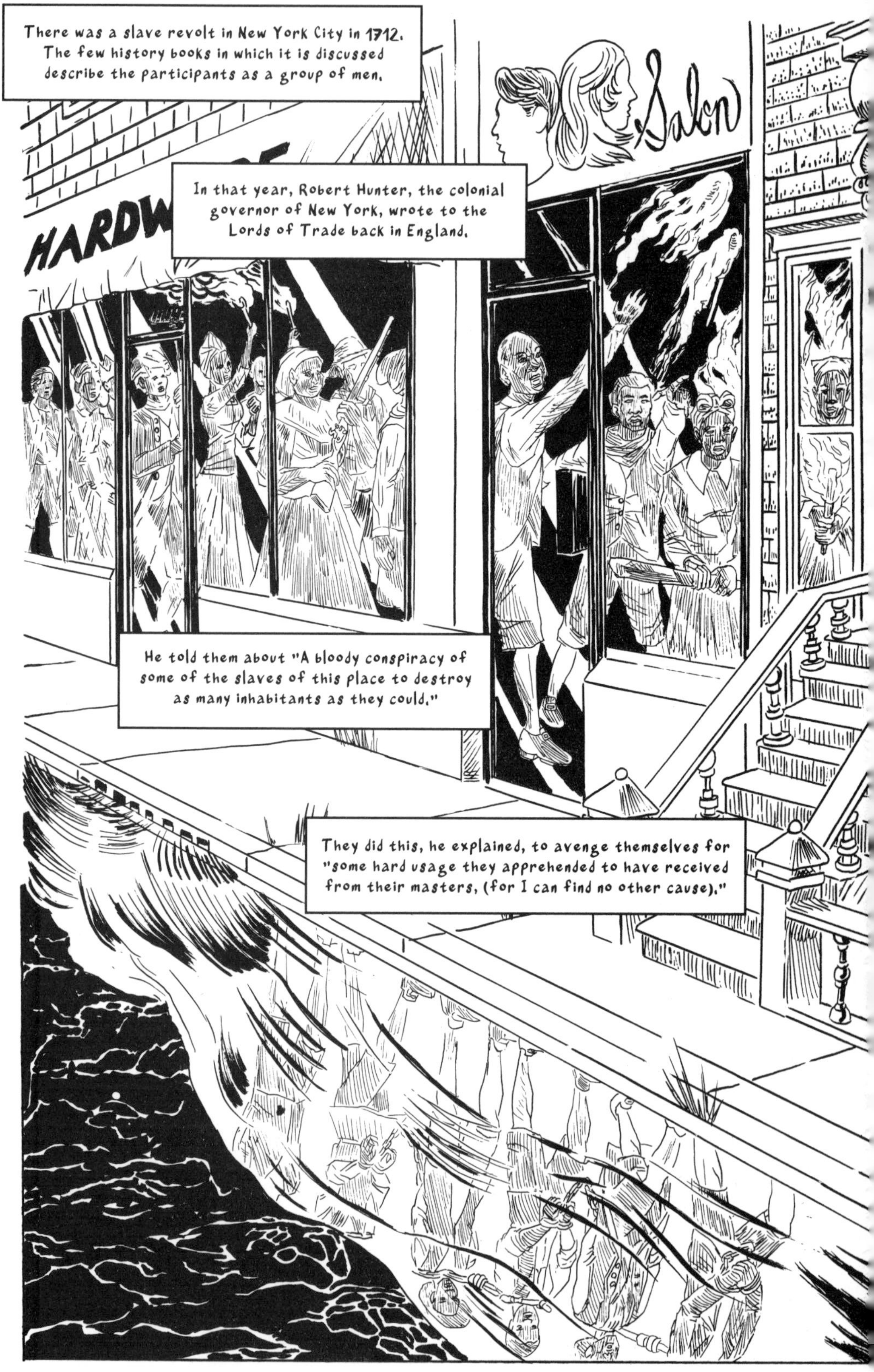

There was a slave revolt in New York City in 1712. The few history books in which it is discussed describe the participants as a group of men.
Salon
HARDW
In that year, Robert Hunter, the colonial governor of New York, wrote to the Lords of Trade back in England.
He told them about "A bloody conspiracy of some of the slaves of this place to destroy as many inhabitants as they could."
They did this, he explained, to avenge themselves for "some hard usage they apprehended to have received from their masters, (for I can find no other cause)."

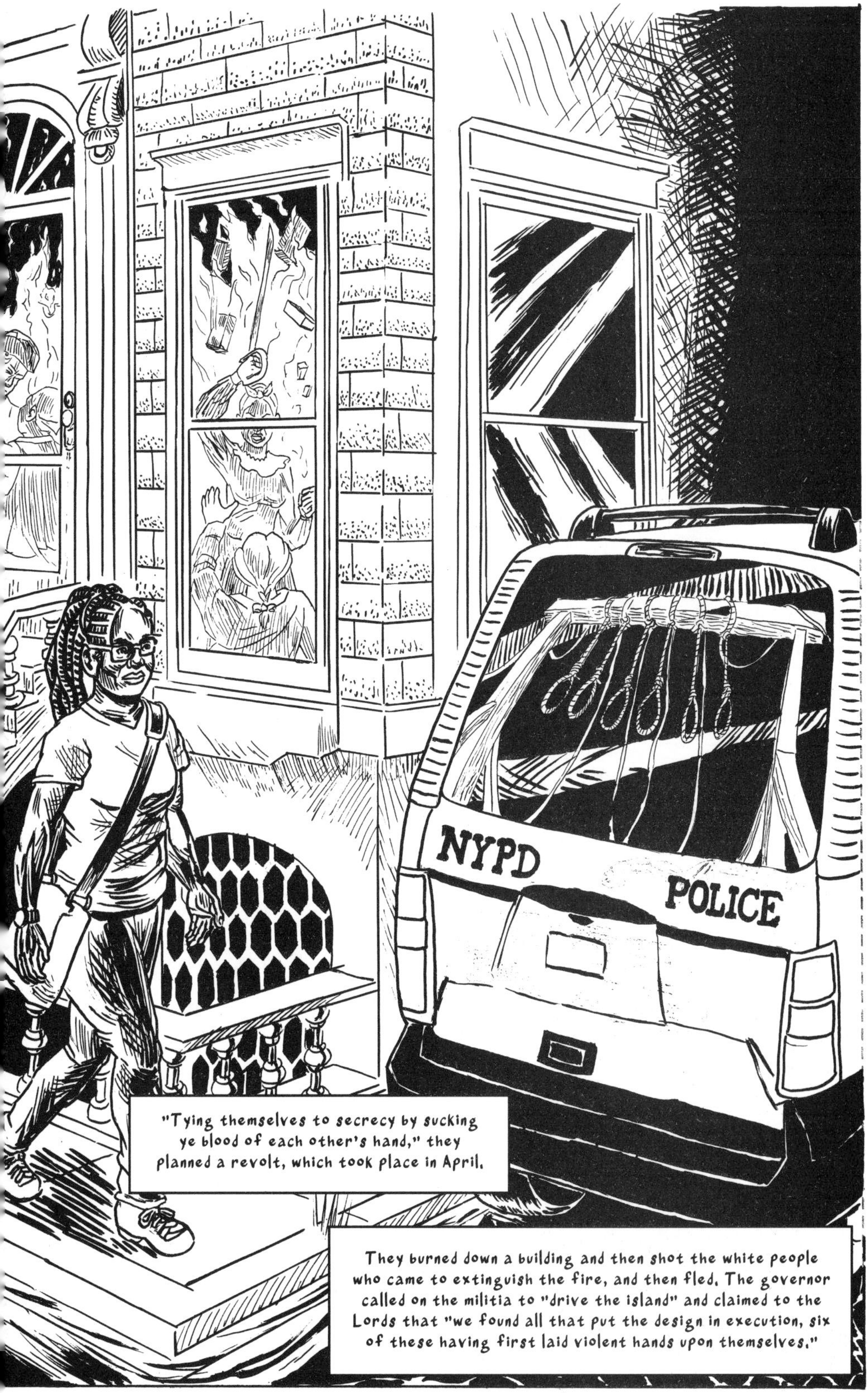
NYPD
POLICE
"Tying themselves to secrecy by sucking ye blood of each other's hand," they planned a revolt, which took place in April.
They burned down a building and then shot the white people who came to extinguish the fire, and then fled. The governor called on the militia to "drive the island" and claimed to the Lords that "we found all that put the design in execution, six of these having first laid violent hands upon themselves."

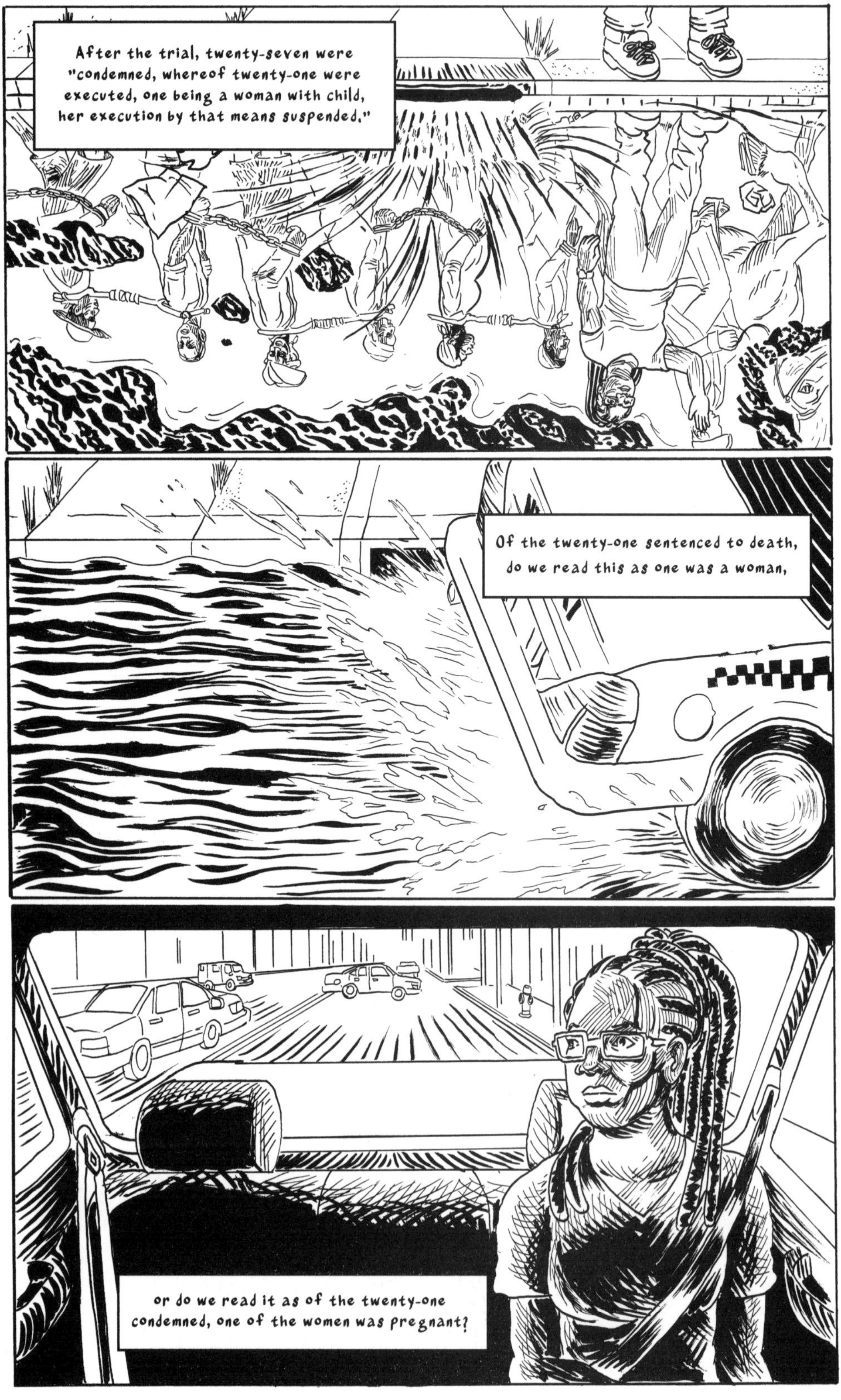

After the trial, twenty-seven were "condemned, whereof twenty-one were executed, one being a woman with child, her execution by that means suspended."
Of the twenty-one sentenced to death, do we read this as one was a woman,
or do we read it as of the twenty-one condemned, one of the women was pregnant?

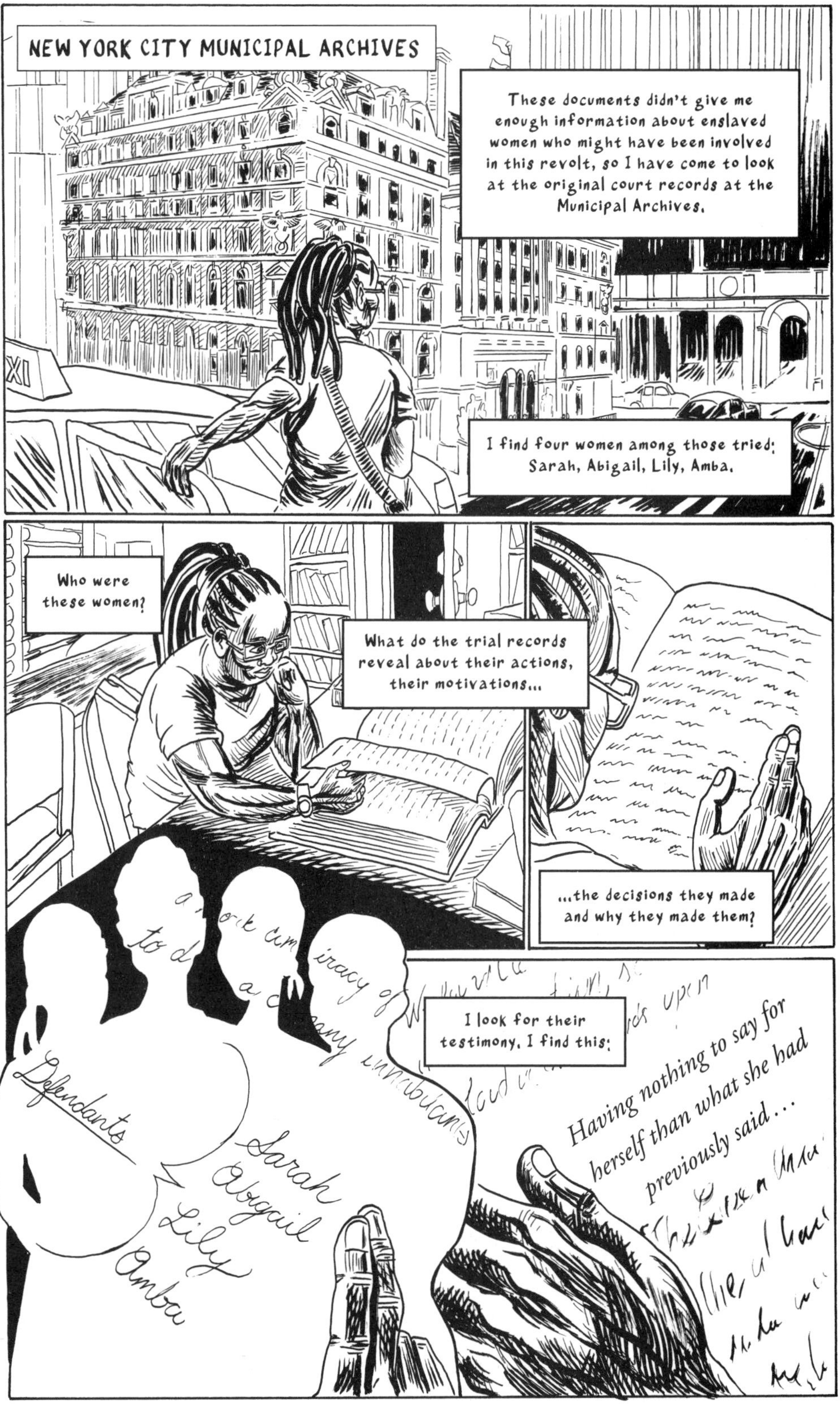
NEW YORK CITY MUNICIPAL ARCHIVES
These documents didn't give me enough information about enslaved women who might have been involved in this revolt, so I have come to look at the original court records at the Municipal Archives.
I find four women among those tried: Sarah, Abigail, Lily, Amba.
Who were these women?
What do the trial records reveal about their actions, their motivations...
...the decisions they made and why they made them?
I look for their testimony. I find this:
Defendants
Sarah
Abigail
Lily
Amba
Having nothing to say for herself than what she had previously said . . .

Wait, what had "she" previously said? Did they record what she said before? Did I miss it, buried in all of the arcane **1700s** British court language?

Let me start over.

In the documents I've unearthed, I find a lot of "Dom Regina."

That means "the queen." Because New York was still a British colony,

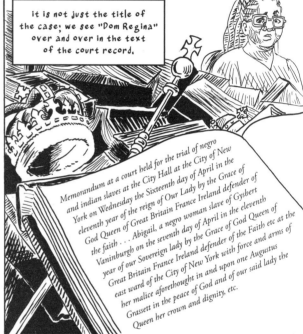

it is not just the title of the case; we see "Dom Regina" over and over in the text of the court record.

Memorandum at a court held for the trial of negro and indian slaves at the City Hall at the City of New York on Wednesday the Sixteenth day of April in the eleventh year of the reign of Our Lady by the Grace of God Queen of Great Britain France Ireland defender of the faith . . . Abigail, a negro woman slave of Gysbert Vaninburgh on the seventh day of April in the eleventh year of our Sovereign lady by the Grace of God Queen of Great Britain France Ireland defender of the Faith etc at the east ward of the City of New York with force and arms of her malice aforethought in and upon one Augustus Grassett in the peace of God and of our said lady the Queen her crown and dignity, etc.

It is invoked every time a crime is alleged because the legal philosophy, then and now, is that crimes are wrongs committed against the state.

In **1712**, Dom Regina was the state, and invoked every time a day or date is mentioned because Dom Regina IS time. Dom Regina is everything and everywhere.

It feels like a playground bully who tells you over and over again that he is the strongest in order to make it true. And in a way, it is that. This is how language creates power.

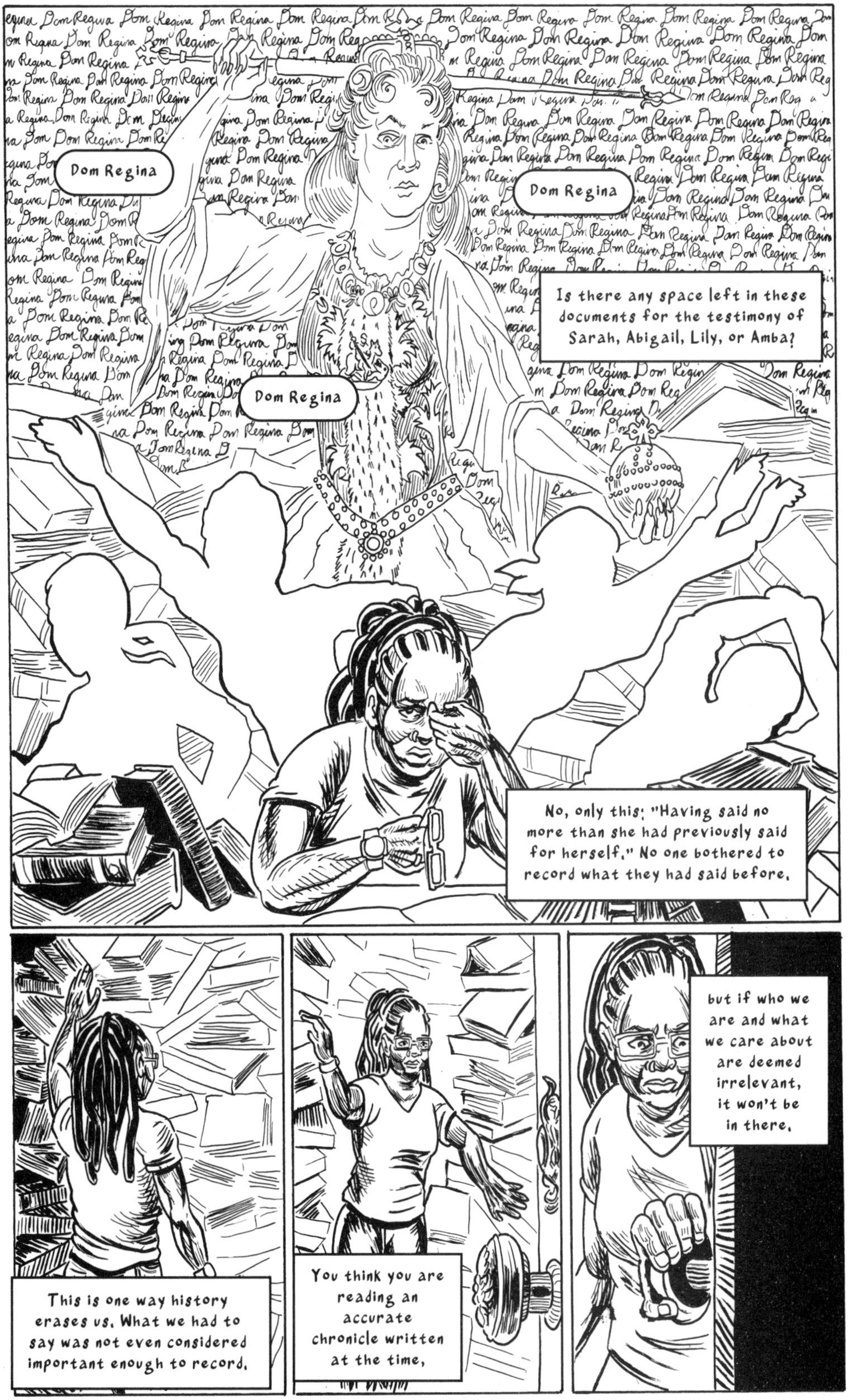

Dom Regina
Dom Regina
Dom Regina
Is there any space left in these documents for the testimony of Sarah, Abigail, Lily, or Amba?
No, only this: "Having said no more than she had previously said for herself." No one bothered to record what they had said before.
This is one way history erases us. What we had to say was not even considered important enough to record.
You think you are reading an accurate chronicle written at the time,
but if who we are and what we care about are deemed irrelevant, it won't be in there.

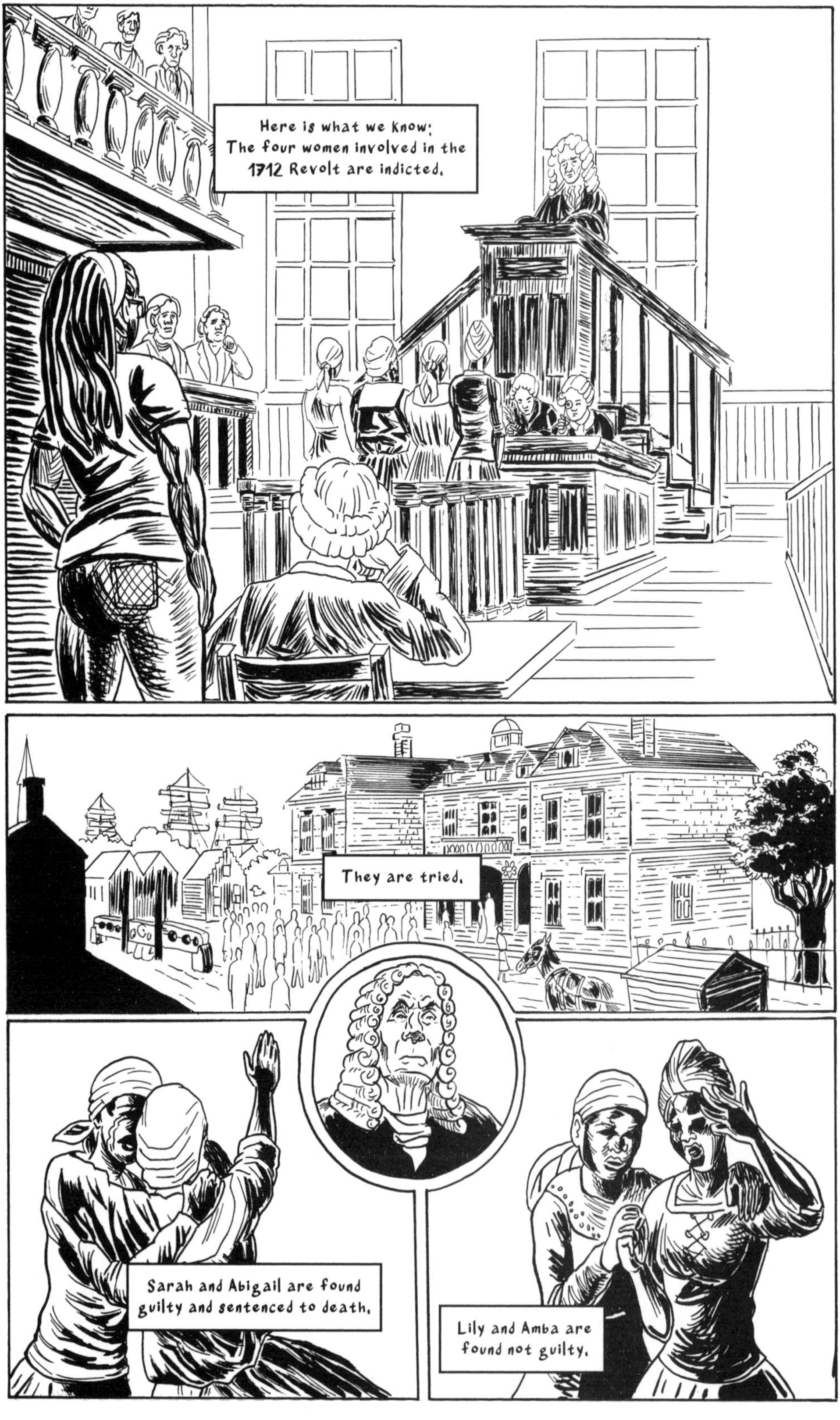
Here is what we know:
The four women involved in the 1712 Revolt are indicted.
They are tried.
Sarah and Abigail are found guilty and sentenced to death.
Lily and Amba are found not guilty.

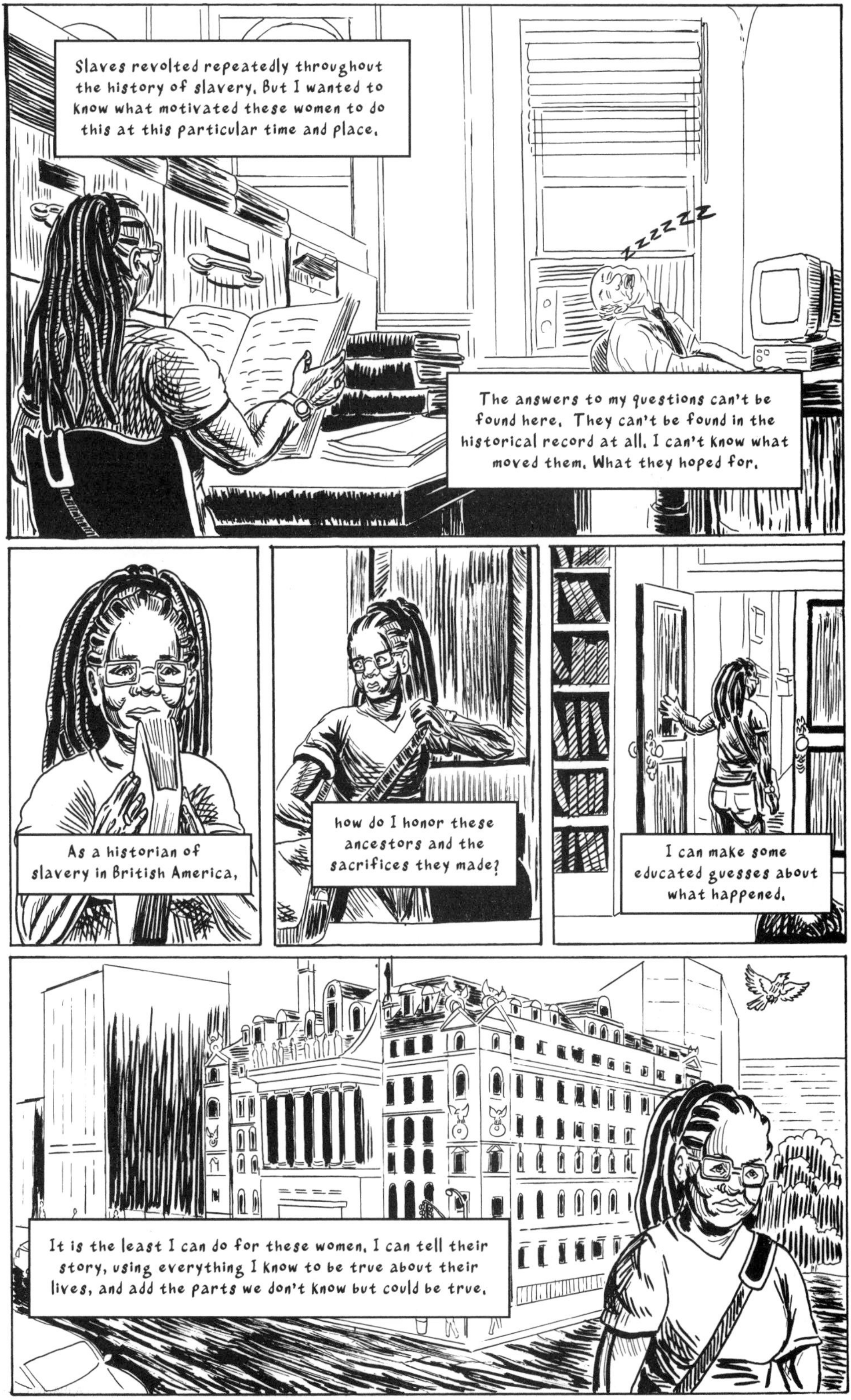
Slaves revolted repeatedly throughout the history of slavery. But I wanted to know what motivated these women to do this at this particular time and place.
ZZZZZZ
The answers to my questions can't be found here. They can't be found in the historical record at all. I can't know what moved them. What they hoped for.
As a historian of slavery in British America,
how do I honor these ancestors and the sacrifices they made?
I can make some educated guesses about what happened.
It is the least I can do for these women. I can tell their story, using everything I know to be true about their lives, and add the parts we don't know but could be true.

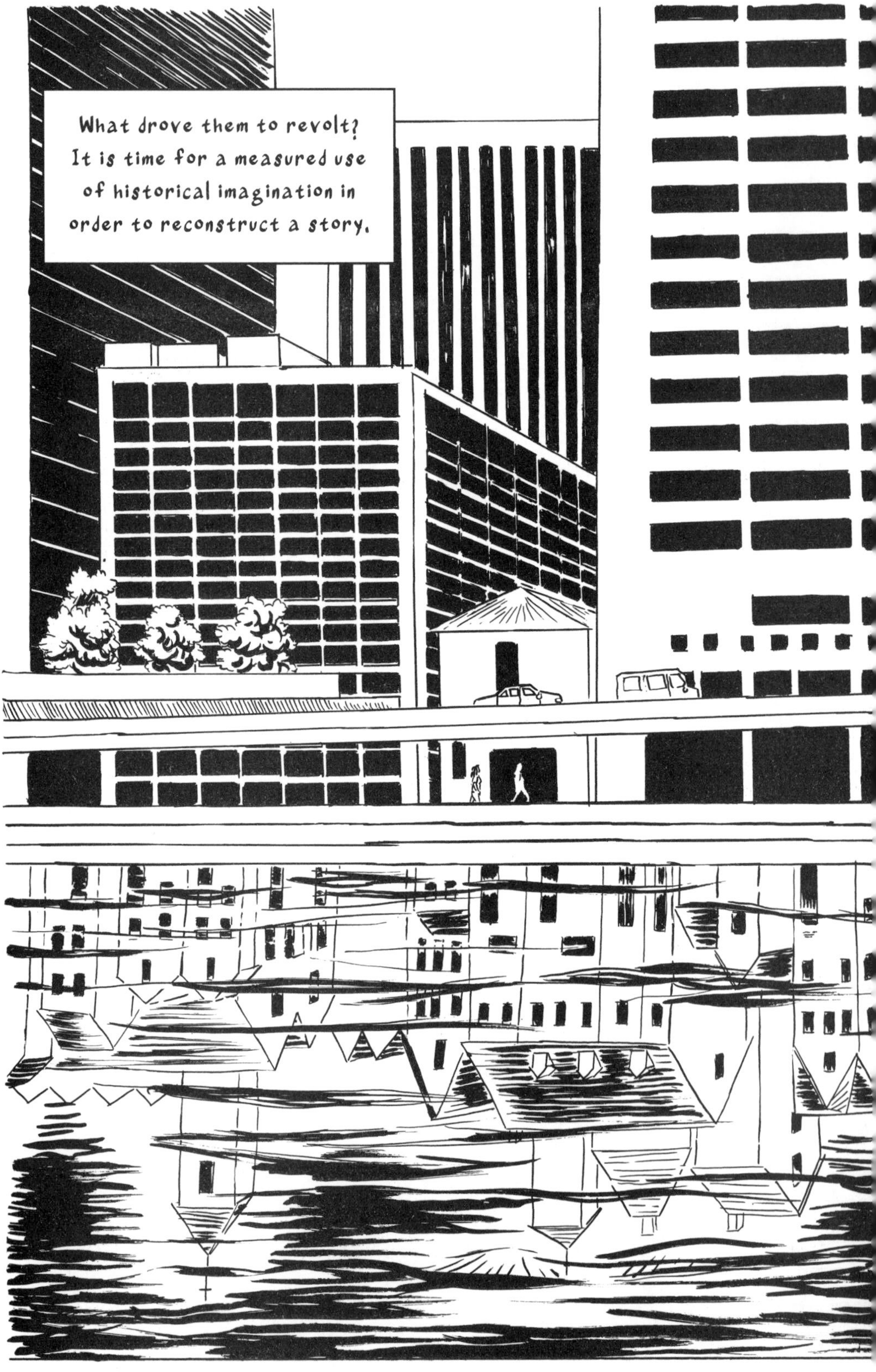
What drove them to revolt? It is time for a measured use of historical imagination in order to reconstruct a story.

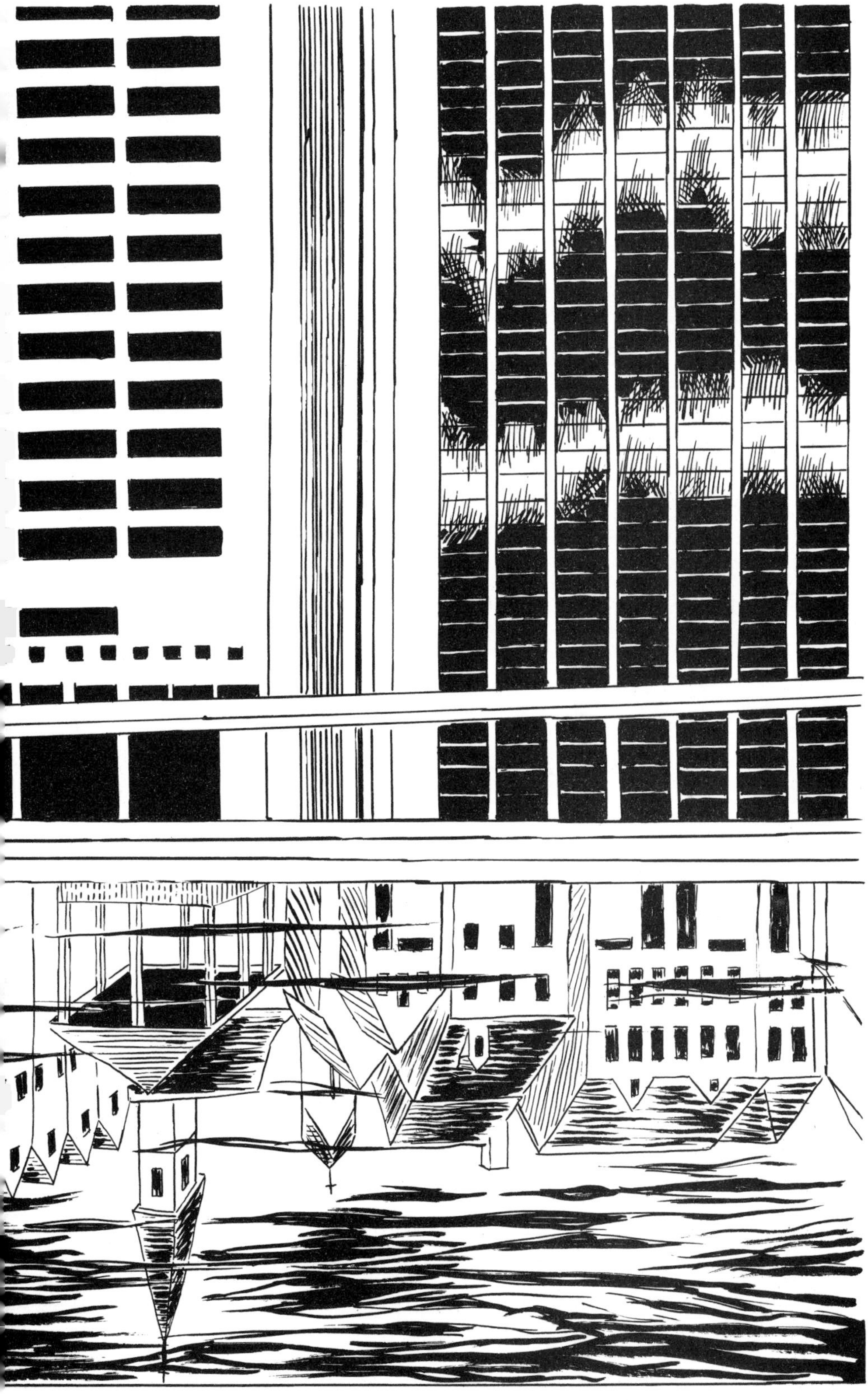

Chapter 3
Some Hard Usage

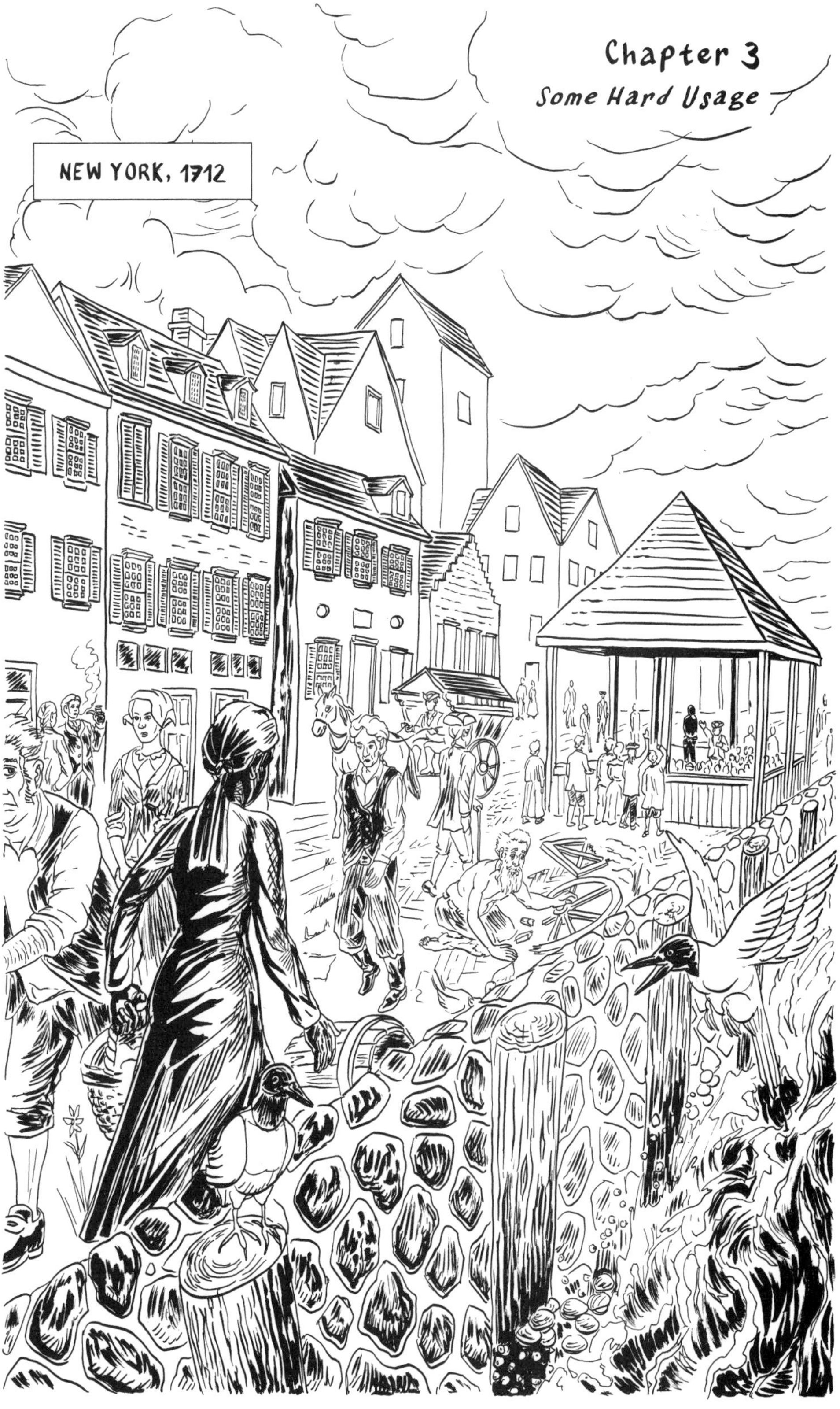
NEW YORK, 1712

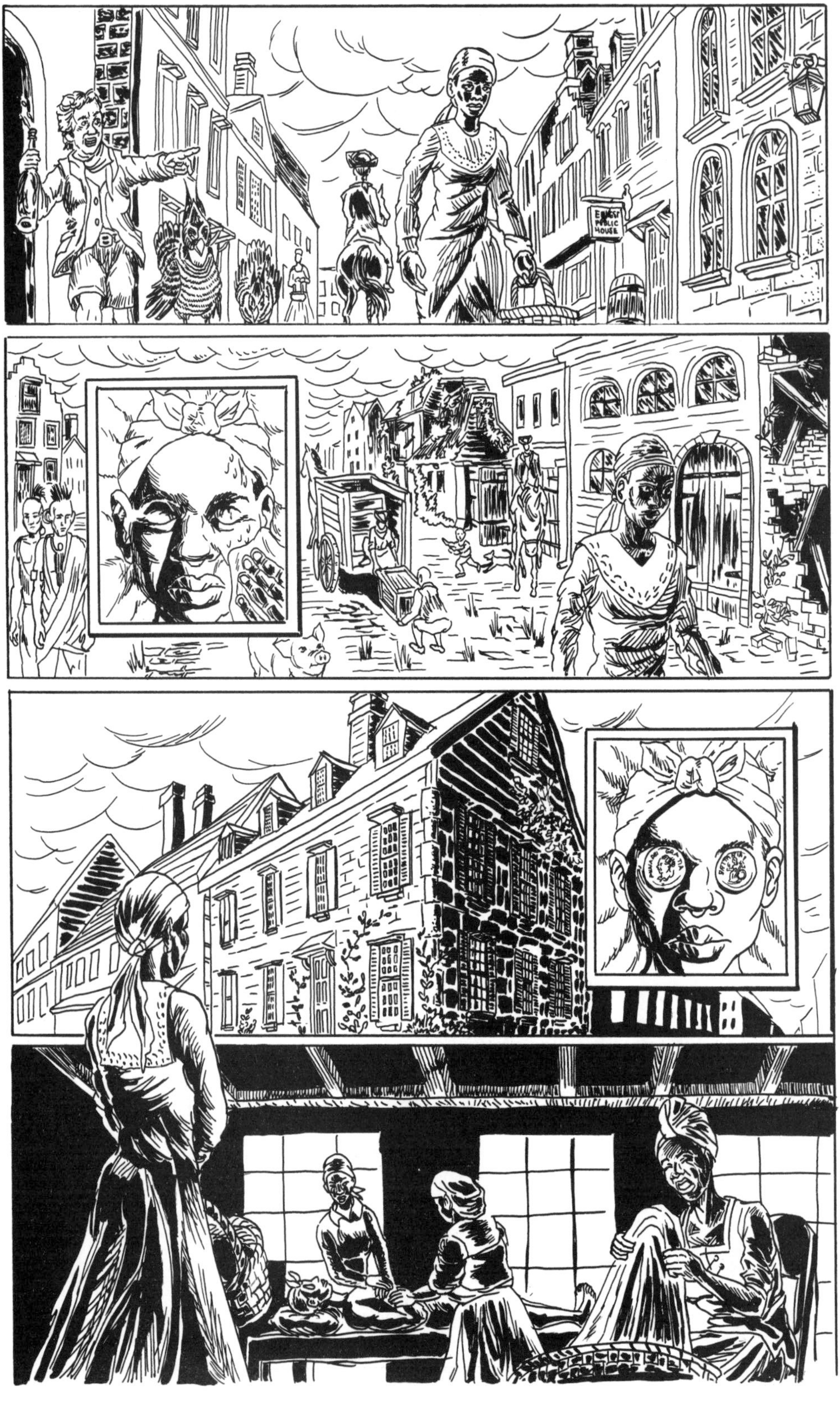
PUBLIC HOUSE

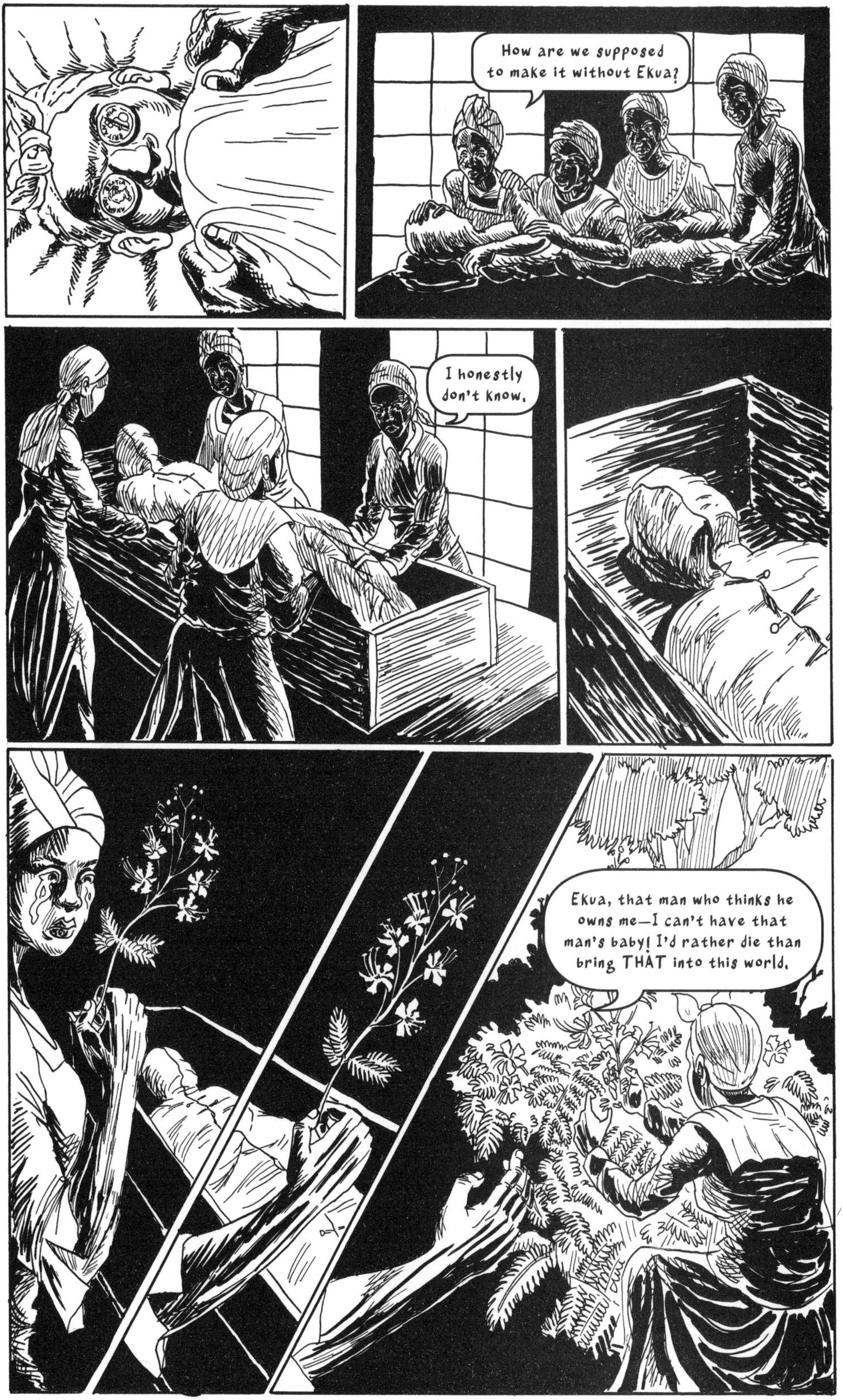
How are we supposed to make it without Ekua?
I honestly don't know.
Ekua, that man who thinks he owns me—I can't have that man's baby! I'd rather die than bring THAT into this world.

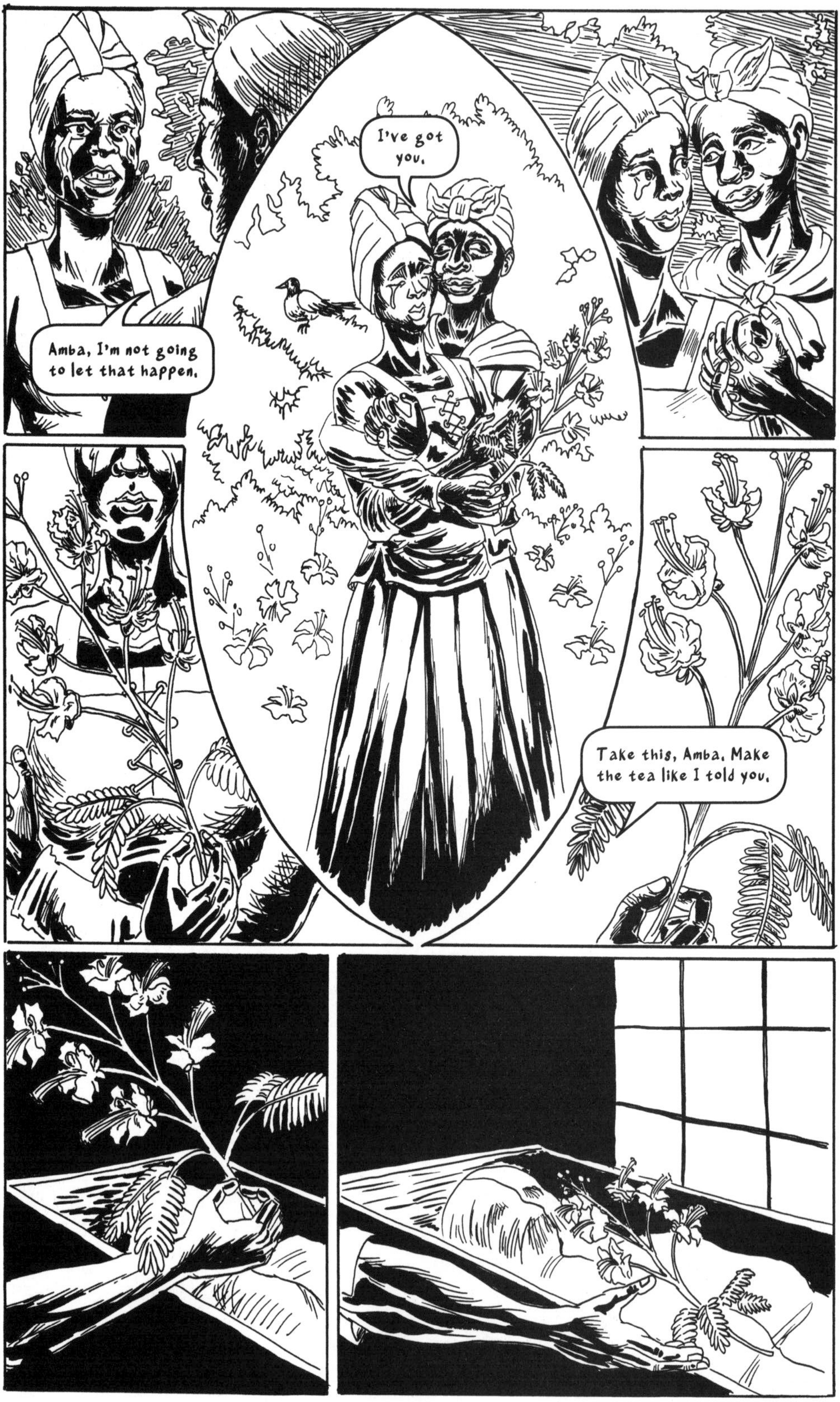
Amba, I'm not going to let that happen.
I've got you.
Take this, Amba. Make the tea like I told you.

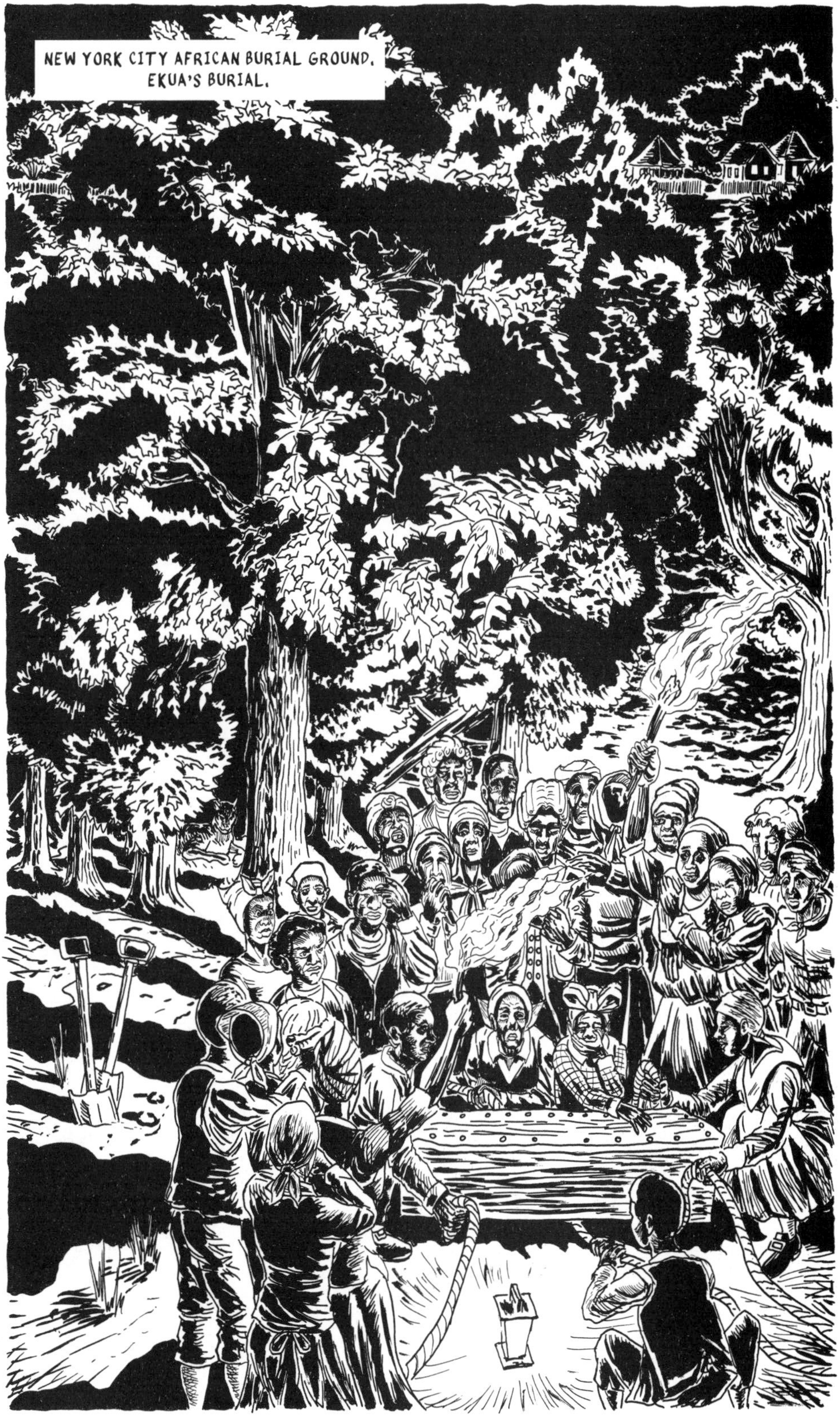
NEW YORK CITY AFRICAN BURIAL GROUND,
EKUA'S BURIAL.

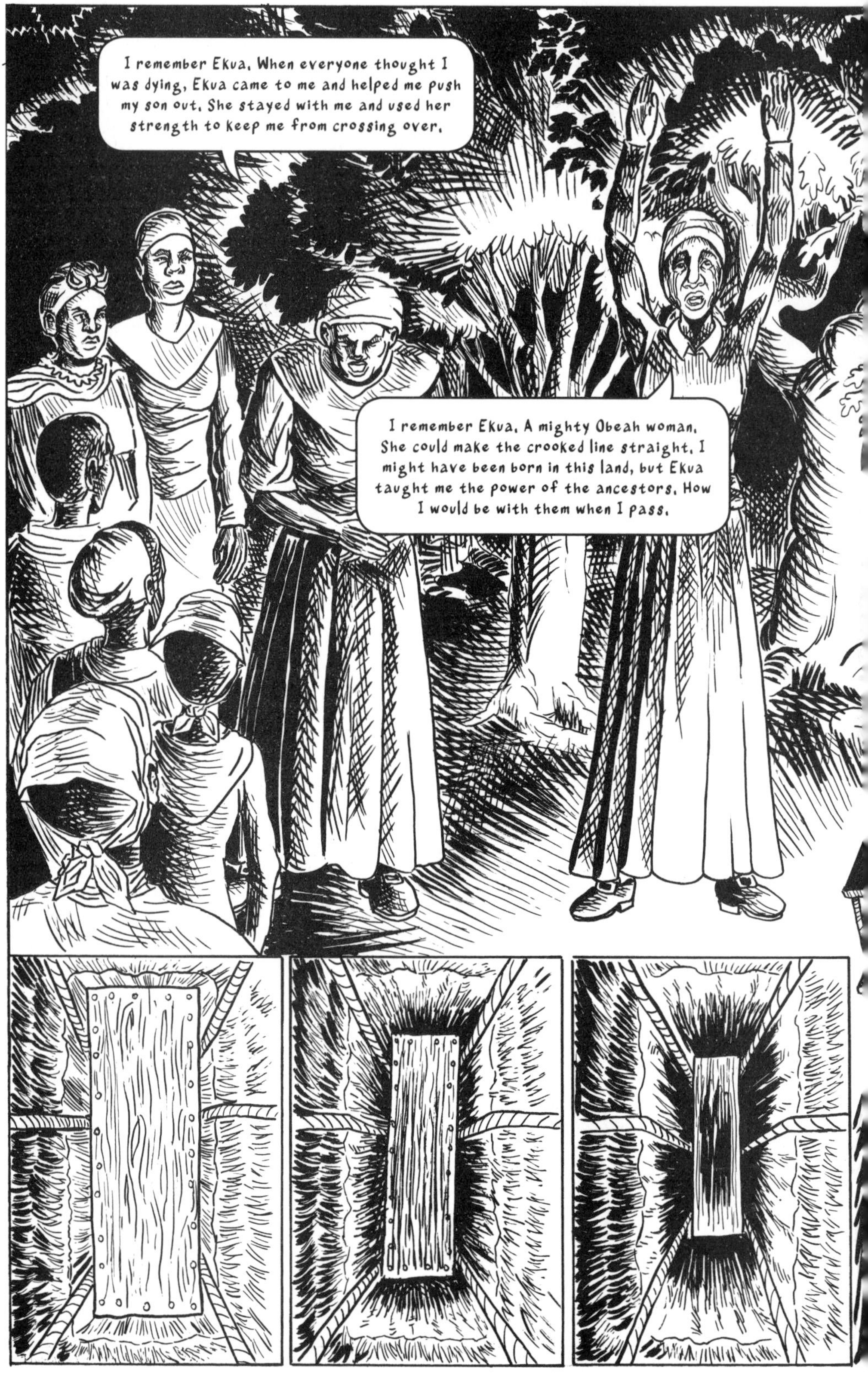
I remember Ekua. When everyone thought I was dying, Ekua came to me and helped me push my son out. She stayed with me and used her strength to keep me from crossing over.
I remember Ekua. A mighty Obeah woman. She could make the crooked line straight. I might have been born in this land, but Ekua taught me the power of the ancestors. How I would be with them when I pass.

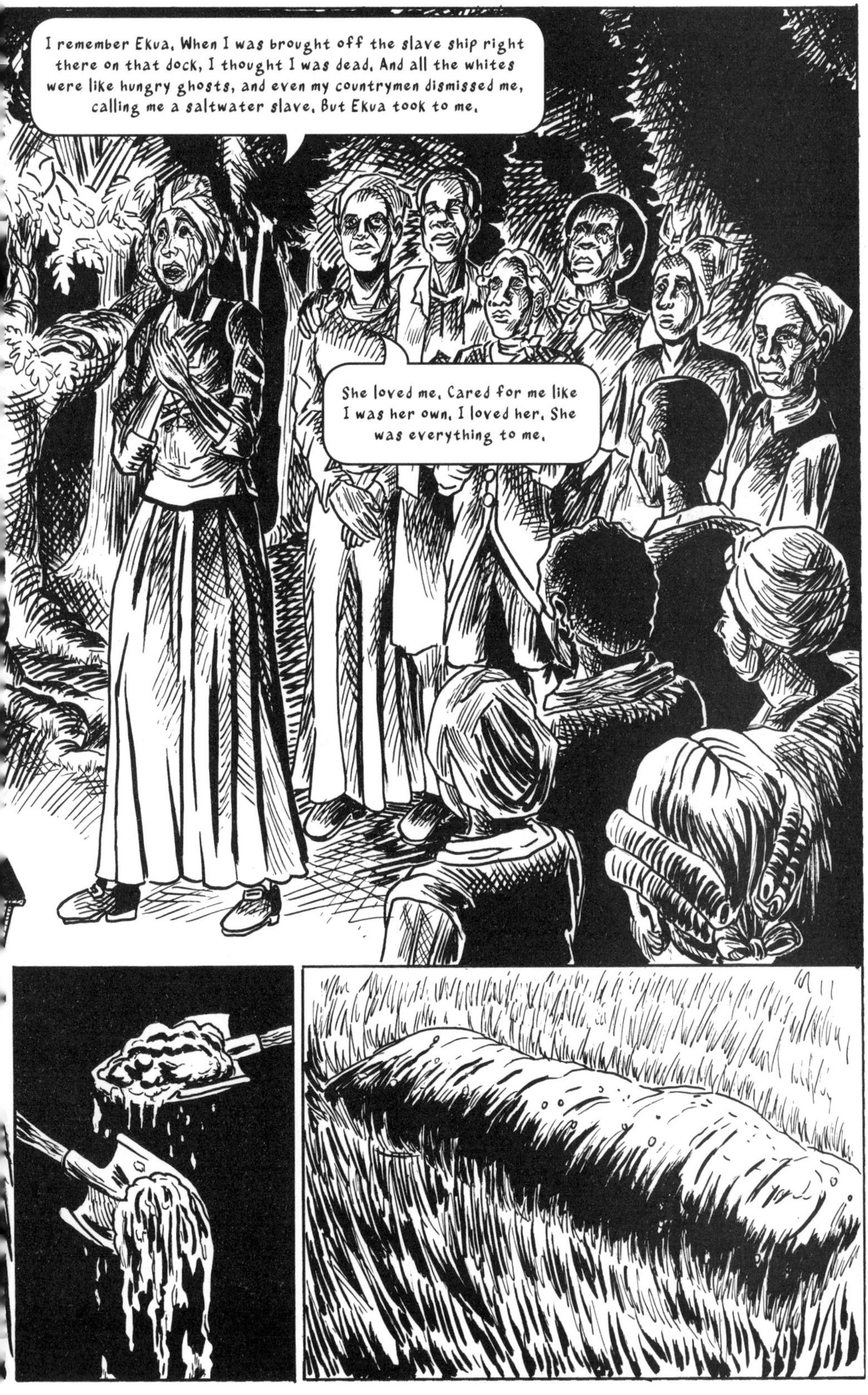
I remember Ekua. When I was brought off the slave ship right there on that dock, I thought I was dead. And all the whites were like hungry ghosts, and even my countrymen dismissed me, calling me a saltwater slave. But Ekua took to me.
She loved me. Cared for me like I was her own. I loved her. She was everything to me.

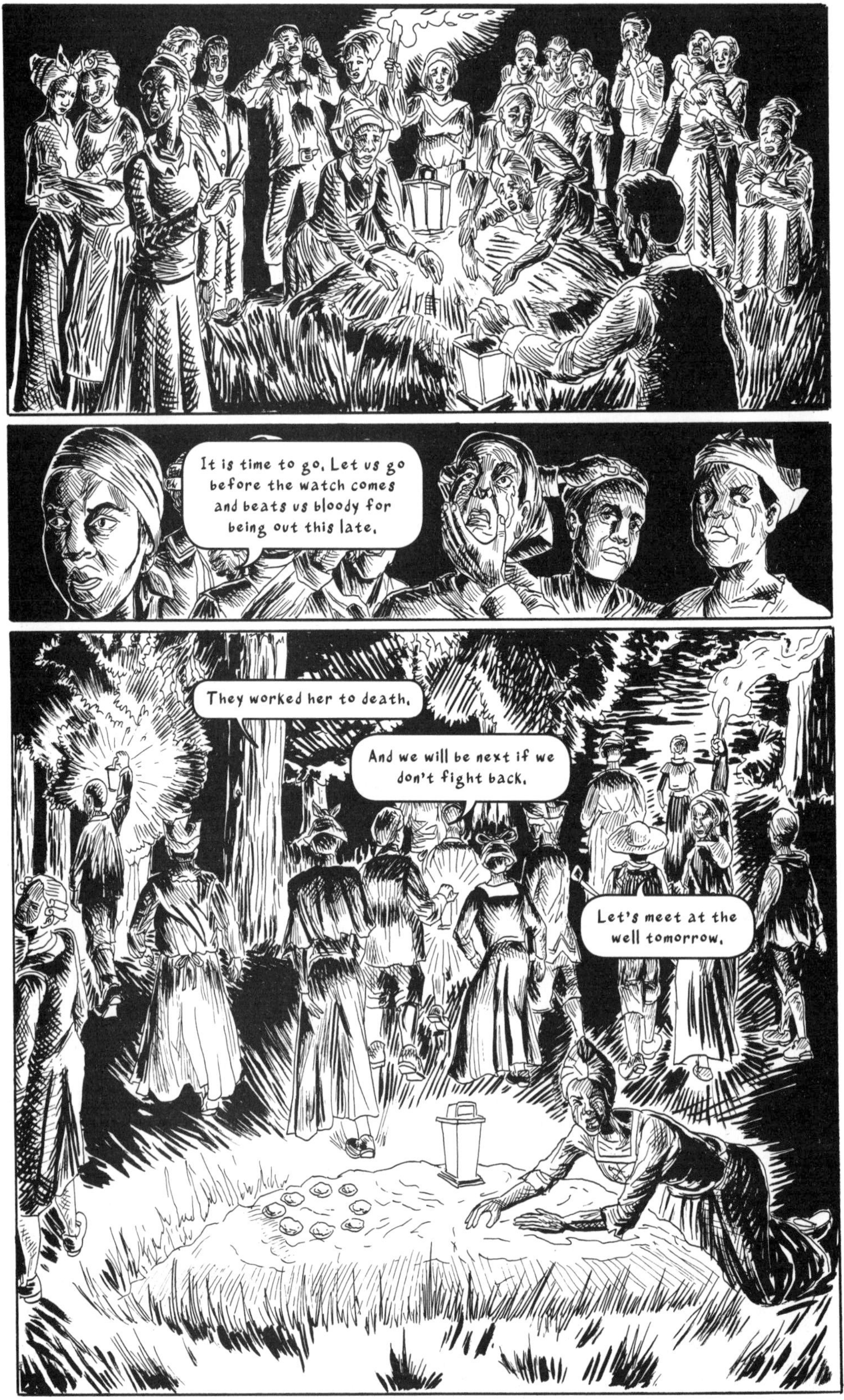
It is time to go. Let us go before the watch comes and beats us bloody for being out this late.
They worked her to death.
And we will be next if we don't fight back.
Let's meet at the well tomorrow.

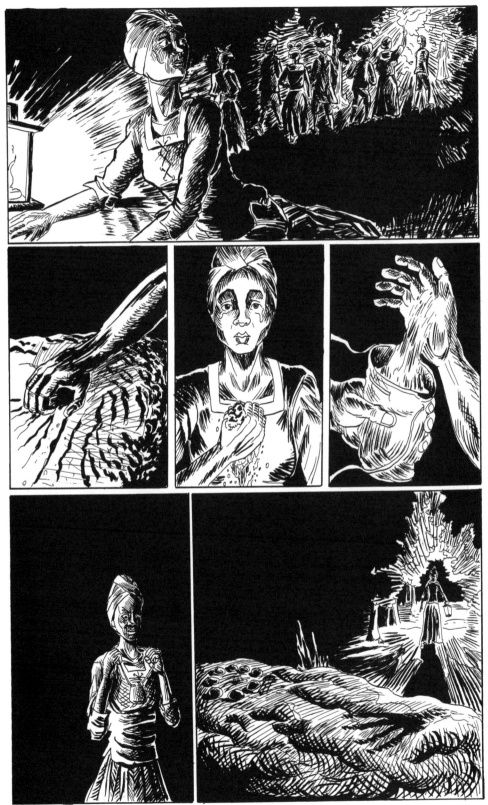

47

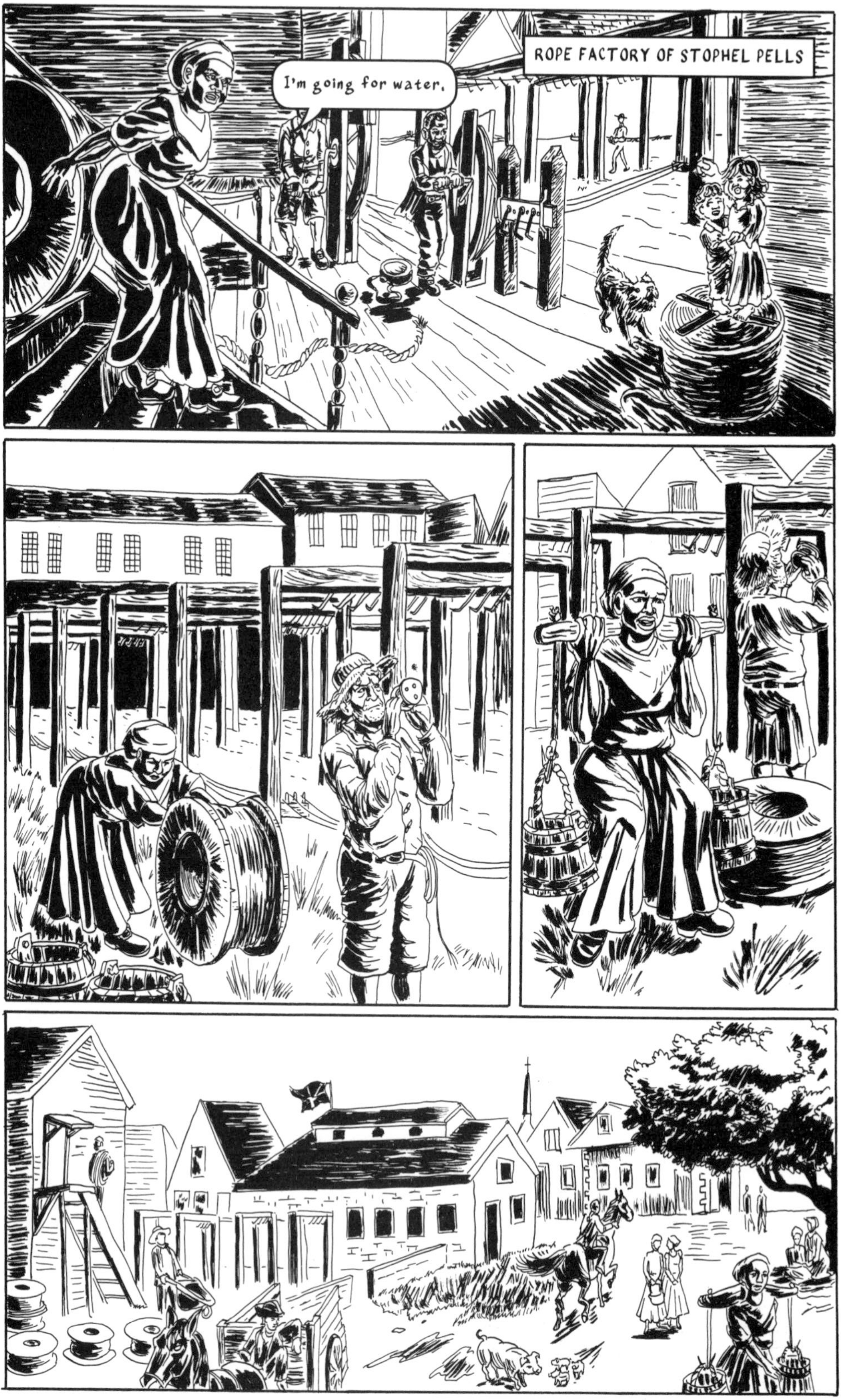
ROPE FACTORY OF STOPHEL PELLS
I'm going for water.

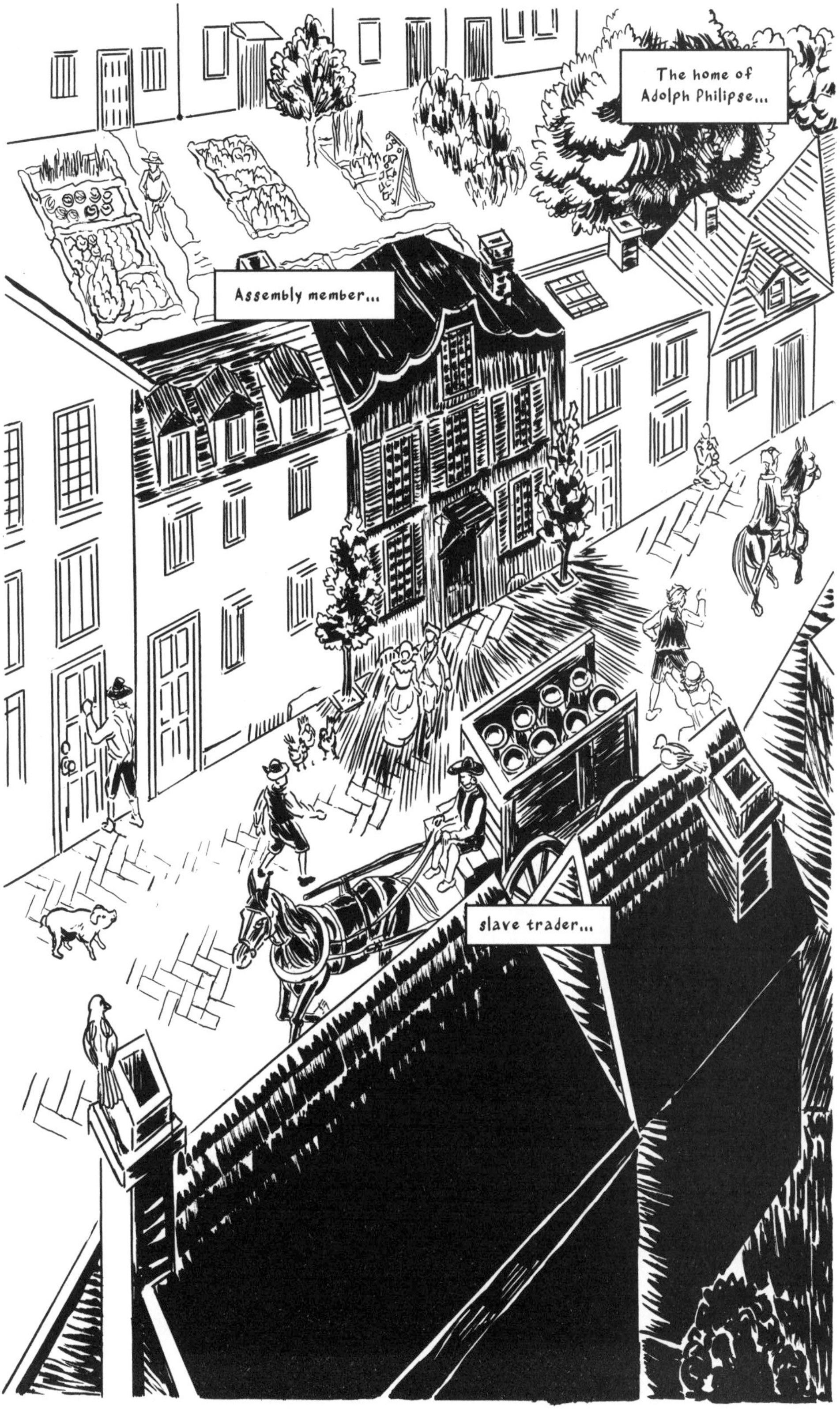
The home of
Adolph Philipse...
Assembly member...
slave trader...

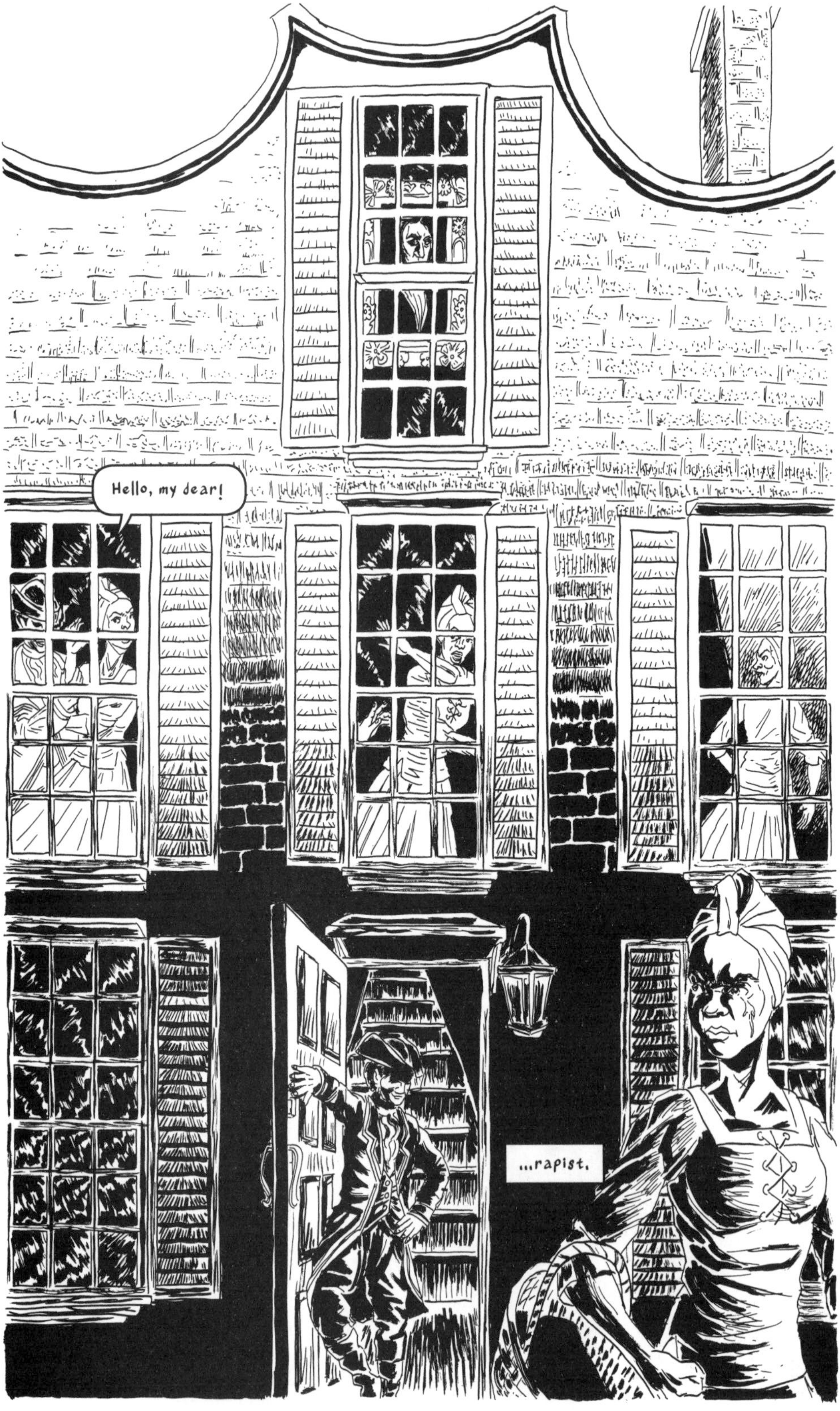
Hello, my dear!
...rapist.

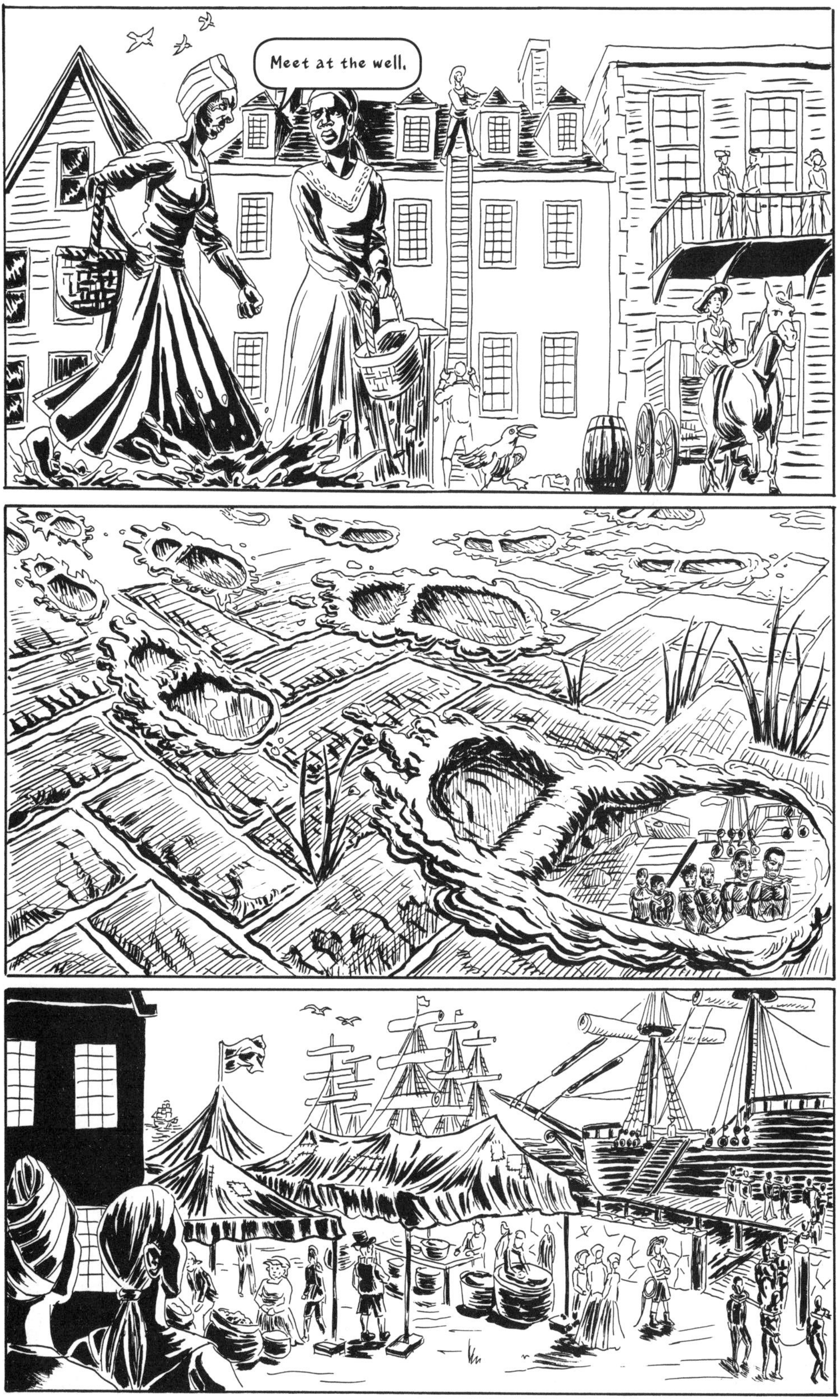
Meet at the well.

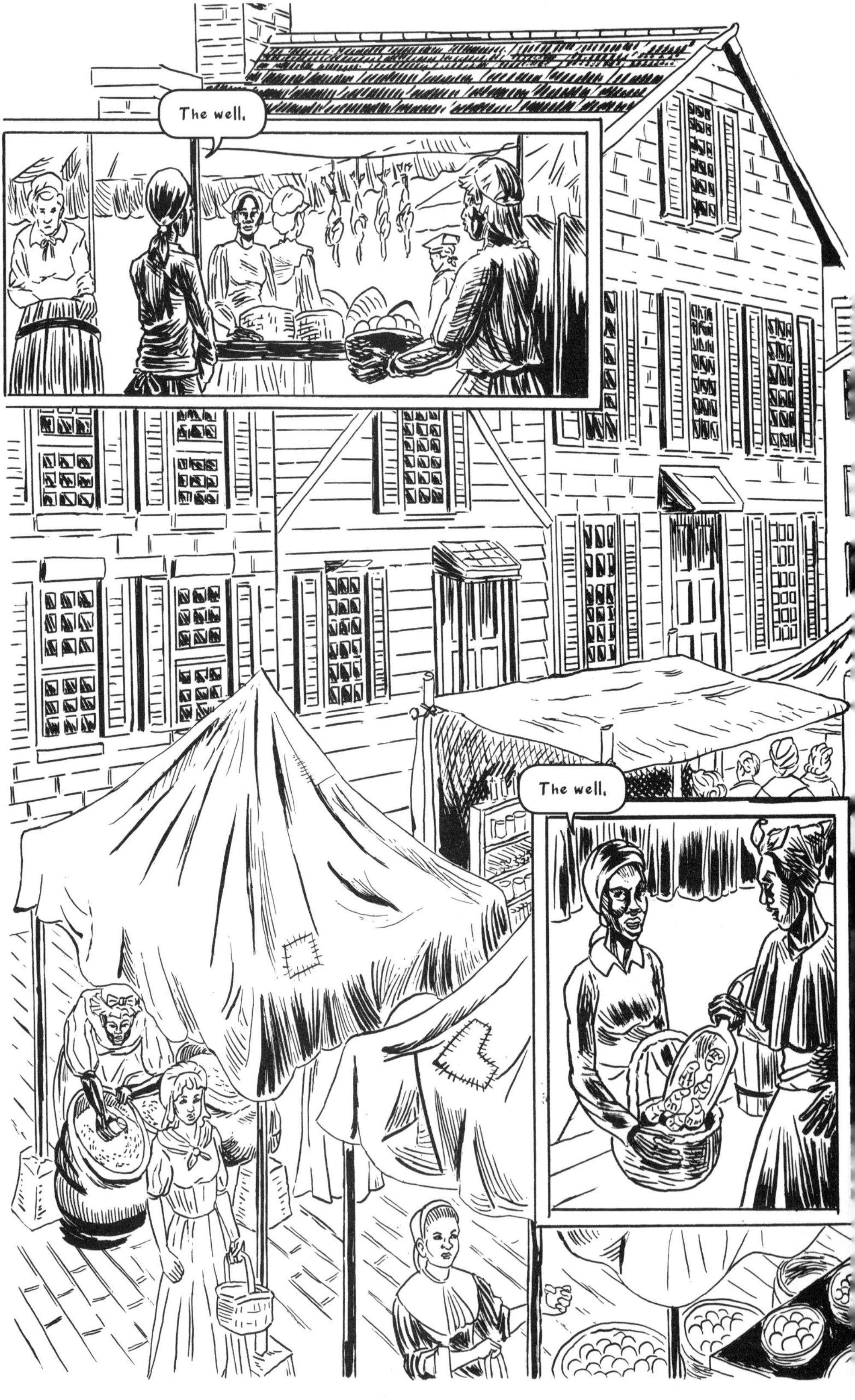
The well.
The well.

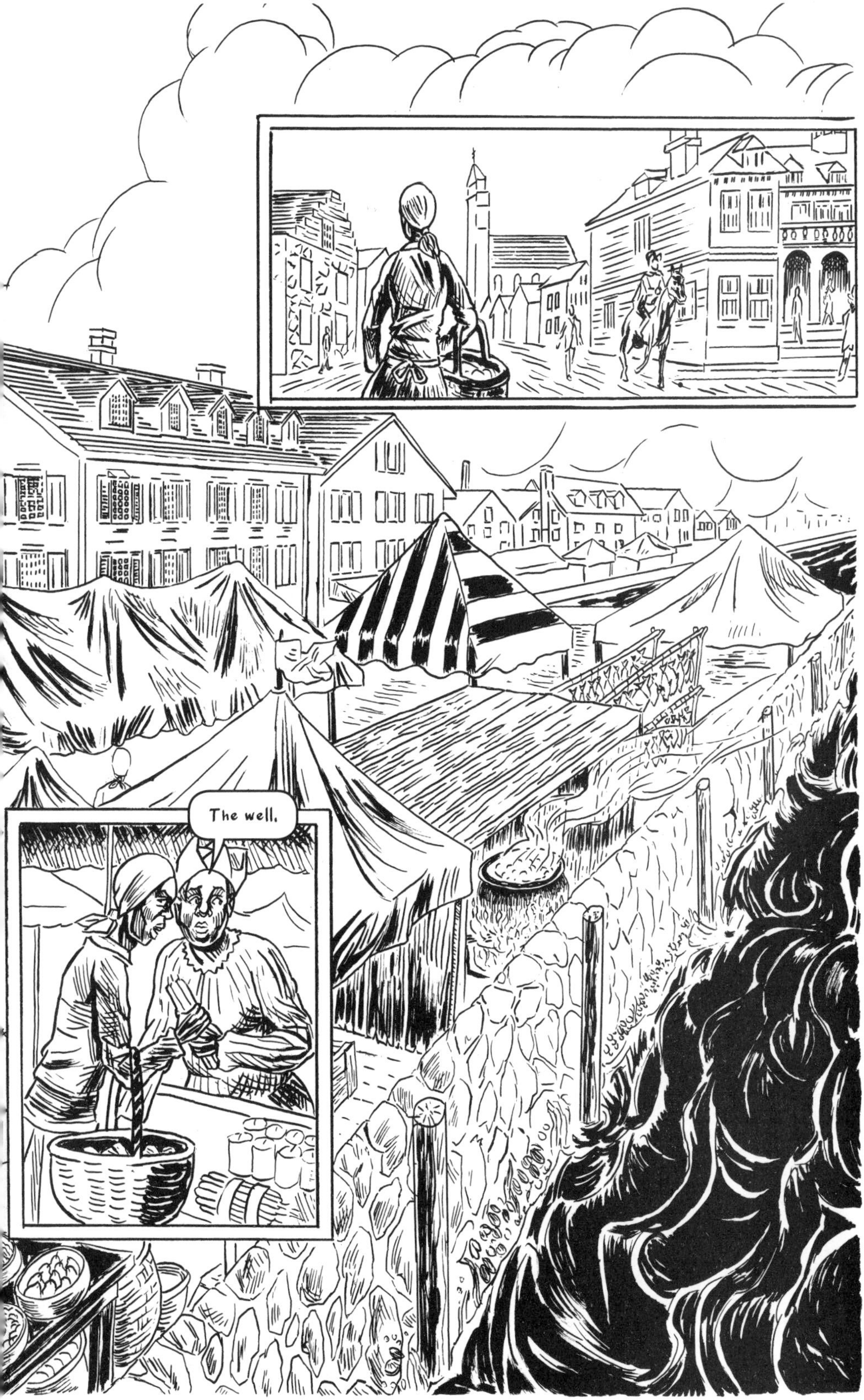
The well.

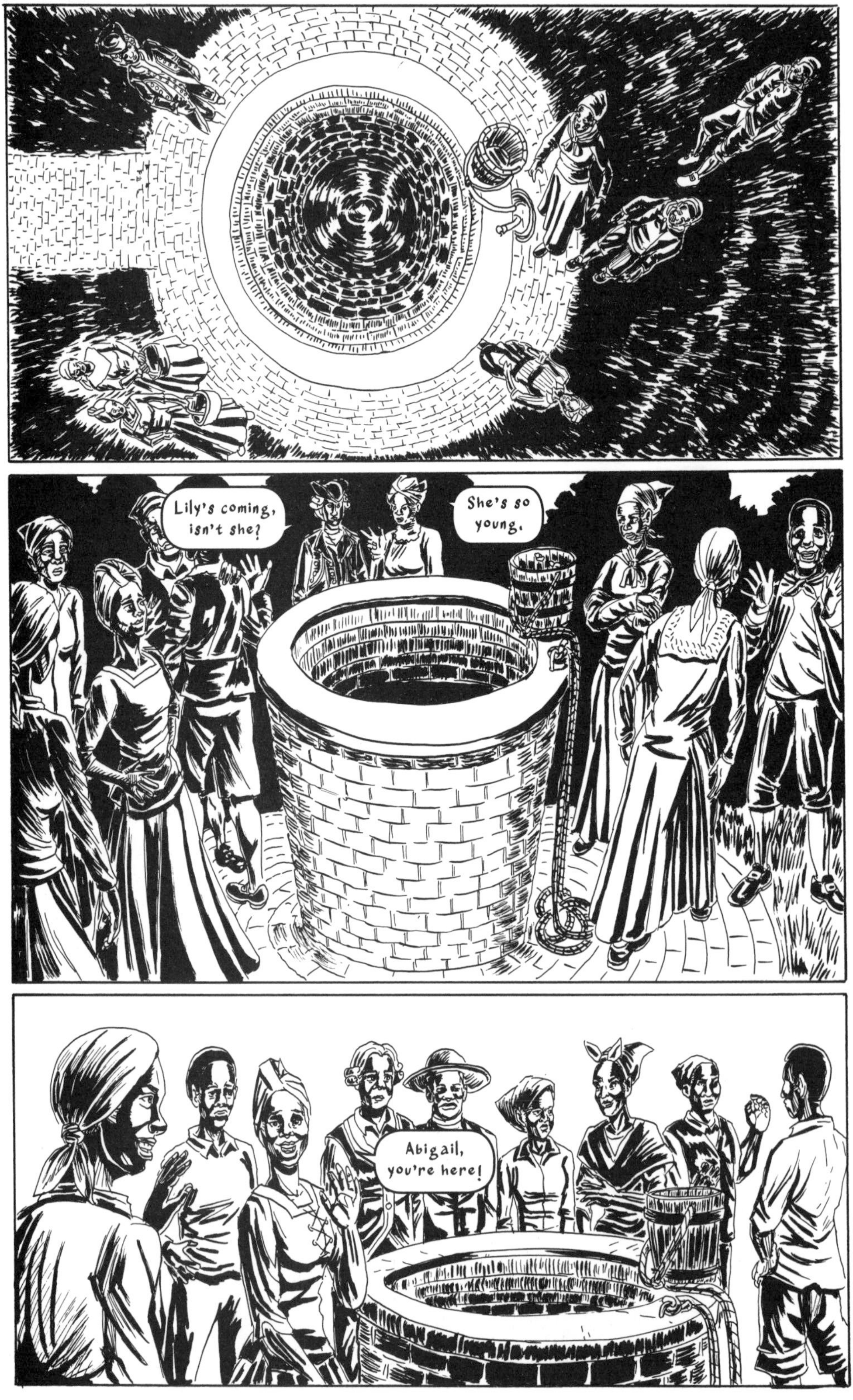
Lily's coming, isn't she?
She's so young.
Abigail, you're here!

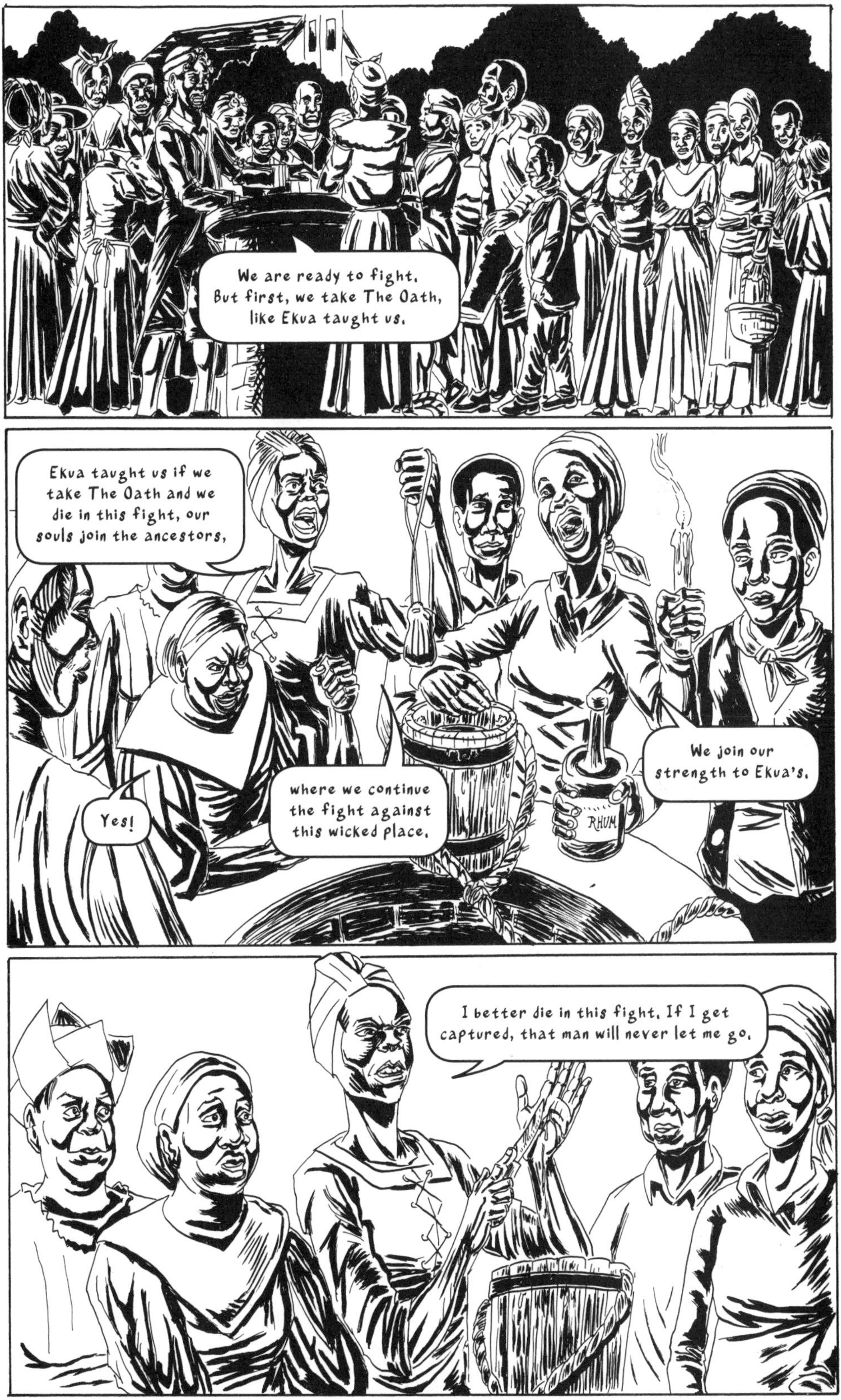
We are ready to fight. But first, we take The Oath, like Ekua taught us.
Ekua taught us if we take The Oath and we die in this fight, our souls join the ancestors,
Yes!
where we continue the fight against this wicked place.
RHUM
We join our strength to Ekua's.
I better die in this fight. If I get captured, that man will never let me go.

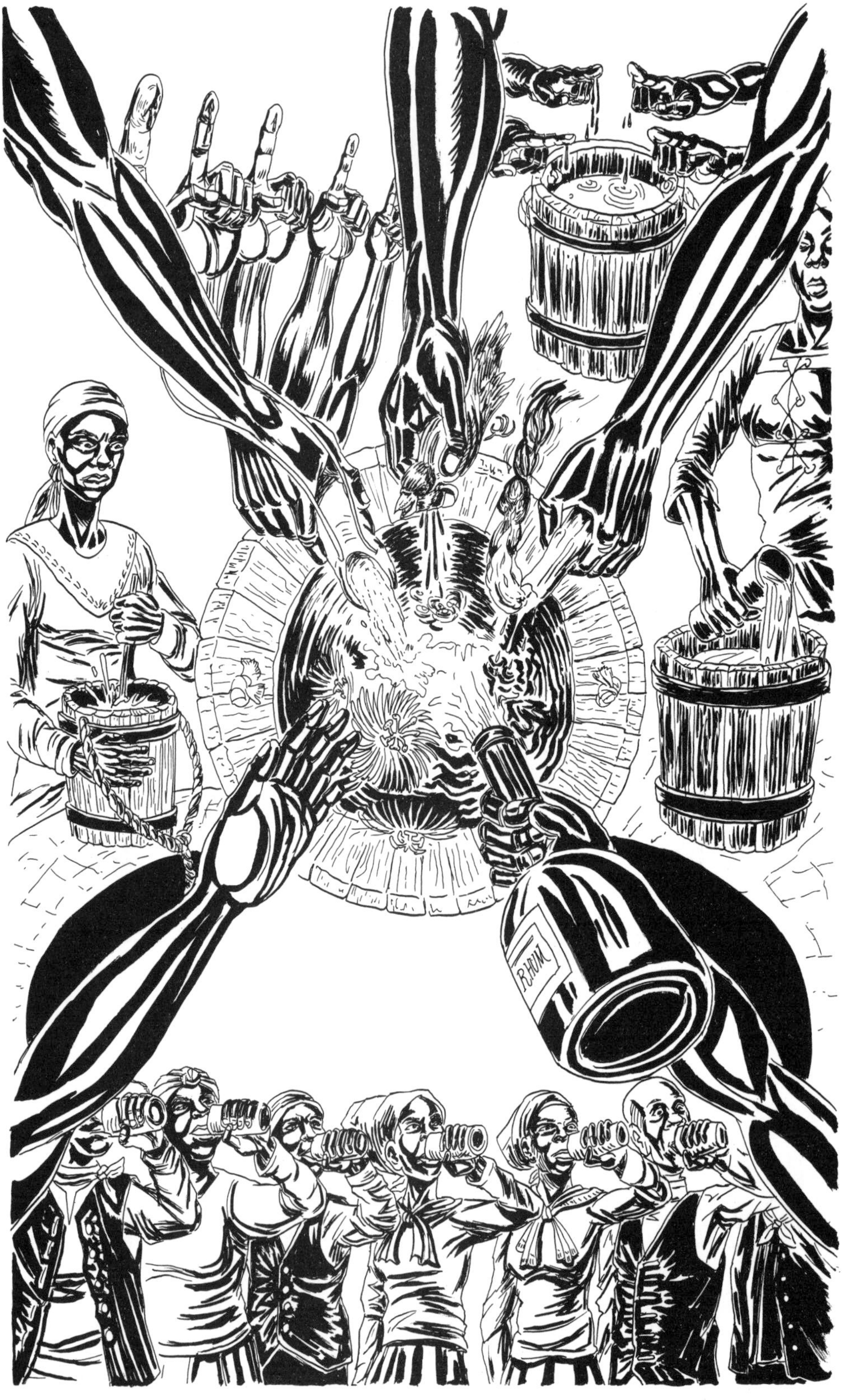
RHUM

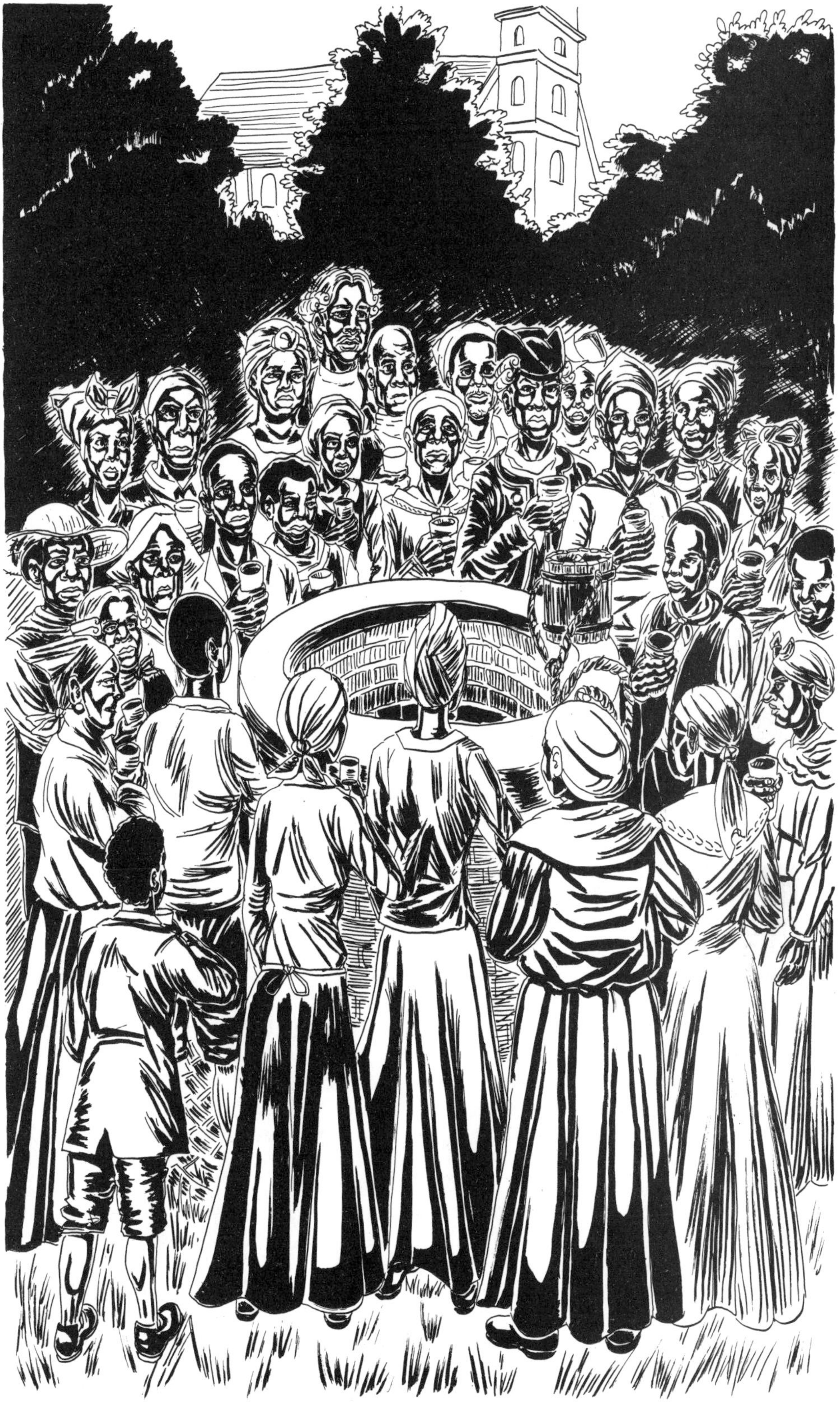

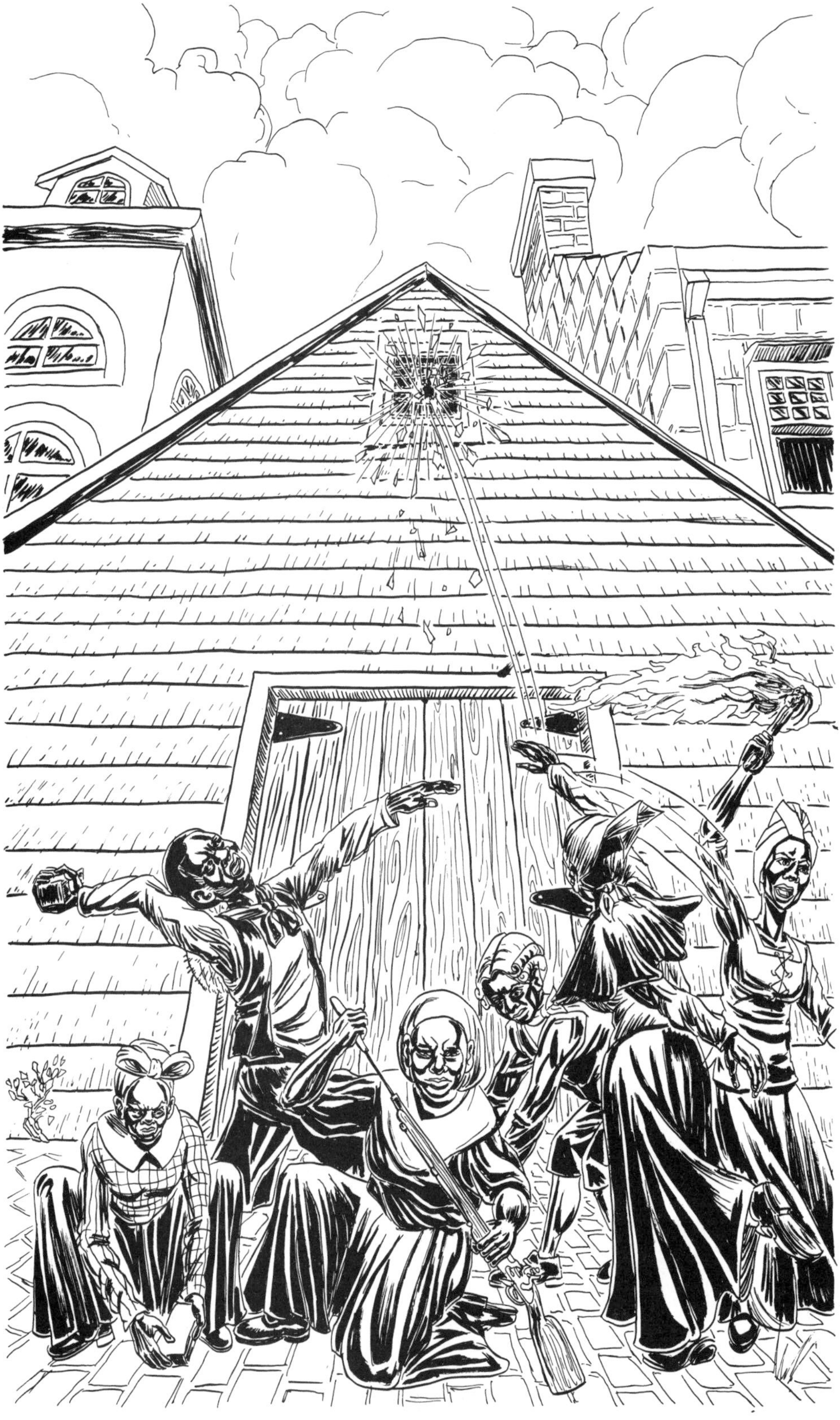

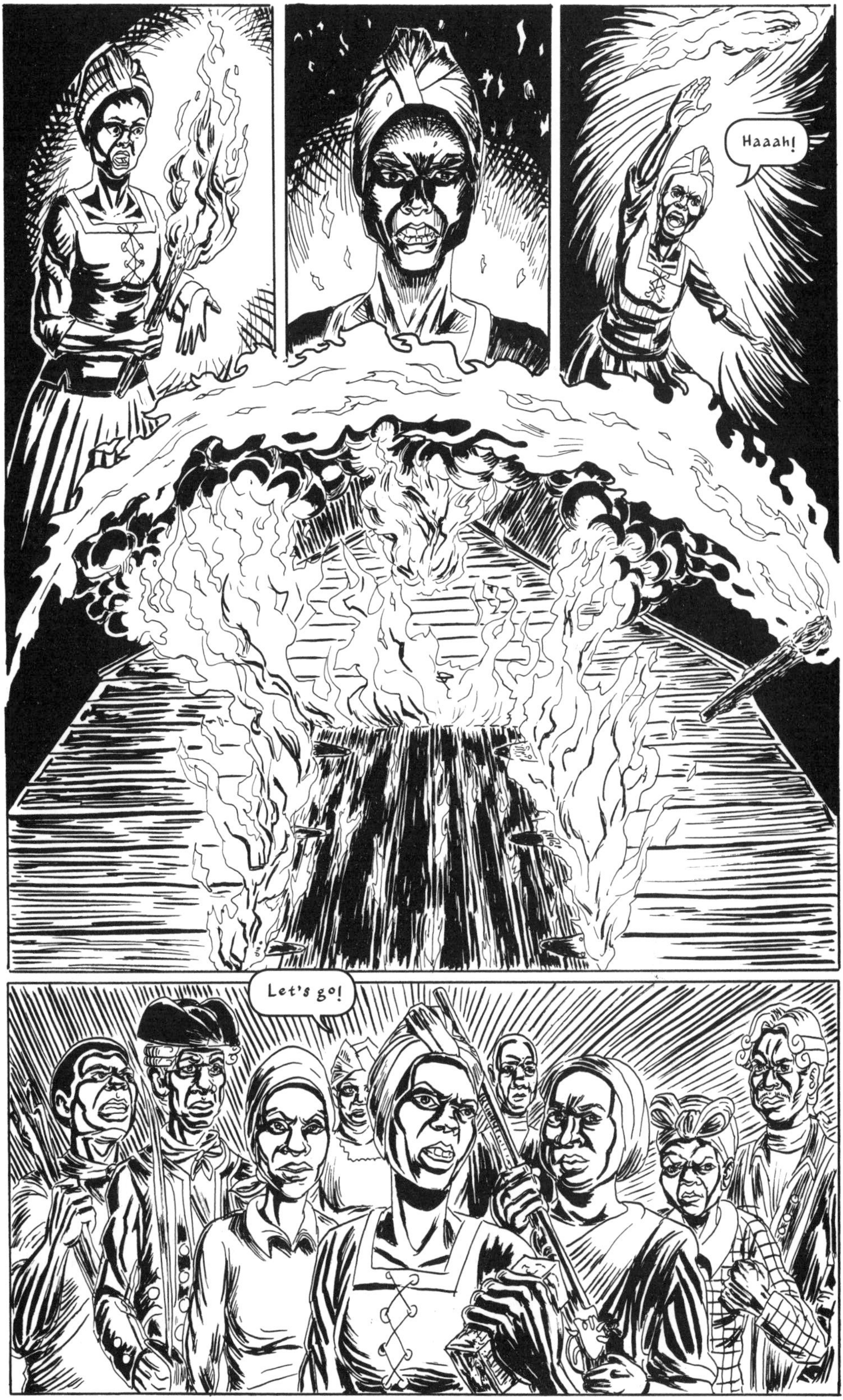
Haaah!
Let's go!

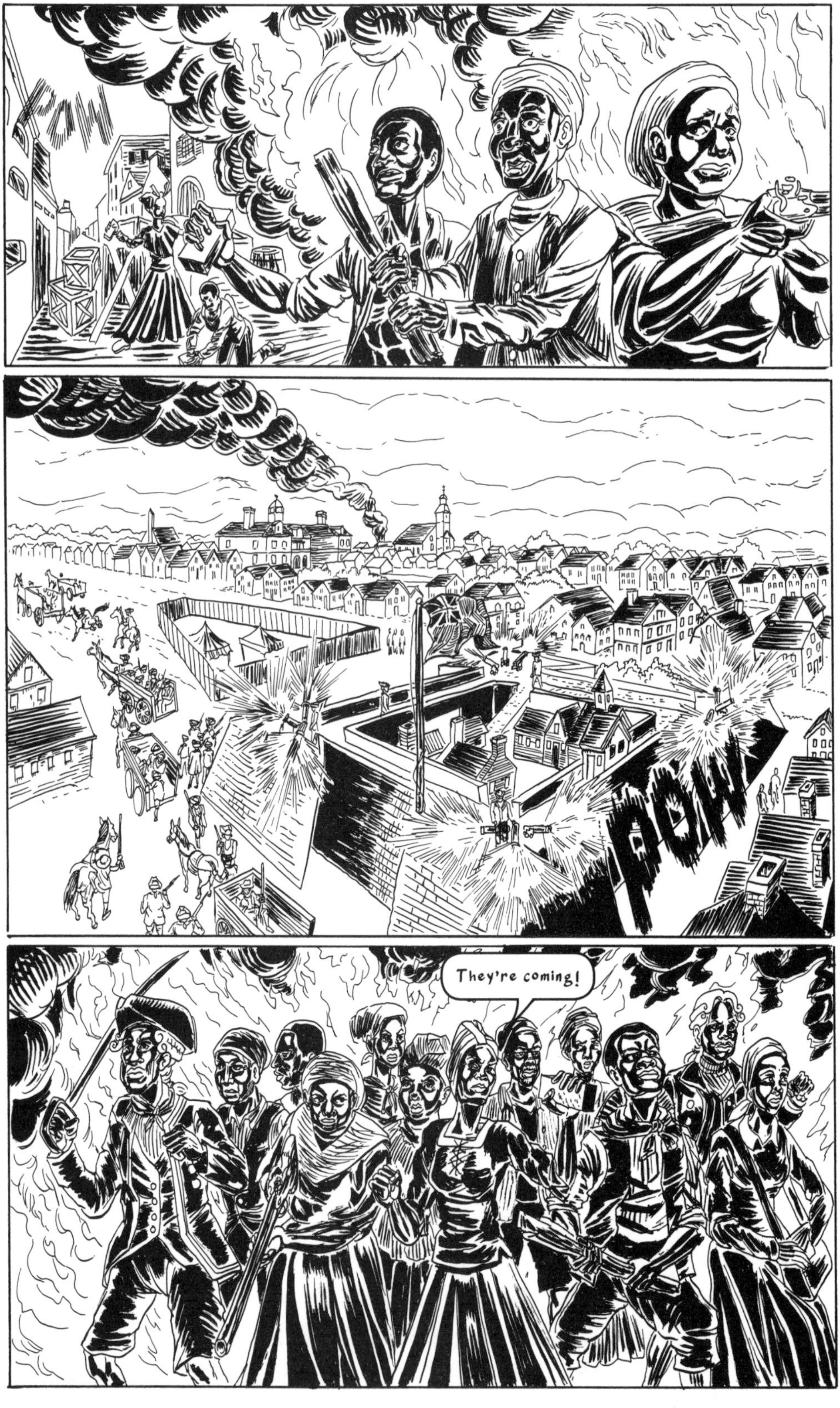
POW
POW
They're coming!

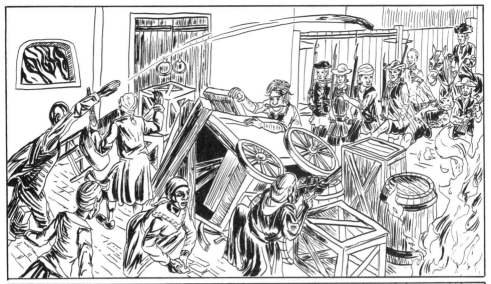

Ugh!

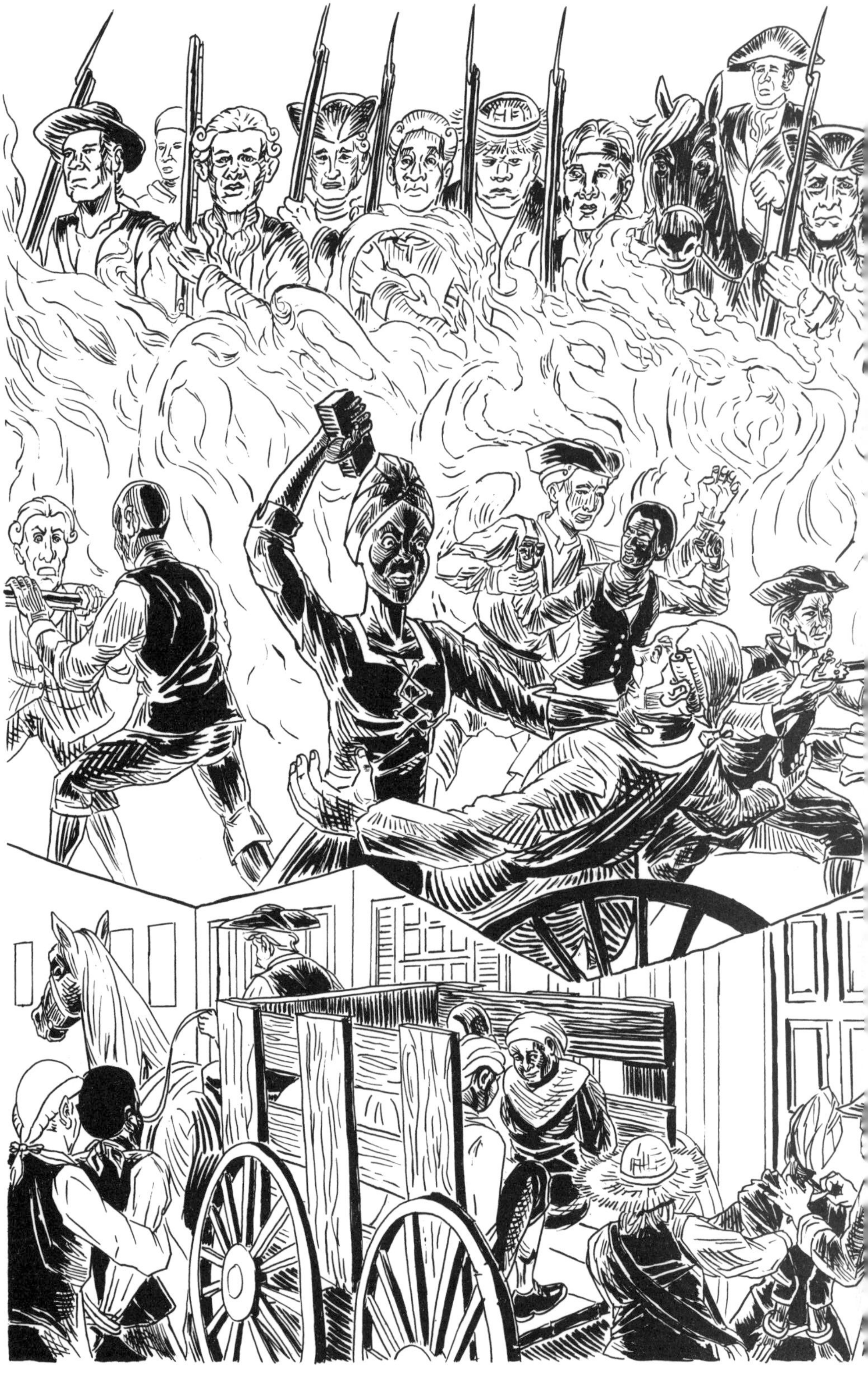

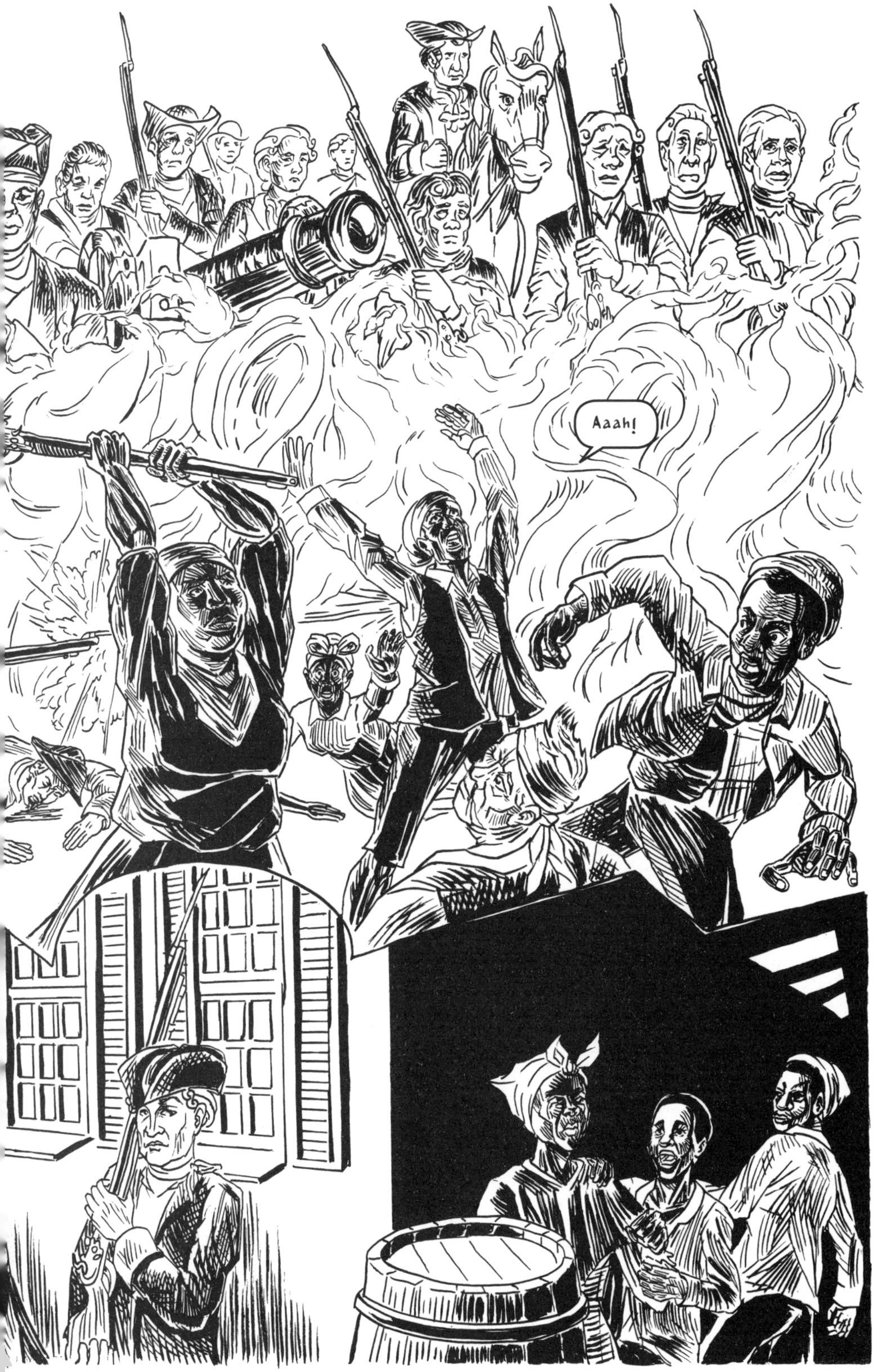
Aaah!

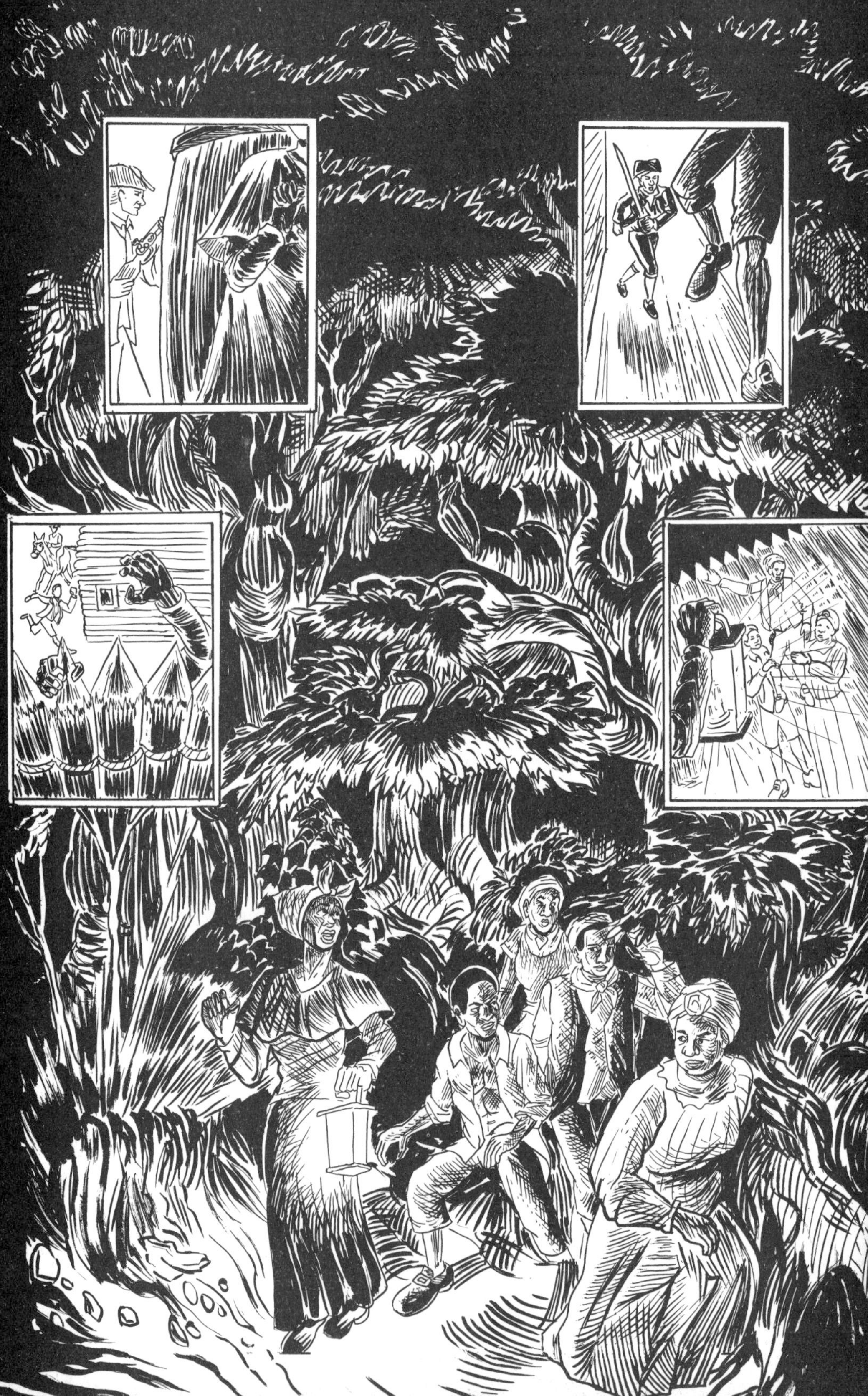

New York governor's letter to Dom Regina

June 23, 1712

We found all that put the design into execution, six of these having first laid violent hands upon themselves, the rest forthwith brought to trial before ye Justices of this place . . .

Twenty-seven condemned, whereof twenty-one were executed, one being a woman with child, her execution by that means suspended . . .

Some were burnt others hanged, one broke on the wheele, and one hung a live in chains in the town, so that there has been the most exemplary punishment inflicted that can possibly be thought of . . .

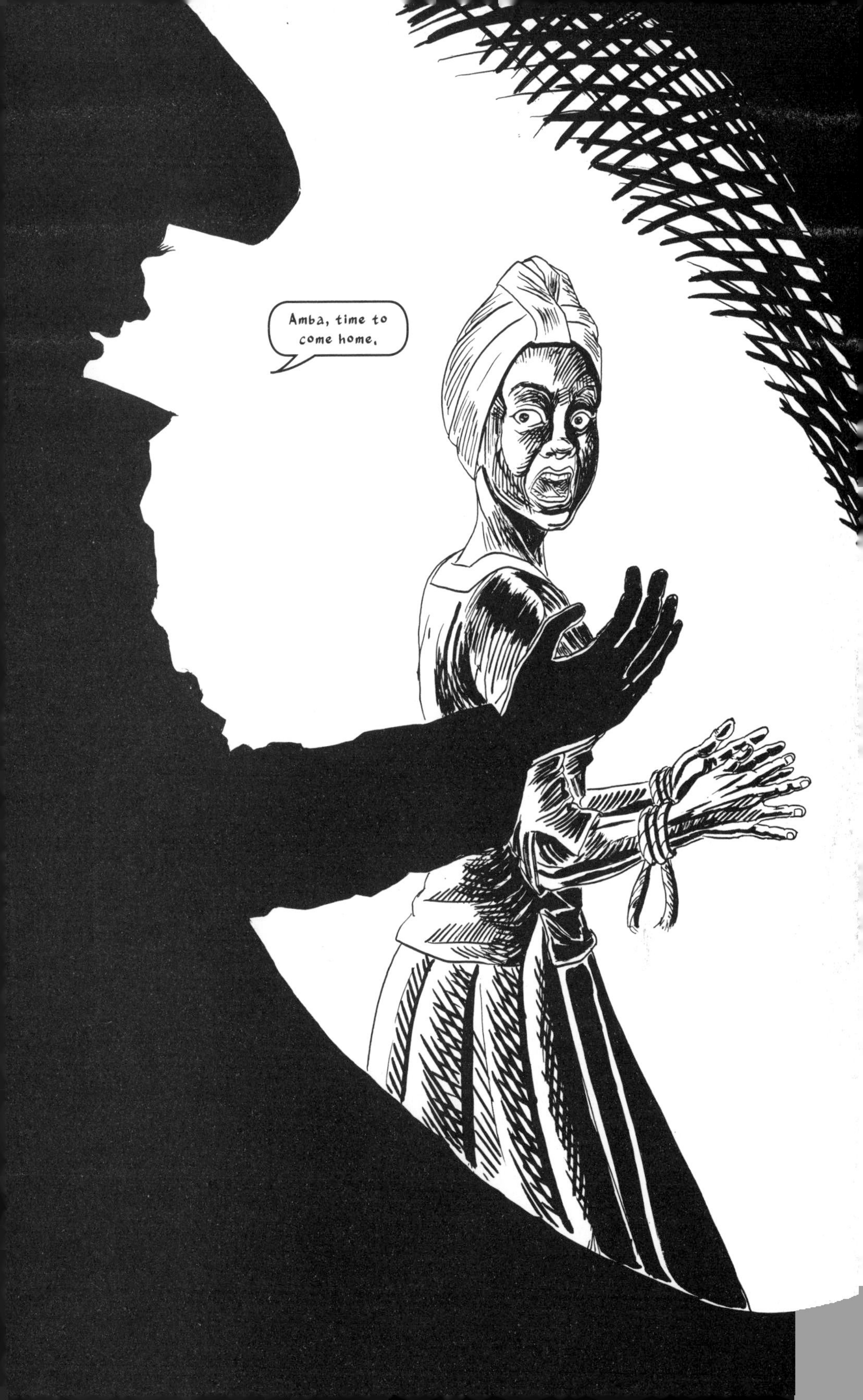
Amba, time to come home.

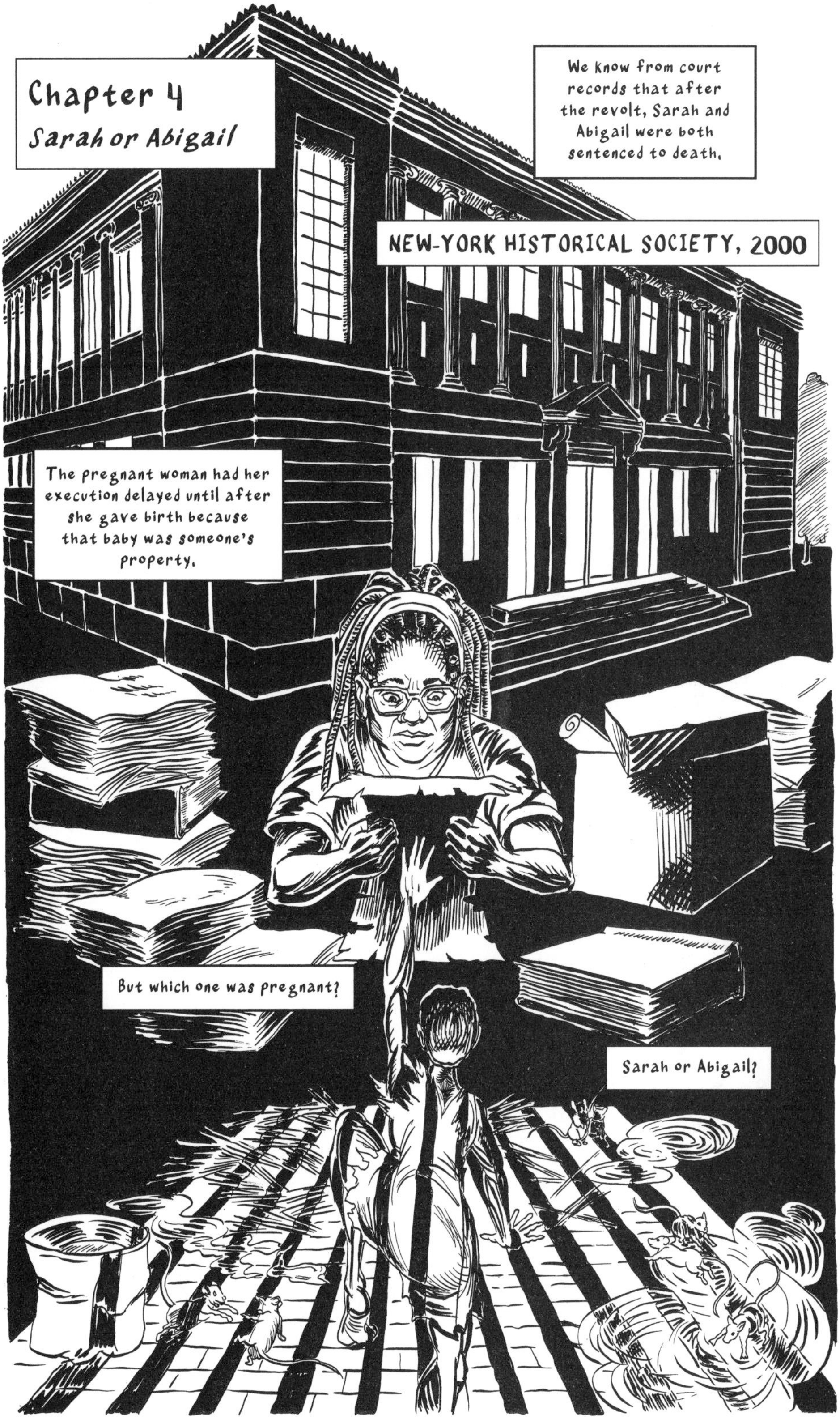
Chapter 4
Sarah or Abigail
We know from court records that after the revolt, Sarah and Abigail were both sentenced to death.
NEW-YORK HISTORICAL SOCIETY, 2000
The pregnant woman had her execution delayed until after she gave birth because that baby was someone's property.
But which one was pregnant?
Sarah or Abigail?

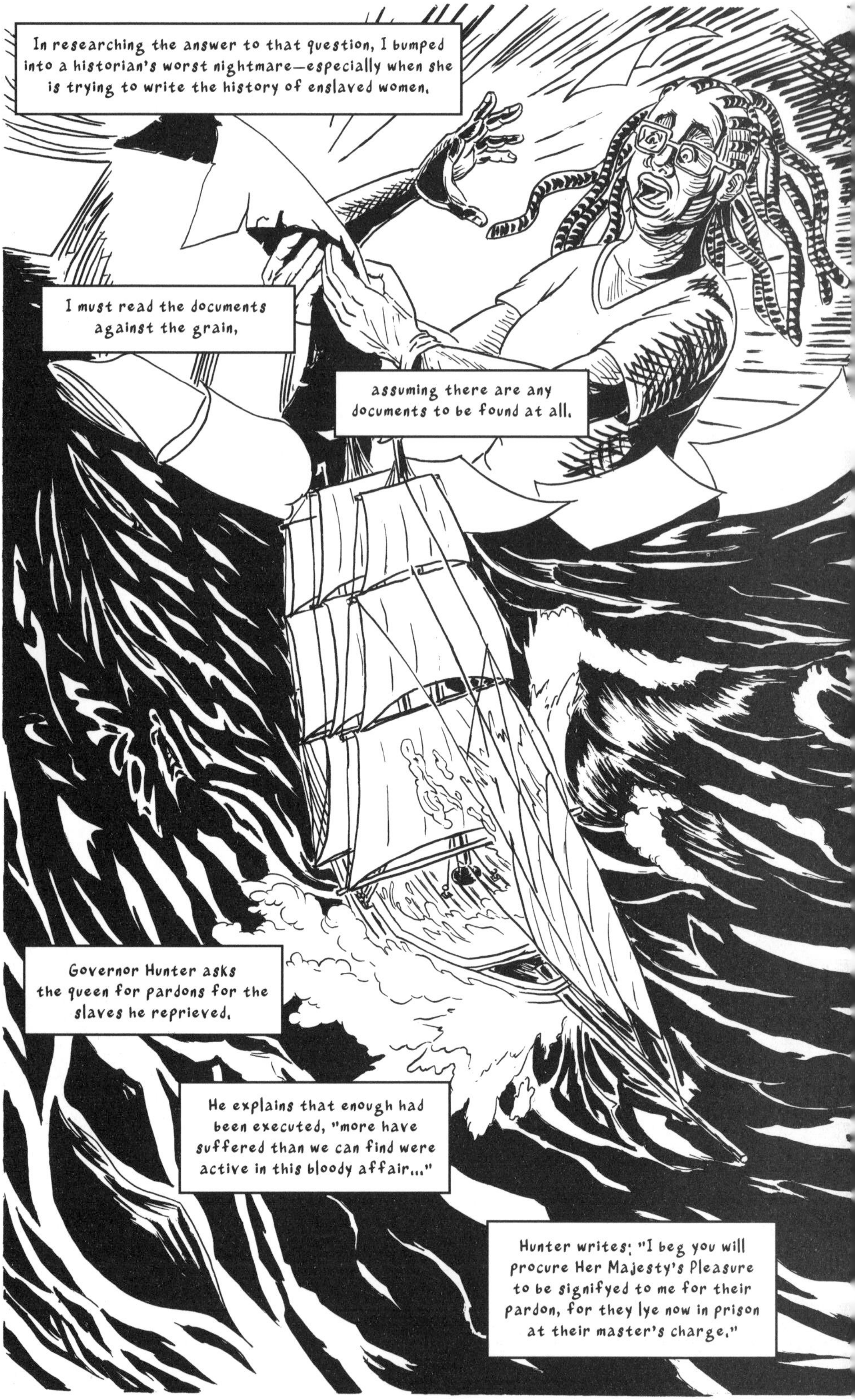
In researching the answer to that question, I bumped into a historian's worst nightmare—especially when she is trying to write the history of enslaved women.
I must read the documents against the grain,
assuming there are any documents to be found at all.
Governor Hunter asks the queen for pardons for the slaves he reprieved.
He explains that enough had been executed, "more have suffered than we can find were active in this bloody affair..."
Hunter writes: "I beg you will procure Her Majesty's Pleasure to be signifyed to me for their pardon, for they lye now in prison at their master's charge."

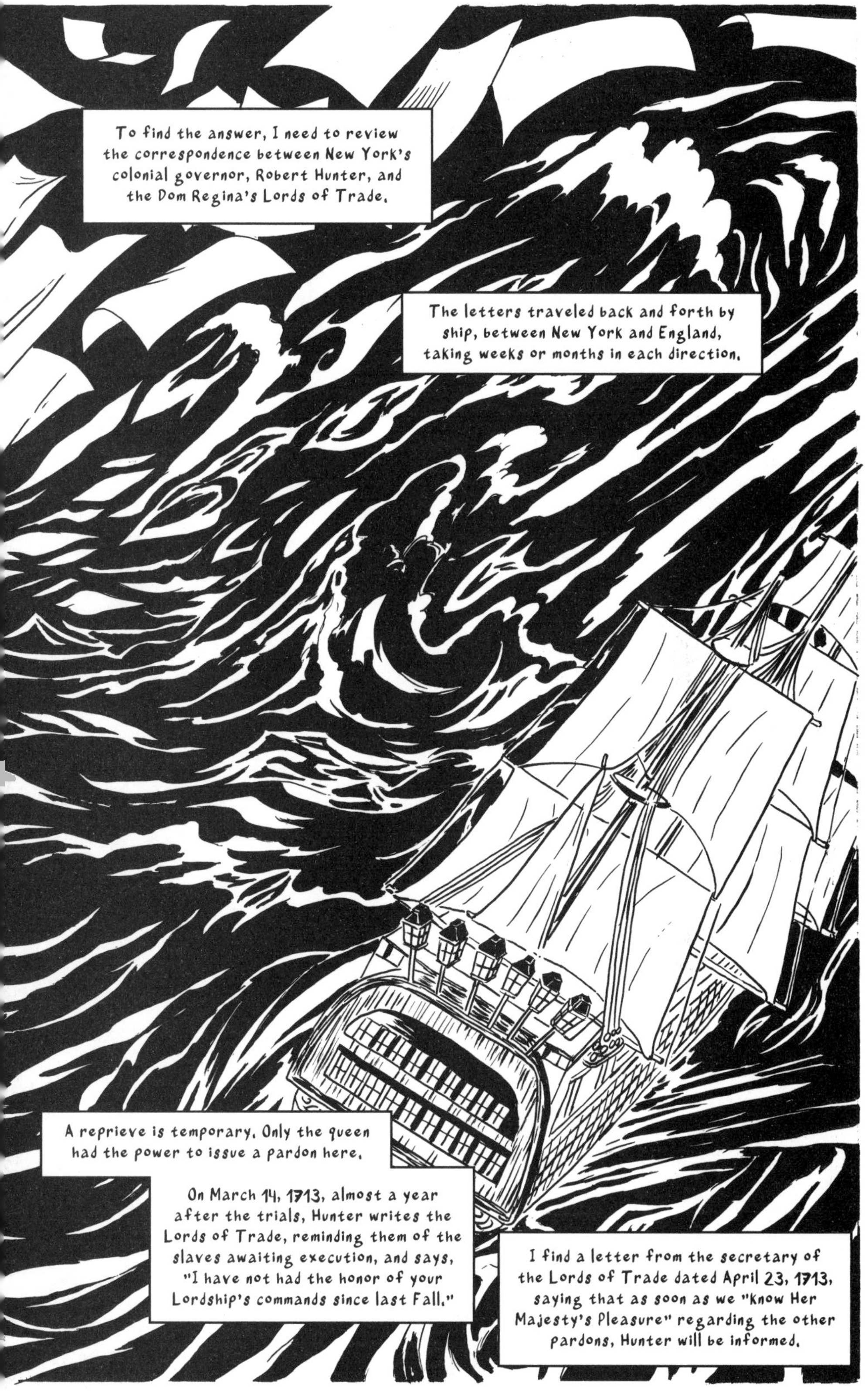
To find the answer, I need to review the correspondence between New York's colonial governor, Robert Hunter, and the Dom Regina's Lords of Trade.
The letters traveled back and forth by ship, between New York and England, taking weeks or months in each direction.
A reprieve is temporary. Only the queen had the power to issue a pardon here.
On March 14, 1713, almost a year after the trials, Hunter writes the Lords of Trade, reminding them of the slaves awaiting execution, and says, "I have not had the honor of your Lordship's commands since last Fall."
I find a letter from the secretary of the Lords of Trade dated April 23, 1713, saying that as soon as we "know Her Majesty's Pleasure" regarding the other pardons, Hunter will be informed.

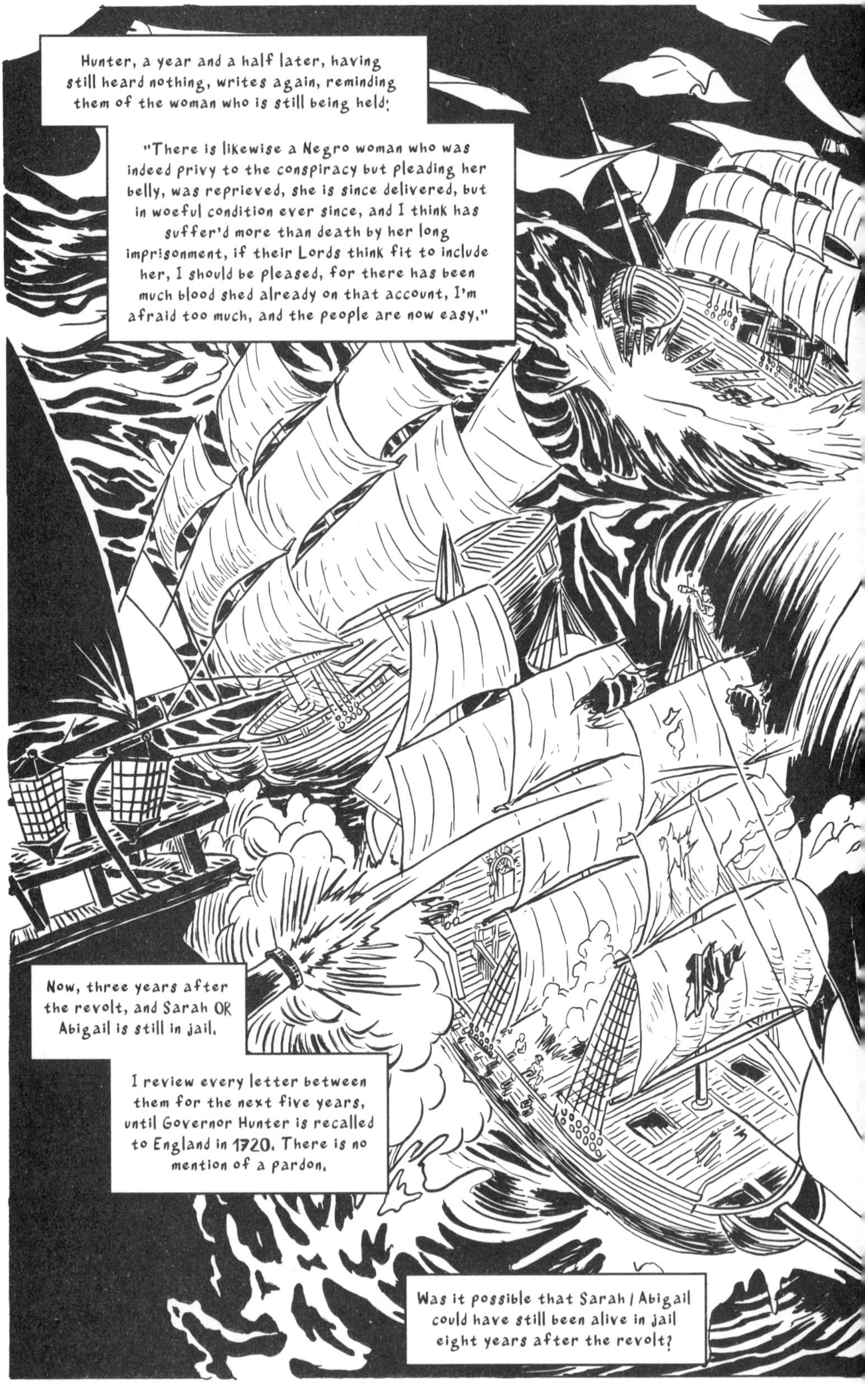
Hunter, a year and a half later, having still heard nothing, writes again, reminding them of the woman who is still being held:
"There is likewise a Negro woman who was indeed privy to the conspiracy but pleading her belly, was reprieved, she is since delivered, but in woeful condition ever since, and I think has suffer'd more than death by her long imprisonment, if their Lords think fit to include her, I should be pleased, for there has been much blood shed already on that account, I'm afraid too much, and the people are now easy."
Now, three years after the revolt, and Sarah OR Abigail is still in jail.
I review every letter between them for the next five years, until Governor Hunter is recalled to England in 1720. There is no mention of a pardon.
Was it possible that Sarah / Abigail could have still been alive in jail eight years after the revolt?

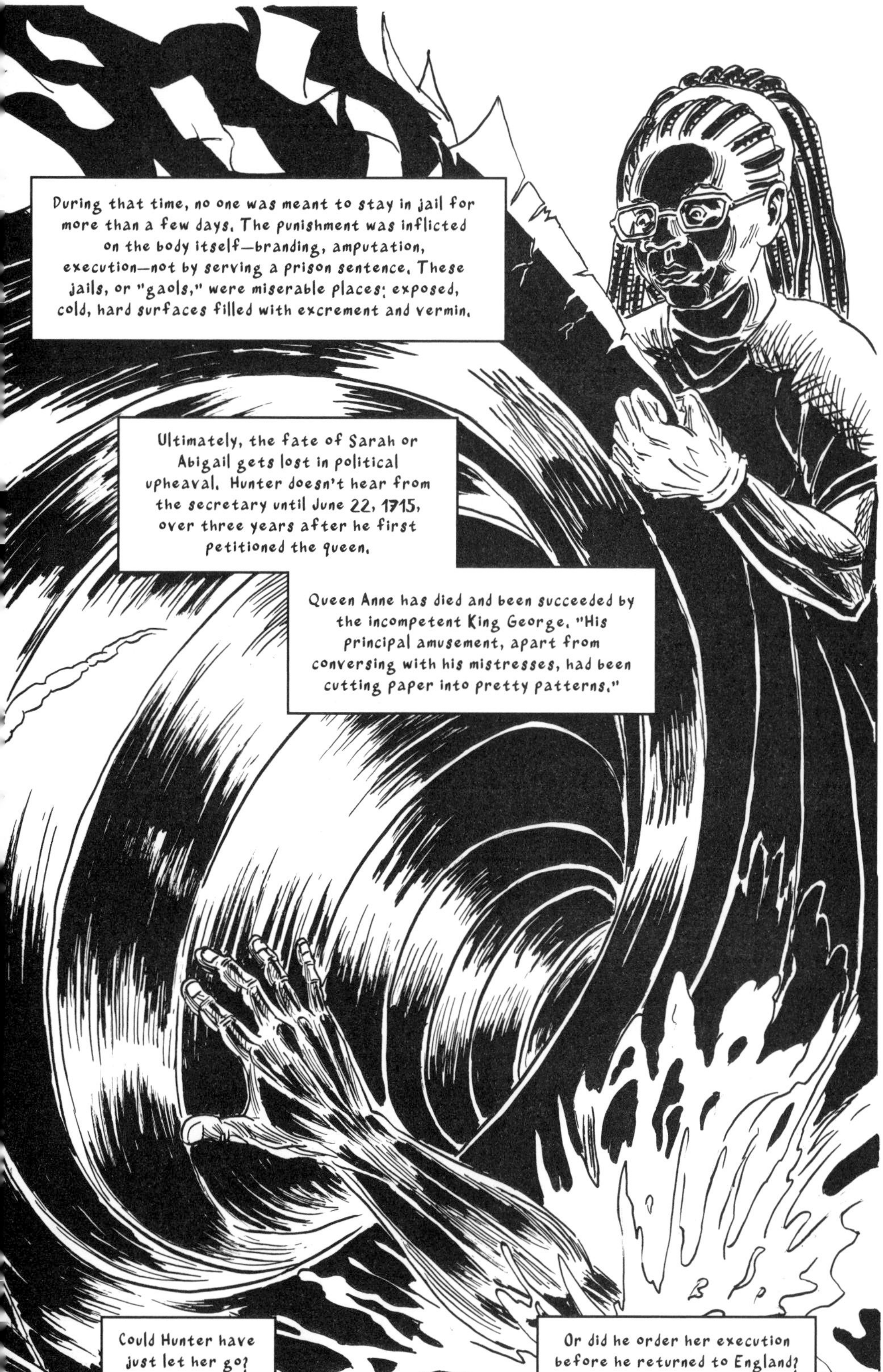

During that time, no one was meant to stay in jail for more than a few days. The punishment was inflicted on the body itself—branding, amputation, execution—not by serving a prison sentence. These jails, or "gaols," were miserable places: exposed, cold, hard surfaces filled with excrement and vermin.
Ultimately, the fate of Sarah or Abigail gets lost in political upheaval. Hunter doesn't hear from the secretary until June 22, 1715, over three years after he first petitioned the queen.
Queen Anne has died and been succeeded by the incompetent King George. "His principal amusement, apart from conversing with his mistresses, had been cutting paper into pretty patterns."
Could Hunter have just let her go?
Or did he order her execution before he returned to England?

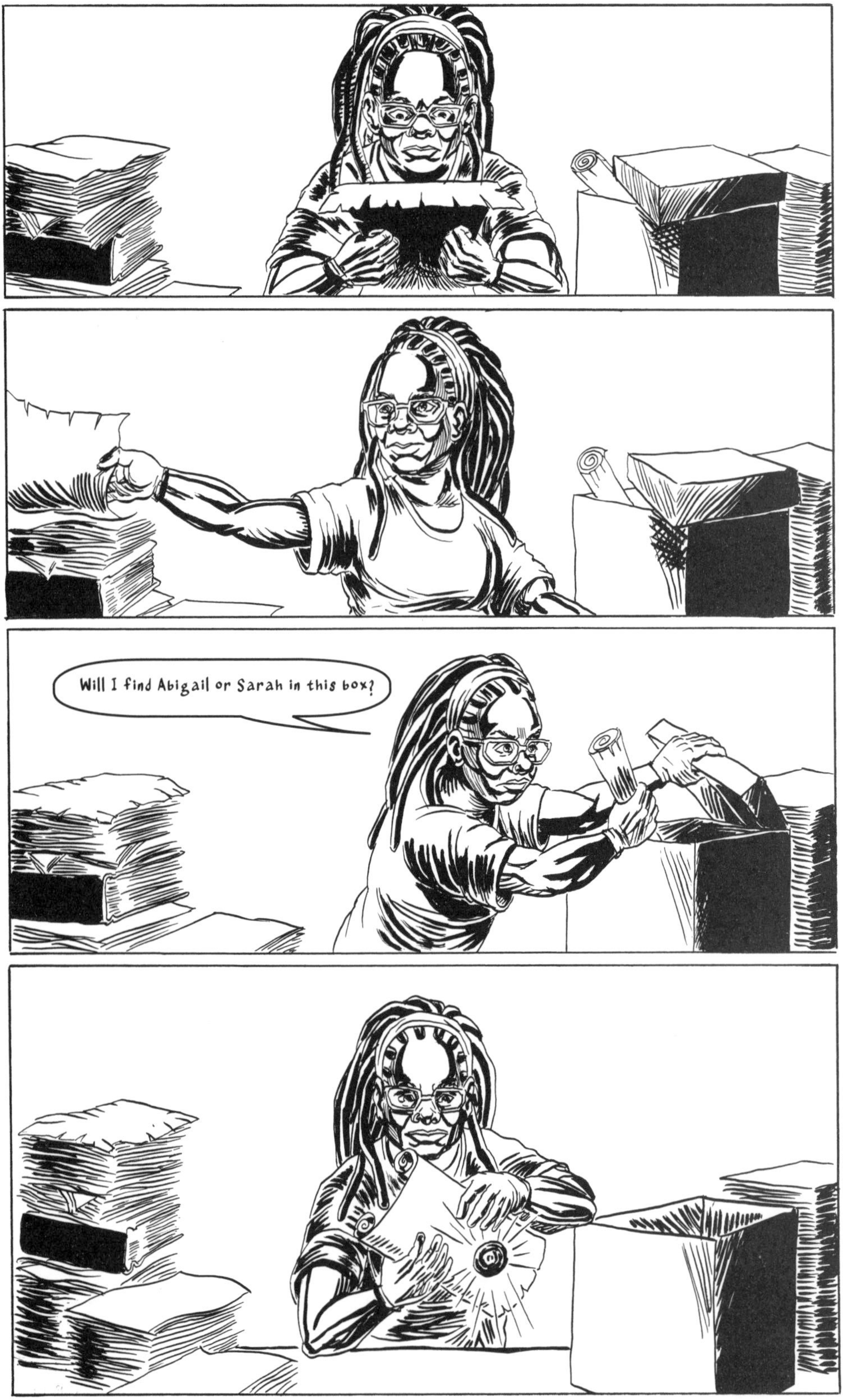
Will I find Abigail or Sarah in this box?

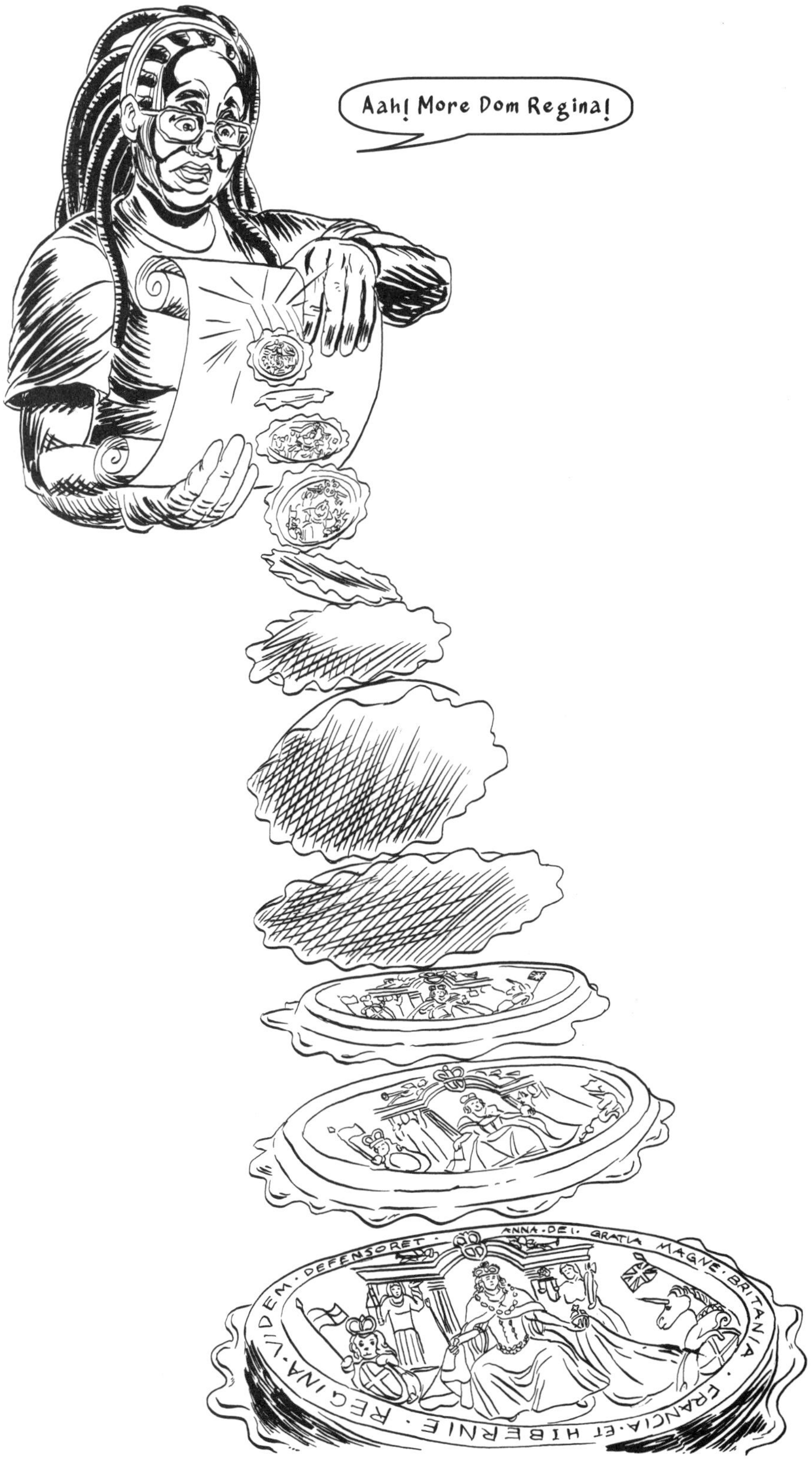
Aah! More Dom Regina!
ANNA·DEI· GRATIA MAGNE·BRITANIA · FRANCIA·ET HIBERNIE · REGINA·VIDEM· DEFENSORET ·

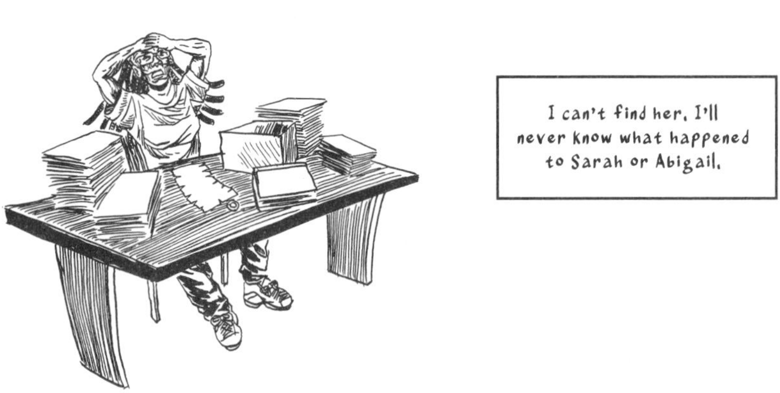
I can't find her. I'll never know what happened to Sarah or Abigail.

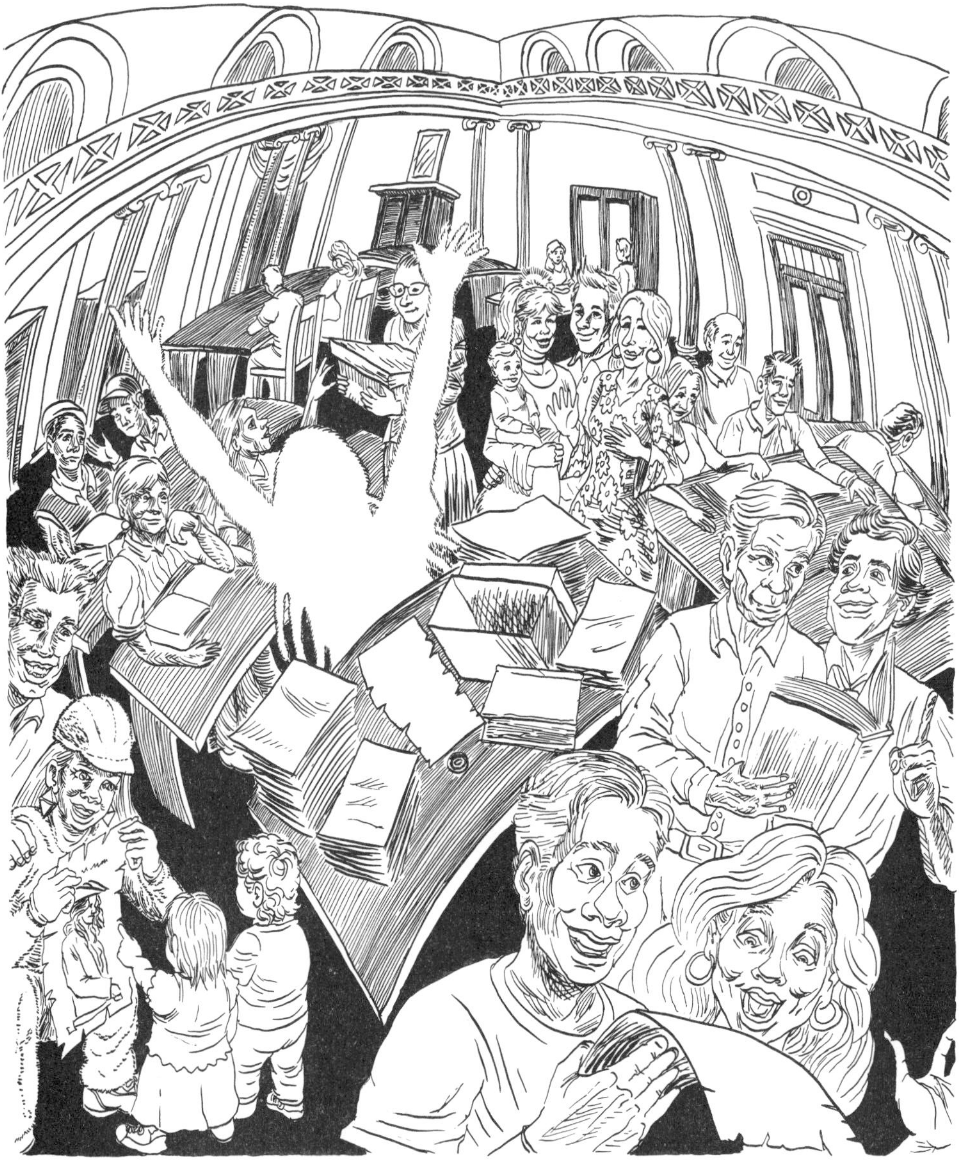

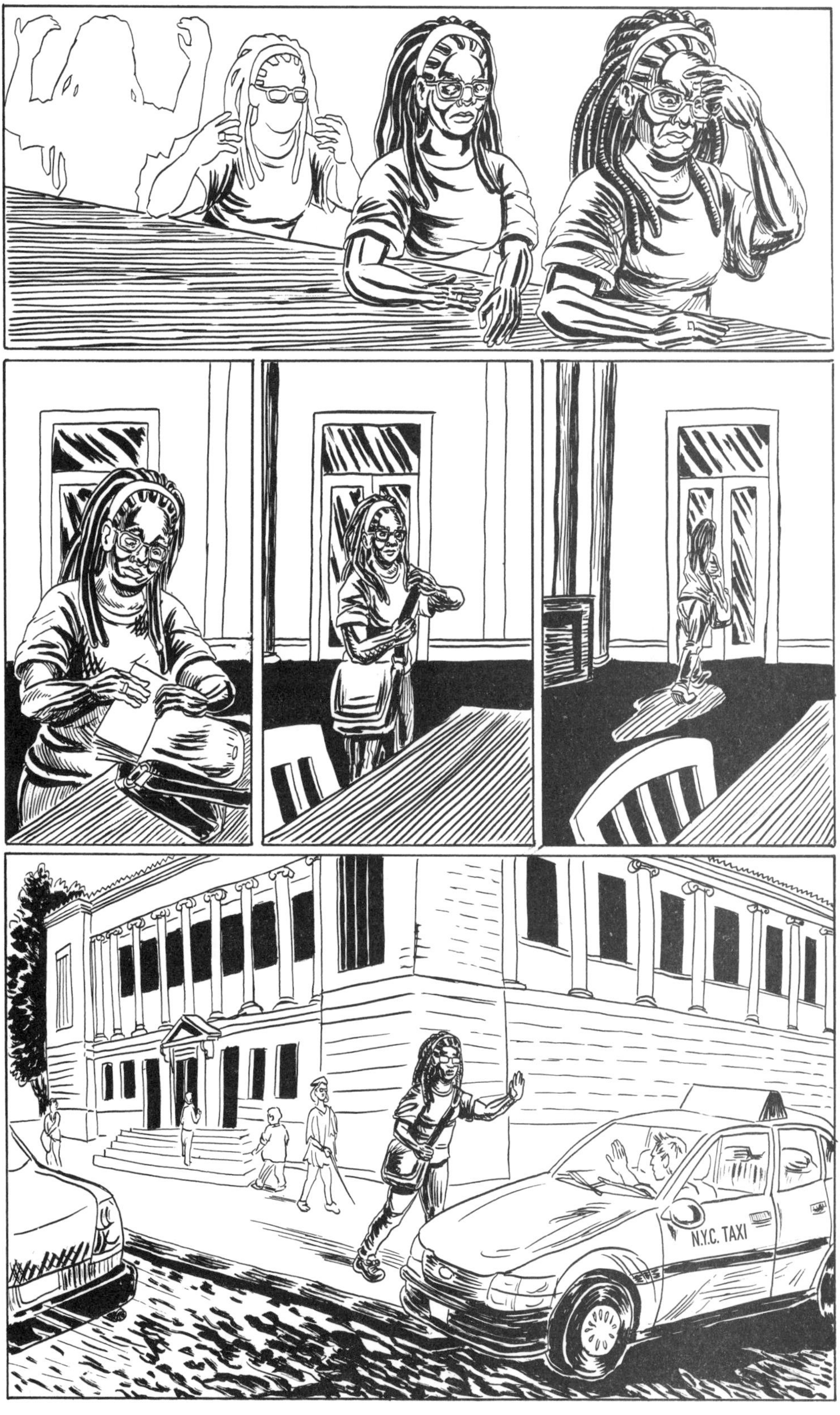
N.Y.C. TAXI

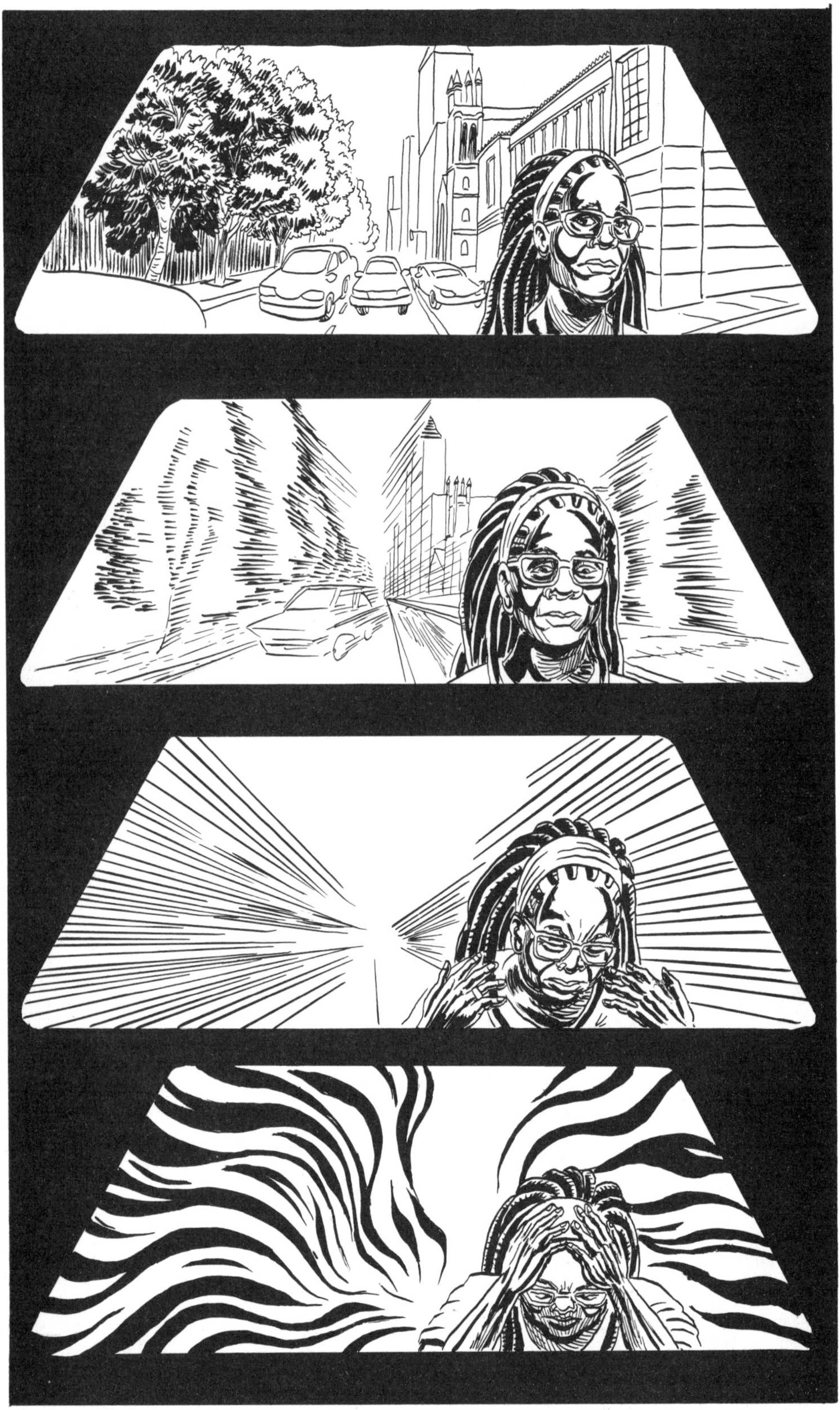

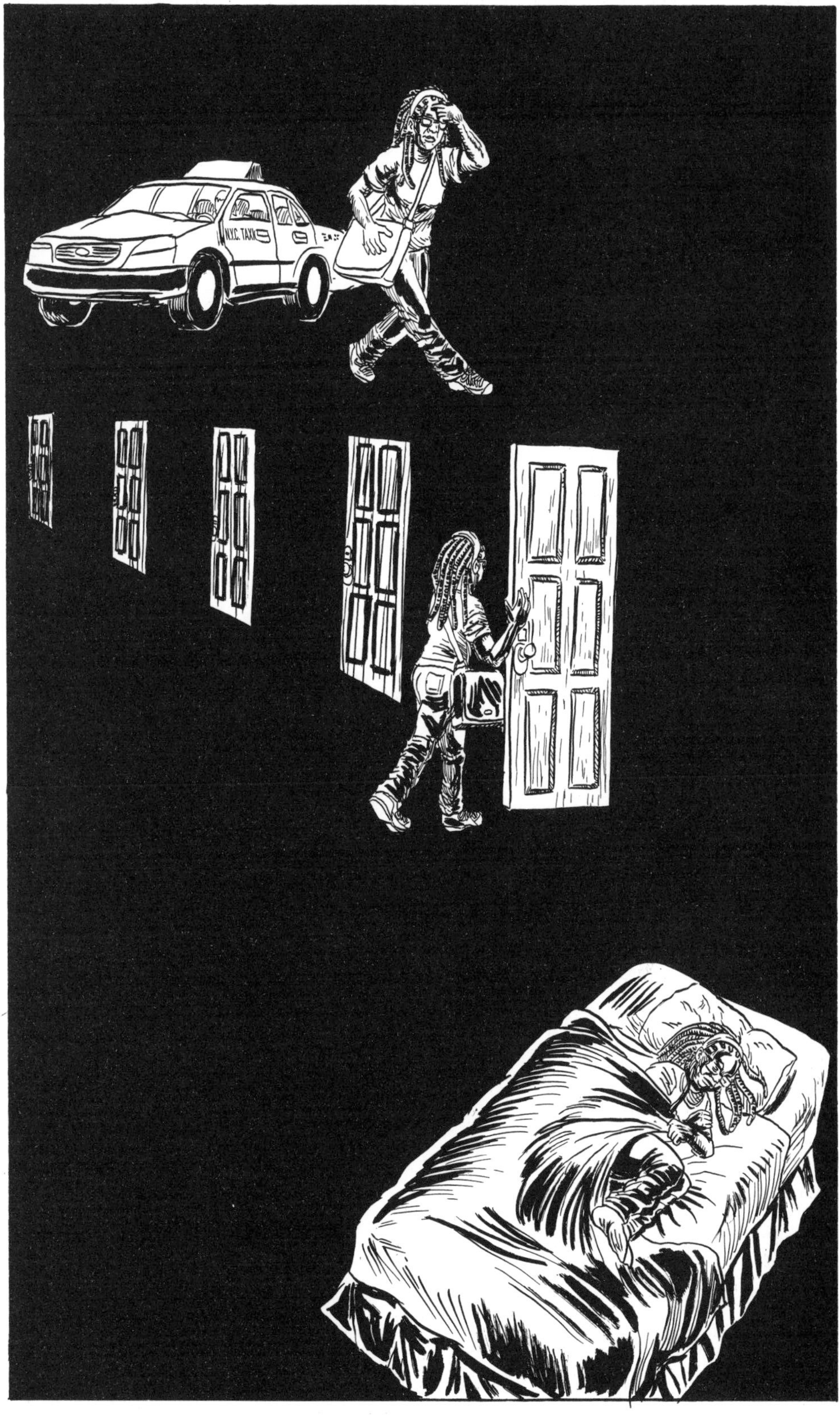
N.Y.C. TAXI

Chapter 5
The Search for the Negro Fiend

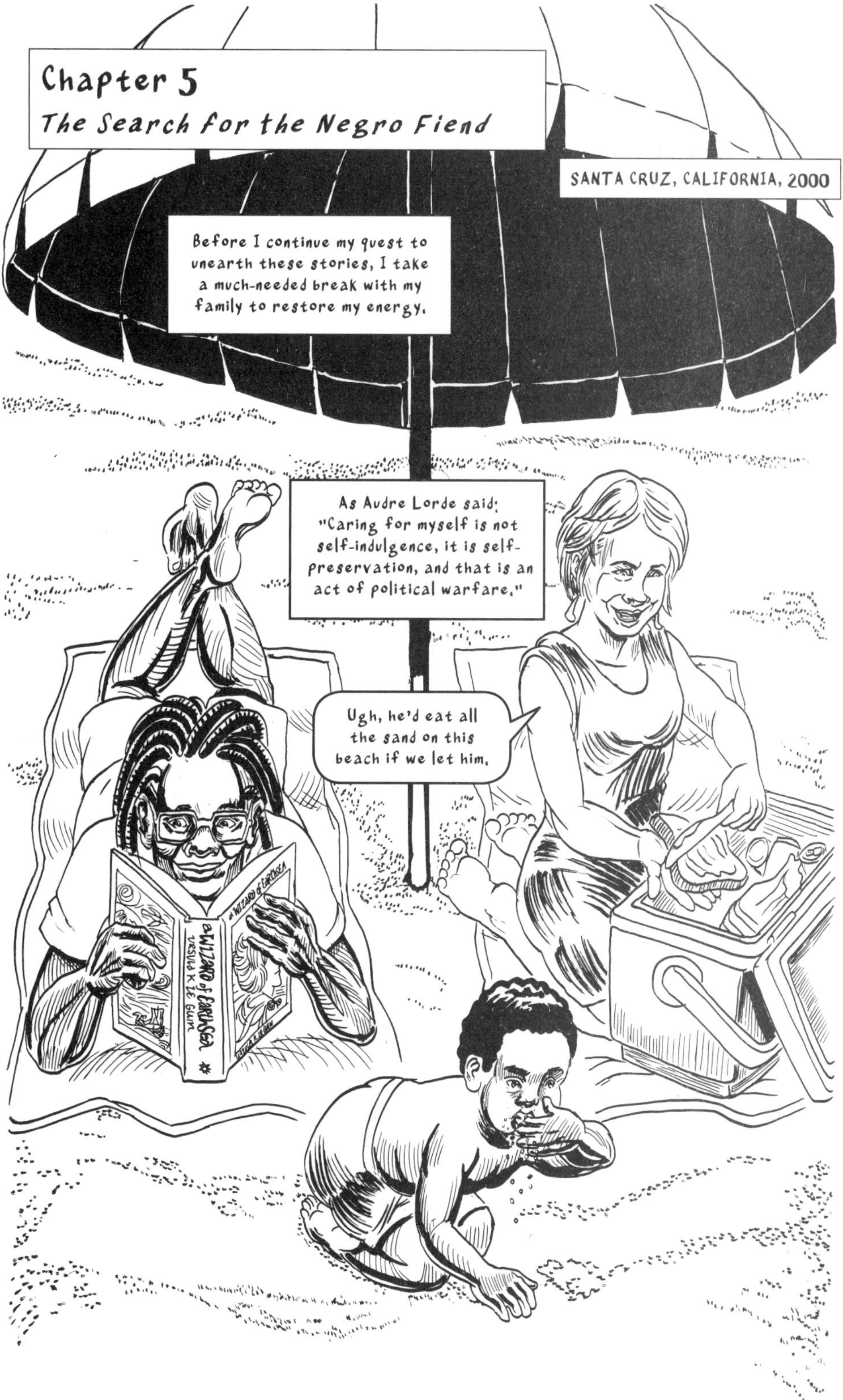

SANTA CRUZ, CALIFORNIA, 2000
Before I continue my quest to unearth these stories, I take a much-needed break with my family to restore my energy.
As Audre Lorde said: "Caring for myself is not self-indulgence, it is self-preservation, and that is an act of political warfare."
Ugh, he'd eat all the sand on this beach if we let him.

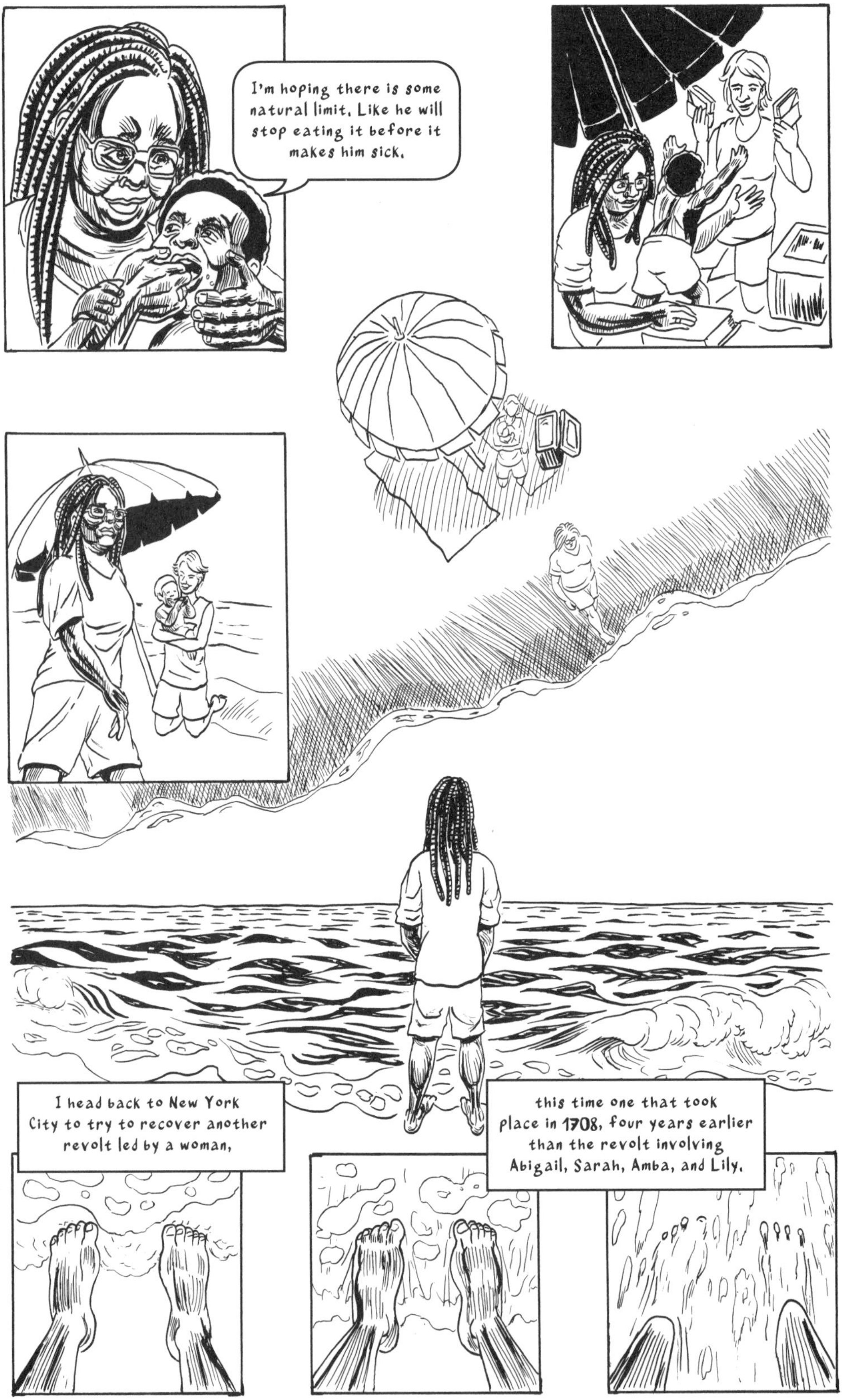
I'm hoping there is some natural limit. Like he will stop eating it before it makes him sick.
I head back to New York City to try to recover another revolt led by a woman,
this time one that took place in 1708, four years earlier than the revolt involving Abigail, Sarah, Amba, and Lily.

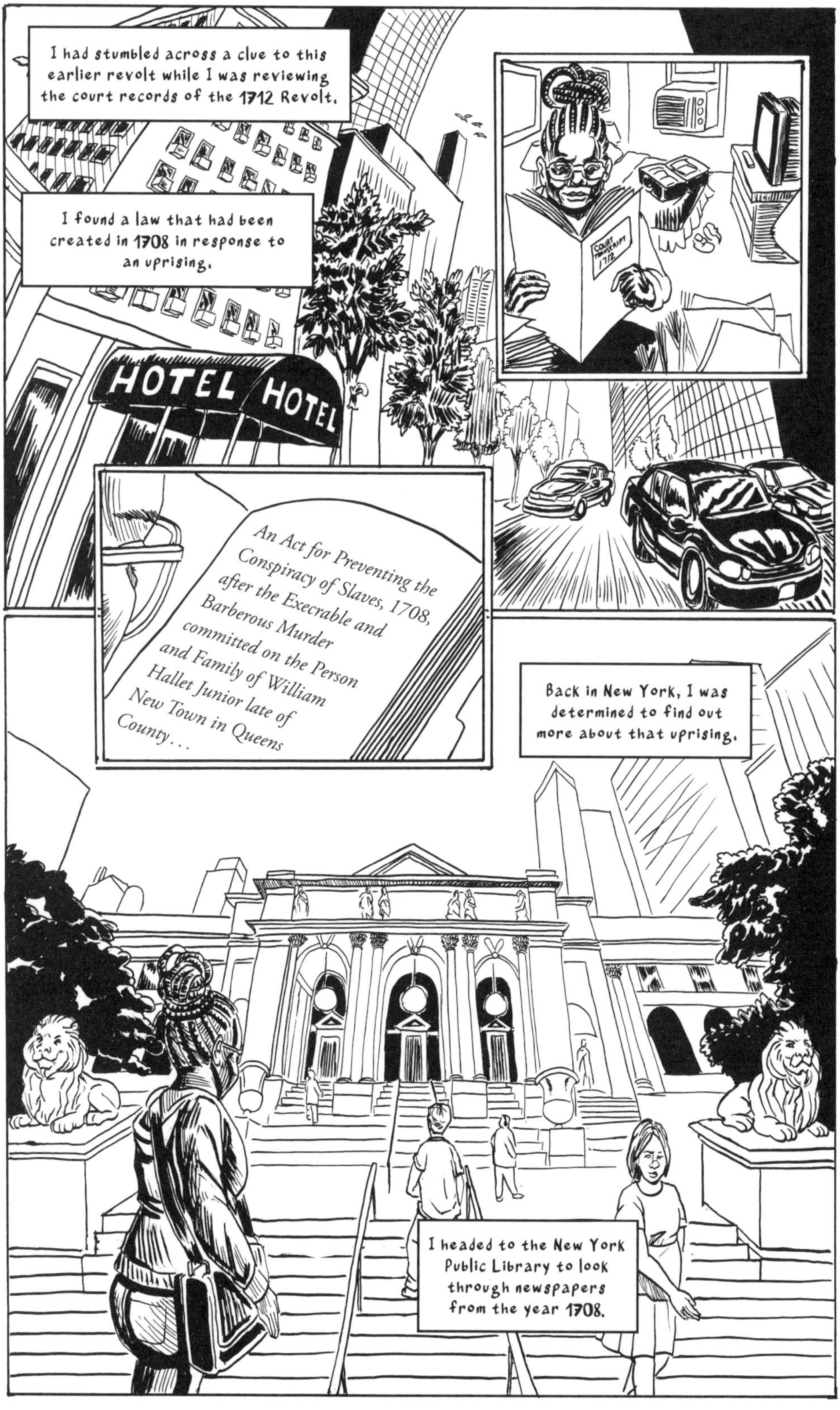
I had stumbled across a clue to this earlier revolt while I was reviewing the court records of the 1712 Revolt.
I found a law that had been created in 1708 in response to an uprising.
COURT TRANSCRIPT 1712
HOTEL
HOTEL
An Act for Preventing the Conspiracy of Slaves, 1708, after the Execrable and Barberous Murder committed on the Person and Family of William Hallet Junior late of New Town in Queens County…
Back in New York, I was determined to find out more about that uprising.
I headed to the New York Public Library to look through newspapers from the year 1708.

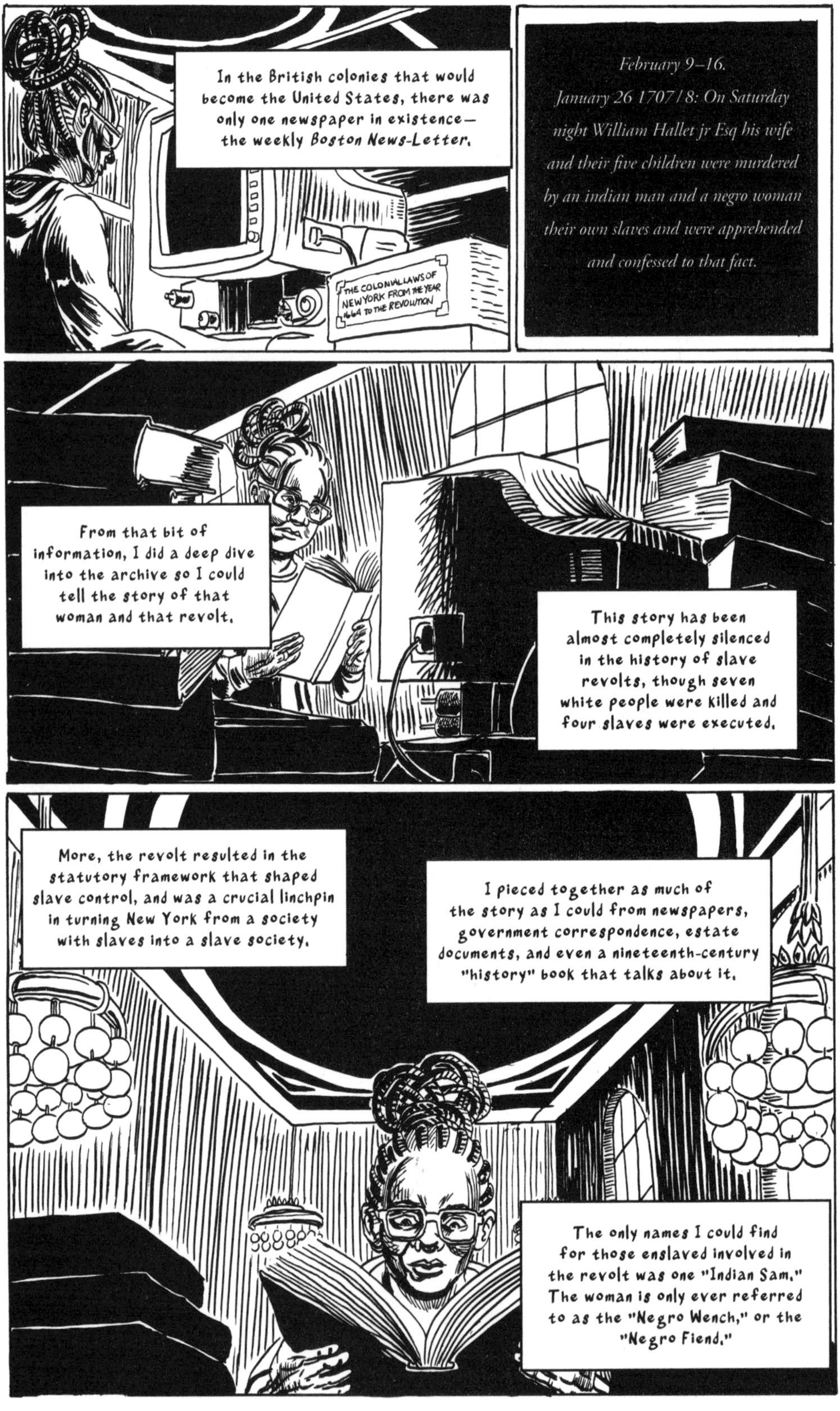
In the British colonies that would become the United States, there was only one newspaper in existence—the weekly *Boston News-Letter*.
THE COLONIAL LAWS OF NEW YORK FROM THE YEAR 1664 TO THE REVOLUTION
February 9–16.
January 26 1707/8: On Saturday night William Hallet jr Esq his wife and their five children were murdered by an indian man and a negro woman their own slaves and were apprehended and confessed to that fact.
From that bit of information, I did a deep dive into the archive so I could tell the story of that woman and that revolt.
This story has been almost completely silenced in the history of slave revolts, though seven white people were killed and four slaves were executed.
More, the revolt resulted in the statutory framework that shaped slave control, and was a crucial linchpin in turning New York from a society with slaves into a slave society.
I pieced together as much of the story as I could from newspapers, government correspondence, estate documents, and even a nineteenth-century "history" book that talks about it.
The only names I could find for those enslaved involved in the revolt was one "Indian Sam." The woman is only ever referred to as the "Negro Wench," or the "Negro Fiend."

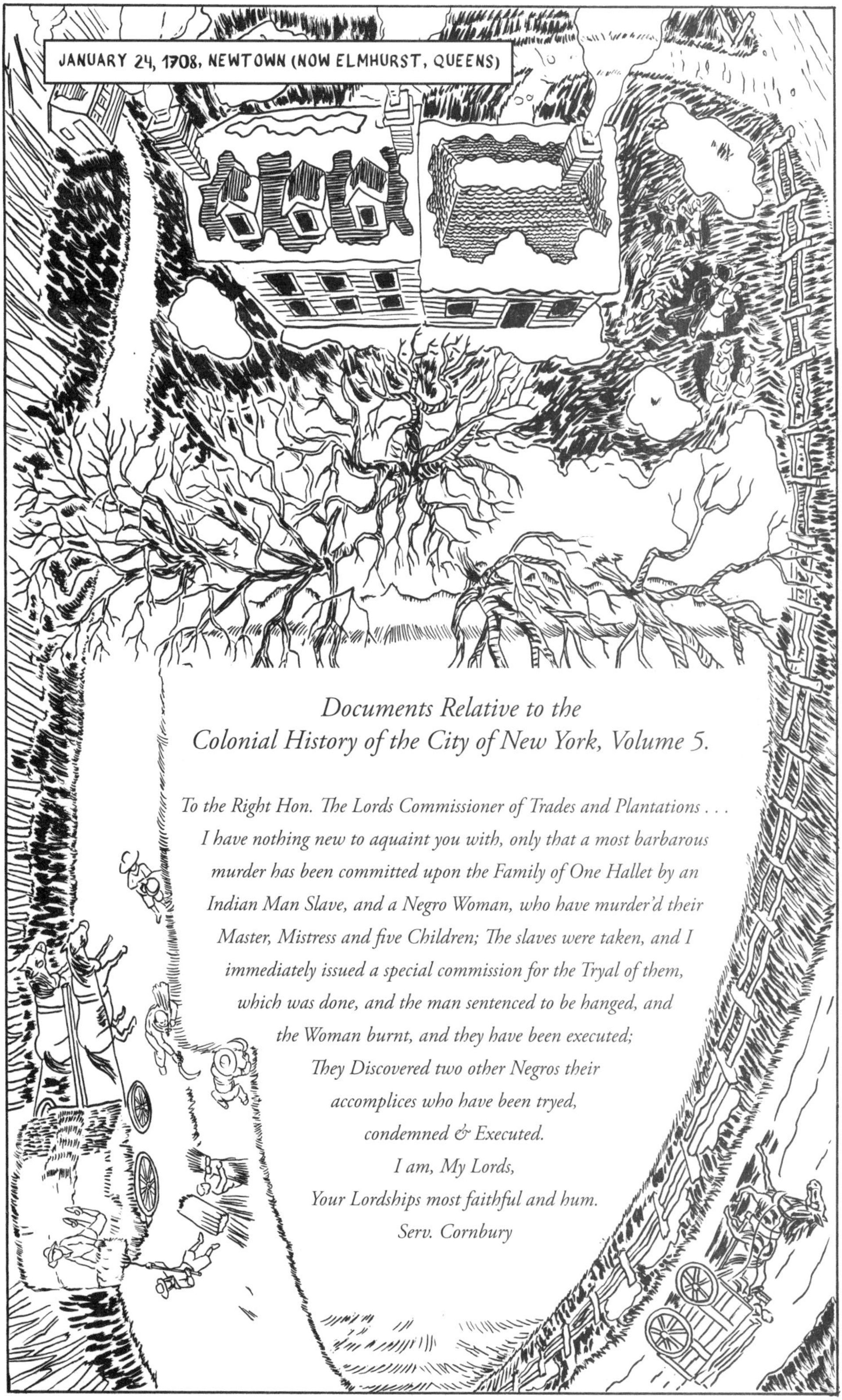
JANUARY 24, 1708, NEWTOWN (NOW ELMHURST, QUEENS)
Documents Relative to the
Colonial History of the City of New York, Volume 5.
To the Right Hon. The Lords Commissioner of Trades and Plantations . . .
I have nothing new to aquaint you with, only that a most barbarous
murder has been committed upon the Family of One Hallet by an
Indian Man Slave, and a Negro Woman, who have murder'd their
Master, Mistress and five Children; The slaves were taken, and I
immediately issued a special commission for the Tryal of them,
which was done, and the man sentenced to be hanged, and
the Woman burnt, and they have been executed;
They Discovered two other Negros their
accomplices who have been tryed,
condemned & Executed.
I am, My Lords,
Your Lordships most faithful and hum.
Serv. Cornbury

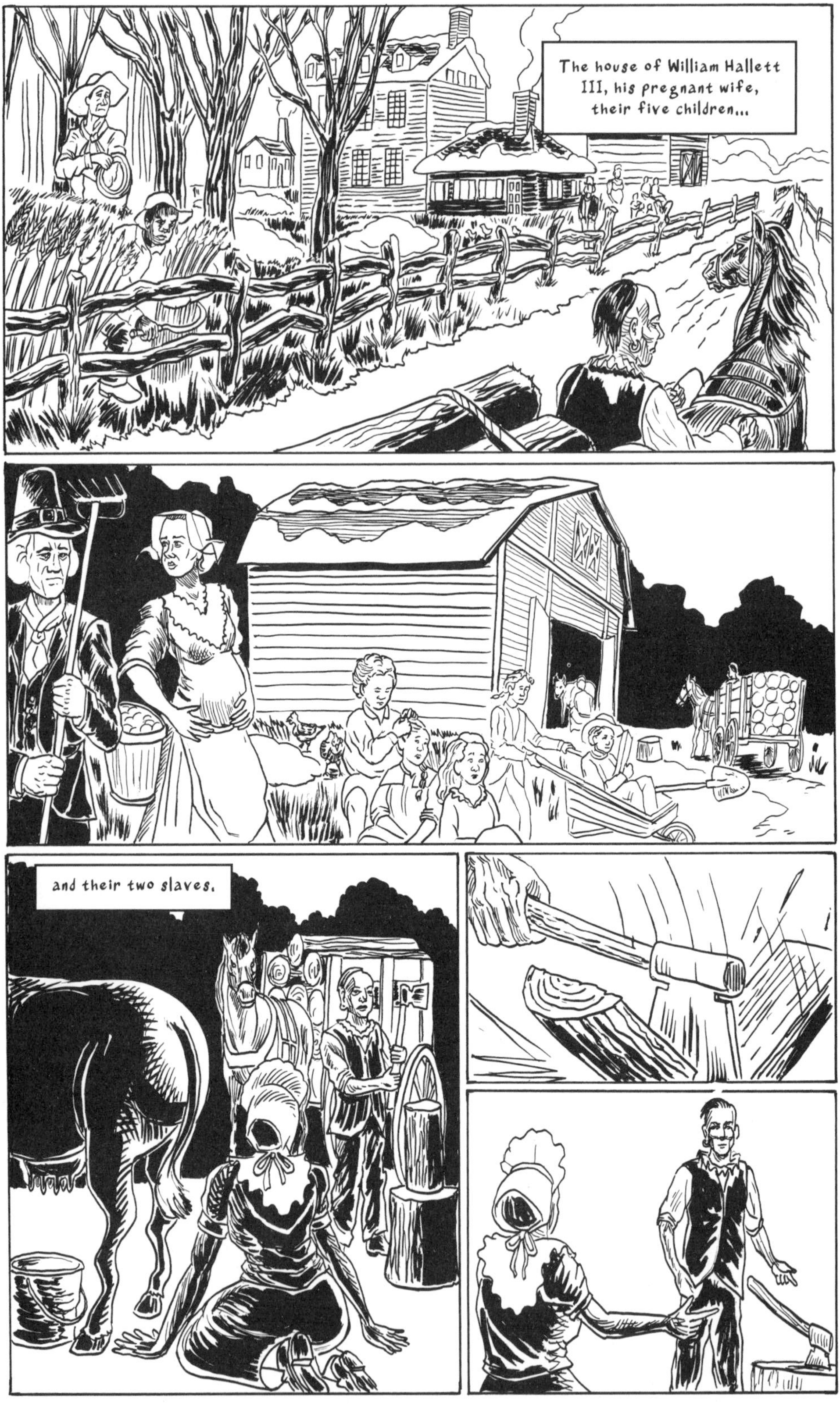
The house of William Hallett III, his pregnant wife, their five children...
and their two slaves.

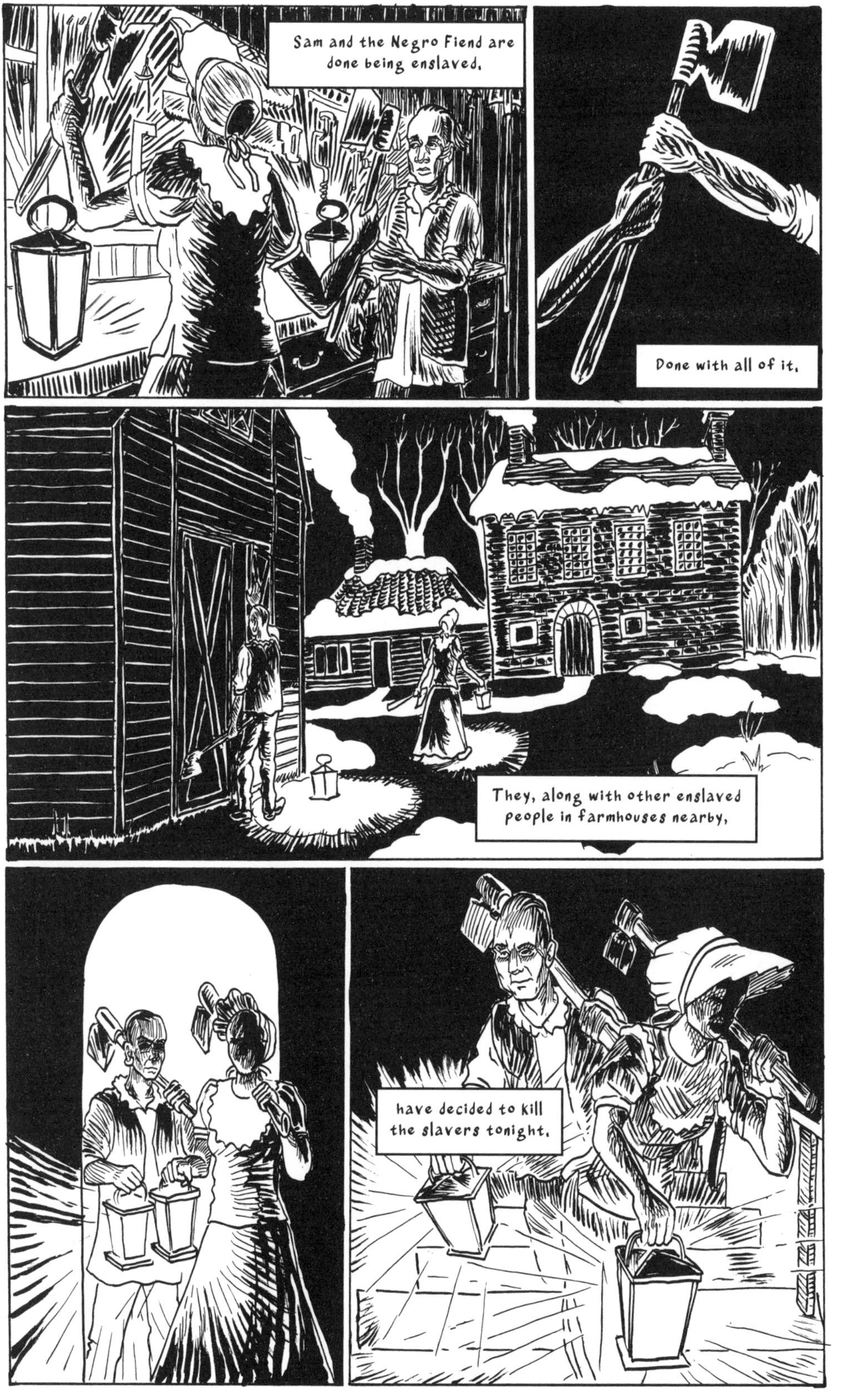
Sam and the Negro Fiend are done being enslaved.
Done with all of it.
They, along with other enslaved people in farmhouses nearby,
have decided to kill the slavers tonight.

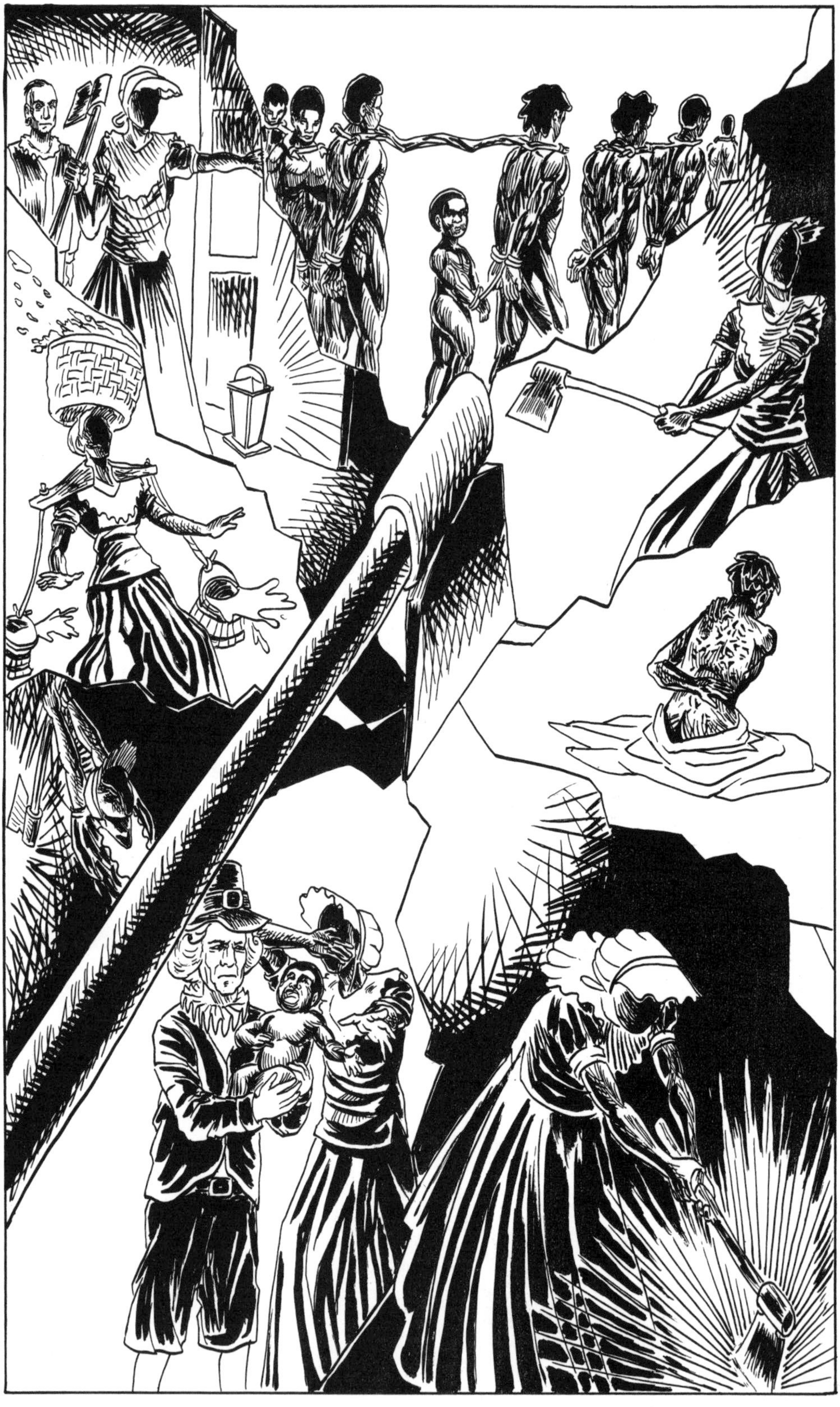

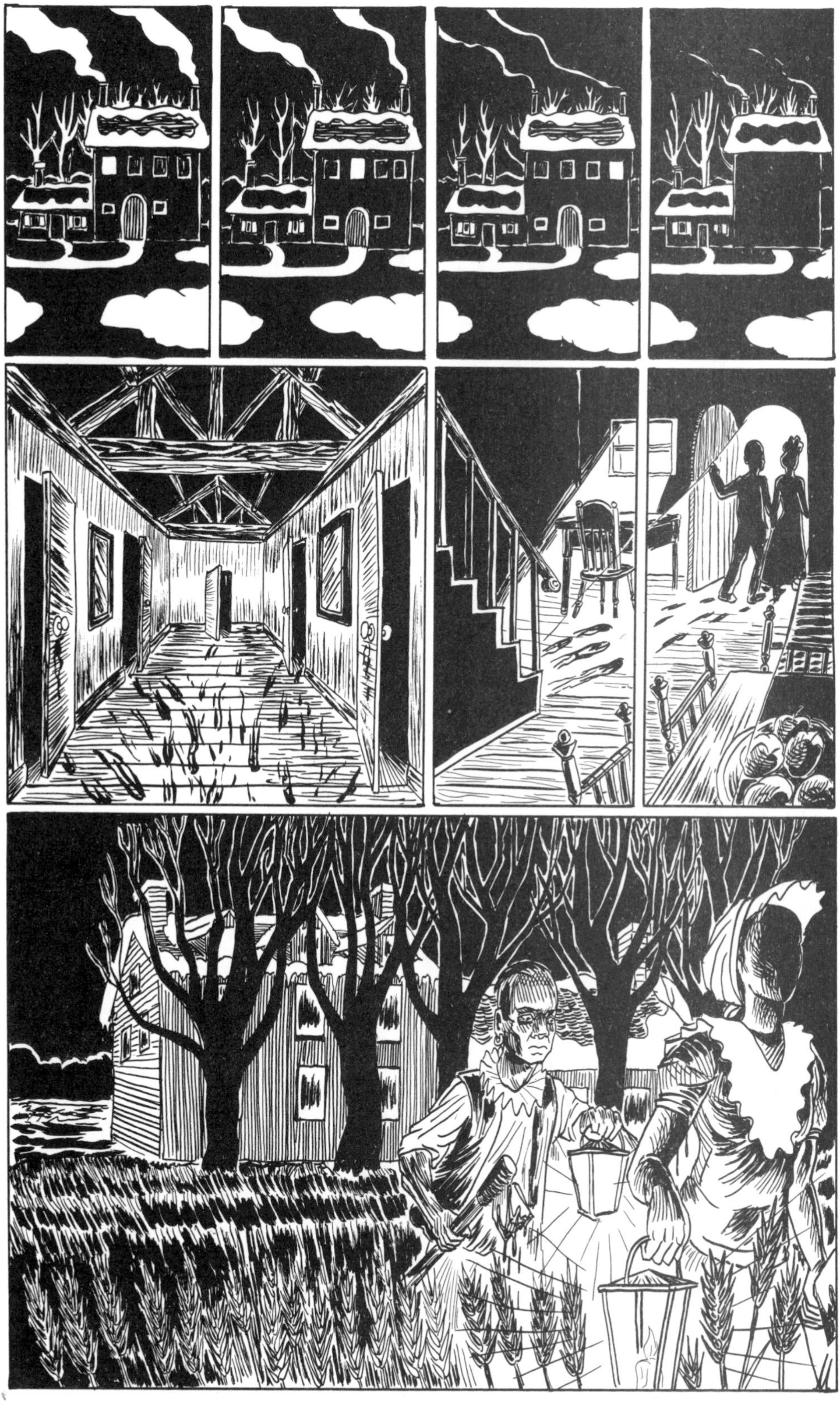

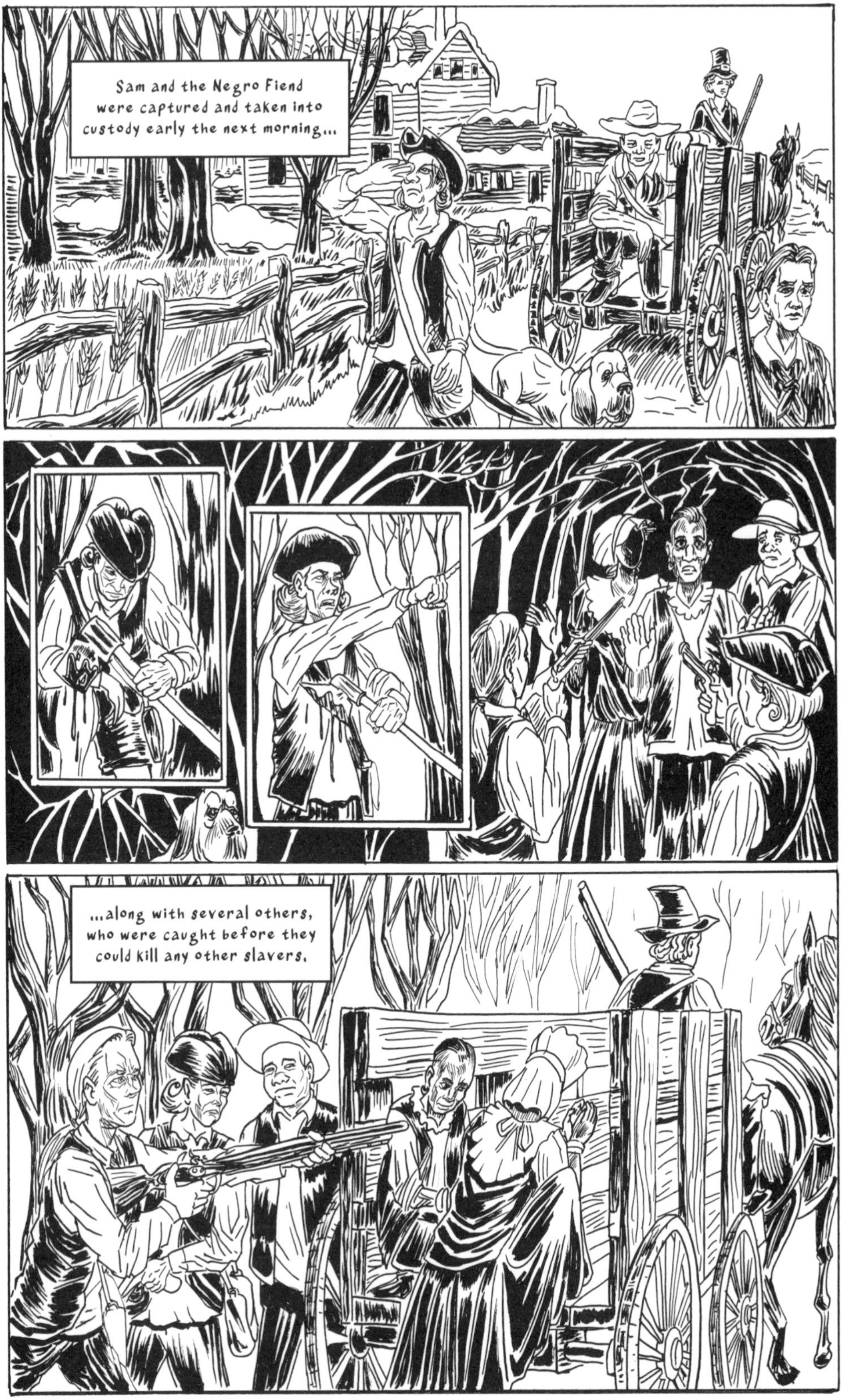
Sam and the Negro Fiend were captured and taken into custody early the next morning...
...along with several others, who were caught before they could kill any other slavers.

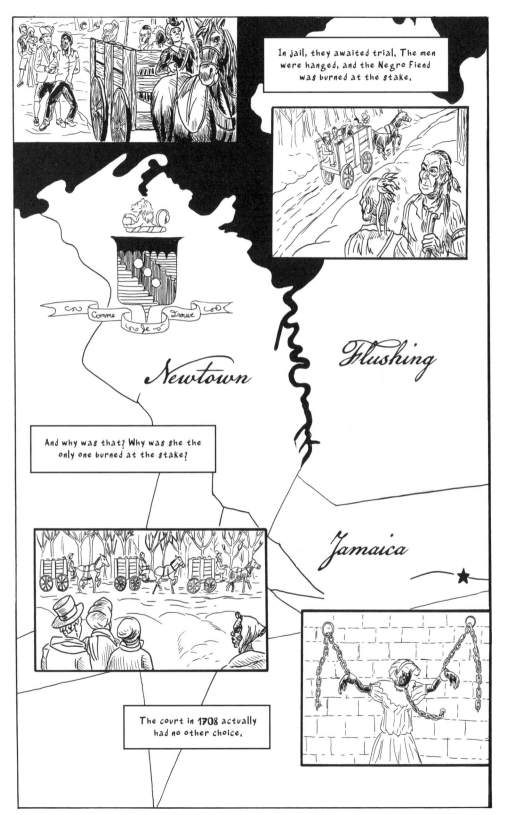

In jail, they awaited trial. The men were hanged, and the Negro Fiend was burned at the stake.

Comme Je Trouve

Newtown

Flushing

And why was that? Why was she the only one burned at the stake?

Jamaica

The court in 1708 actually had no other choice.

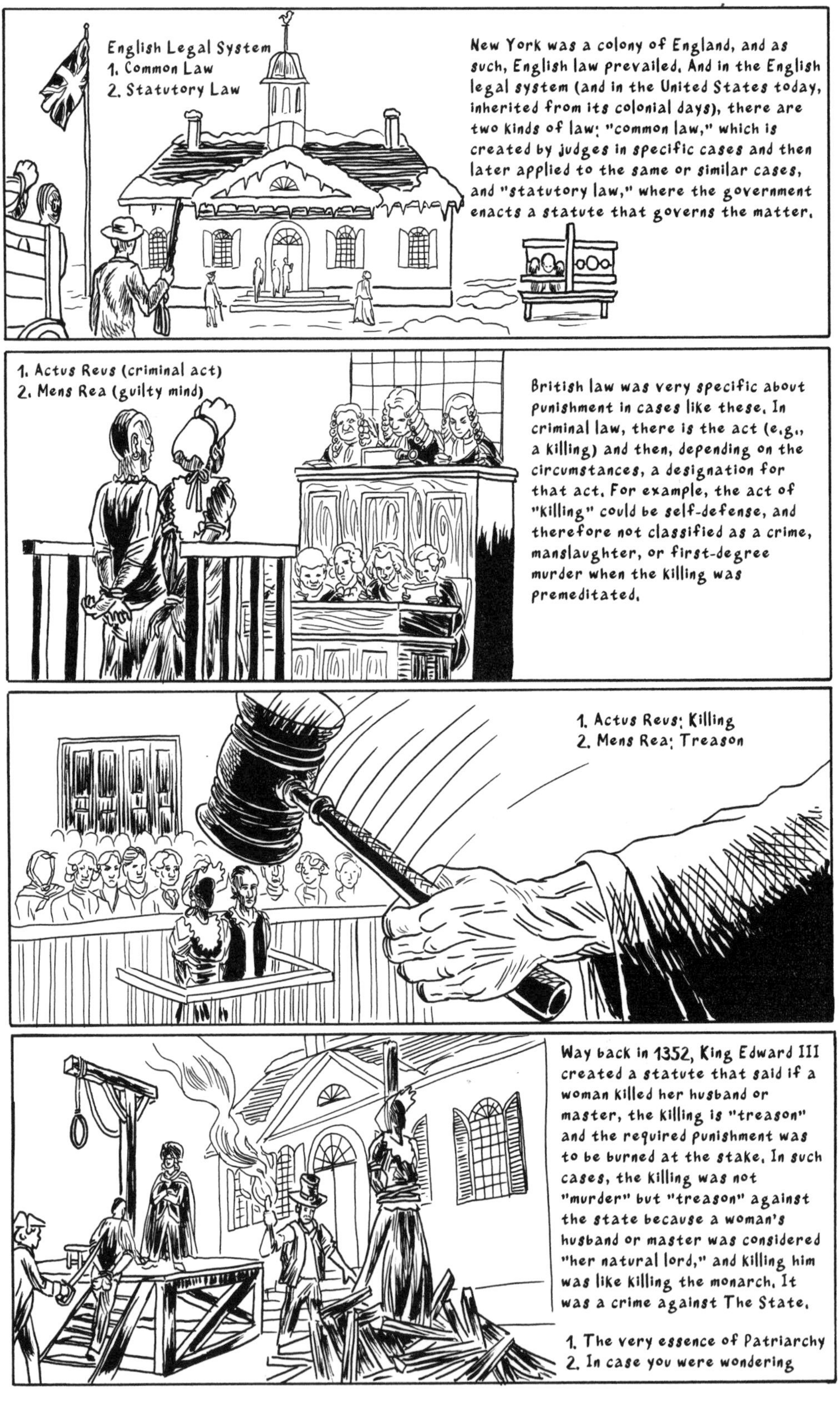
English Legal System
1. Common Law
2. Statutory Law
New York was a colony of England, and as such, English law prevailed. And in the English legal system (and in the United States today, inherited from its colonial days), there are two kinds of law: "common law," which is created by judges in specific cases and then later applied to the same or similar cases, and "statutory law," where the government enacts a statute that governs the matter.
1. Actus Reus (criminal act)
2. Mens Rea (guilty mind)
British law was very specific about punishment in cases like these. In criminal law, there is the act (e.g., a killing) and then, depending on the circumstances, a designation for that act. For example, the act of "killing" could be self-defense, and therefore not classified as a crime, manslaughter, or first-degree murder when the killing was premeditated.
1. Actus Reus: Killing
2. Mens Rea: Treason
Way back in 1352, King Edward III created a statute that said if a woman killed her husband or master, the killing is "treason" and the required punishment was to be burned at the stake. In such cases, the killing was not "murder" but "treason" against the state because a woman's husband or master was considered "her natural lord," and killing him was like killing the monarch. It was a crime against The State.
1. The very essence of Patriarchy
2. In case you were wondering

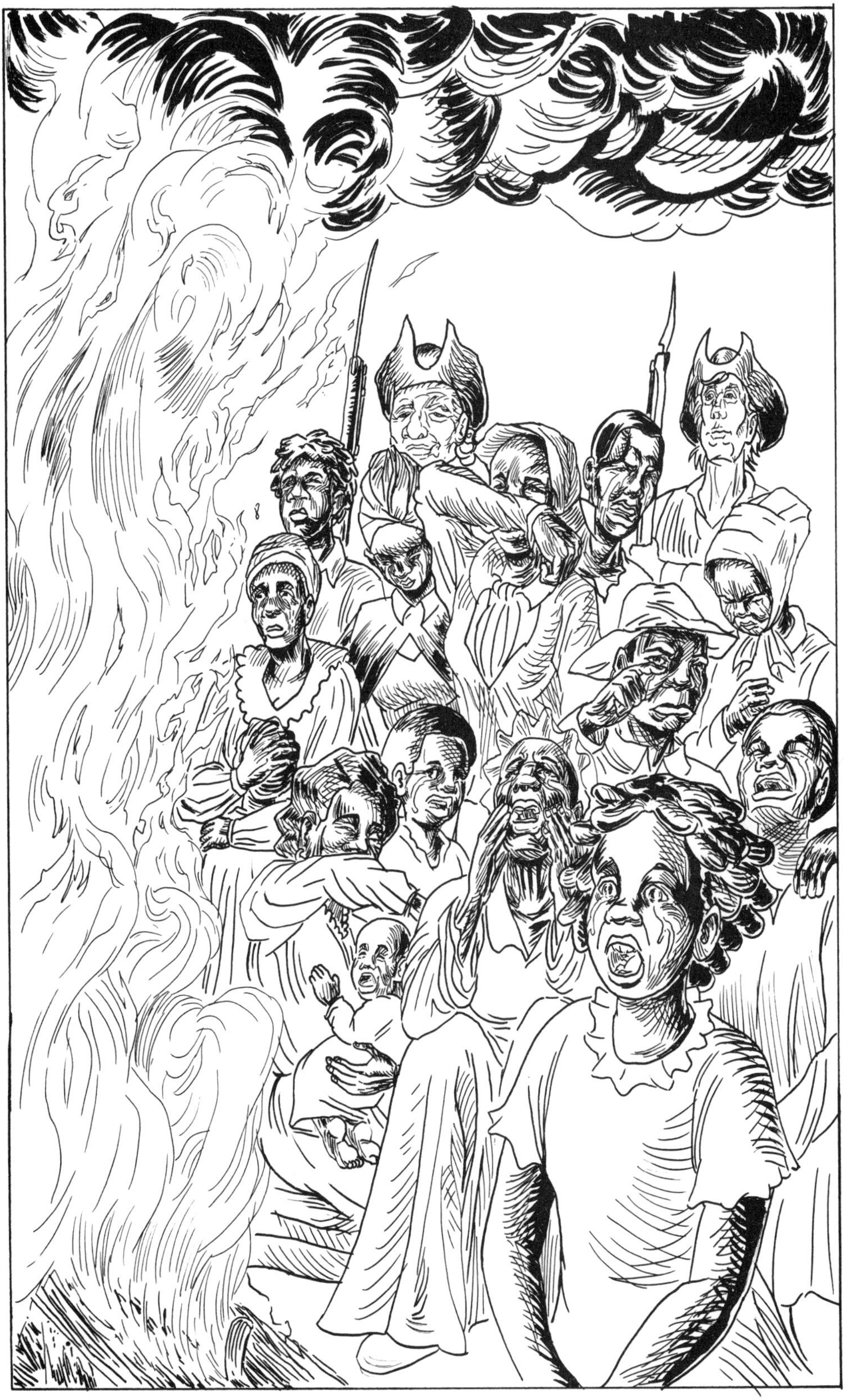

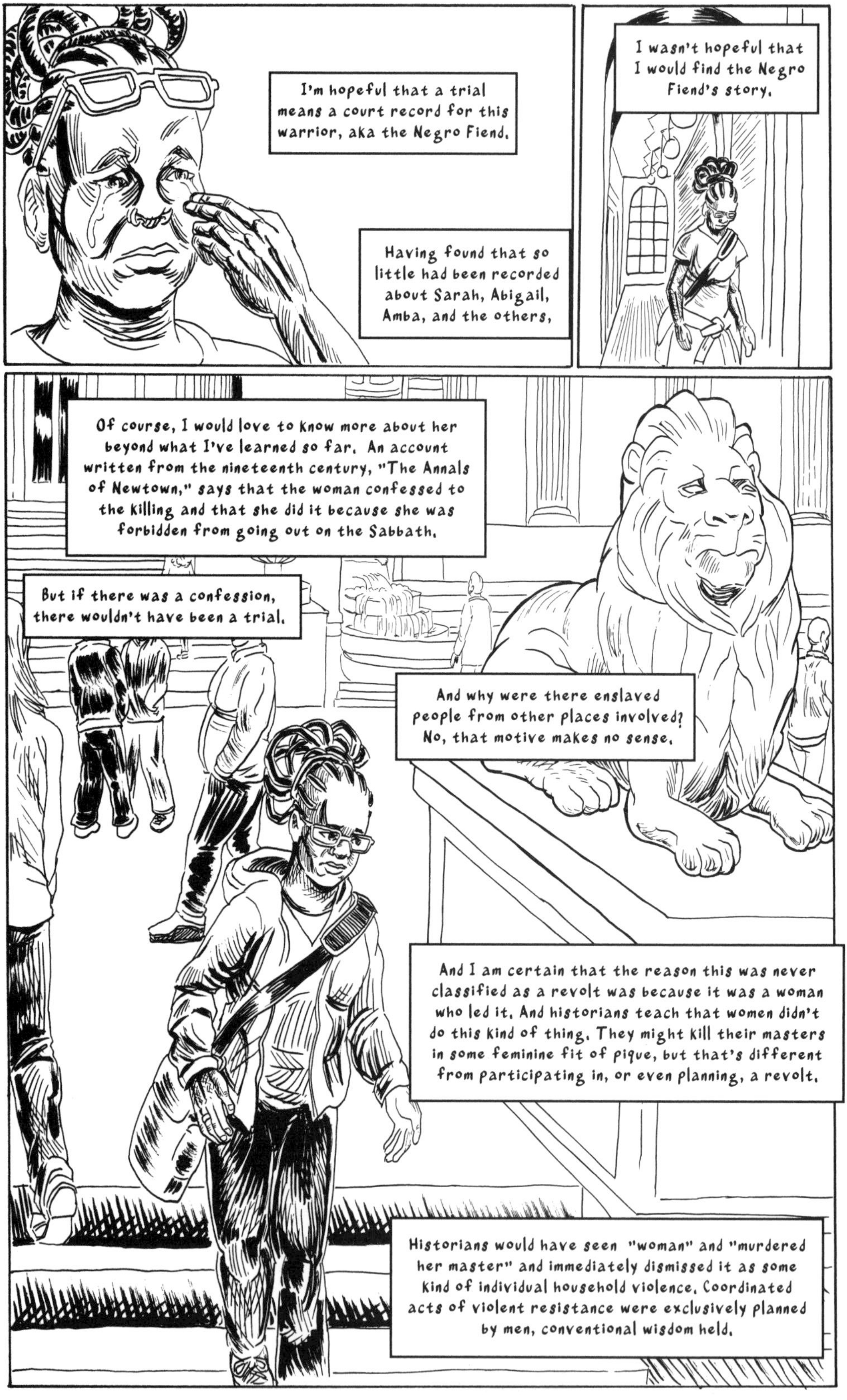
I'm hopeful that a trial means a court record for this warrior, aka the Negro Fiend.
Having found that so little had been recorded about Sarah, Abigail, Amba, and the others,
I wasn't hopeful that I would find the Negro Fiend's story.
Of course, I would love to know more about her beyond what I've learned so far. An account written from the nineteenth century, "The Annals of Newtown," says that the woman confessed to the killing and that she did it because she was forbidden from going out on the Sabbath.
But if there was a confession, there wouldn't have been a trial.
And why were there enslaved people from other places involved? No, that motive makes no sense.
And I am certain that the reason this was never classified as a revolt was because it was a woman who led it. And historians teach that women didn't do this kind of thing. They might kill their masters in some feminine fit of pique, but that's different from participating in, or even planning, a revolt.
Historians would have seen "woman" and "murdered her master" and immediately dismissed it as some kind of individual household violence. Coordinated acts of violent resistance were exclusively planned by men, conventional wisdom held.

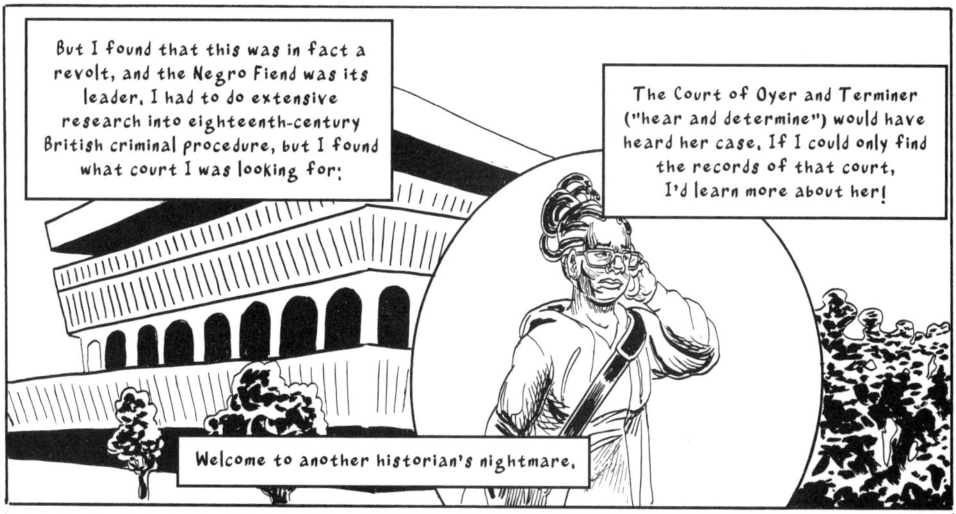

But I found that this was in fact a revolt, and the Negro Fiend was its leader. I had to do extensive research into eighteenth-century British criminal procedure, but I found what court I was looking for:
The Court of Oyer and Terminer ("hear and determine") would have heard her case. If I could only find the records of that court, I'd learn more about her!
Welcome to another historian's nightmare.

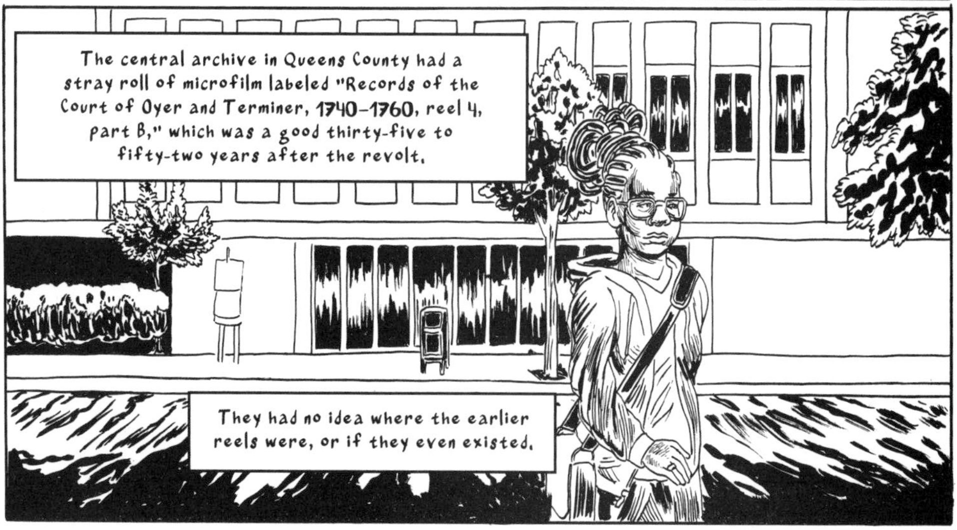

The central archive in Queens County had a stray roll of microfilm labeled "Records of the Court of Oyer and Terminer, 1740–1760, reel 4, part B," which was a good thirty-five to fifty-two years after the revolt.
They had no idea where the earlier reels were, or if they even existed.

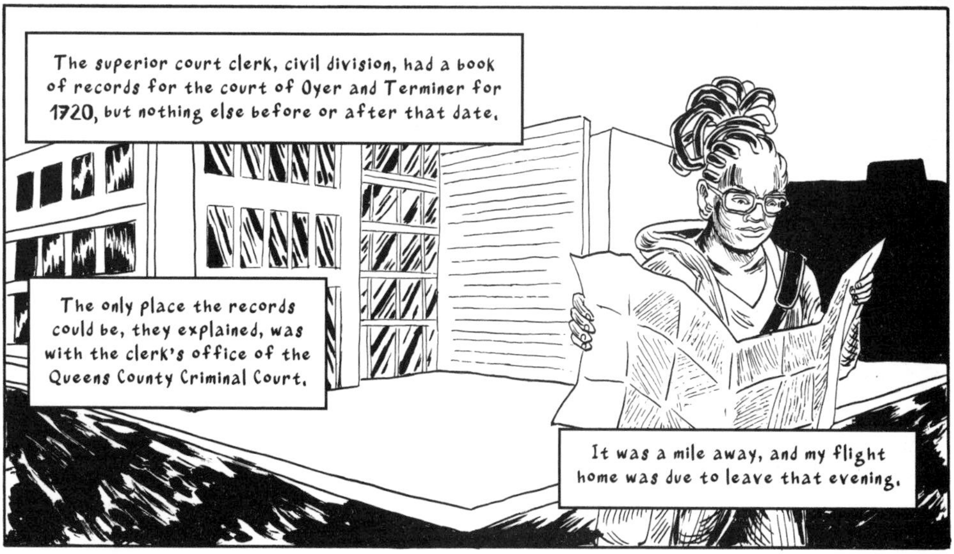

The superior court clerk, civil division, had a book of records for the court of Oyer and Terminer for 1720, but nothing else before or after that date.
The only place the records could be, they explained, was with the clerk's office of the Queens County Criminal Court.
It was a mile away, and my flight home was due to leave that evening.

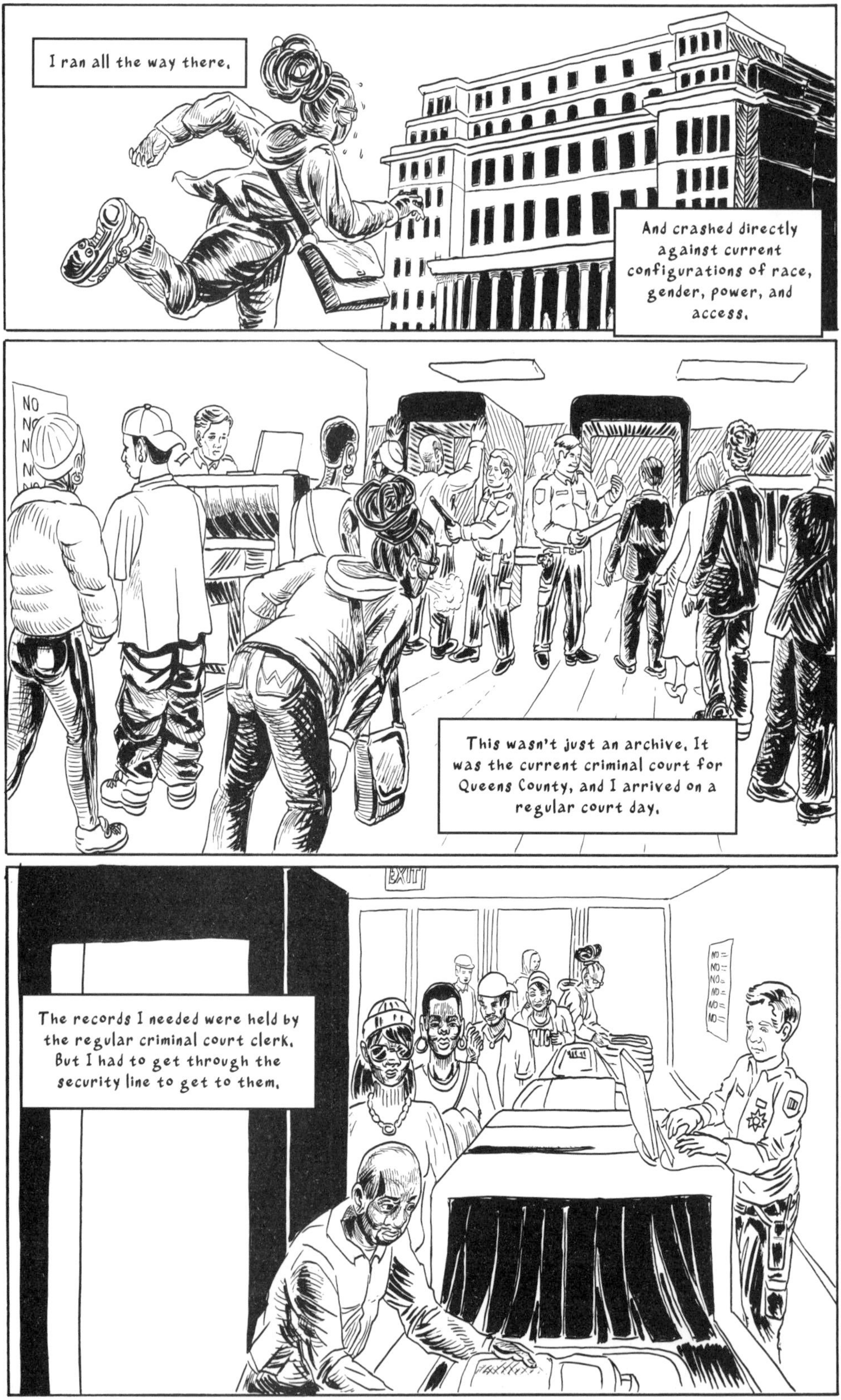
I ran all the way there.
And crashed directly against current configurations of race, gender, power, and access.
This wasn't just an archive. It was the current criminal court for Queens County, and I arrived on a regular court day.
EXIT
The records I needed were held by the regular criminal court clerk. But I had to get through the security line to get to them.

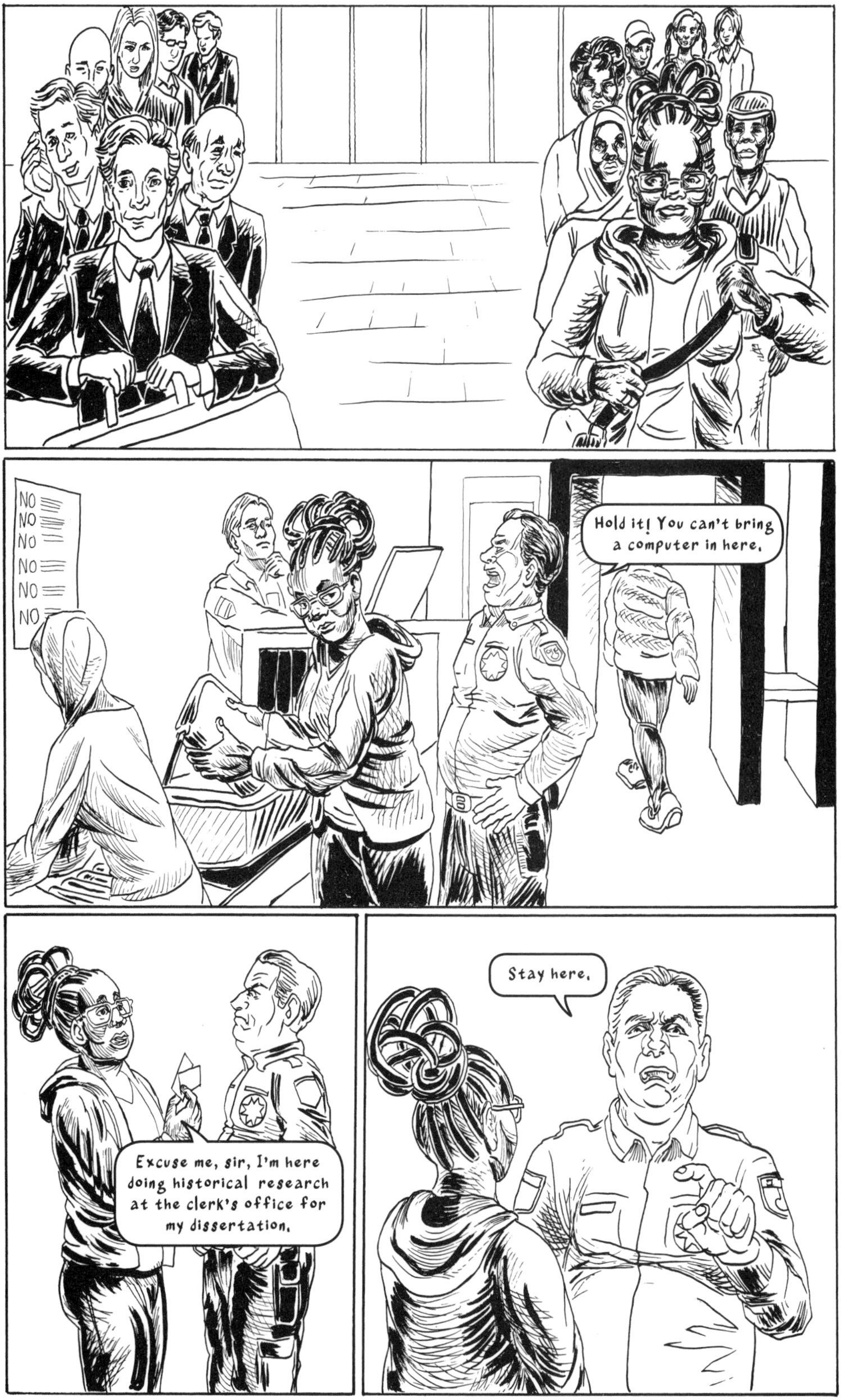
NO
NO
NO
NO
NO
NO
Hold it! You can't bring a computer in here.
Excuse me, sir, I'm here doing historical research at the clerk's office for my dissertation.
Stay here.

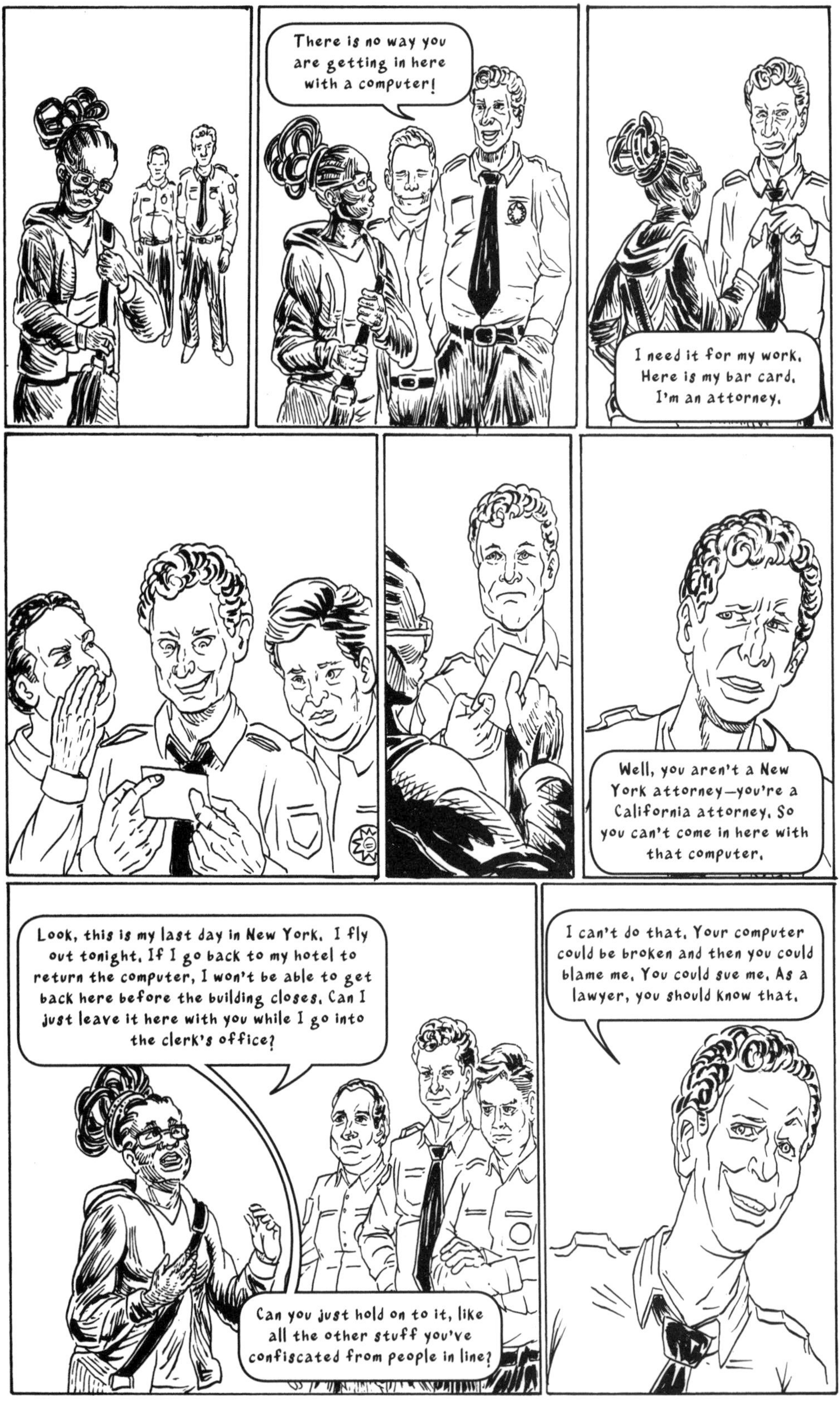
There is no way you are getting in here with a computer!
I need it for my work. Here is my bar card. I'm an attorney.
Well, you aren't a New York attorney—you're a California attorney. So you can't come in here with that computer.
Look, this is my last day in New York. I fly out tonight. If I go back to my hotel to return the computer, I won't be able to get back here before the building closes. Can I just leave it here with you while I go into the clerk's office?
Can you just hold on to it, like all the other stuff you've confiscated from people in line?
I can't do that. Your computer could be broken and then you could blame me. You could sue me. As a lawyer, you should know that.

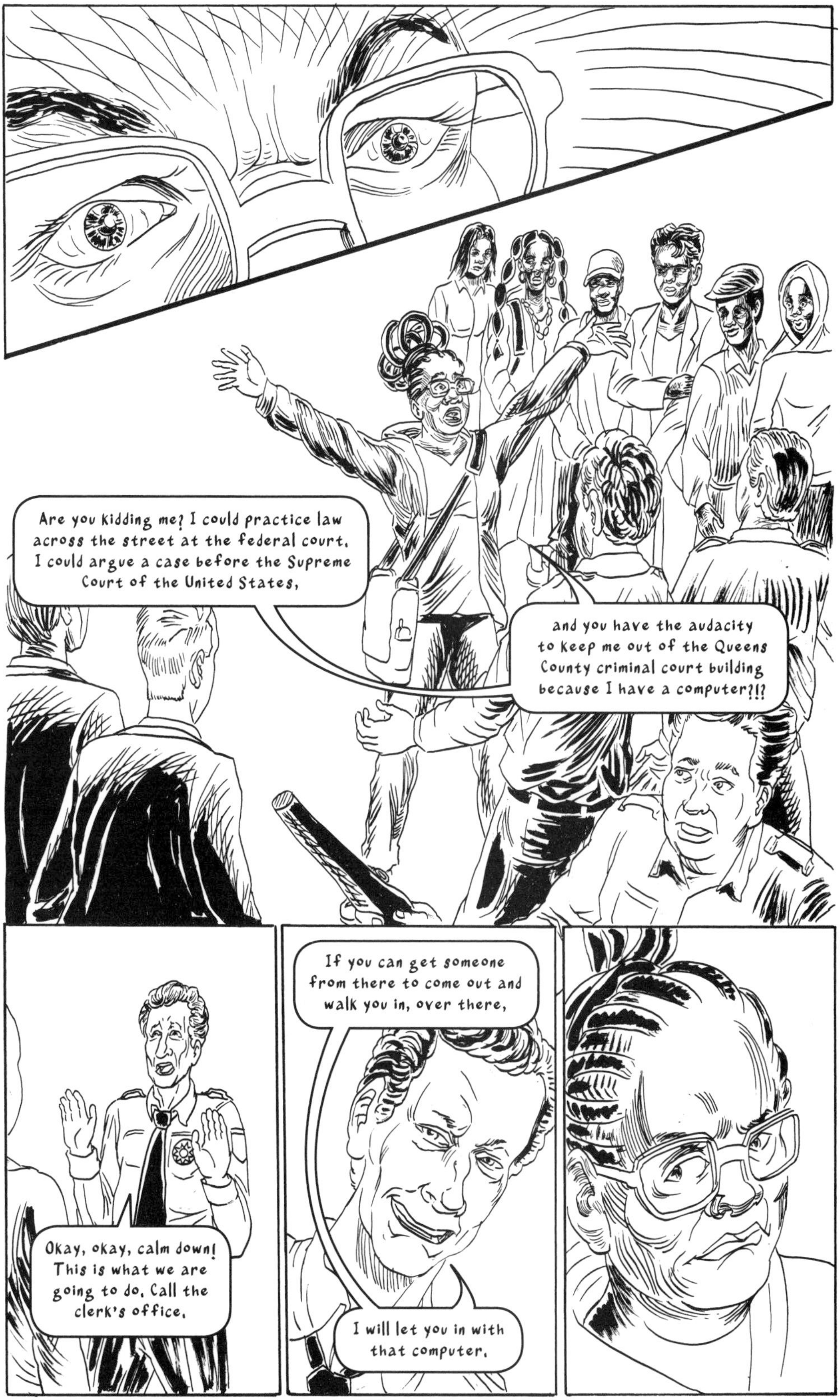
Are you kidding me? I could practice law across the street at the federal court. I could argue a case before the Supreme Court of the United States,
and you have the audacity to keep me out of the Queens County criminal court building because I have a computer?!?
Okay, okay, calm down! This is what we are going to do. Call the clerk's office.
If you can get someone from there to come out and walk you in, over there,
I will let you in with that computer.

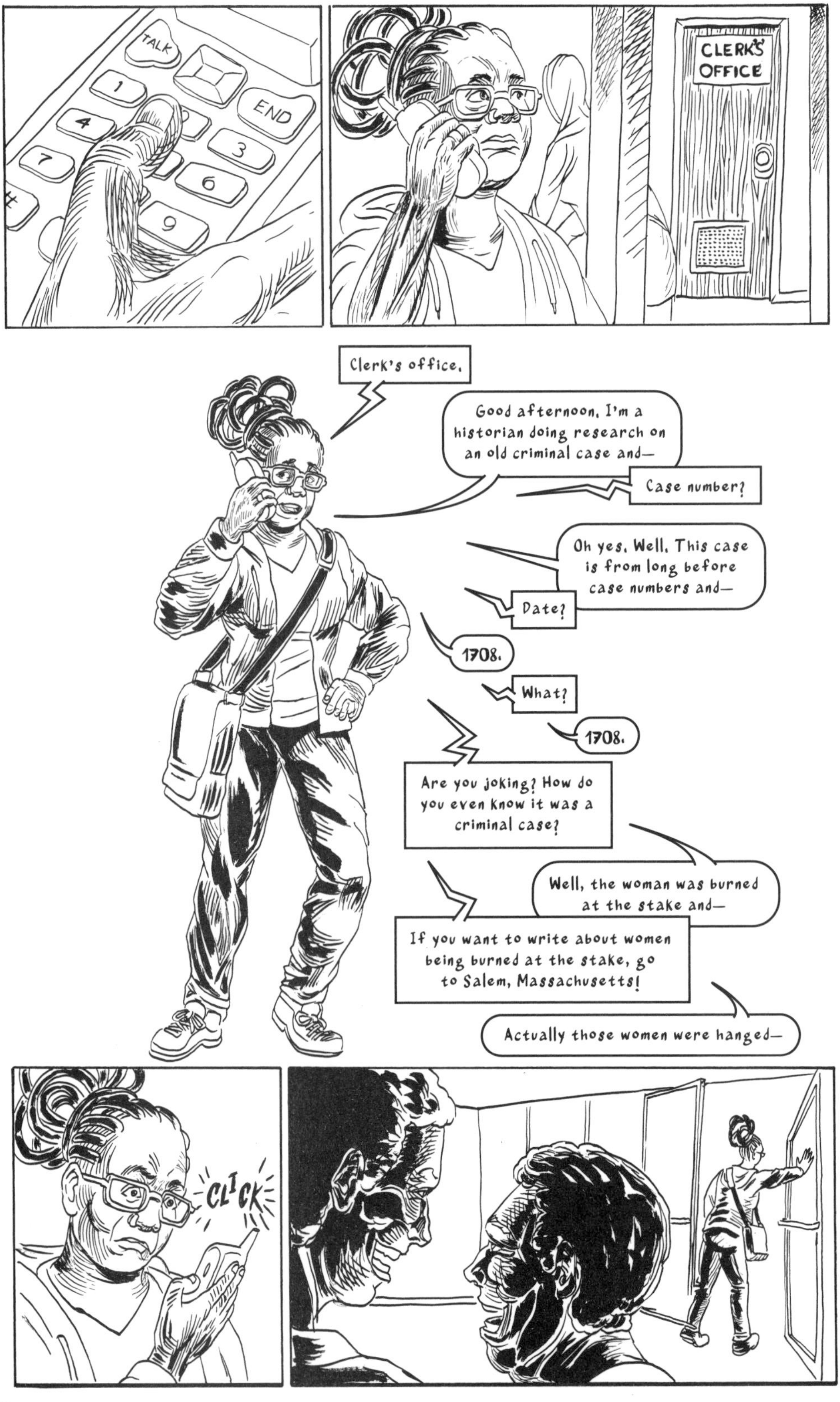
TALK
END
CLERK'S OFFICE
Clerk's office.
Good afternoon. I'm a historian doing research on an old criminal case and—
Case number?
Oh yes. Well. This case is from long before case numbers and—
Date?
1708.
What?
1708.
Are you joking? How do you even know it was a criminal case?
Well, the woman was burned at the stake and—
If you want to write about women being burned at the stake, go to Salem, Massachusetts!
Actually those women were hanged—
CLICK

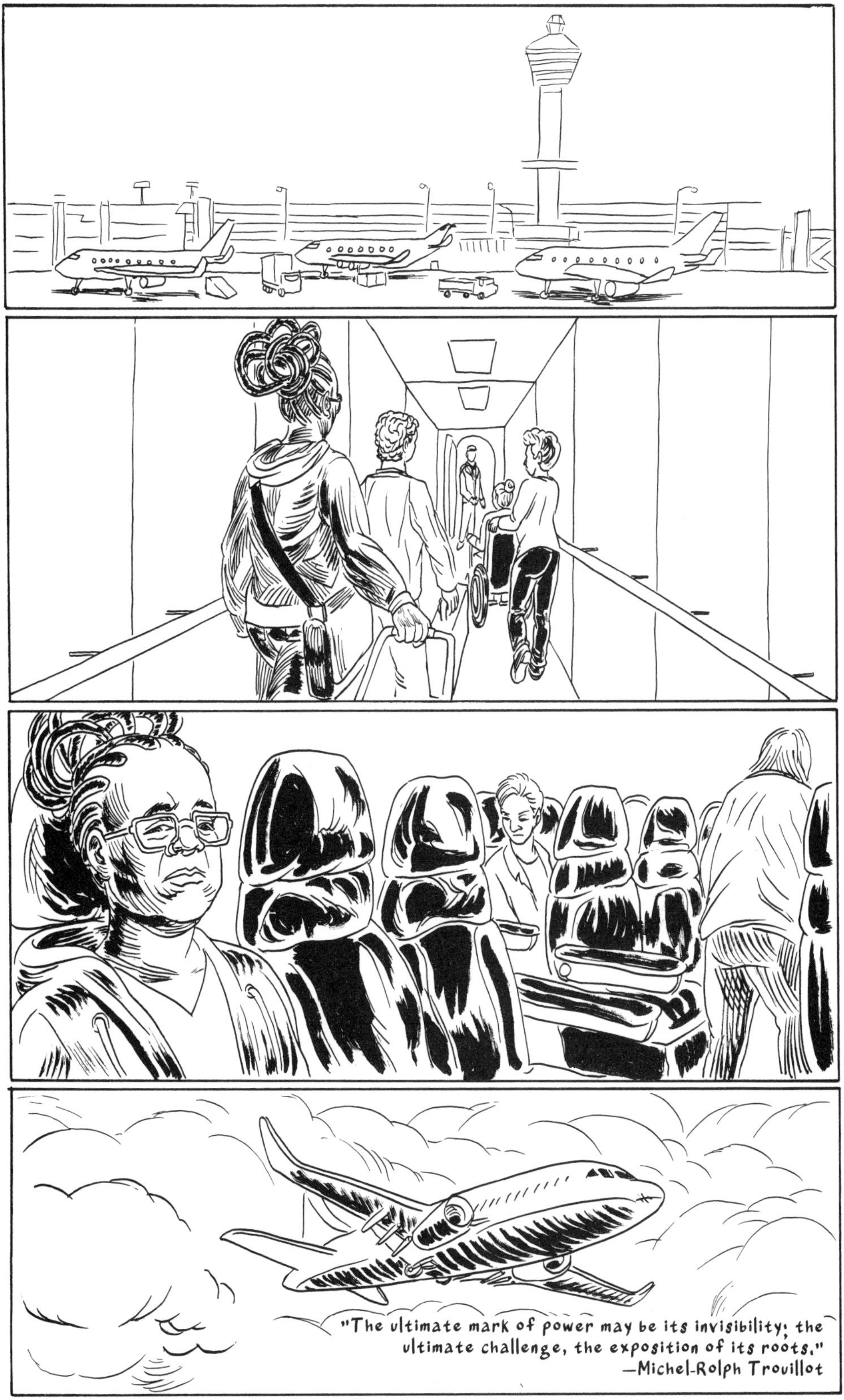
"The ultimate mark of power may be its invisibility; the ultimate challenge, the exposition of its roots."
—Michel-Rolph Trouillot

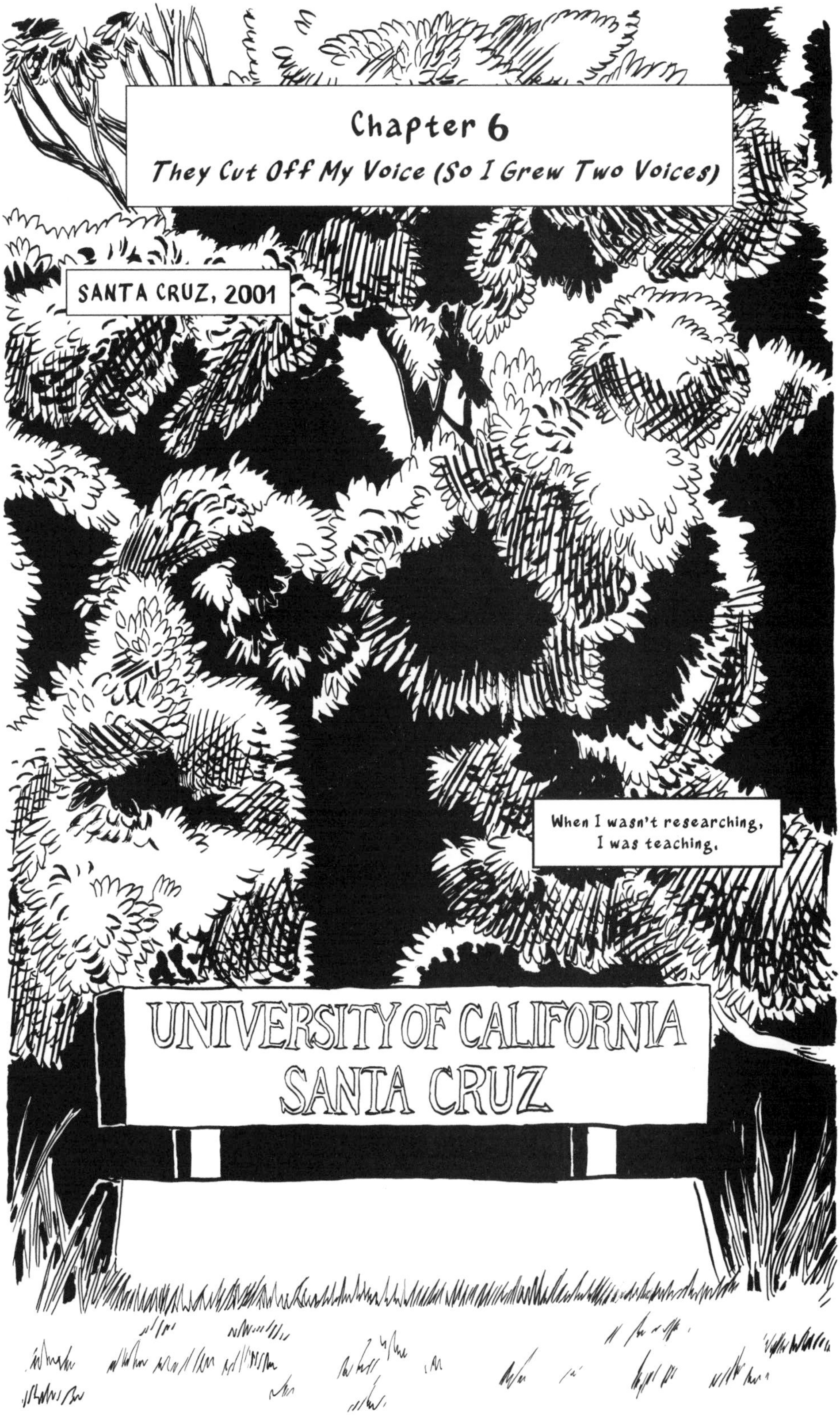
Chapter 6
They Cut Off My Voice (So I Grew Two Voices)
SANTA CRUZ, 2001
When I wasn't researching, I was teaching.
UNIVERSITY OF CALIFORNIA
SANTA CRUZ

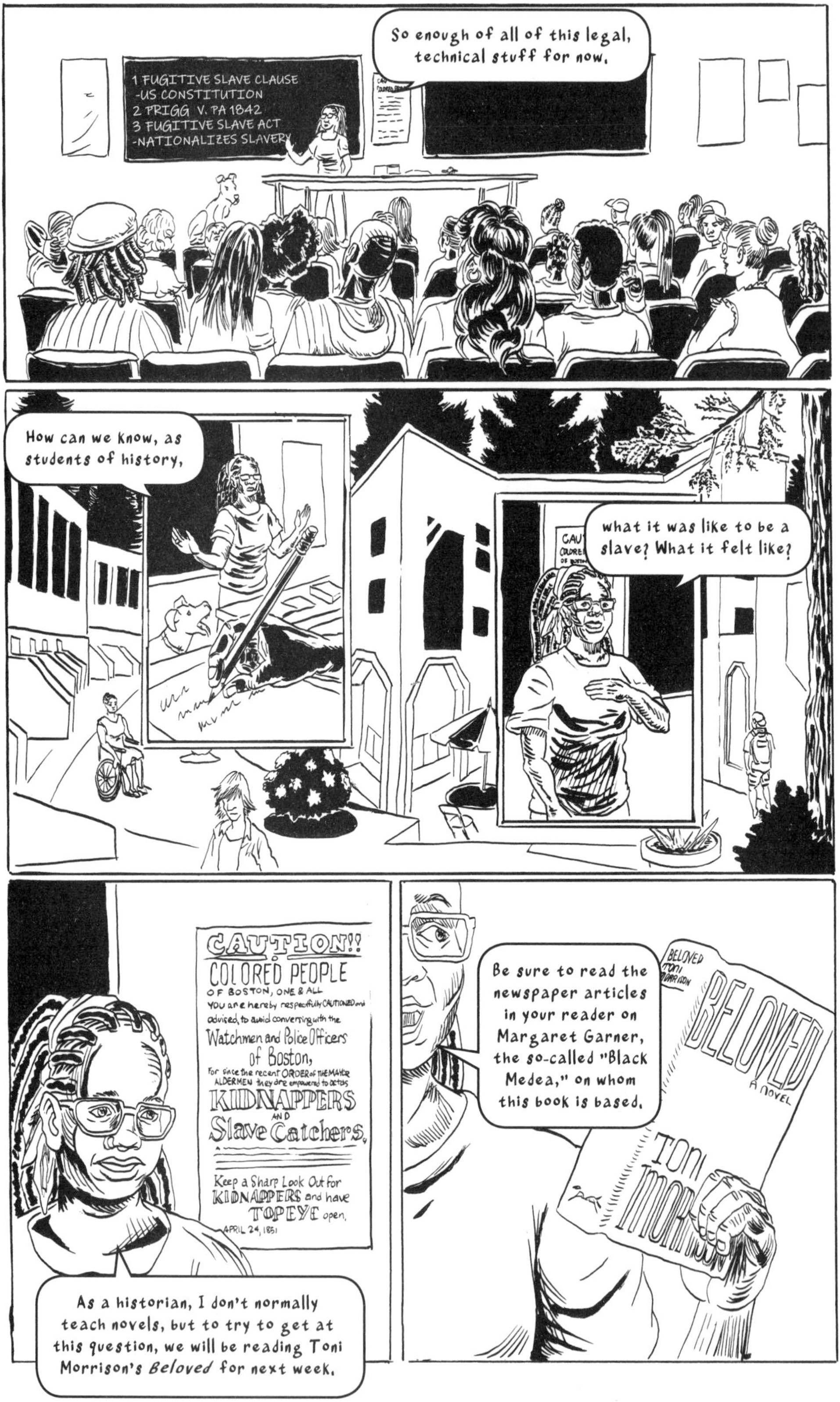

1 FUGITIVE SLAVE CLAUSE
-US CONSTITUTION
2 PRIGG V. PA 1842
3 FUGITIVE SLAVE ACT
-NATIONALIZES SLAVERY
So enough of all of this legal, technical stuff for now.
How can we know, as students of history,
what it was like to be a slave? What it felt like?
CAUTION!!
COLORED PEOPLE
OF BOSTON, ONE & ALL
You are hereby respectfully CAUTIONED and advised, to avoid conversing with the
Watchmen and Police Officers
of Boston,
For since the recent ORDER OF THE MAYOR & ALDERMEN they are empowered to act as
KIDNAPPERS
AND
Slave Catchers,
Keep a Sharp Look Out for KIDNAPPERS and have TOP EYE open.
APRIL 24, 1851
As a historian, I don't normally teach novels, but to try to get at this question, we will be reading Toni Morrison's *Beloved* for next week.
Be sure to read the newspaper articles in your reader on Margaret Garner, the so-called "Black Medea," on whom this book is based.
BELOVED
Toni Morrison
BELOVED
A NOVEL

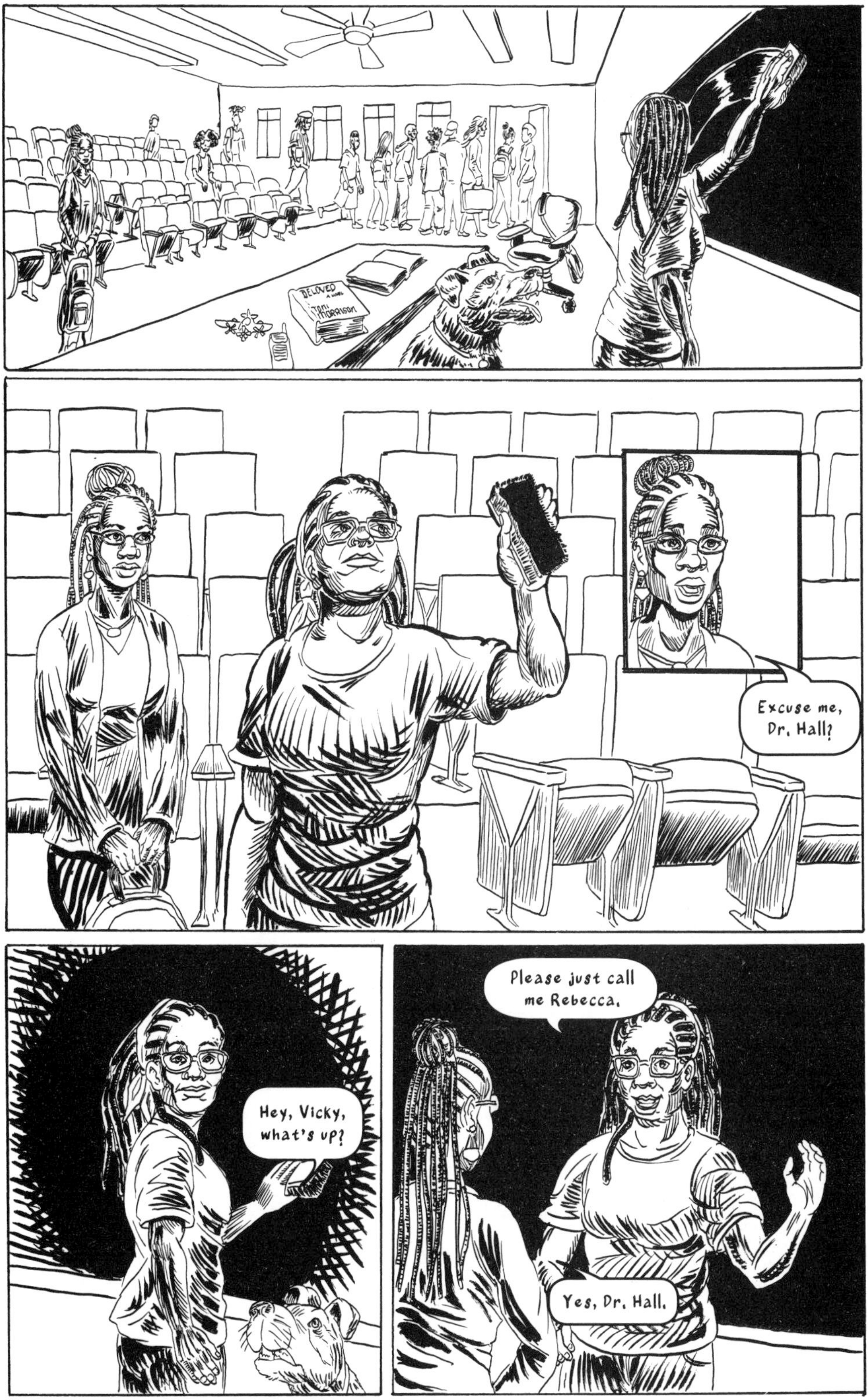
BELOVED
A NOVEL
TONI MORRISON
Excuse me, Dr. Hall?
Hey, Vicky, what's up?
Please just call me Rebecca.
Yes, Dr. Hall.

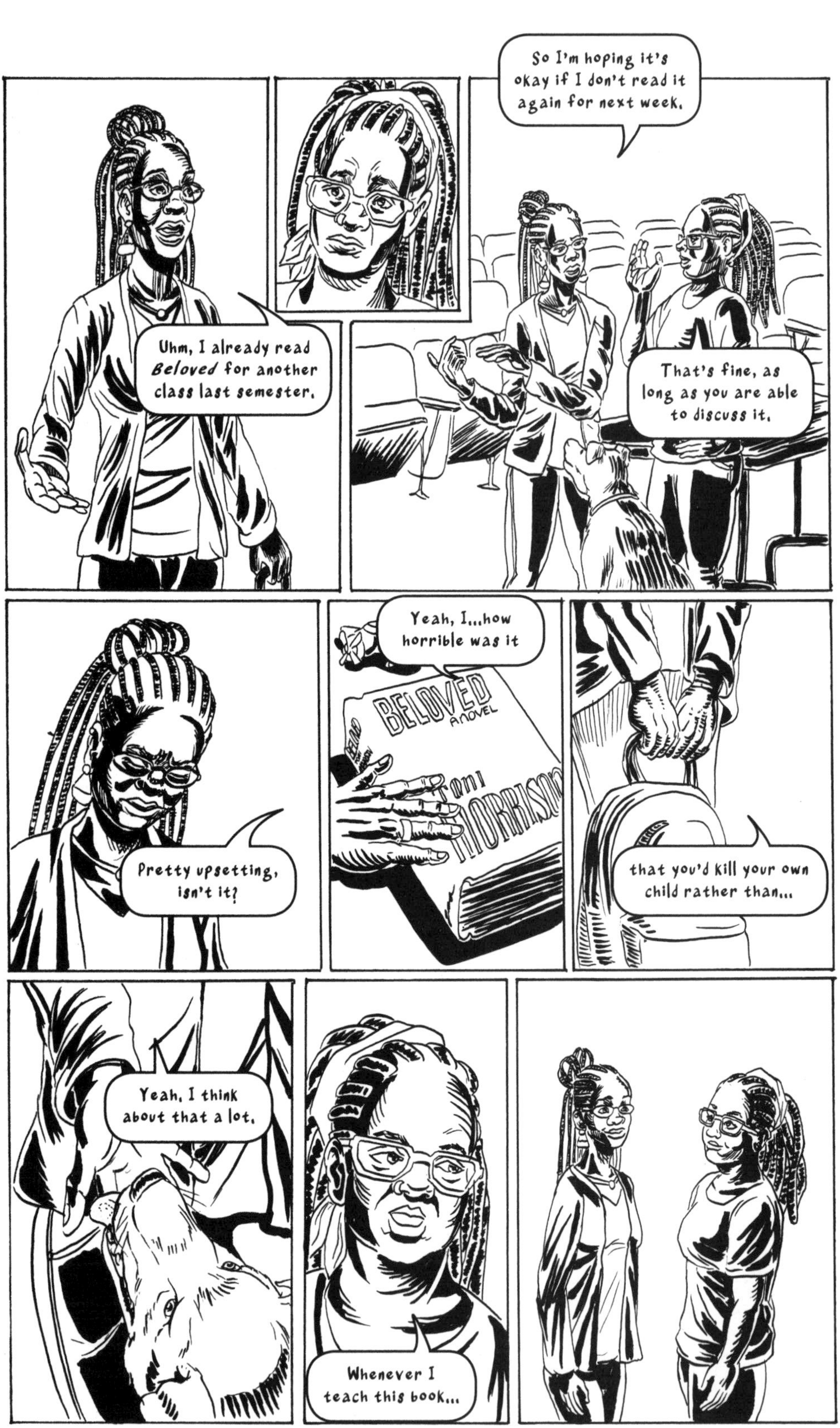
Uhm, I already read *Beloved* for another class last semester.
So I'm hoping it's okay if I don't read it again for next week.
That's fine, as long as you are able to discuss it.
Pretty upsetting, isn't it?
Yeah, I...how horrible was it
BELOVED
A NOVEL
Toni
MORRISON
that you'd kill your own child rather than...
Yeah, I think about that a lot.
Whenever I teach this book...

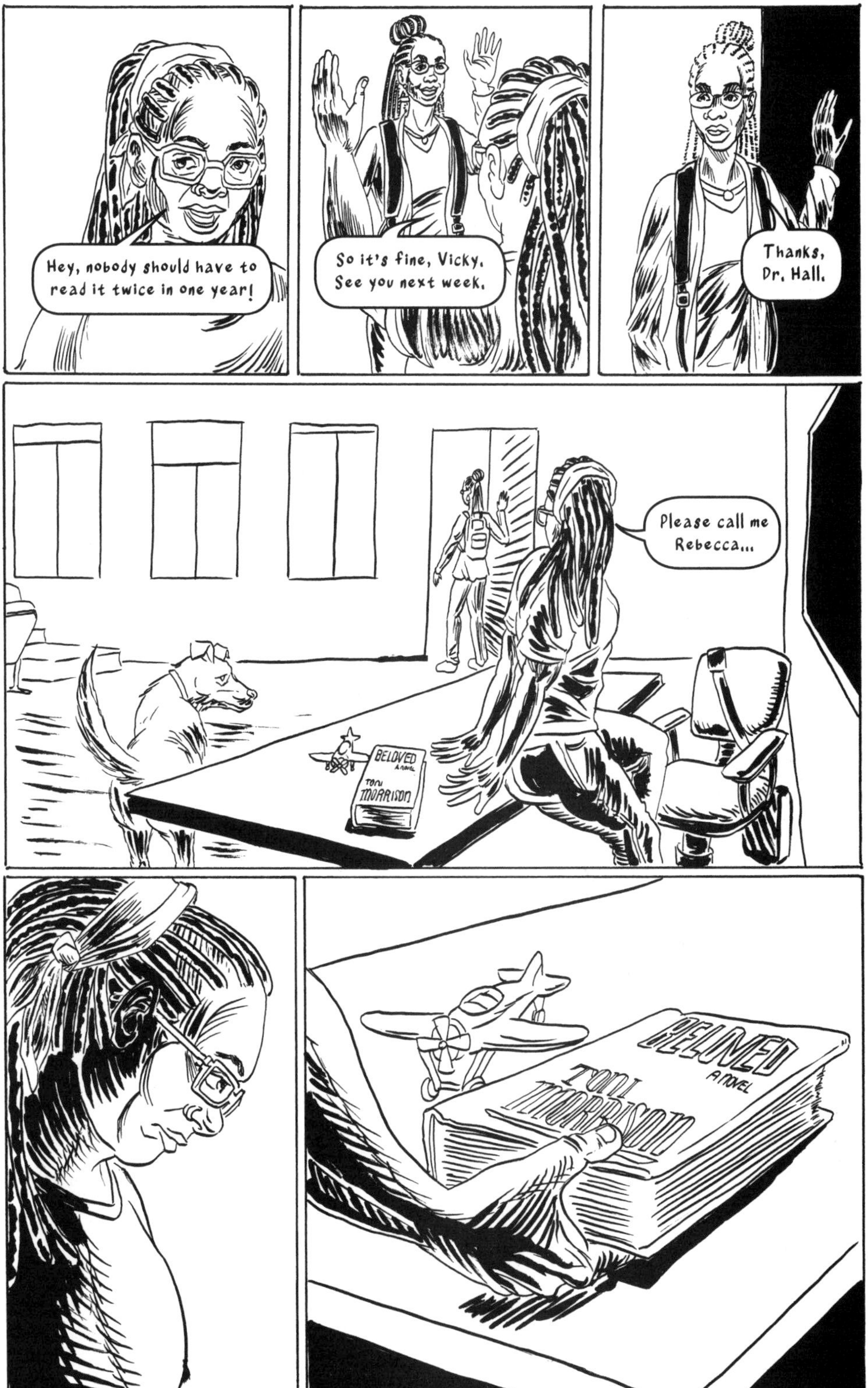
Hey, nobody should have to read it twice in one year!
So it's fine, Vicky. See you next week.
Thanks, Dr. Hall.
Please call me Rebecca...
BELOVED A NOVEL TONI MORRISON
BELOVED A NOVEL TONI MORRISON

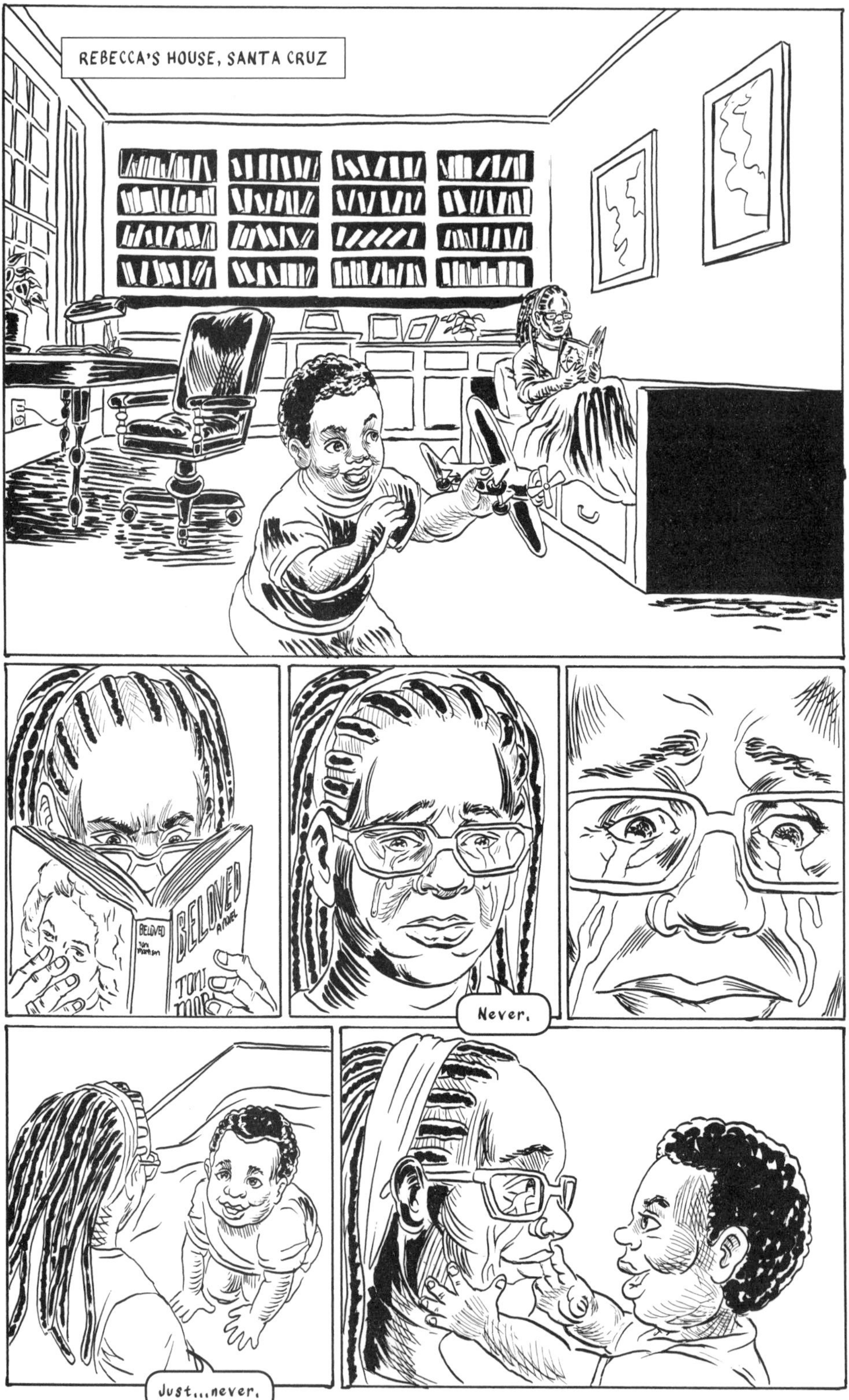
REBECCA'S HOUSE, SANTA CRUZ
BELOVED
Never.
Just...never.

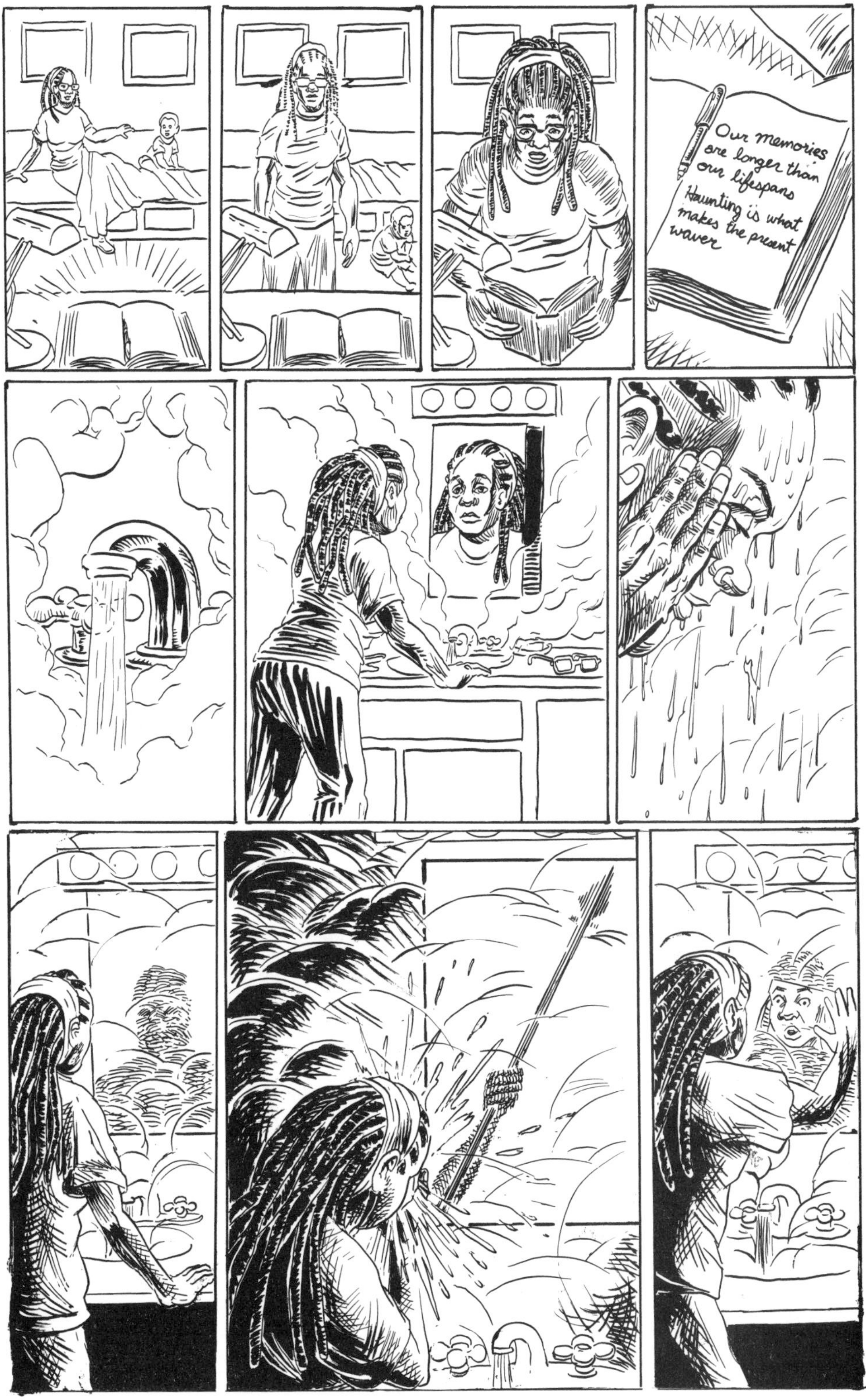
Our memories are longer than our lifespans
Haunting is what makes the present waver

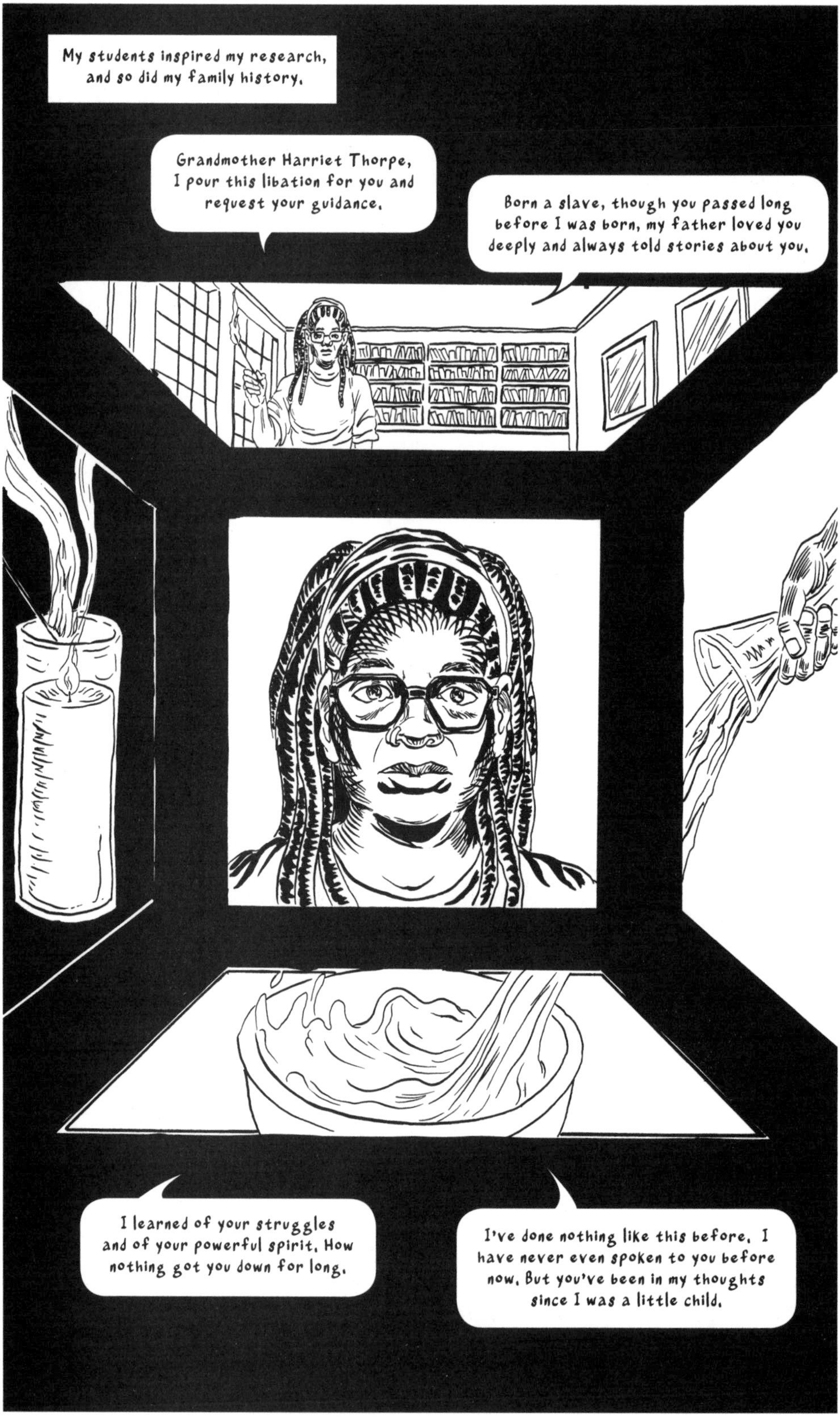
My students inspired my research, and so did my family history.
Grandmother Harriet Thorpe, I pour this libation for you and request your guidance.
Born a slave, though you passed long before I was born, my father loved you deeply and always told stories about you.
I learned of your struggles and of your powerful spirit. How nothing got you down for long.
I've done nothing like this before. I have never even spoken to you before now. But you've been in my thoughts since I was a little child.

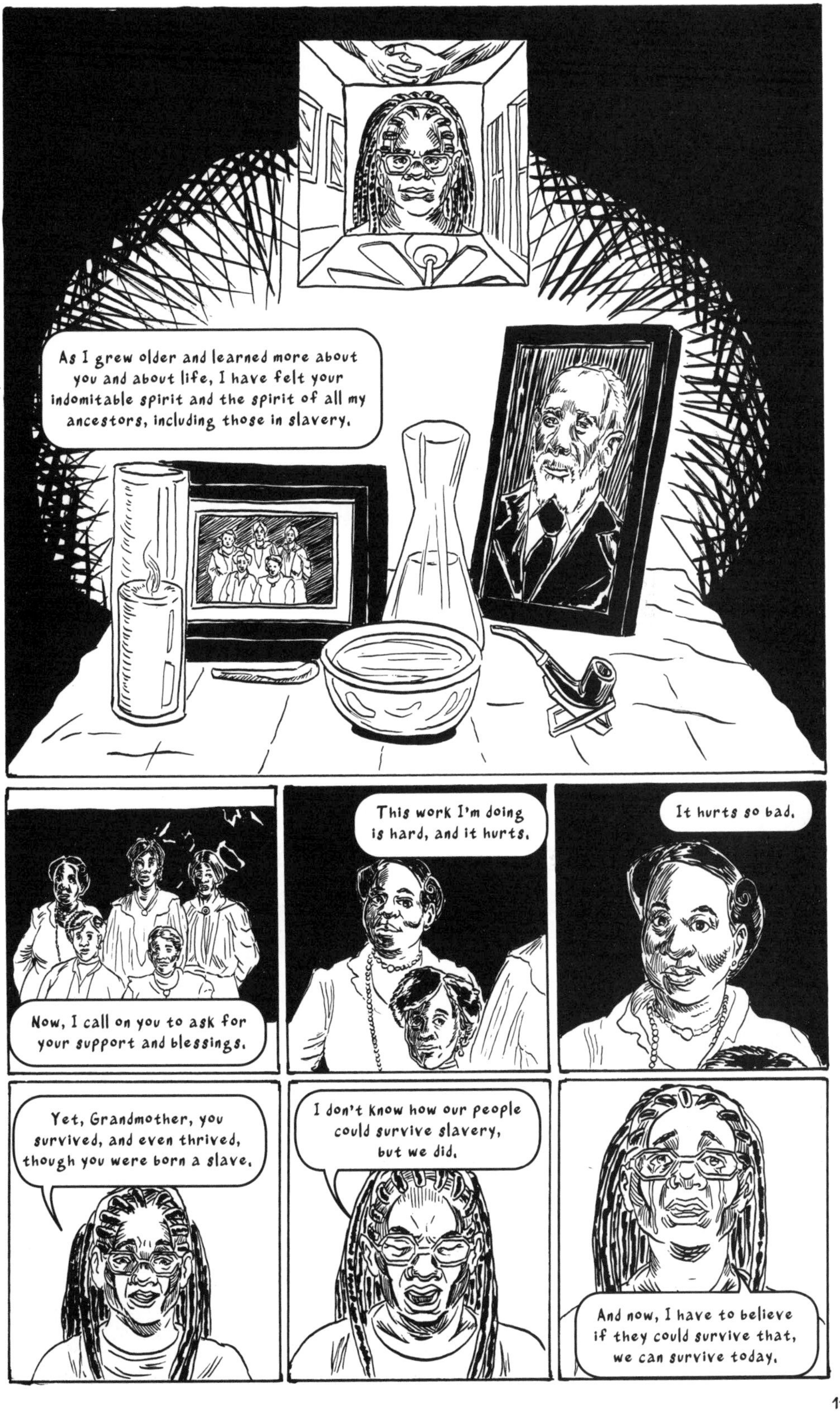

As I grew older and learned more about you and about life, I have felt your indomitable spirit and the spirit of all my ancestors, including those in slavery.
Now, I call on you to ask for your support and blessings.
This work I'm doing is hard, and it hurts.
It hurts so bad.
Yet, Grandmother, you survived, and even thrived, though you were born a slave.
I don't know how our people could survive slavery, but we did.
And now, I have to believe if they could survive that, we can survive today.

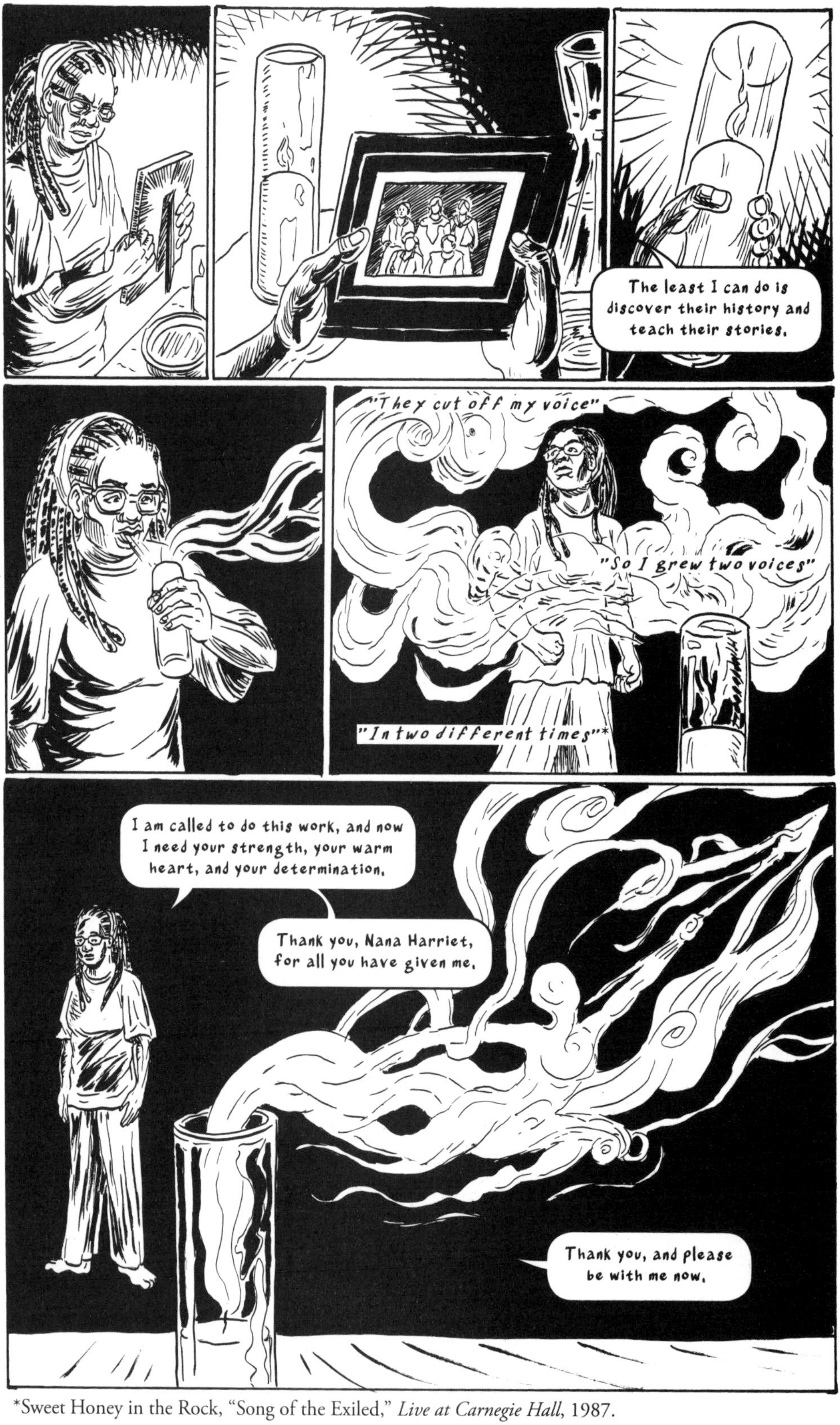
The least I can do is discover their history and teach their stories.
"They cut off my voice"
"So I grew two voices"
"In two different times"*
I am called to do this work, and now I need your strength, your warm heart, and your determination.
Thank you, Nana Harriet, for all you have given me.
Thank you, and please be with me now.

*Sweet Honey in the Rock, "Song of the Exiled," *Live at Carnegie Hall*, 1987.

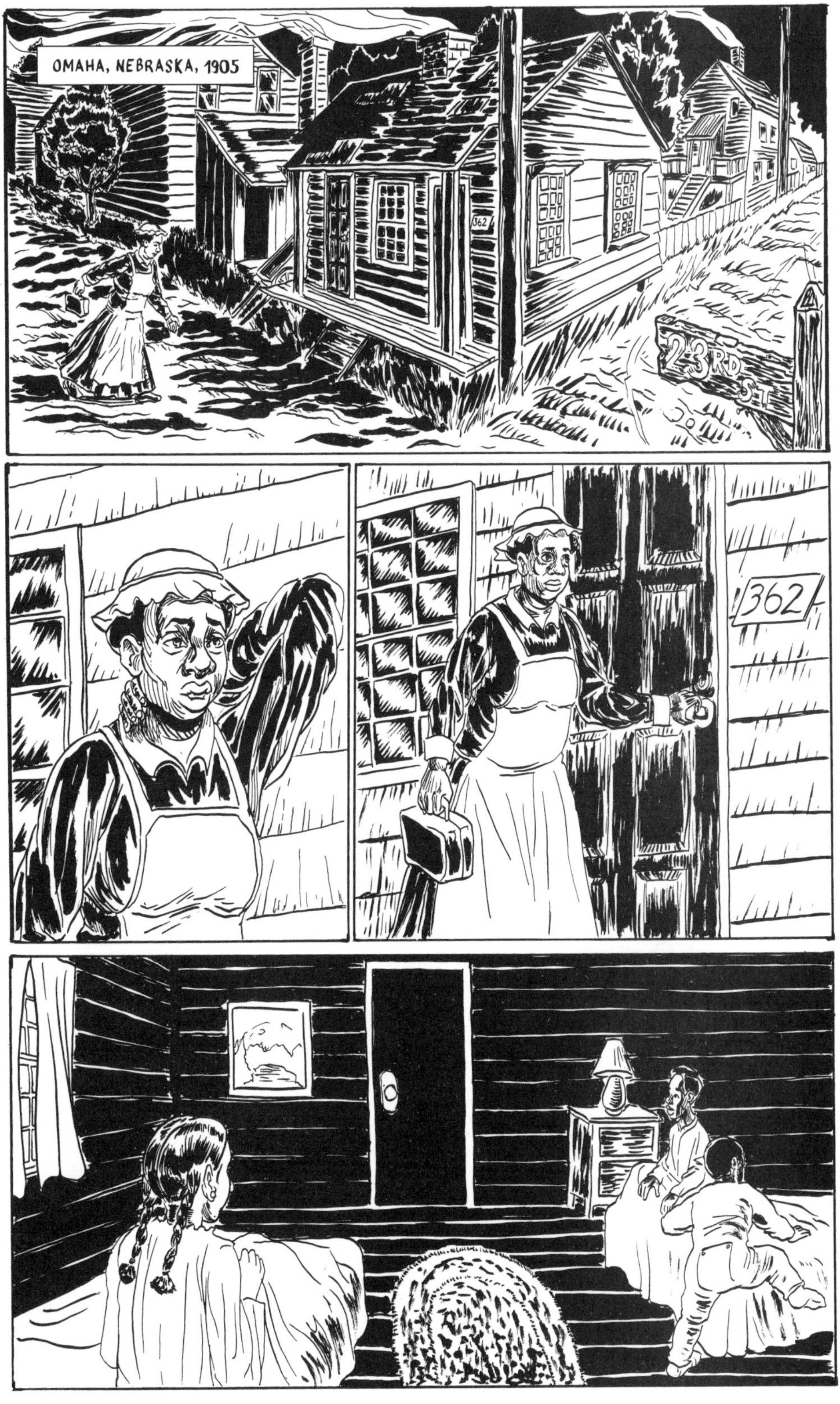
OMAHA, NEBRASKA, 1905
362
23RD ST
362

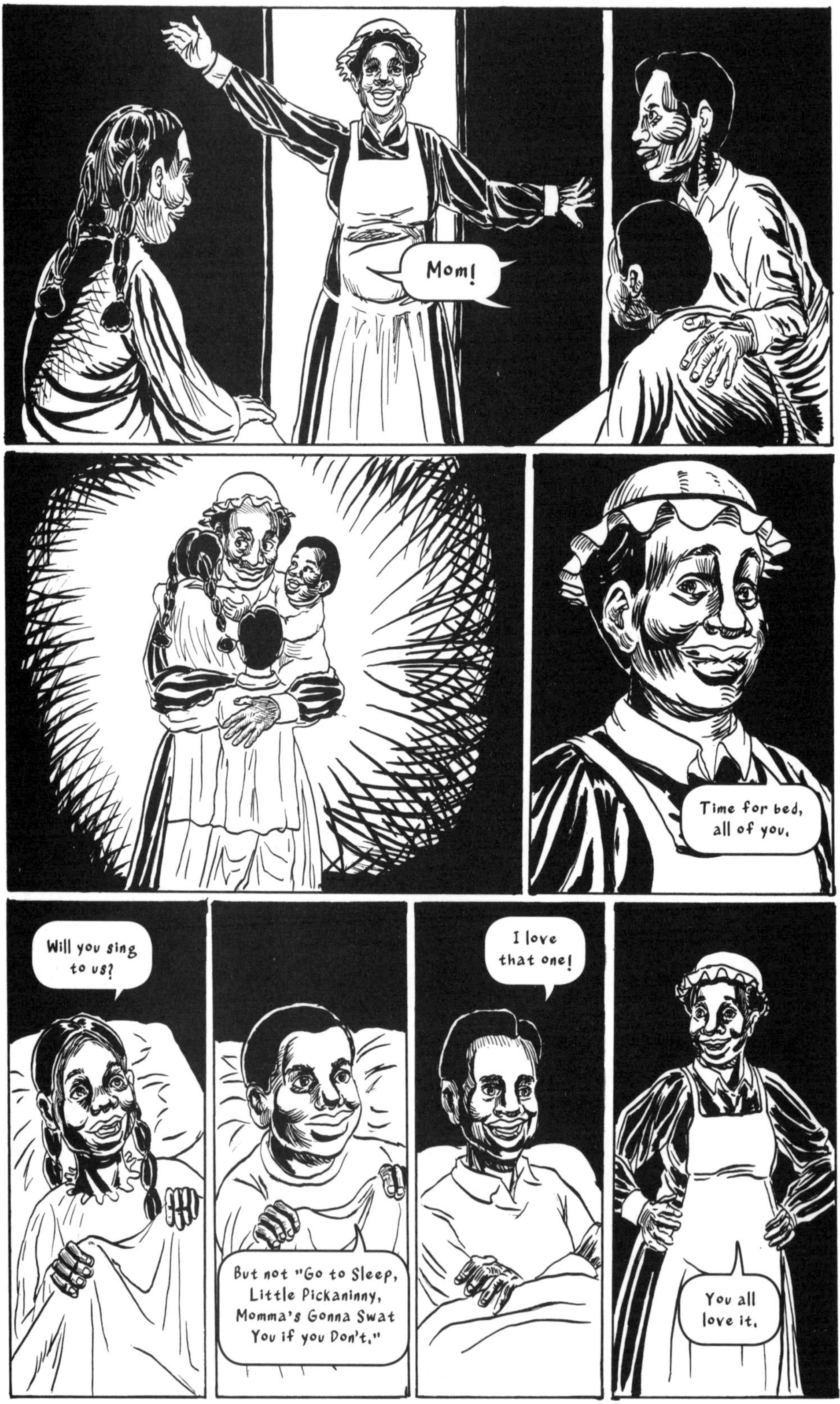
Mom!
Time for bed, all of you.
Will you sing to us?
But not "Go to Sleep, Little Pickaninny, Momma's Gonna Swat You if you Don't."
I love that one!
You all love it.

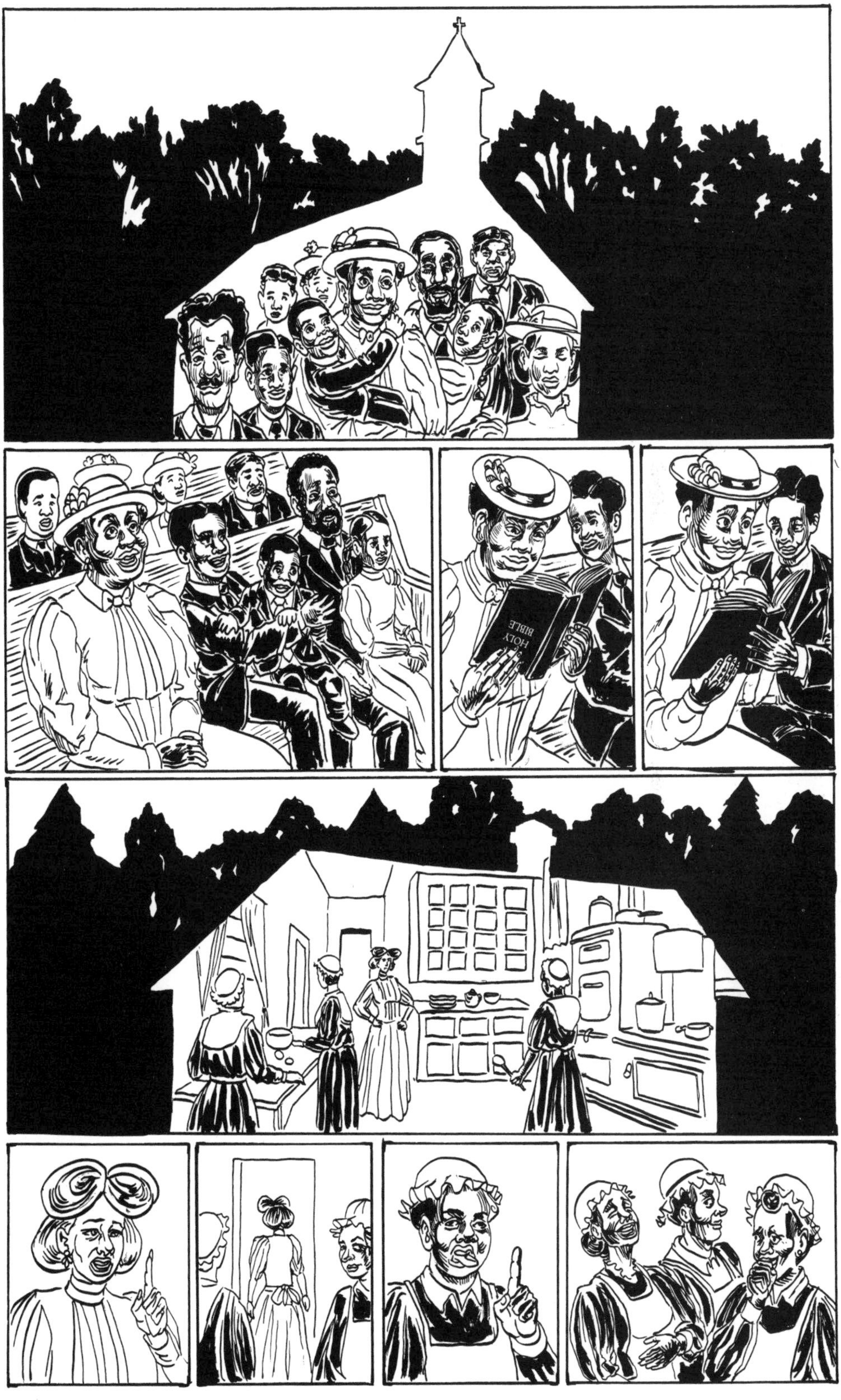
HOLY BIBLE

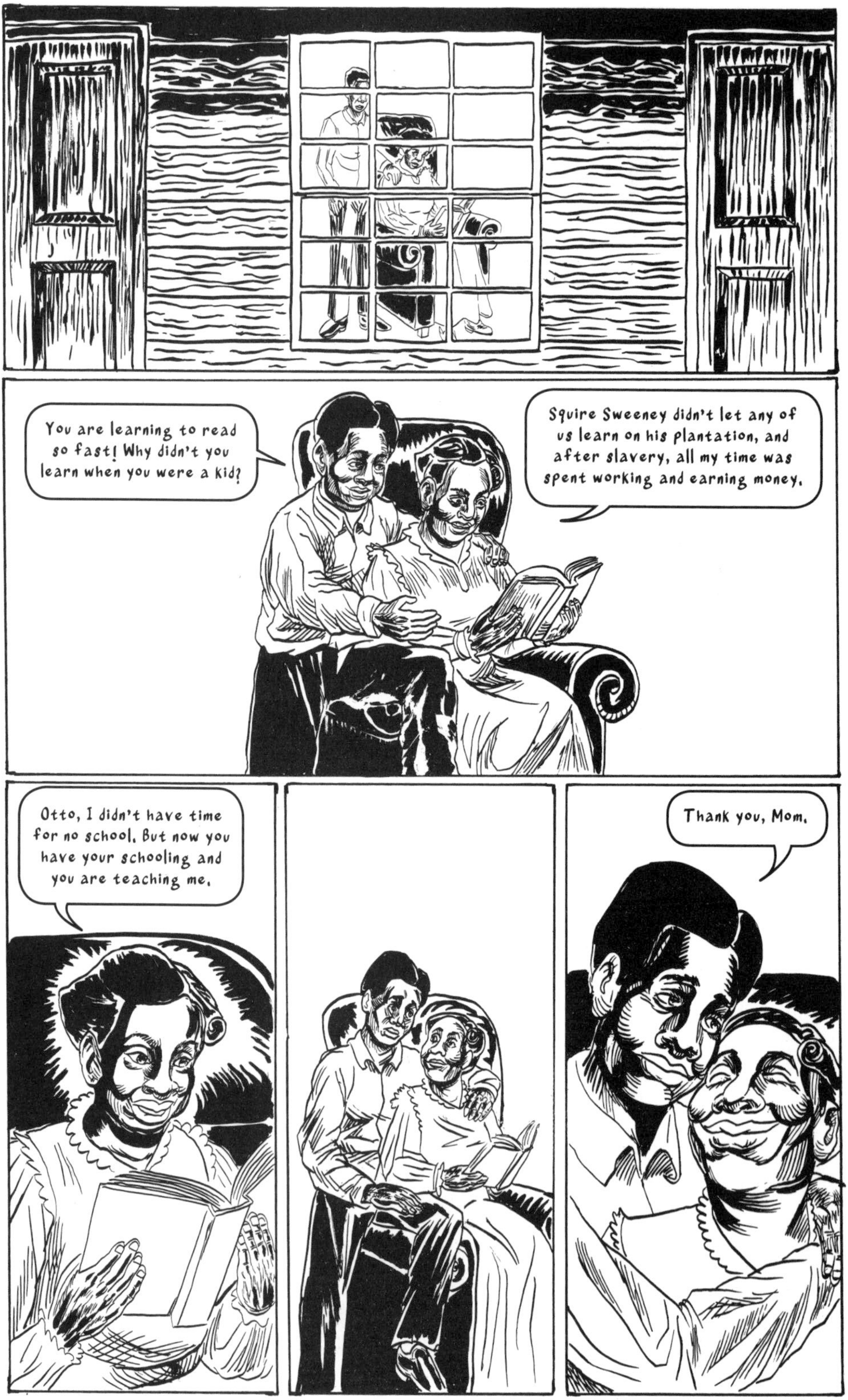
You are learning to read so fast! Why didn't you learn when you were a kid?
Squire Sweeney didn't let any of us learn on his plantation, and after slavery, all my time was spent working and earning money.
Otto, I didn't have time for no school. But now you have your schooling and you are teaching me.
Thank you, Mom.

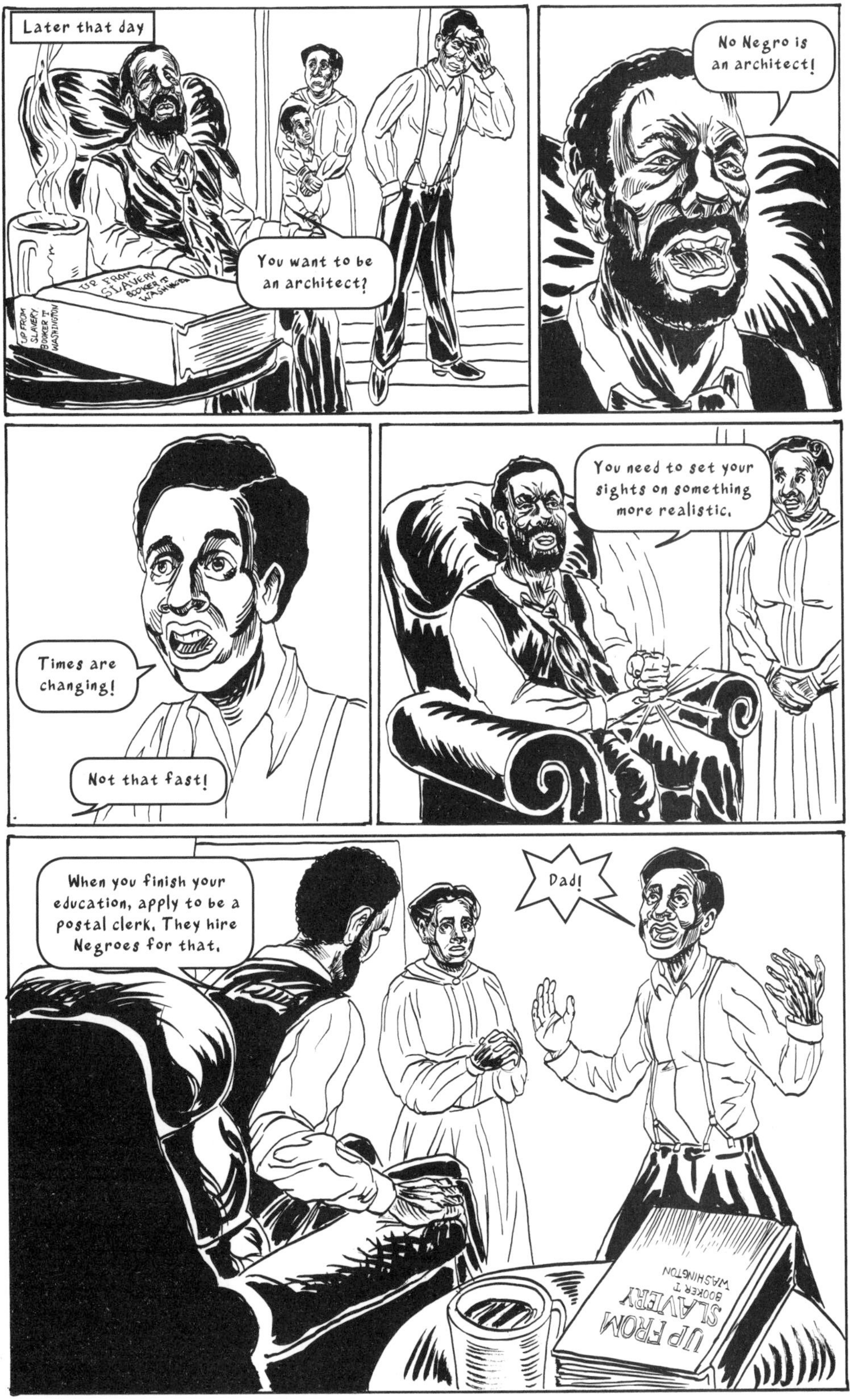

Later that day
UP FROM SLAVERY BOOKER T. WASHINGTON
You want to be an architect?
No Negro is an architect!
Times are changing!
Not that fast!
You need to set your sights on something more realistic.
When you finish your education, apply to be a postal clerk. They hire Negroes for that.
Dad!
UP FROM SLAVERY BOOKER T. WASHINGTON

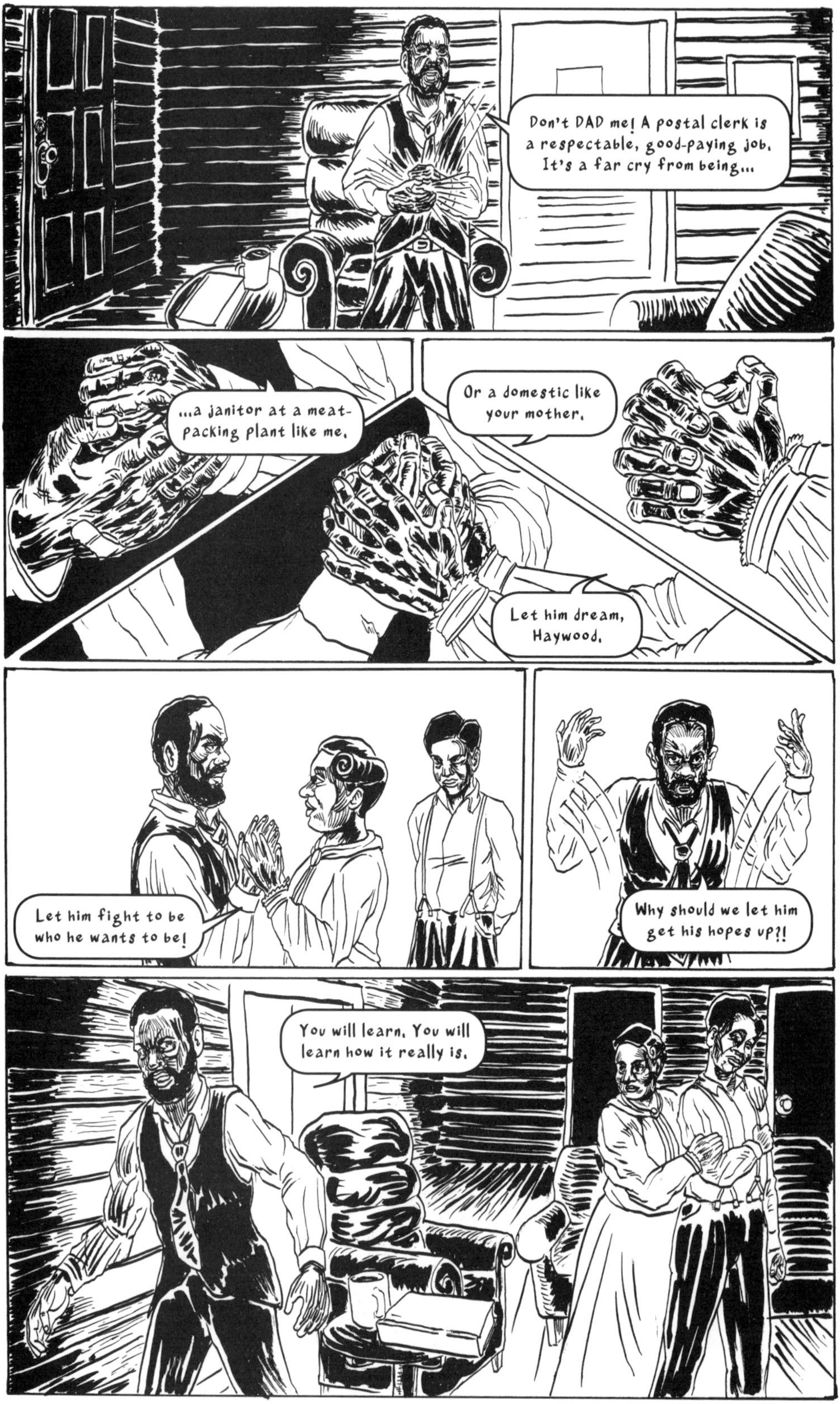
Don't DAD me! A postal clerk is a respectable, good-paying job. It's a far cry from being...
...a janitor at a meat-packing plant like me.
Or a domestic like your mother.
Let him dream, Haywood.
Let him fight to be who he wants to be!
Why should we let him get his hopes up?!
You will learn. You will learn how it really is.

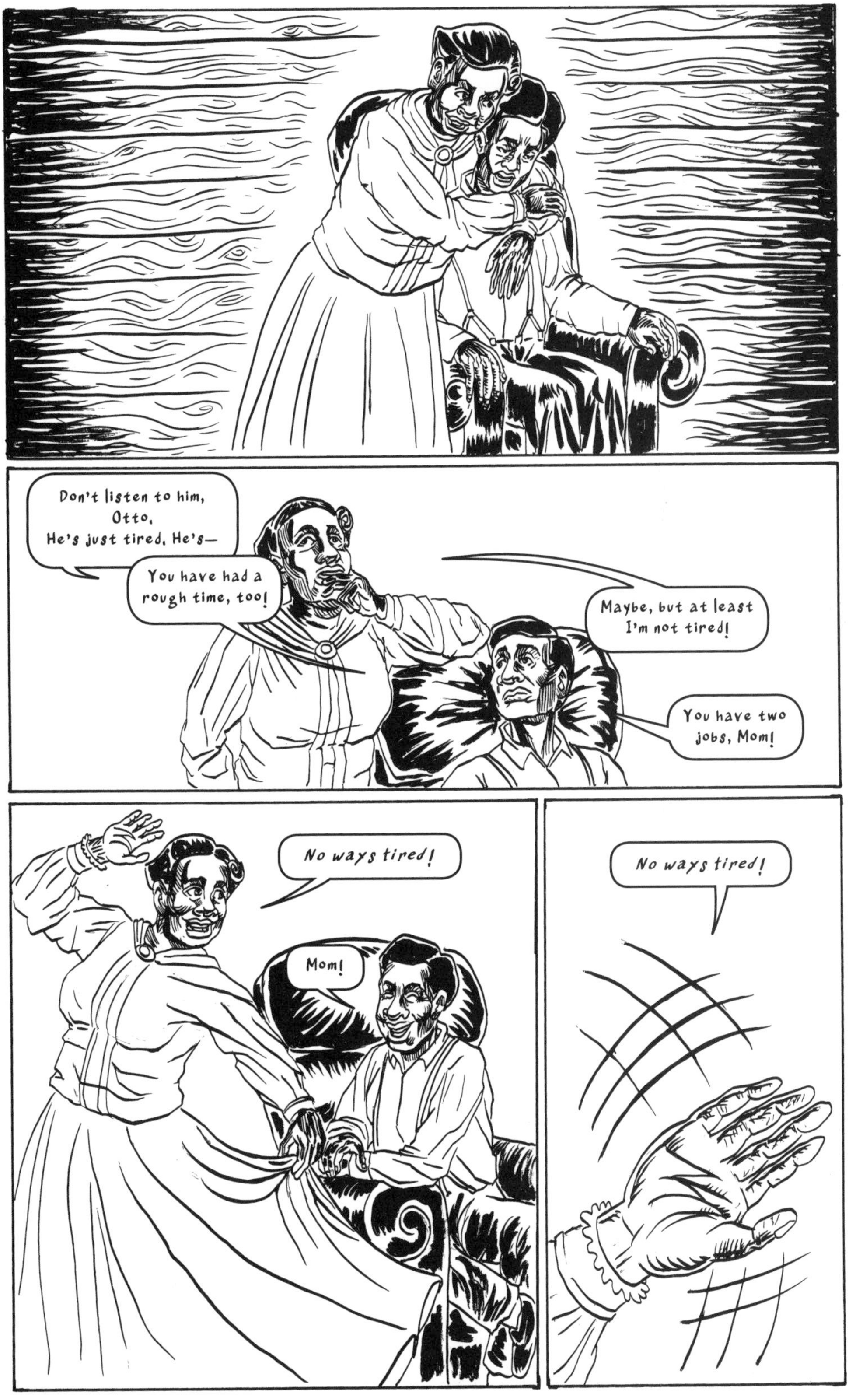
Don't listen to him, Otto. He's just tired. He's—
You have had a rough time, too!
Maybe, but at least I'm not tired!
You have two jobs, Mom!
No ways tired!
Mom!
No ways tired!

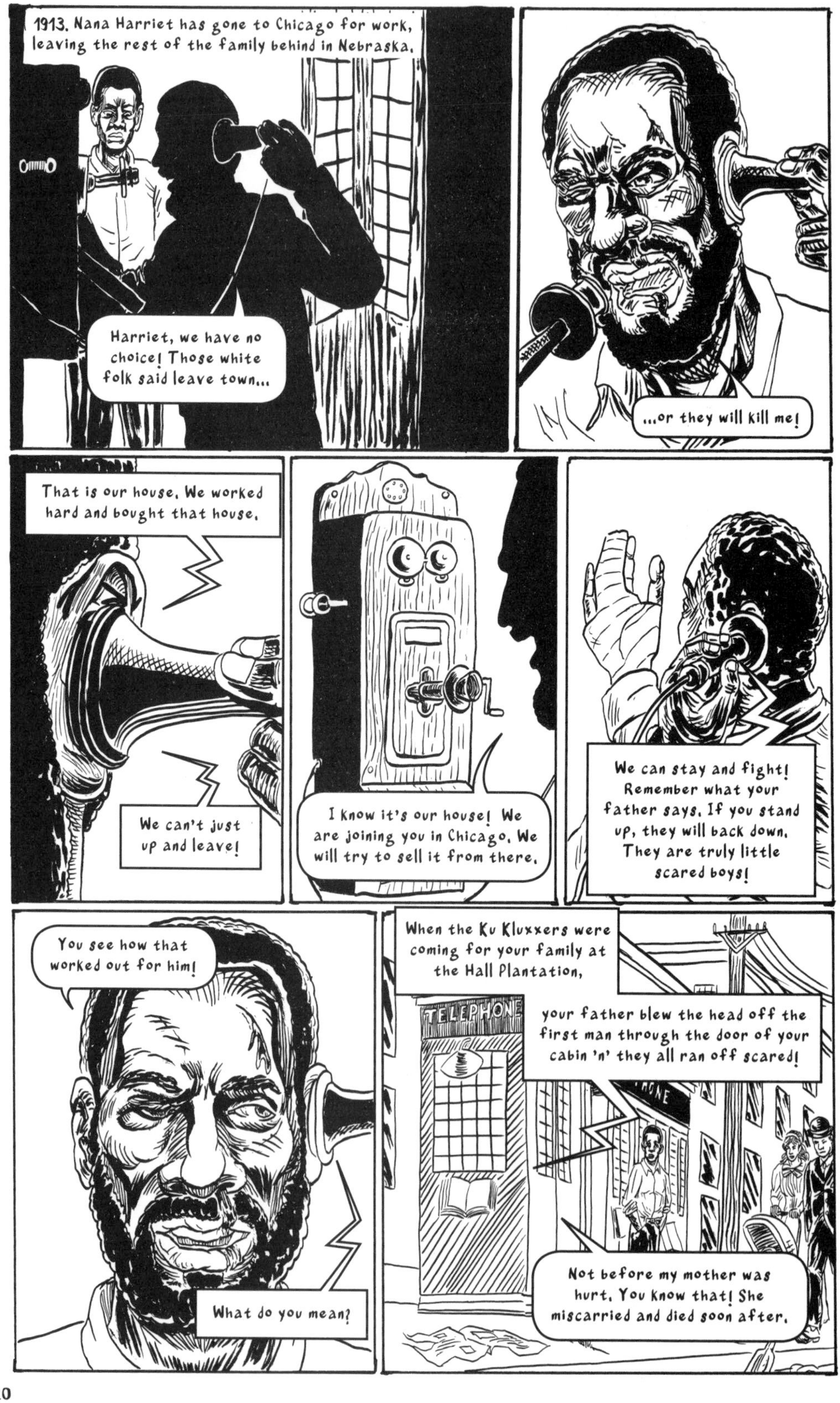
1913. Nana Harriet has gone to Chicago for work, leaving the rest of the family behind in Nebraska.
Harriet, we have no choice! Those white folk said leave town...
...or they will kill me!
That is our house. We worked hard and bought that house.
We can't just up and leave!
I know it's our house! We are joining you in Chicago. We will try to sell it from there.
We can stay and fight! Remember what your father says. If you stand up, they will back down. They are truly little scared boys!
You see how that worked out for him!
What do you mean?
When the Ku Kluxxers were coming for your family at the Hall Plantation,
your father blew the head off the first man through the door of your cabin 'n' they all ran off scared!
TELEPHONE
Not before my mother was hurt. You know that! She miscarried and died soon after.

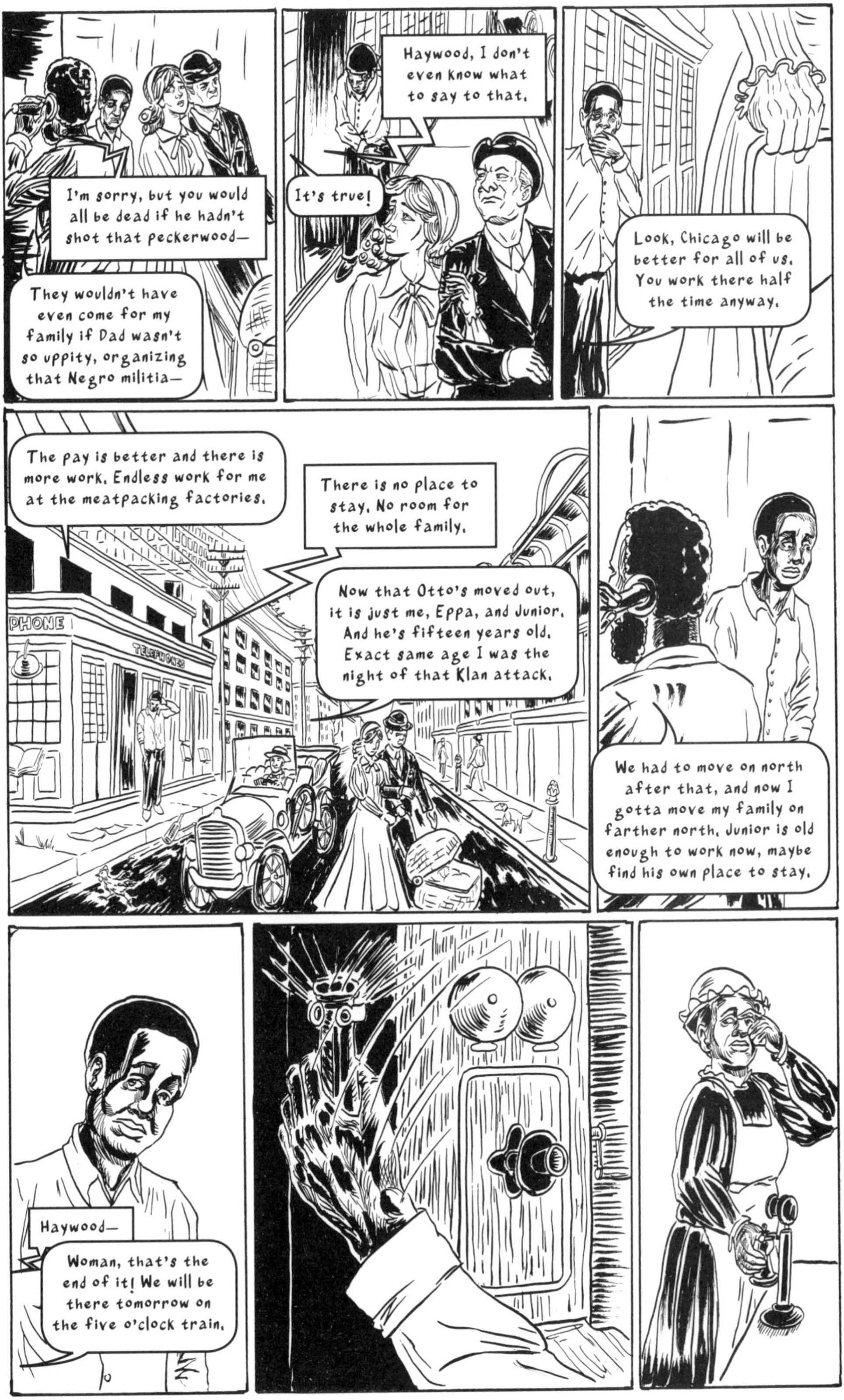
I'm sorry, but you would all be dead if he hadn't shot that peckerwood—
They wouldn't have even come for my family if Dad wasn't so uppity, organizing that Negro militia—
Haywood, I don't even know what to say to that.
It's true!
Look, Chicago will be better for all of us. You work there half the time anyway.
The pay is better and there is more work. Endless work for me at the meatpacking factories.
There is no place to stay. No room for the whole family.
Now that Otto's moved out, it is just me, Eppa, and Junior. And he's fifteen years old. Exact same age I was the night of that Klan attack.
PHONE
TELEPHONES
We had to move on north after that, and now I gotta move my family on farther north. Junior is old enough to work now, maybe find his own place to stay.
Haywood—
Woman, that's the end of it! We will be there tomorrow on the five o'clock train.

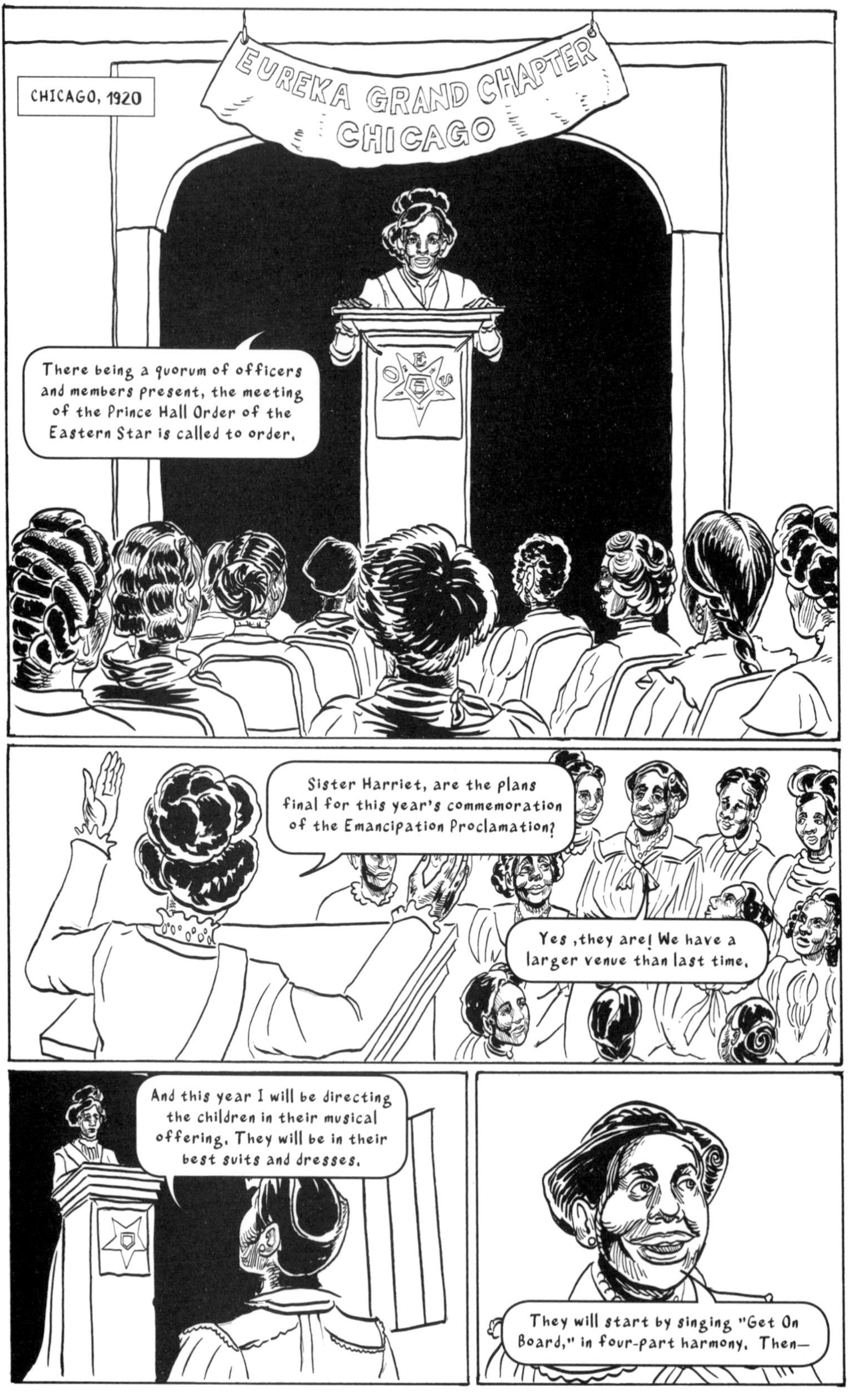

CHICAGO, 1920
EUREKA GRAND CHAPTER CHICAGO
There being a quorum of officers and members present, the meeting of the Prince Hall Order of the Eastern Star is called to order.
Sister Harriet, are the plans final for this year's commemoration of the Emancipation Proclamation?
Yes ,they are! We have a larger venue than last time.
And this year I will be directing the children in their musical offering. They will be in their best suits and dresses.
They will start by singing "Get On Board," in four-part harmony. Then—

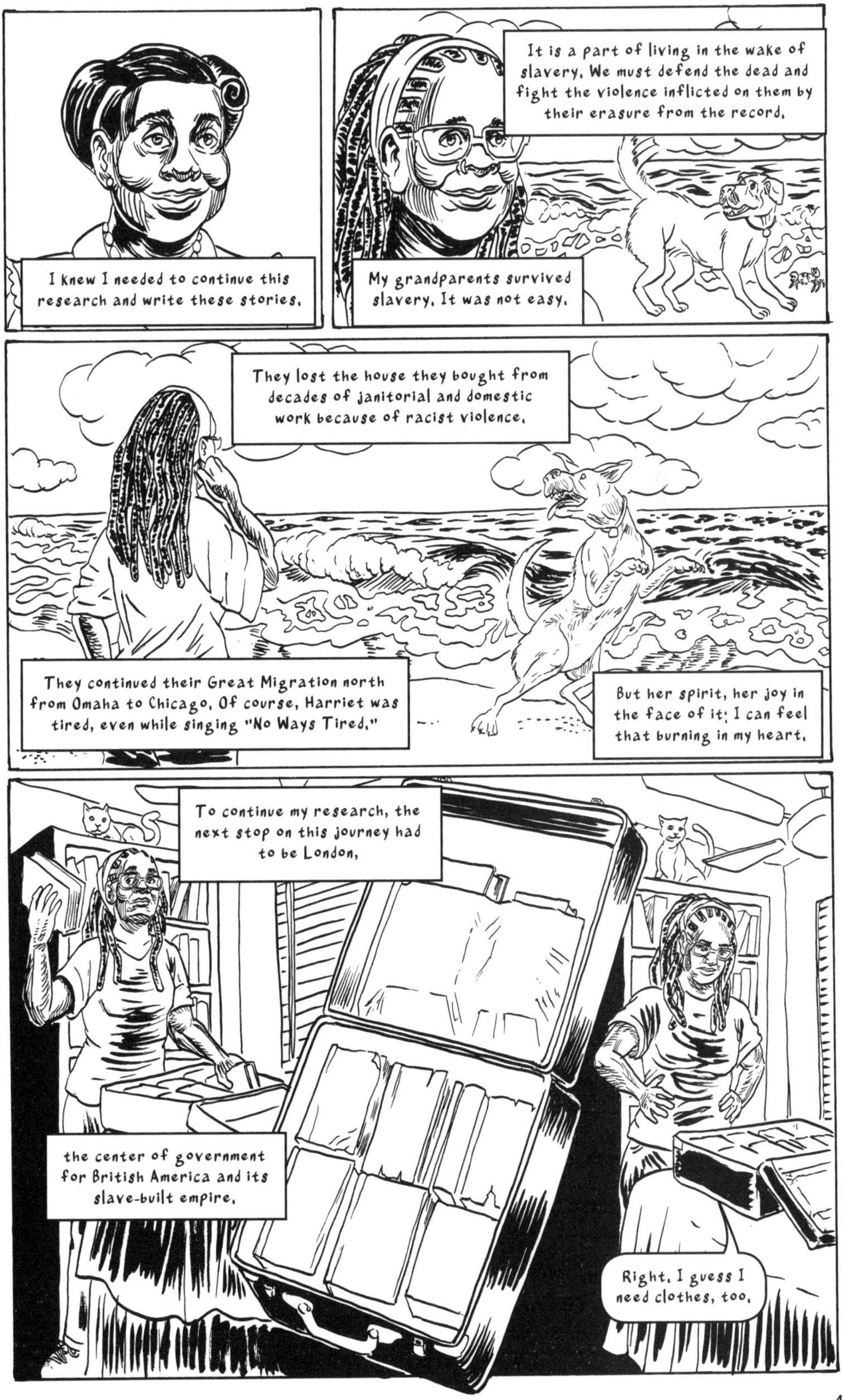
I knew I needed to continue this research and write these stories.
It is a part of living in the wake of slavery. We must defend the dead and fight the violence inflicted on them by their erasure from the record.
My grandparents survived slavery. It was not easy.
They lost the house they bought from decades of janitorial and domestic work because of racist violence.
They continued their Great Migration north from Omaha to Chicago. Of course, Harriet was tired, even while singing "No Ways Tired."
But her spirit, her joy in the face of it; I can feel that burning in my heart.
To continue my research, the next stop on this journey had to be London,
the center of government for British America and its slave-built empire.
Right. I guess I need clothes, too.

Chapter 7
England and the Slave Trade

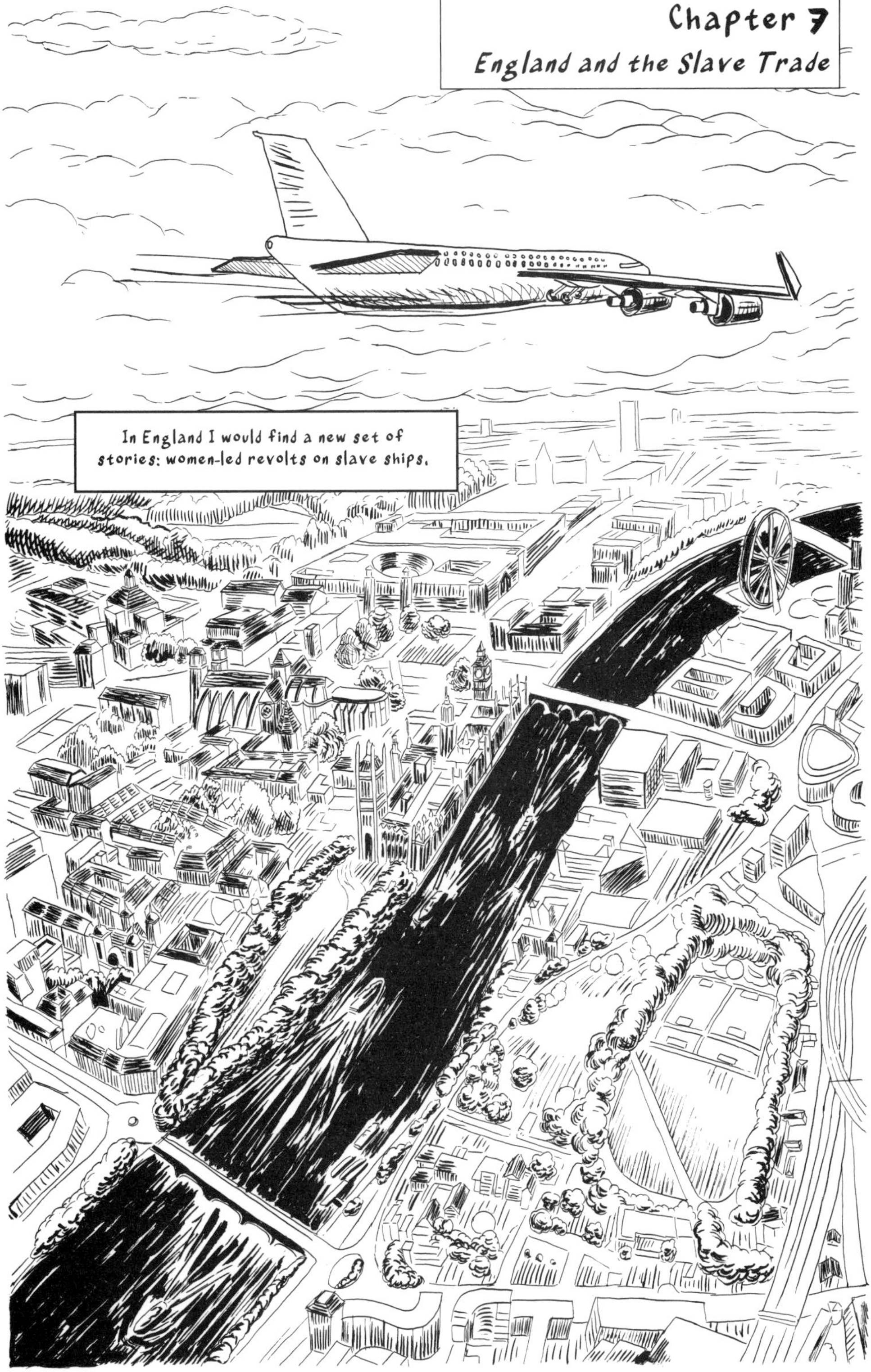
In England I would find a new set of stories: women-led revolts on slave ships.

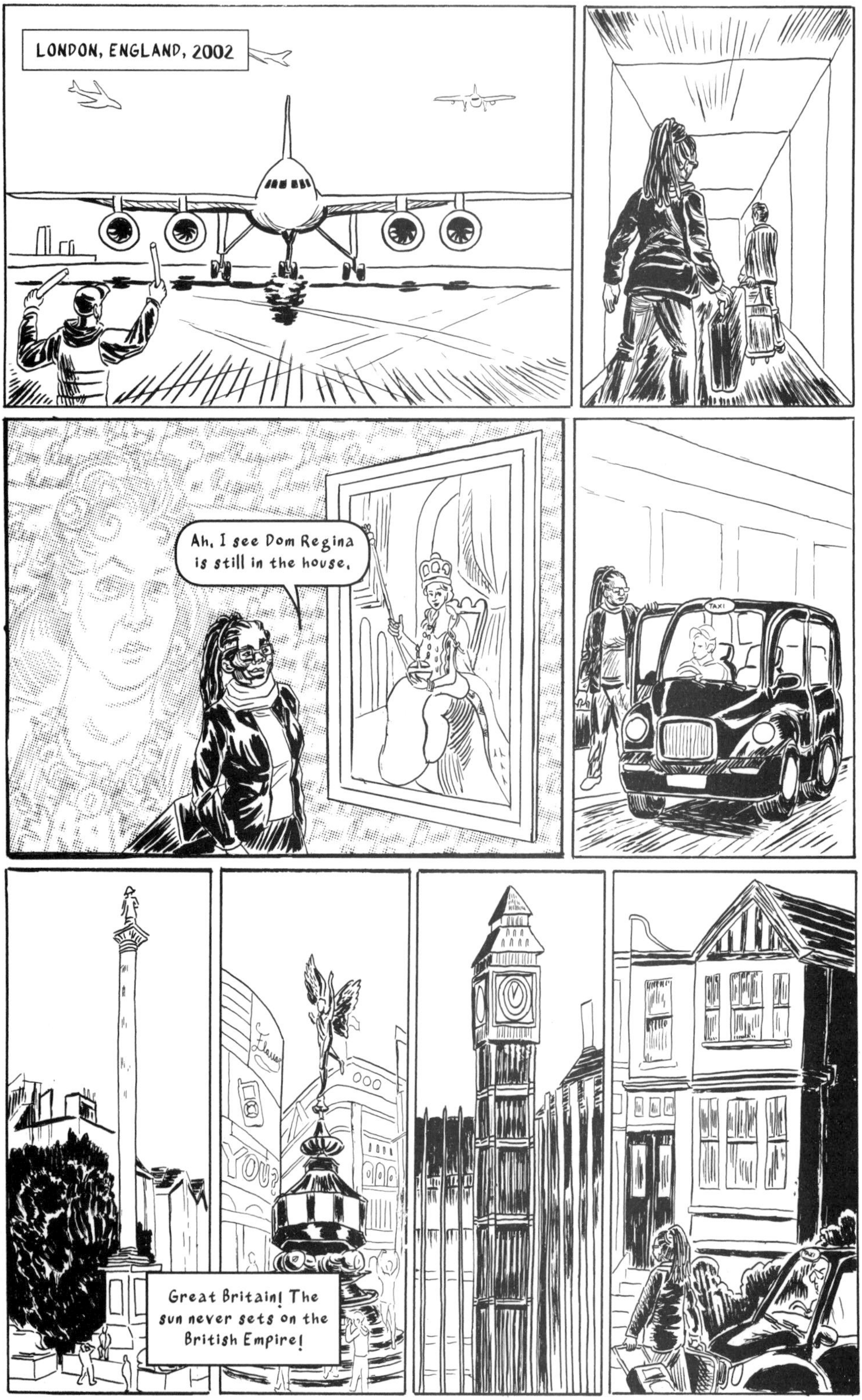
LONDON, ENGLAND, 2002
Ah, I see Dom Regina is still in the house.
TAXI
YOU?
Great Britain! The sun never sets on the British Empire!

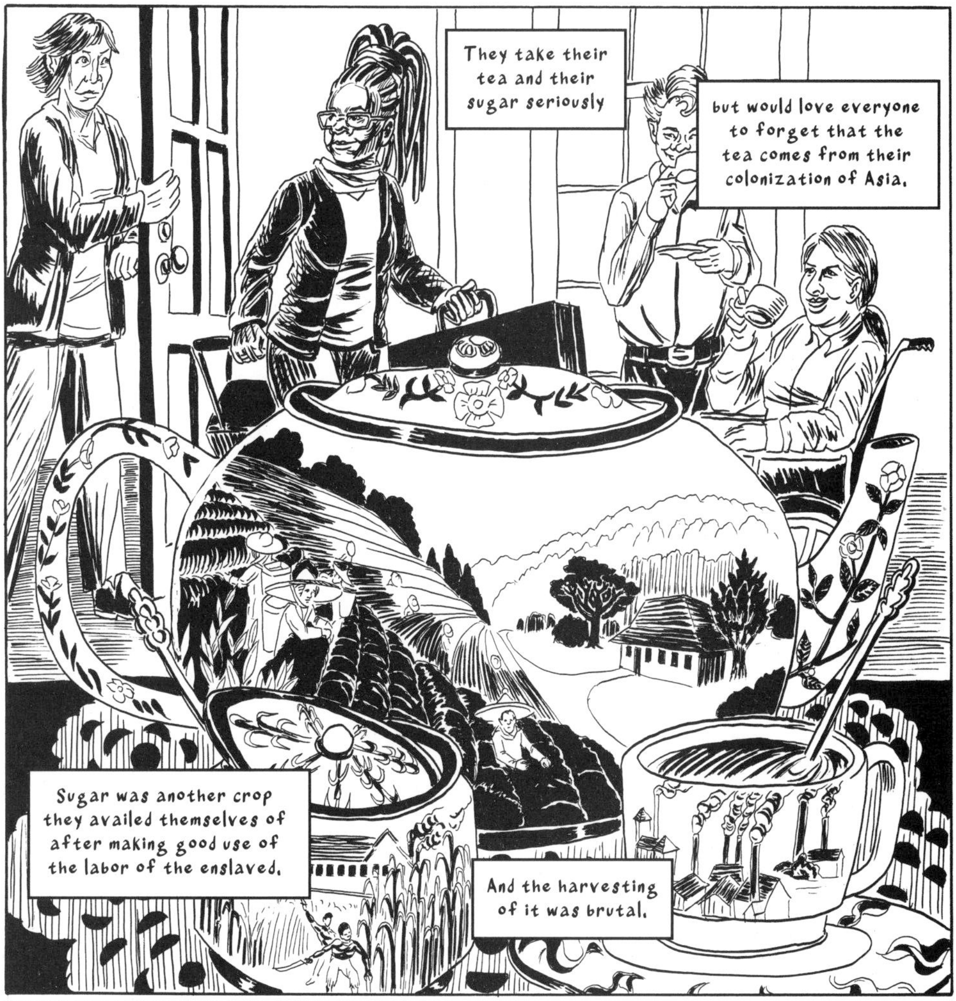
They take their tea and their sugar seriously
but would love everyone to forget that the tea comes from their colonization of Asia.
Sugar was another crop they availed themselves of after making good use of the labor of the enslaved.
And the harvesting of it was brutal.

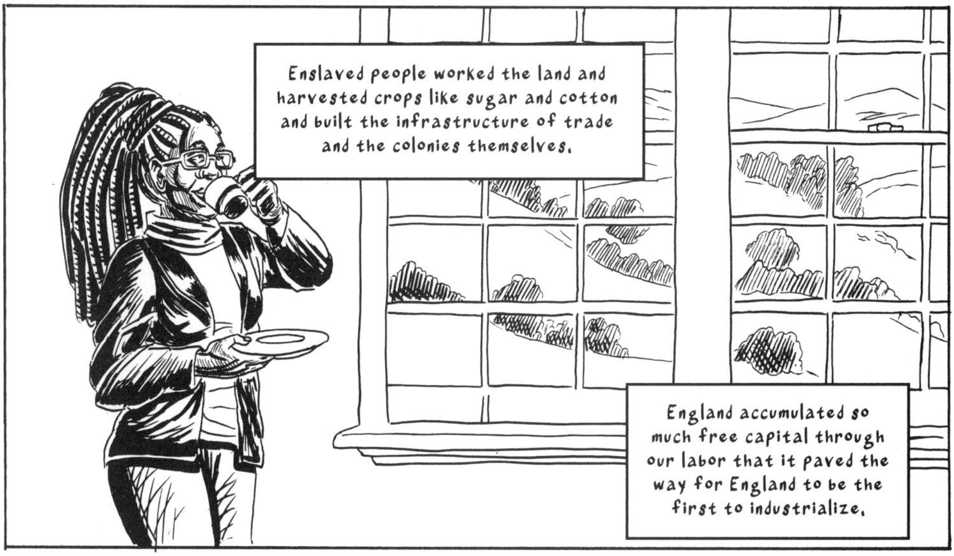
Enslaved people worked the land and harvested crops like sugar and cotton and built the infrastructure of trade and the colonies themselves.
England accumulated so much free capital through our labor that it paved the way for England to be the first to industrialize.

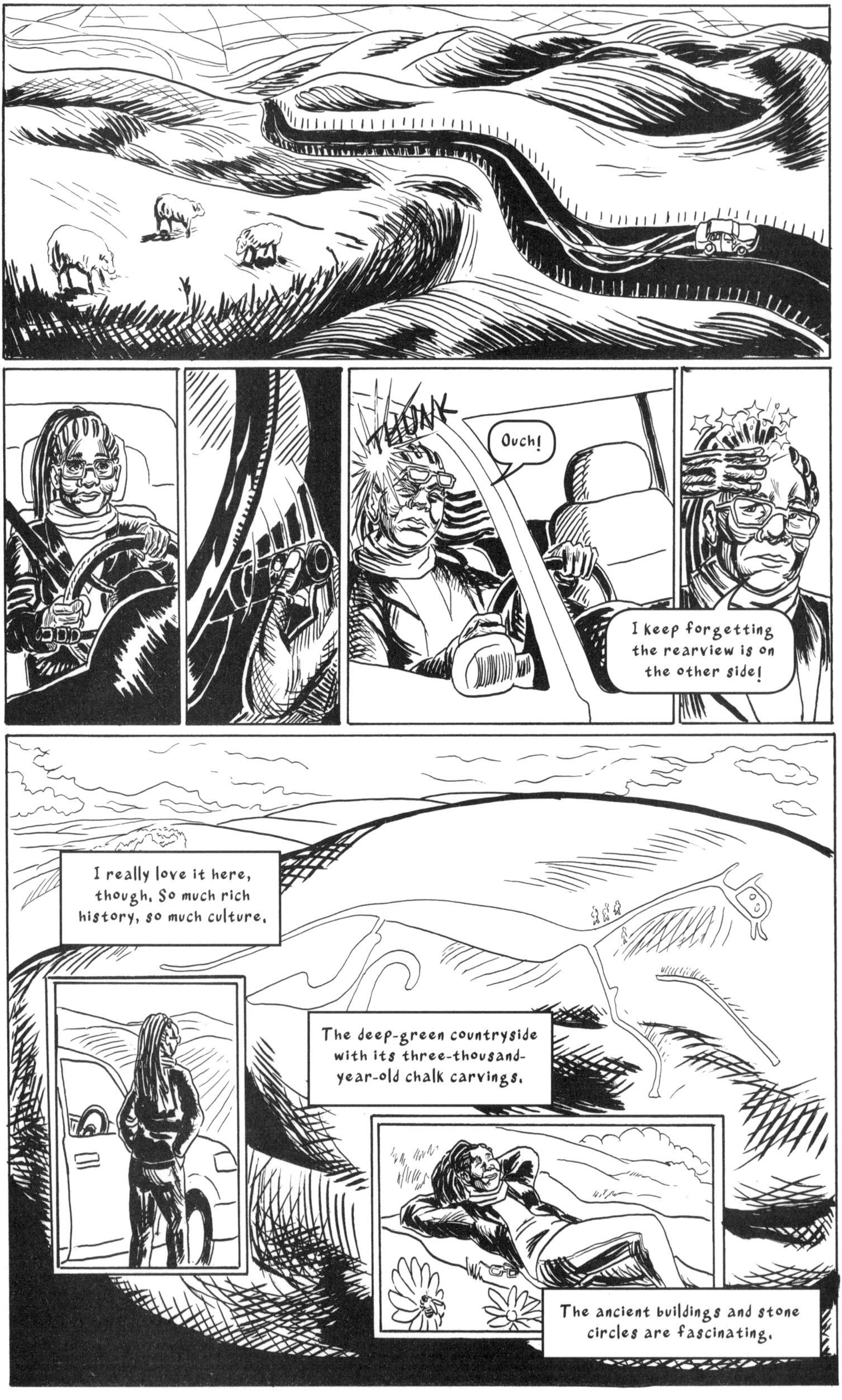
THUNK
Ouch!
I keep forgetting the rearview is on the other side!
I really love it here, though. So much rich history, so much culture.
The deep-green countryside with its three-thousand-year-old chalk carvings.
The ancient buildings and stone circles are fascinating.

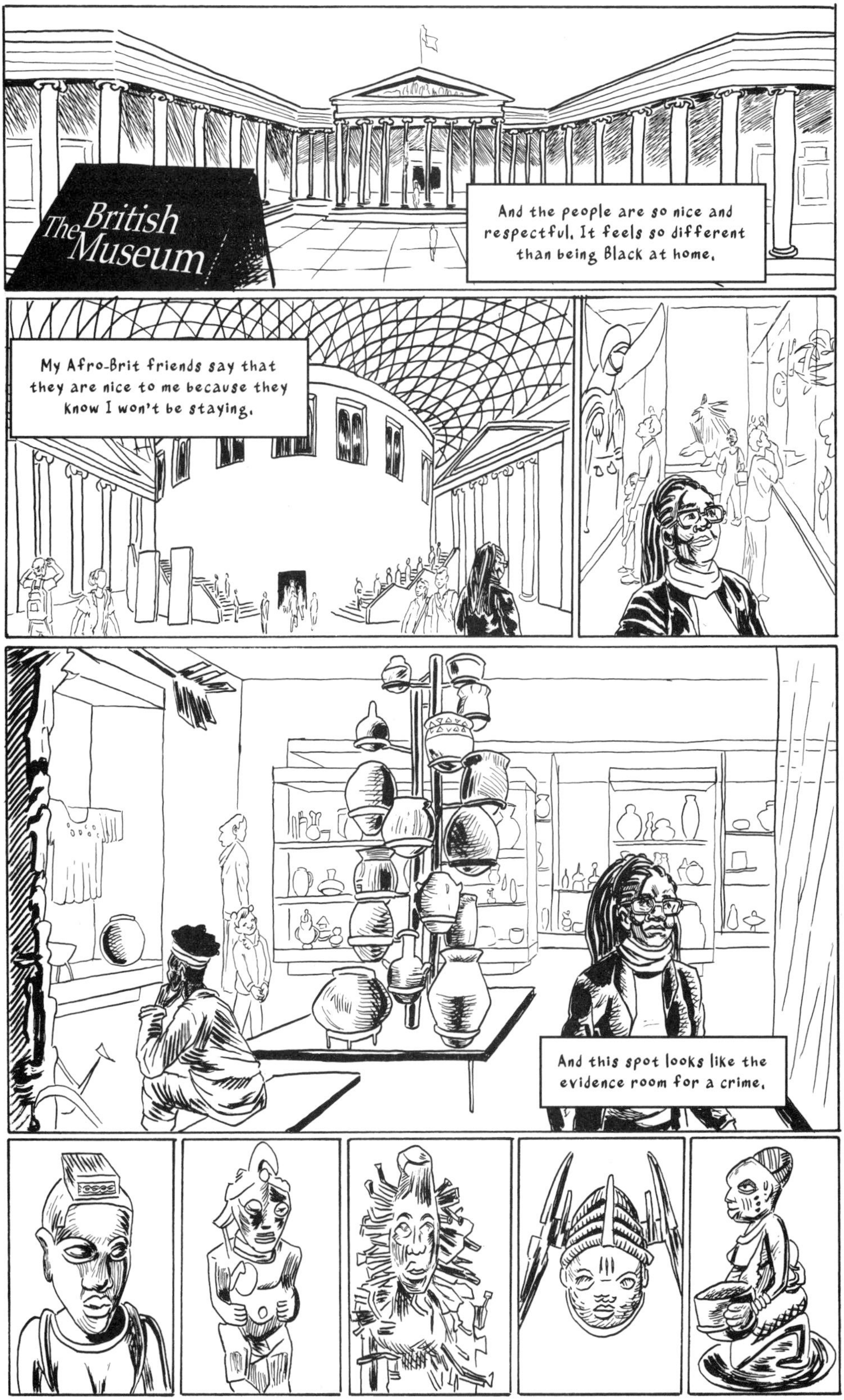
The British Museum
And the people are so nice and respectful. It feels so different than being Black at home.
My Afro-Brit friends say that they are nice to me because they know I won't be staying.
And this spot looks like the evidence room for a crime.

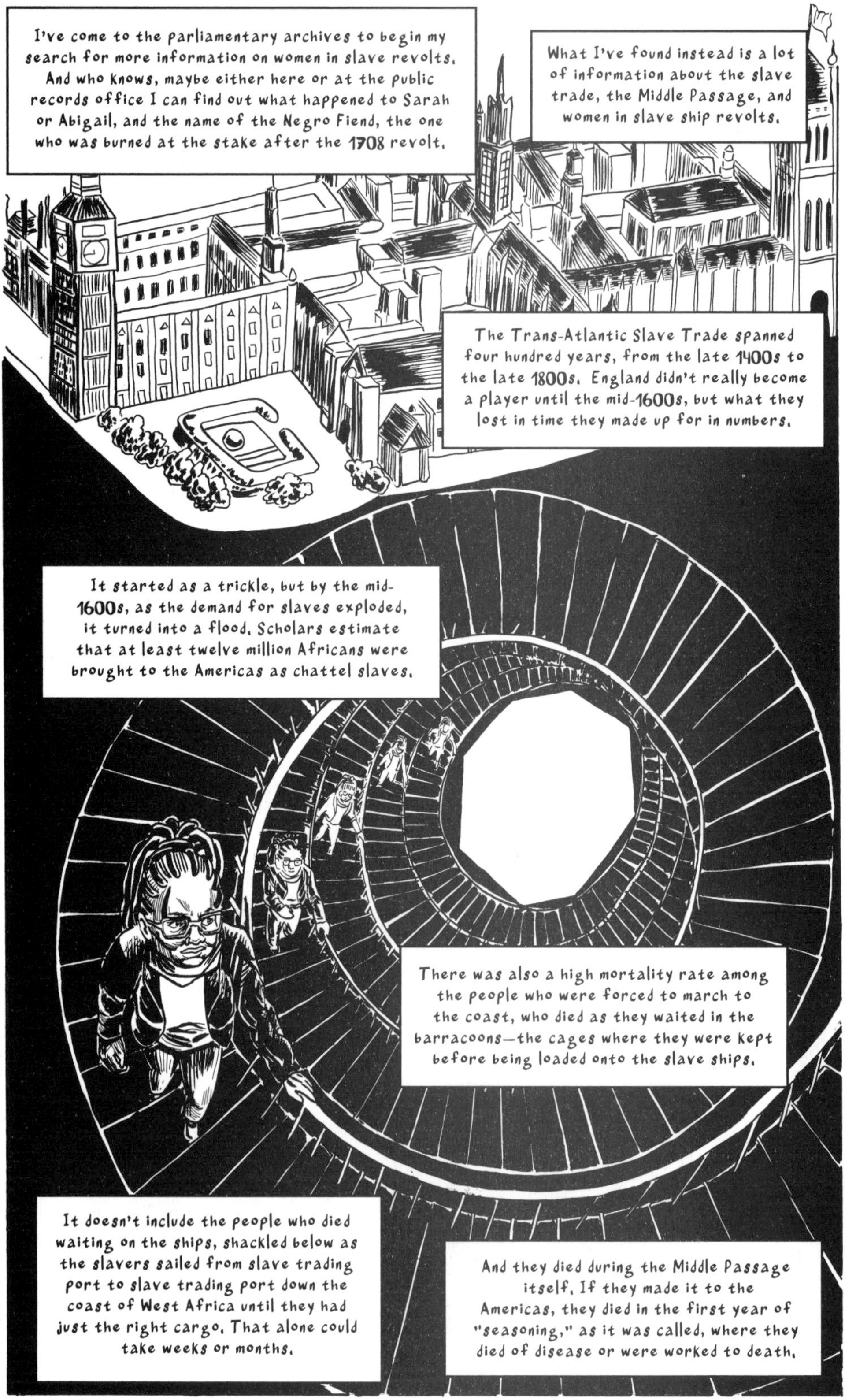
I've come to the parliamentary archives to begin my search for more information on women in slave revolts. And who knows, maybe either here or at the public records office I can find out what happened to Sarah or Abigail, and the name of the Negro Fiend, the one who was burned at the stake after the 1708 revolt.
What I've found instead is a lot of information about the slave trade, the Middle Passage, and women in slave ship revolts.
The Trans-Atlantic Slave Trade spanned four hundred years, from the late 1400s to the late 1800s. England didn't really become a player until the mid-1600s, but what they lost in time they made up for in numbers.
It started as a trickle, but by the mid-1600s, as the demand for slaves exploded, it turned into a flood. Scholars estimate that at least twelve million Africans were brought to the Americas as chattel slaves.
There was also a high mortality rate among the people who were forced to march to the coast, who died as they waited in the barracoons—the cages where they were kept before being loaded onto the slave ships.
It doesn't include the people who died waiting on the ships, shackled below as the slavers sailed from slave trading port to slave trading port down the coast of West Africa until they had just the right cargo. That alone could take weeks or months.
And they died during the Middle Passage itself. If they made it to the Americas, they died in the first year of "seasoning," as it was called, where they died of disease or were worked to death.

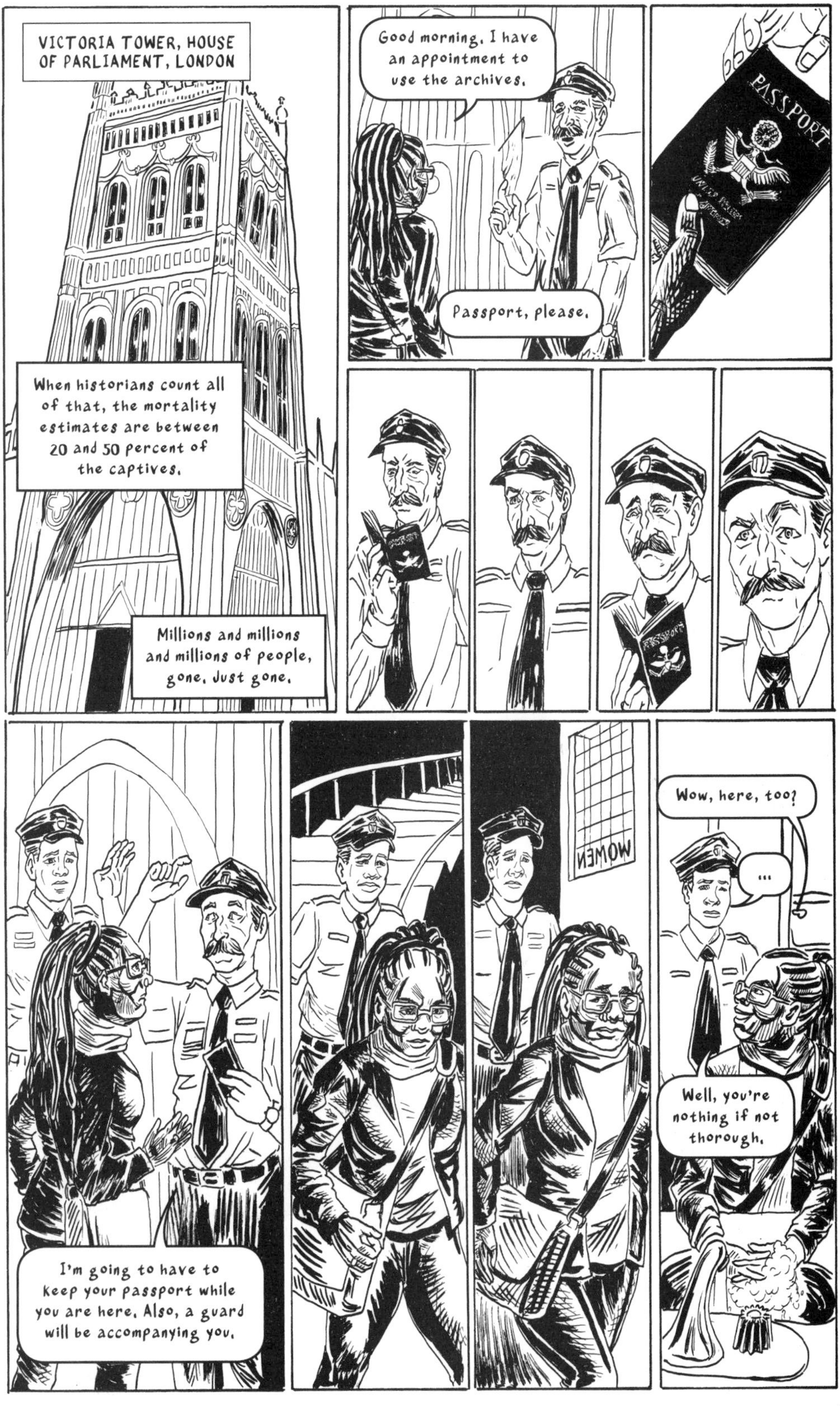
VICTORIA TOWER, HOUSE OF PARLIAMENT, LONDON
When historians count all of that, the mortality estimates are between 20 and 50 percent of the captives.
Millions and millions and millions of people, gone. Just gone.
Good morning. I have an appointment to use the archives.
Passport, please.
PASSPORT
I'm going to have to keep your passport while you are here. Also, a guard will be accompanying you.
WOMEN
Wow, here, too?
...
Well, you're nothing if not thorough.

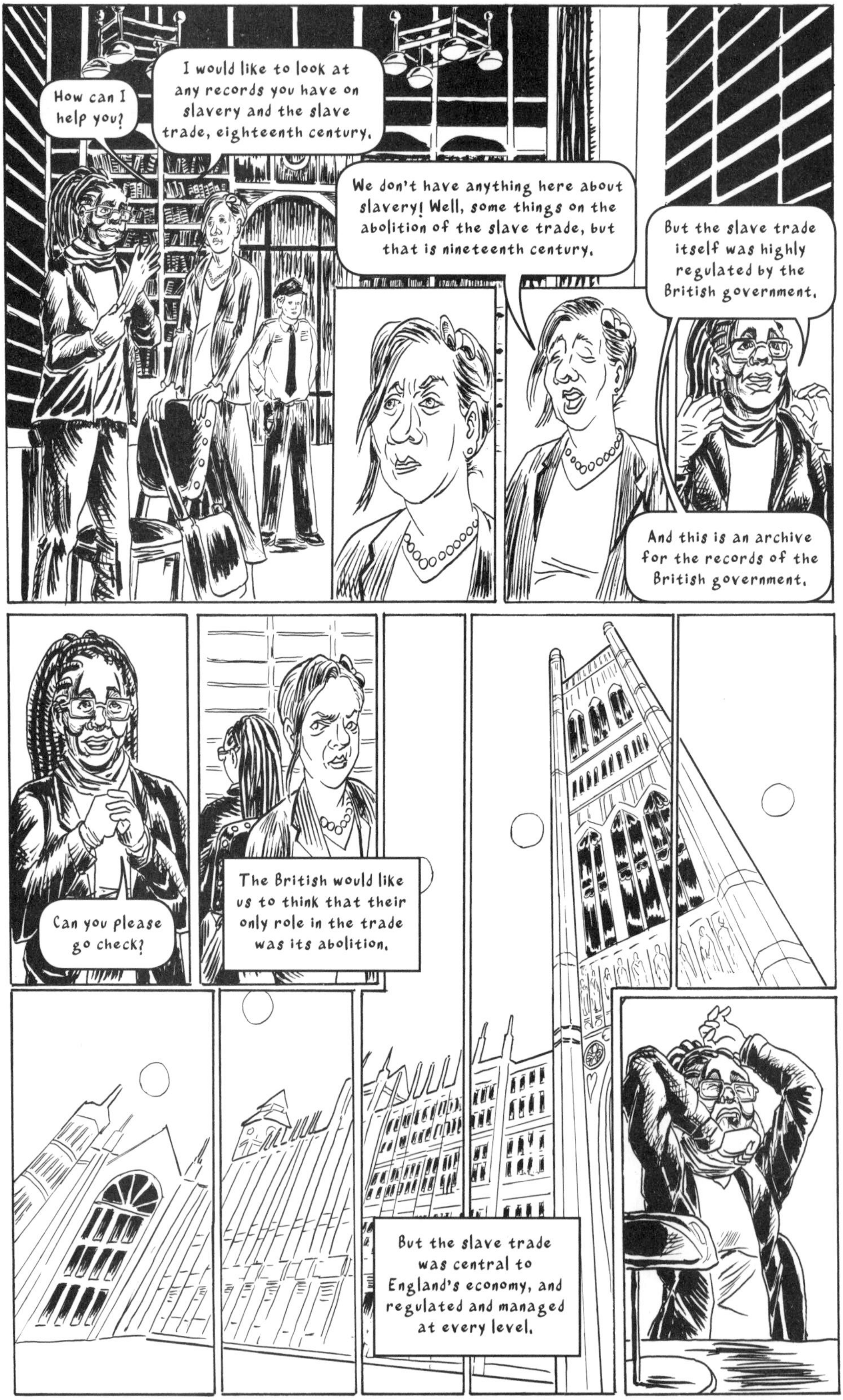
How can I help you?
I would like to look at any records you have on slavery and the slave trade, eighteenth century.
We don't have anything here about slavery! Well, some things on the abolition of the slave trade, but that is nineteenth century.
But the slave trade itself was highly regulated by the British government.
And this is an archive for the records of the British government.
Can you please go check?
The British would like us to think that their only role in the trade was its abolition.
But the slave trade was central to England's economy, and regulated and managed at every level.

Laws created and maintained the trade, and the Crown gave out a monopoly on the trade to a company called the Royal African Company. John Locke, a luminary of the Enlightenment and perhaps the central theorist of American democracy, was a stockholder.

The infamous Brookes Diagram was itself created from the regulation of the slave trade.

You can see that if you look closely at the top: "Stowage of the British Slave Ship Brookes under the REGULATED SLAVE TRADE." It demonstrated the maximum number of slaves allowed under the Slave Trade Act of 1788.

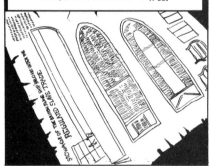

STOWAGE OF THE BRITISH SLAVE SHIP BROOKES UNDER THE REGULATED SLAVE TRADE

Can you reproduce these, and have them shipped to me in the United States?

These also?

And these.

This is crucial history, and if it is taught in school at all, it is taught horribly. We are either told that Europeans went into West Africa and kidnapped helpless Africans living in Stone Age conditions,

or we are taught the opposite: that Africans sold their own brothers and sisters into slavery while Europe innocently tapped into an existing supply.

Both of these paradigms are wrong. History is more complicated than either of these accounts, and history, by definition, is the study of change over time. A lot changed in the four-hundred-year sweep of Atlantic slave trade history.

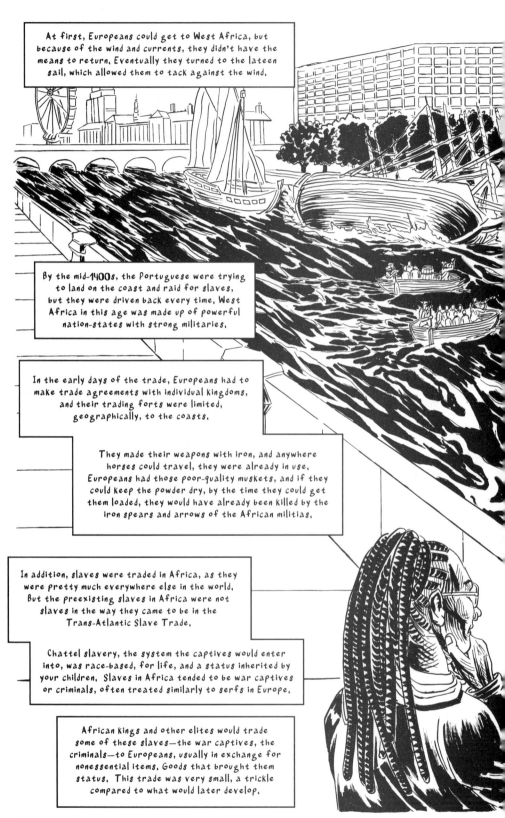

At first, Europeans could get to West Africa, but because of the wind and currents, they didn't have the means to return. Eventually they turned to the lateen sail, which allowed them to tack against the wind.

By the mid-1400s, the Portuguese were trying to land on the coast and raid for slaves, but they were driven back every time. West Africa in this age was made up of powerful nation-states with strong militaries.

In the early days of the trade, Europeans had to make trade agreements with individual kingdoms, and their trading forts were limited, geographically, to the coasts.

They made their weapons with iron, and anywhere horses could travel, they were already in use. Europeans had those poor-quality muskets, and if they could keep the powder dry, by the time they could get them loaded, they would have already been killed by the iron spears and arrows of the African militias.

In addition, slaves were traded in Africa, as they were pretty much everywhere else in the world. But the preexisting slaves in Africa were not slaves in the way they came to be in the Trans-Atlantic Slave Trade.

Chattel slavery, the system the captives would enter into, was race-based, for life, and a status inherited by your children. Slaves in Africa tended to be war captives or criminals, often treated similarly to serfs in Europe.

African kings and other elites would trade some of these slaves—the war captives, the criminals—to Europeans, usually in exchange for nonessential items. Goods that brought them status. This trade was very small, a trickle compared to what would later develop.

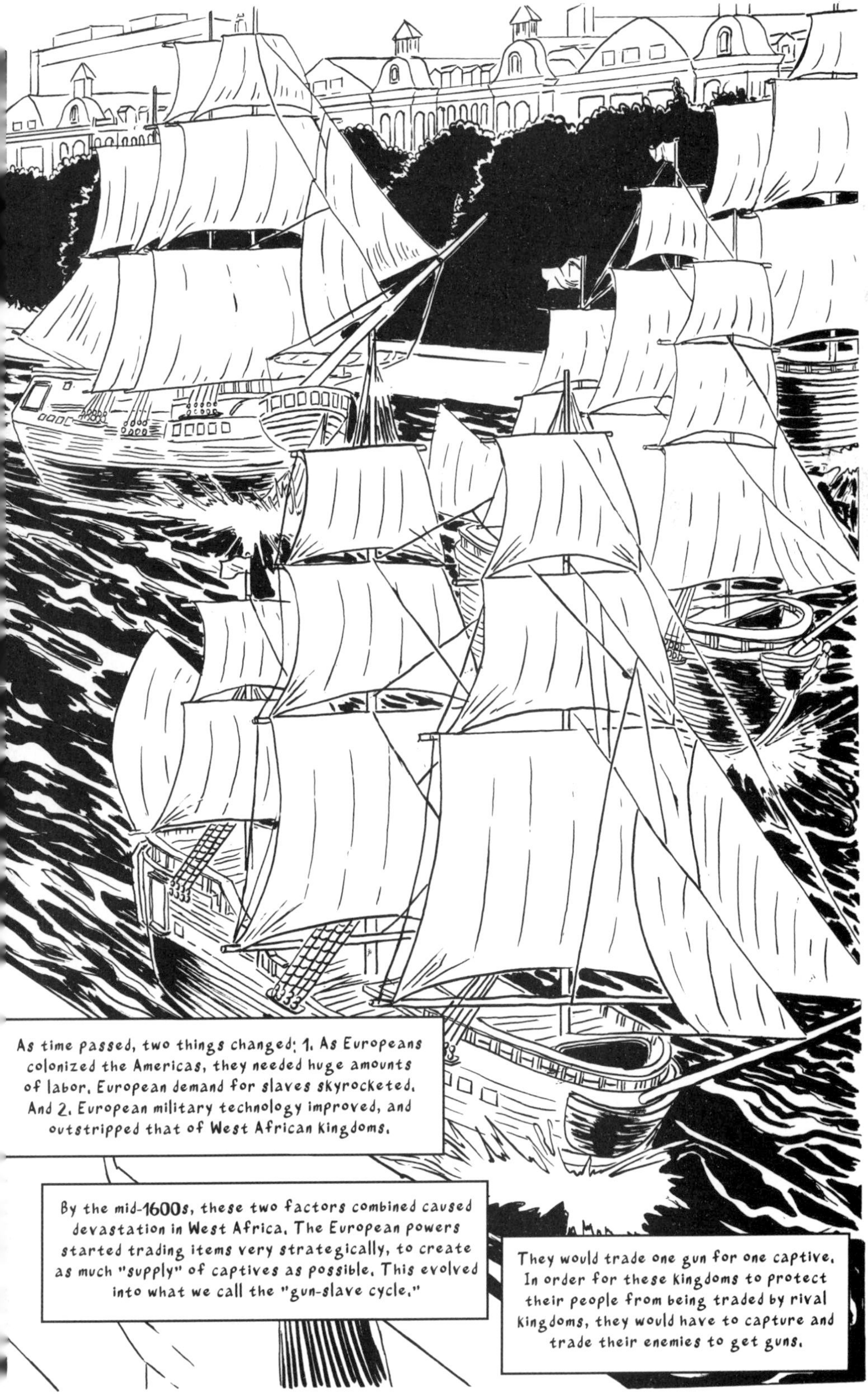
As time passed, two things changed: 1. As Europeans colonized the Americas, they needed huge amounts of labor. European demand for slaves skyrocketed. And 2. European military technology improved, and outstripped that of West African kingdoms.
By the mid-1600s, these two factors combined caused devastation in West Africa. The European powers started trading items very strategically, to create as much "supply" of captives as possible. This evolved into what we call the "gun-slave cycle."
They would trade one gun for one captive. In order for these kingdoms to protect their people from being traded by rival kingdoms, they would have to capture and trade their enemies to get guns.

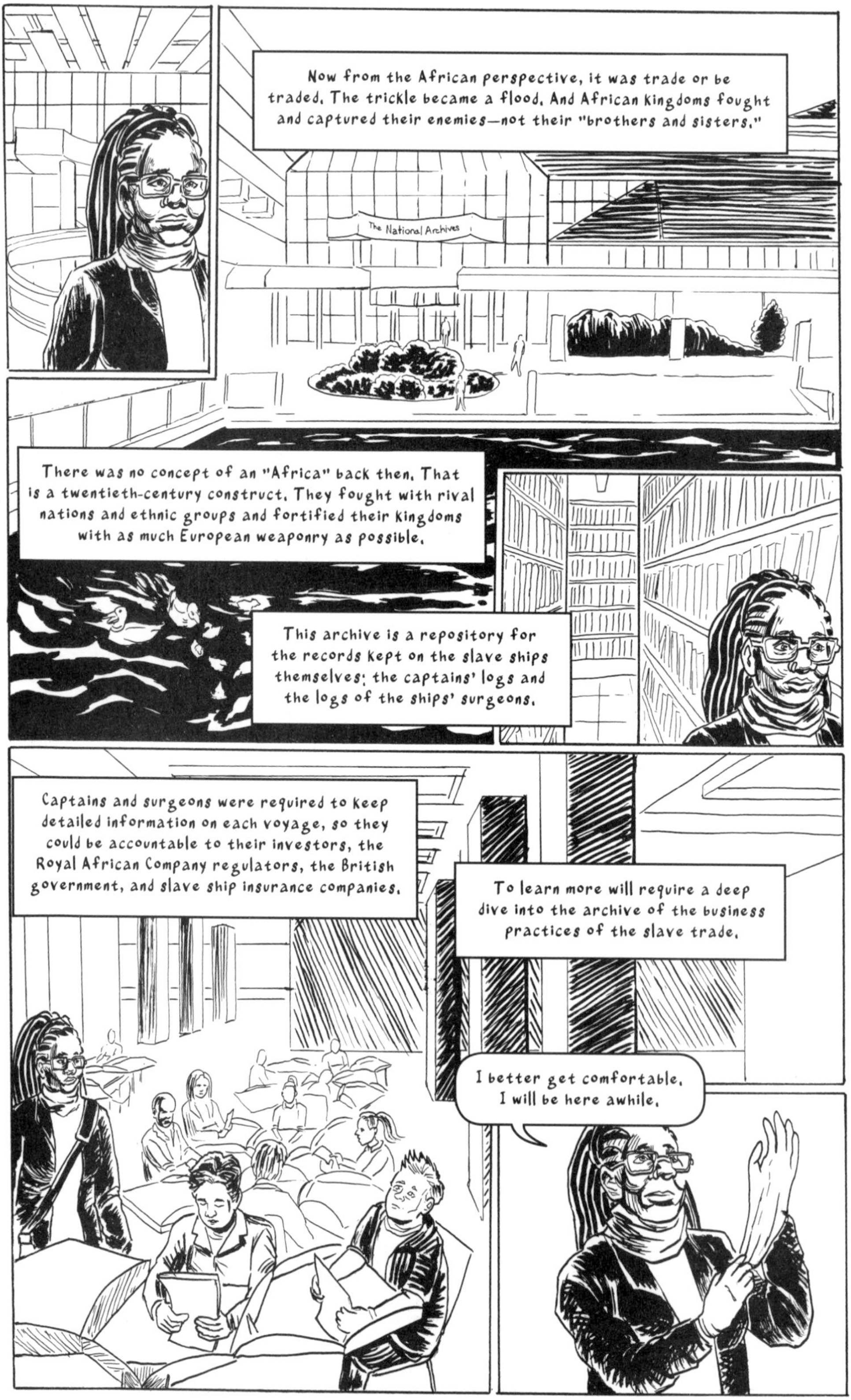

Now from the African perspective, it was trade or be traded. The trickle became a flood. And African kingdoms fought and captured their enemies—not their "brothers and sisters."
The National Archives
There was no concept of an "Africa" back then. That is a twentieth-century construct. They fought with rival nations and ethnic groups and fortified their kingdoms with as much European weaponry as possible.
This archive is a repository for the records kept on the slave ships themselves: the captains' logs and the logs of the ships' surgeons.
Captains and surgeons were required to keep detailed information on each voyage, so they could be accountable to their investors, the Royal African Company regulators, the British government, and slave ship insurance companies.
To learn more will require a deep dive into the archive of the business practices of the slave trade.
I better get comfortable. I will be here awhile.

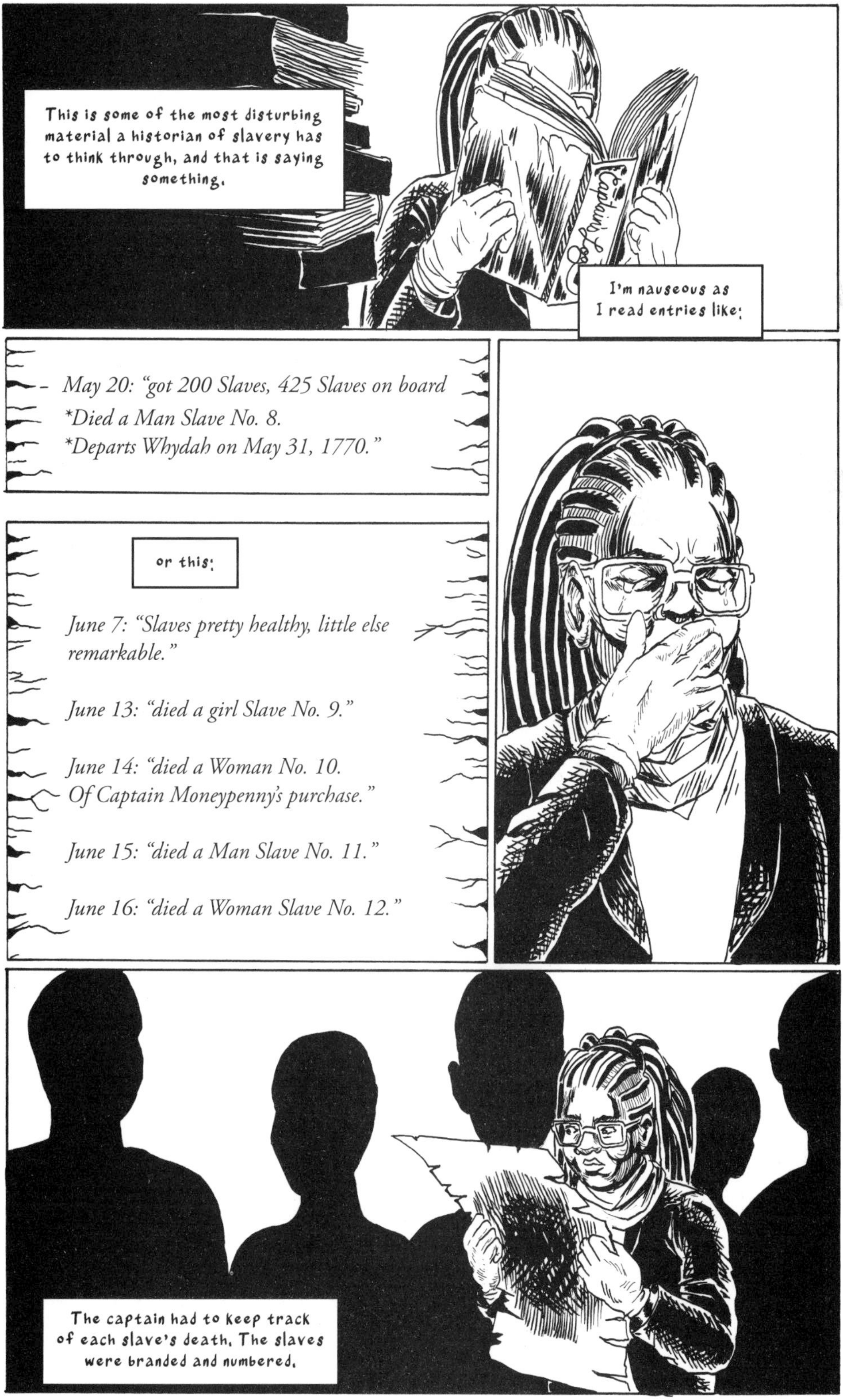
This is some of the most disturbing material a historian of slavery has to think through, and that is saying something.
Captain's Log
I'm nauseous as I read entries like:
May 20: "got 200 Slaves, 425 Slaves on board
*Died a Man Slave No. 8.
*Departs Whydah on May 31, 1770."
or this:
June 7: "Slaves pretty healthy, little else remarkable."
June 13: "died a girl Slave No. 9."
June 14: "died a Woman No. 10. Of Captain Moneypenny's purchase."
June 15: "died a Man Slave No. 11."
June 16: "died a Woman Slave No. 12."
The captain had to keep track of each slave's death. The slaves were branded and numbered.

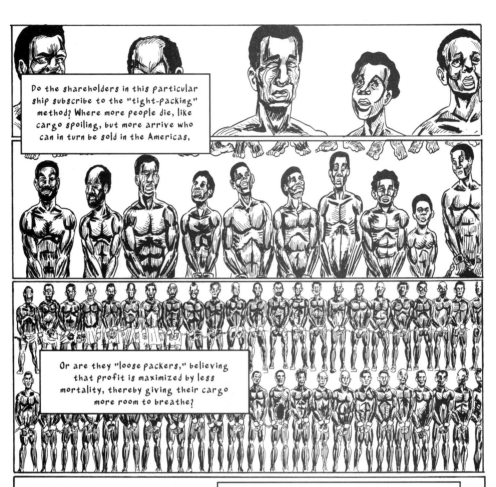

Do the shareholders in this particular ship subscribe to the "tight-packing" method? Where more people die, like cargo spoiling, but more arrive who can in turn be sold in the Americas.

Or are they "loose packers," believing that profit is maximized by less mortality, thereby giving their cargo more room to breathe?

It is a complex business turning people into things. Things that can be stored, shipped, and sold.

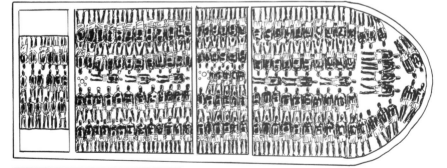

PLAN OF LOWER DECK WITH STORAGE OF 292 SLAVES

130 OF THESE SLAVES BEING STOWED UNDER THE SHELVES AS SHEWN IN FIGURES 5 & FIGURES 6

My eyes glaze at the calculations on person-to-tonnage ratios, and how to be most efficient in arranging the cargo.

And it is not easy for a historian to comb through these documents, feeling a combination of stultifying boredom, anger, and constant nausea.

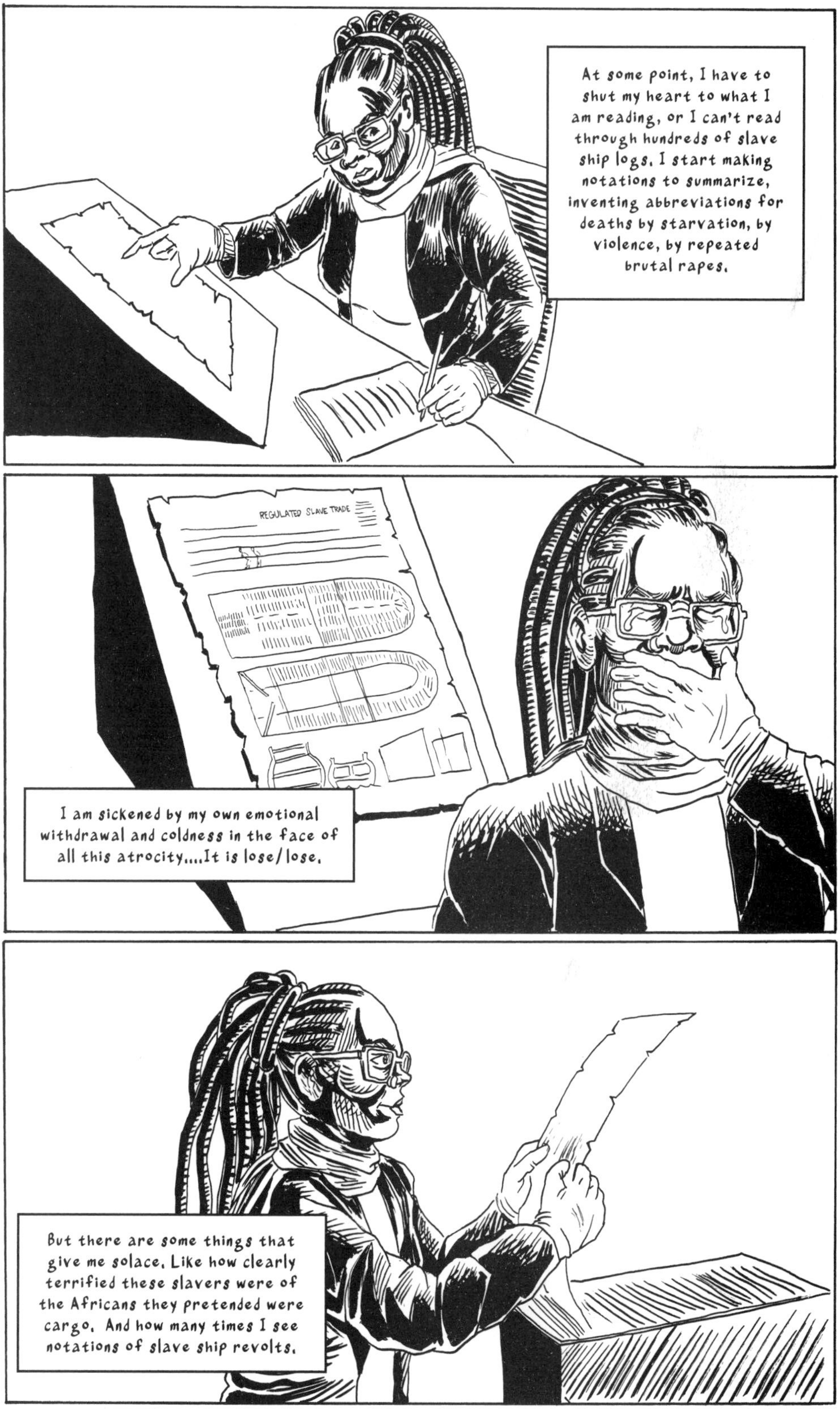
At some point, I have to shut my heart to what I am reading, or I can't read through hundreds of slave ship logs. I start making notations to summarize, inventing abbreviations for deaths by starvation, by violence, by repeated brutal rapes.
REGULATED SLAVE TRADE
I am sickened by my own emotional withdrawal and coldness in the face of all this atrocity....It is lose/lose.
But there are some things that give me solace. Like how clearly terrified these slavers were of the Africans they pretended were cargo. And how many times I see notations of slave ship revolts.

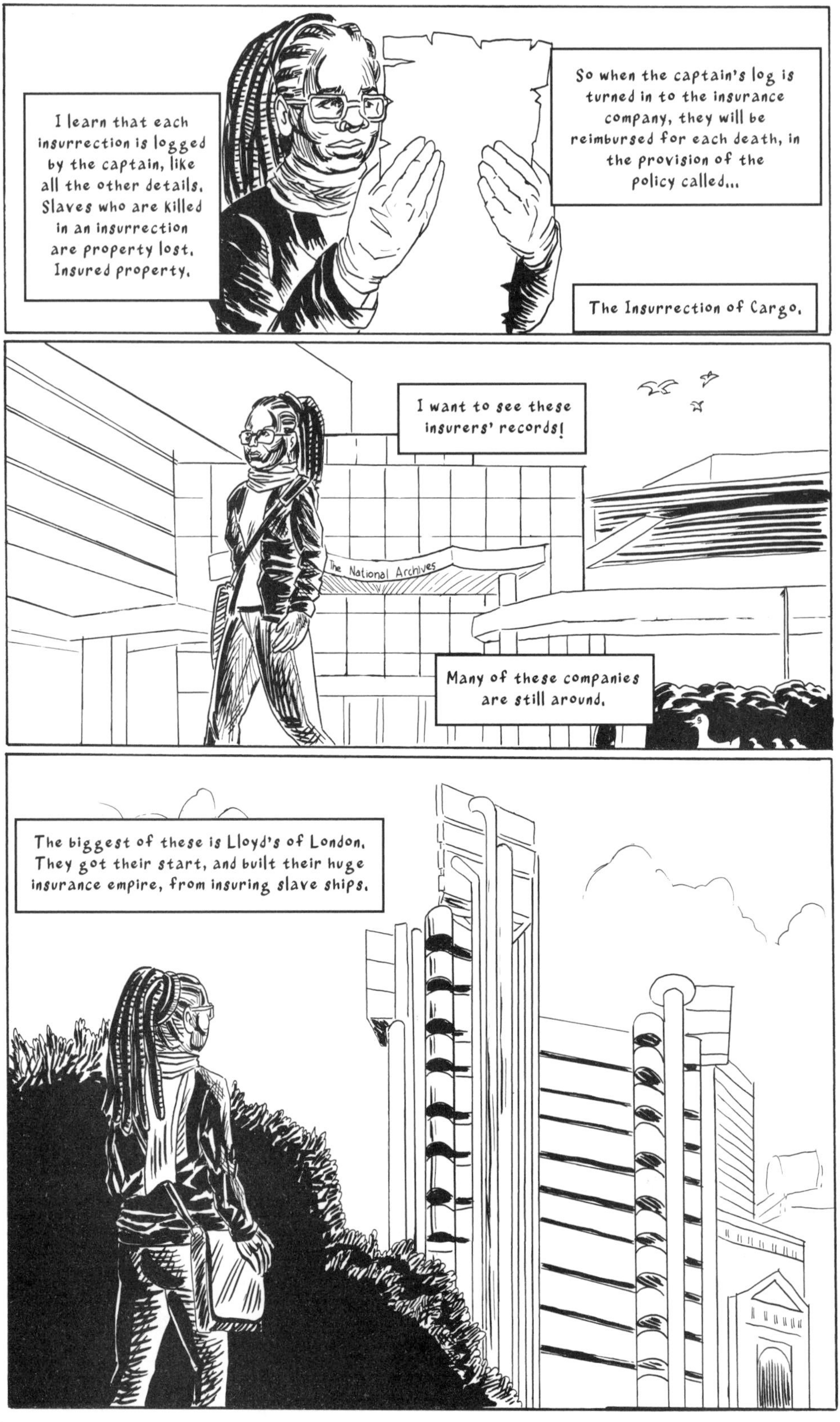
I learn that each insurrection is logged by the captain, like all the other details. Slaves who are killed in an insurrection are property lost. Insured property.
So when the captain's log is turned in to the insurance company, they will be reimbursed for each death, in the provision of the policy called...
The Insurrection of Cargo.
I want to see these insurers' records!
The National Archives
Many of these companies are still around.
The biggest of these is Lloyd's of London. They got their start, and built their huge insurance empire, from insuring slave ships.

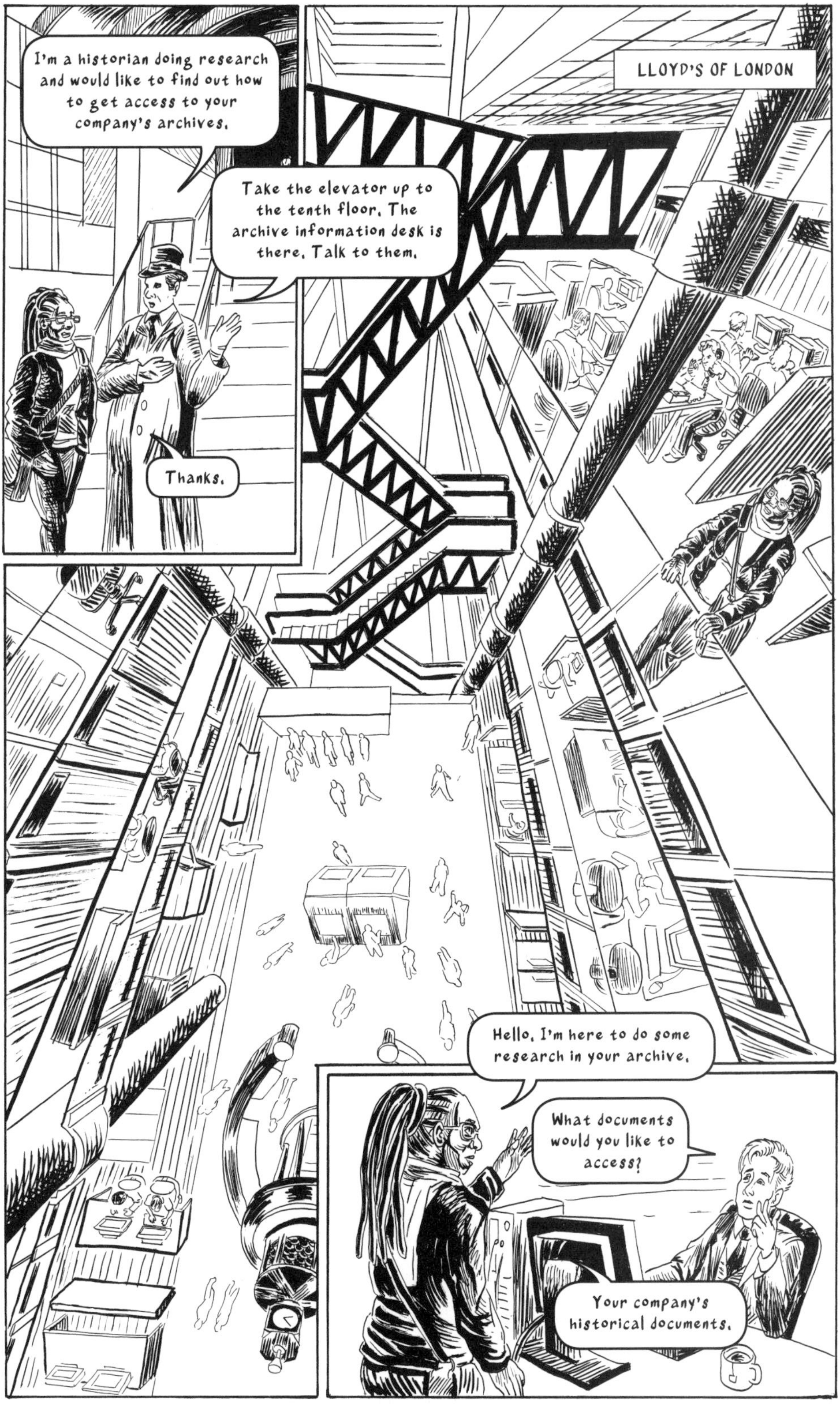
I'm a historian doing research and would like to find out how to get access to your company's archives.
Take the elevator up to the tenth floor. The archive information desk is there. Talk to them.
Thanks.
LLOYD'S OF LONDON
Hello, I'm here to do some research in your archive.
What documents would you like to access?
Your company's historical documents.

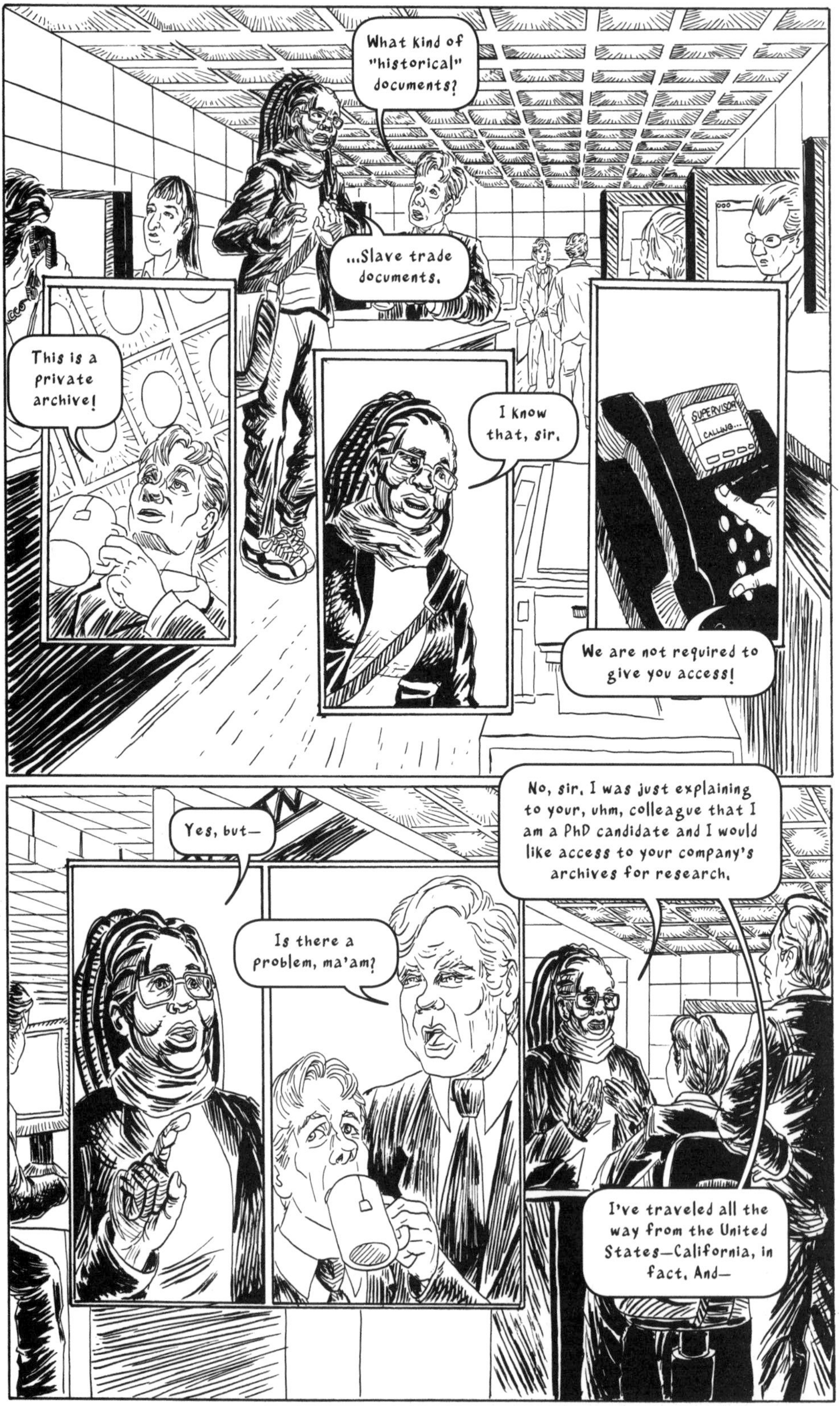
What kind of "historical" documents?
...Slave trade documents.
This is a private archive!
I know that, sir.
SUPERVISOR CALLING...
We are not required to give you access!
Yes, but—
Is there a problem, ma'am?
No, sir. I was just explaining to your, uhm, colleague that I am a PhD candidate and I would like access to your company's archives for research.
I've traveled all the way from the United States—California, in fact. And—

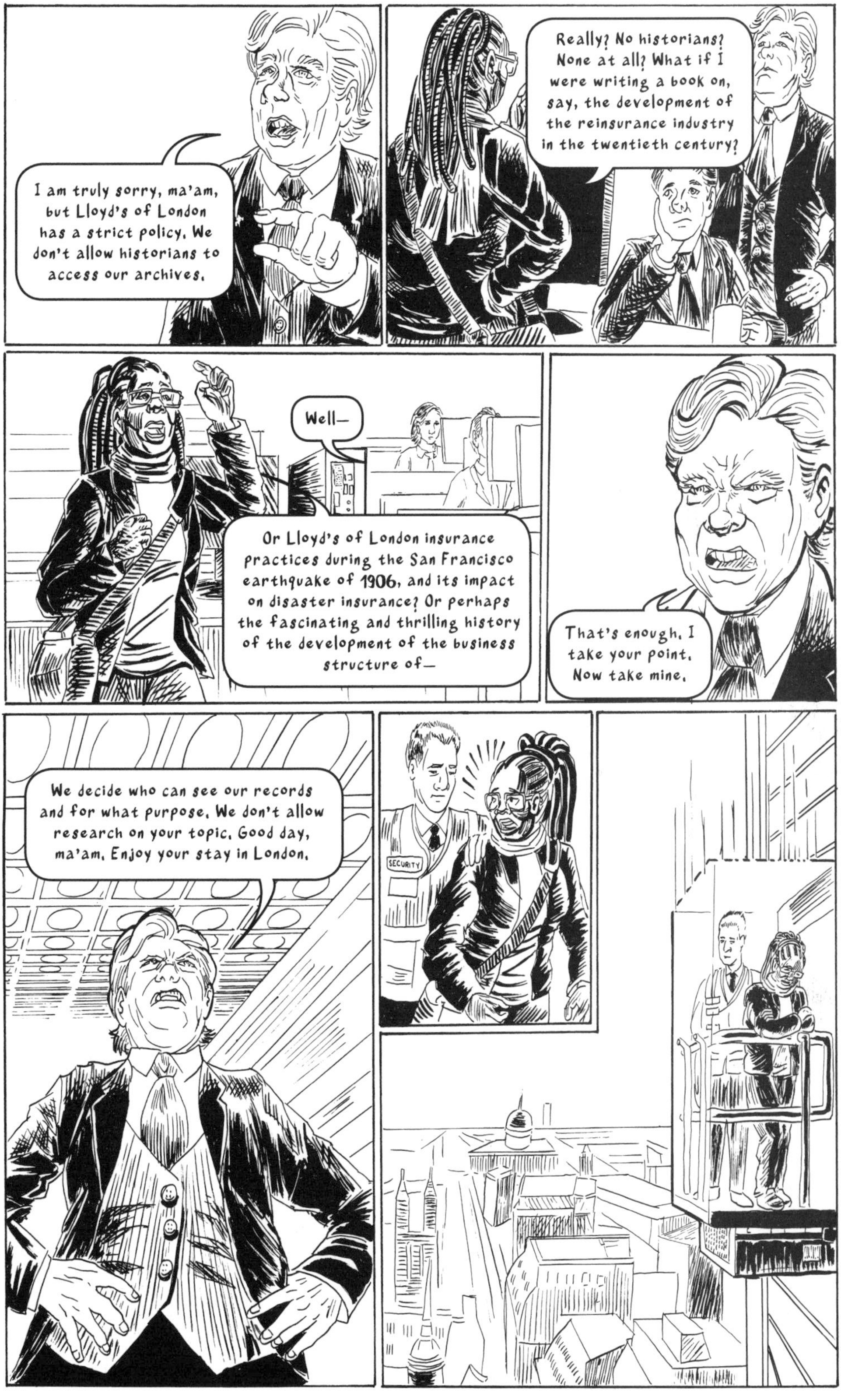

I am truly sorry, ma'am, but Lloyd's of London has a strict policy. We don't allow historians to access our archives.
Really? No historians? None at all? What if I were writing a book on, say, the development of the reinsurance industry in the twentieth century?
Well—
Or Lloyd's of London insurance practices during the San Francisco earthquake of 1906, and its impact on disaster insurance? Or perhaps the fascinating and thrilling history of the development of the business structure of—
That's enough. I take your point. Now take mine.
We decide who can see our records and for what purpose. We don't allow research on your topic. Good day, ma'am. Enjoy your stay in London.
SECURITY

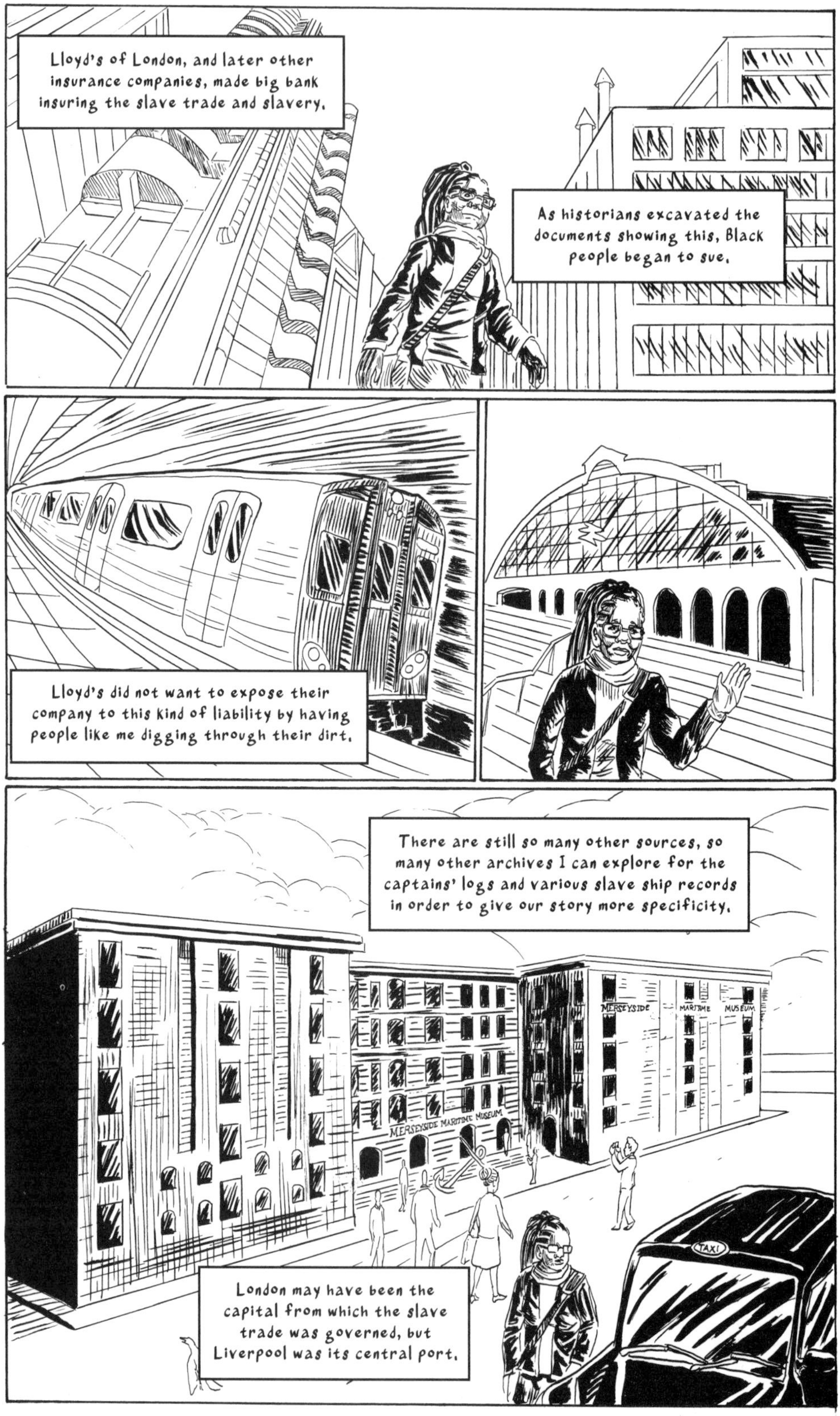
Lloyd's of London, and later other insurance companies, made big bank insuring the slave trade and slavery.
As historians excavated the documents showing this, Black people began to sue.
Lloyd's did not want to expose their company to this kind of liability by having people like me digging through their dirt.
There are still so many other sources, so many other archives I can explore for the captains' logs and various slave ship records in order to give our story more specificity.
MERSEYSIDE MARITIME MUSEUM
MERSEYSIDE MARITIME MUSEUM
TAXI
London may have been the capital from which the slave trade was governed, but Liverpool was its central port.

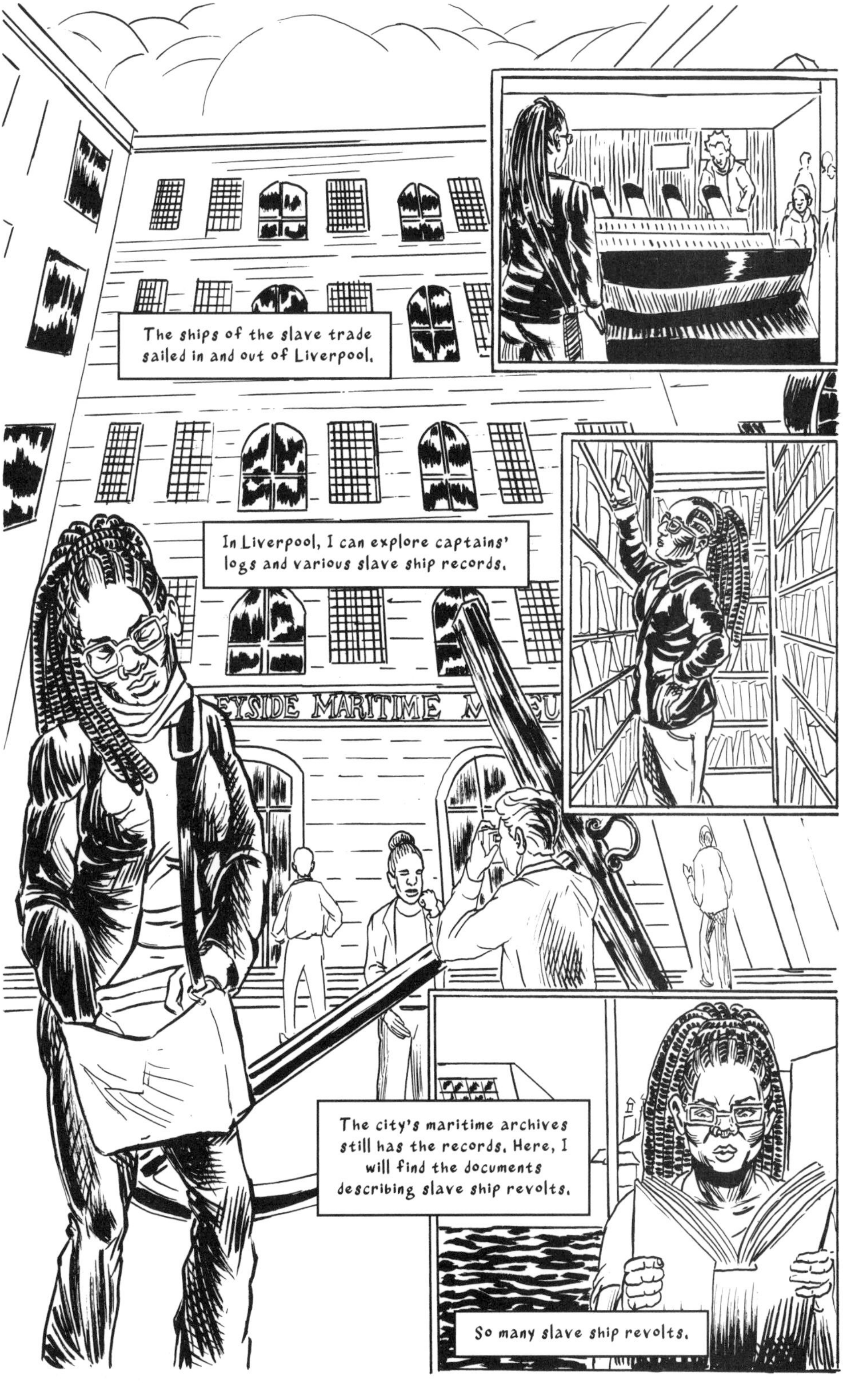
The ships of the slave trade sailed in and out of Liverpool.
In Liverpool, I can explore captains' logs and various slave ship records.
EYSIDE MARITIME M EU
The city's maritime archives still has the records. Here, I will find the documents describing slave ship revolts.
So many slave ship revolts.

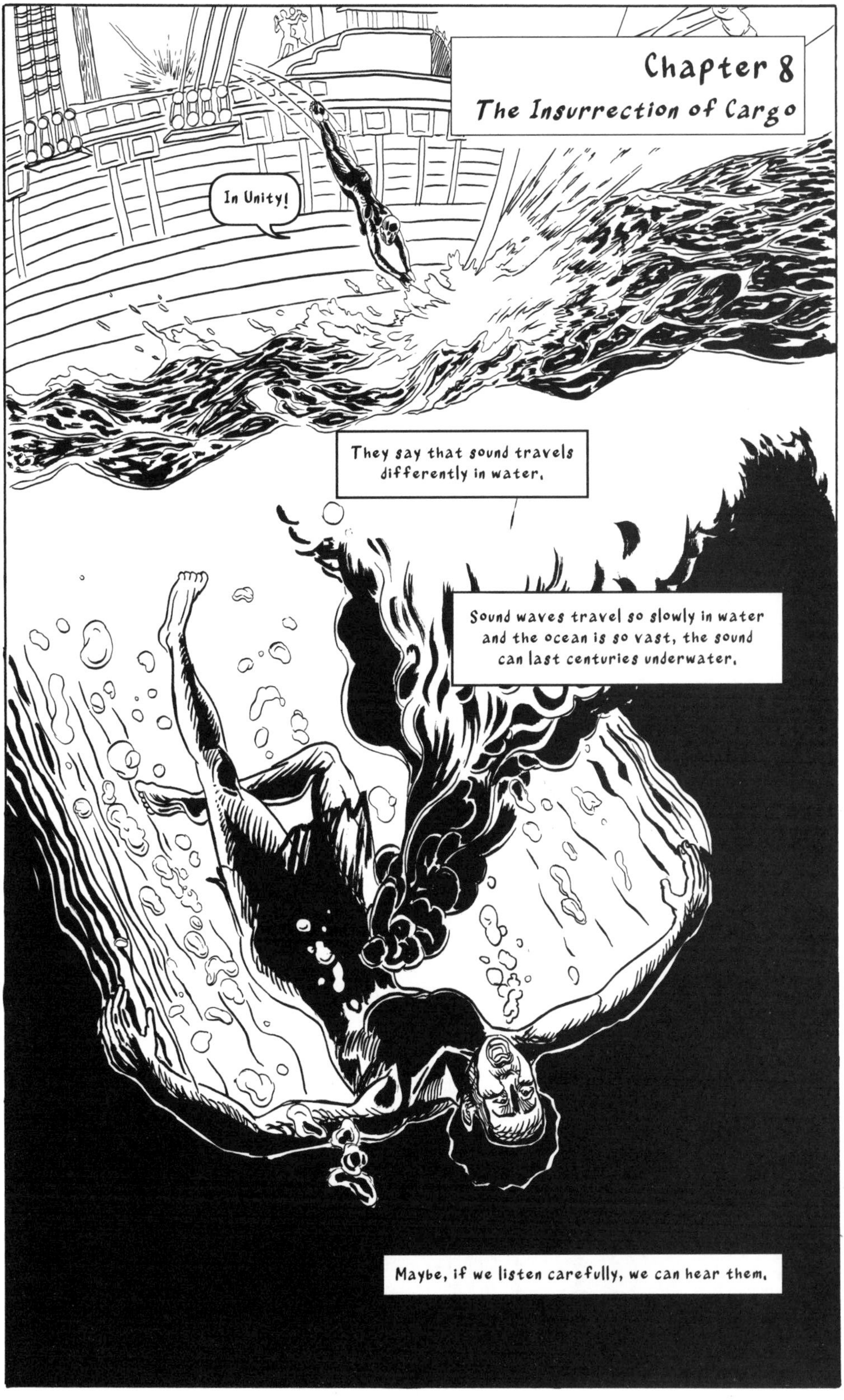
Chapter 8
The Insurrection of Cargo
In Unity!
They say that sound travels differently in water.
Sound waves travel so slowly in water and the ocean is so vast, the sound can last centuries underwater.
Maybe, if we listen carefully, we can hear them.

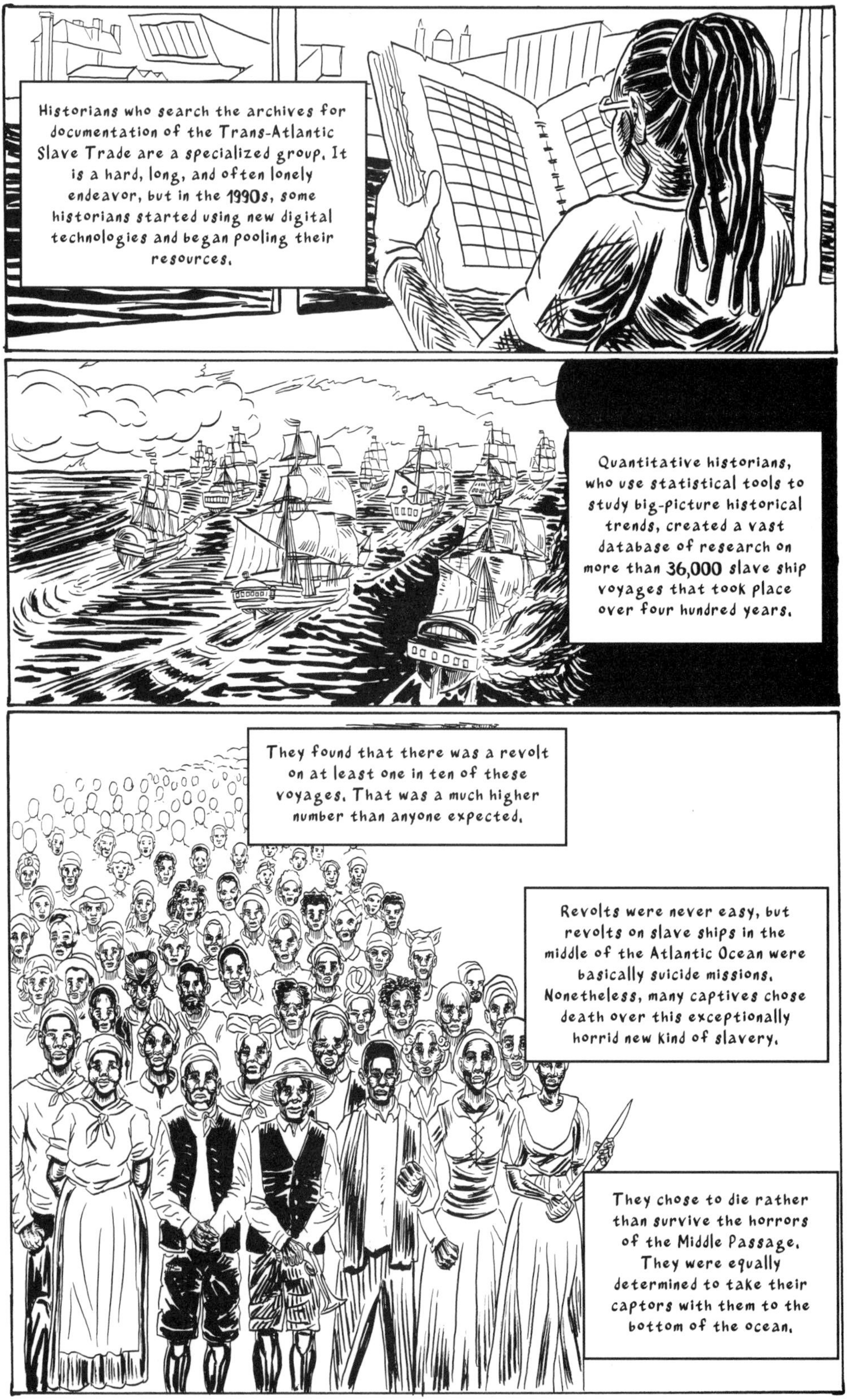
Historians who search the archives for documentation of the Trans-Atlantic Slave Trade are a specialized group. It is a hard, long, and often lonely endeavor, but in the 1990s, some historians started using new digital technologies and began pooling their resources.
Quantitative historians, who use statistical tools to study big-picture historical trends, created a vast database of research on more than 36,000 slave ship voyages that took place over four hundred years.
They found that there was a revolt on at least one in ten of these voyages. That was a much higher number than anyone expected.
Revolts were never easy, but revolts on slave ships in the middle of the Atlantic Ocean were basically suicide missions. Nonetheless, many captives chose death over this exceptionally horrid new kind of slavery.
They chose to die rather than survive the horrors of the Middle Passage. They were equally determined to take their captors with them to the bottom of the ocean.

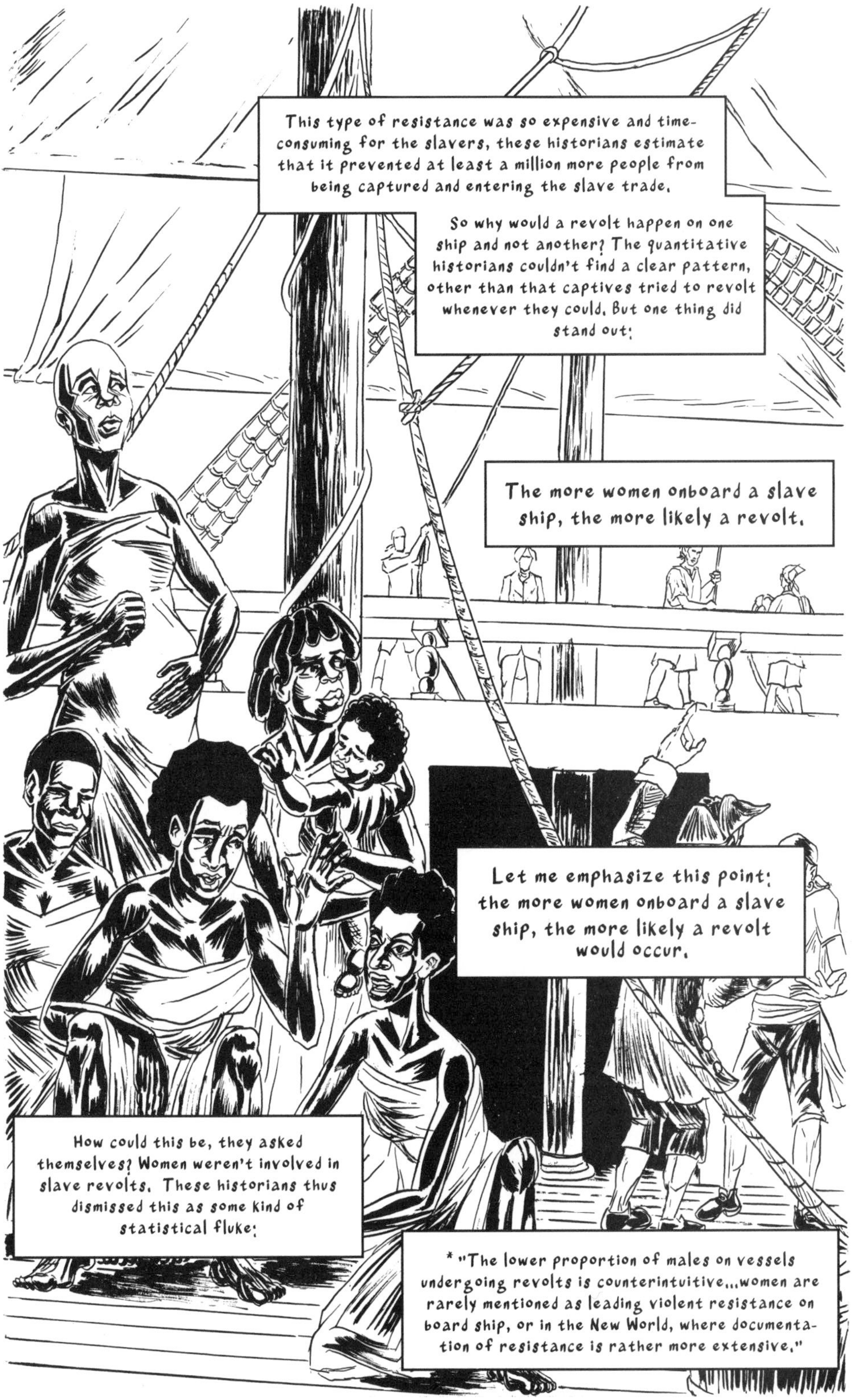
This type of resistance was so expensive and time-consuming for the slavers, these historians estimate that it prevented at least a million more people from being captured and entering the slave trade.
So why would a revolt happen on one ship and not another? The quantitative historians couldn't find a clear pattern, other than that captives tried to revolt whenever they could. But one thing did stand out:
The more women onboard a slave ship, the more likely a revolt.
Let me emphasize this point: the more women onboard a slave ship, the more likely a revolt would occur.
How could this be, they asked themselves? Women weren't involved in slave revolts. These historians thus dismissed this as some kind of statistical fluke:
* "The lower proportion of males on vessels undergoing revolts is counterintuitive...women are rarely mentioned as leading violent resistance on board ship, or in the New World, where documentation of resistance is rather more extensive."

*Behrendt et al., "The Costs of Coercion," *The Economic History Review* vol. 54, No 3 (August 2001): 460.

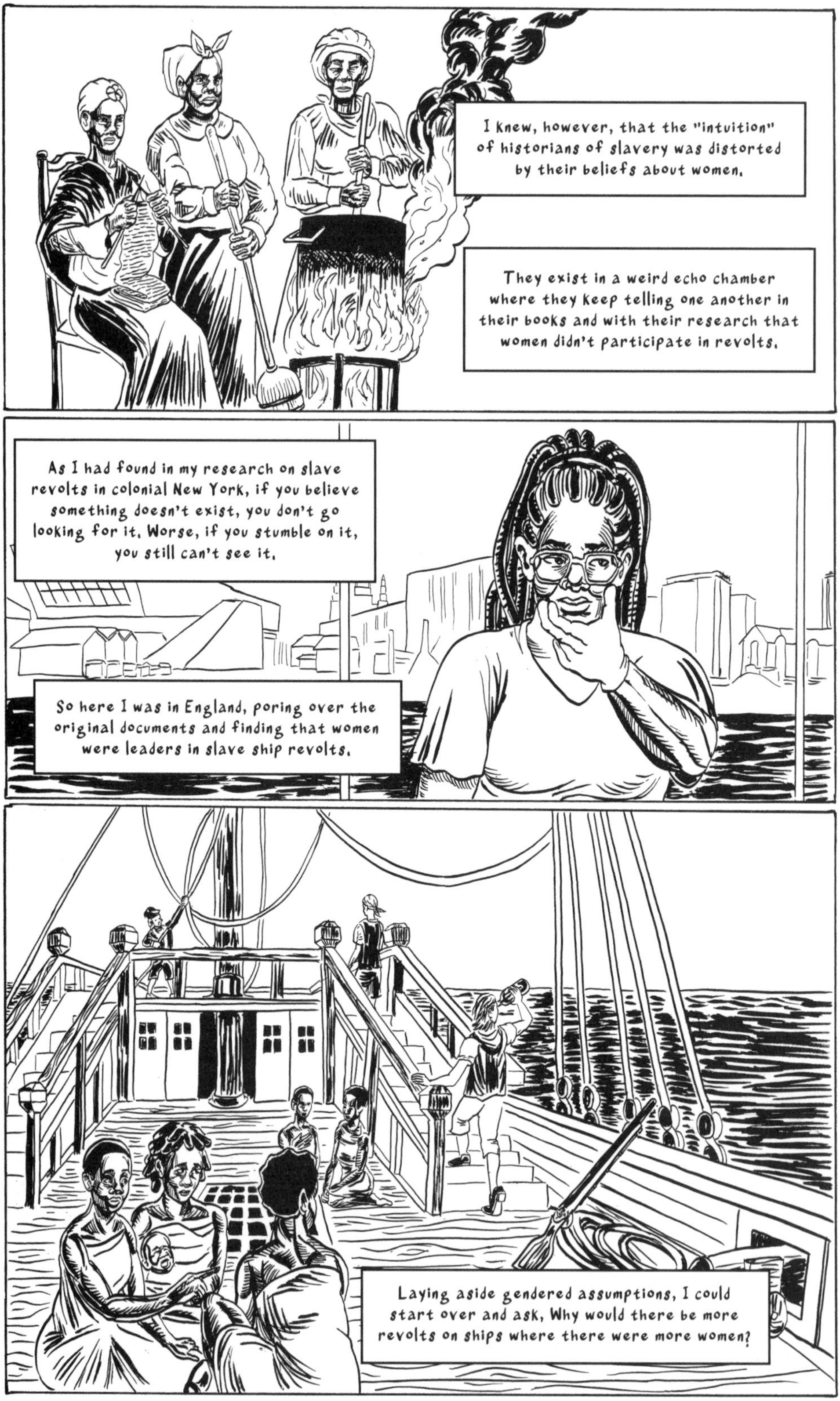
I knew, however, that the "intuition" of historians of slavery was distorted by their beliefs about women.
They exist in a weird echo chamber where they keep telling one another in their books and with their research that women didn't participate in revolts.
As I had found in my research on slave revolts in colonial New York, if you believe something doesn't exist, you don't go looking for it. Worse, if you stumble on it, you still can't see it.
So here I was in England, poring over the original documents and finding that women were leaders in slave ship revolts.
Laying aside gendered assumptions, I could start over and ask, Why would there be more revolts on ships where there were more women?

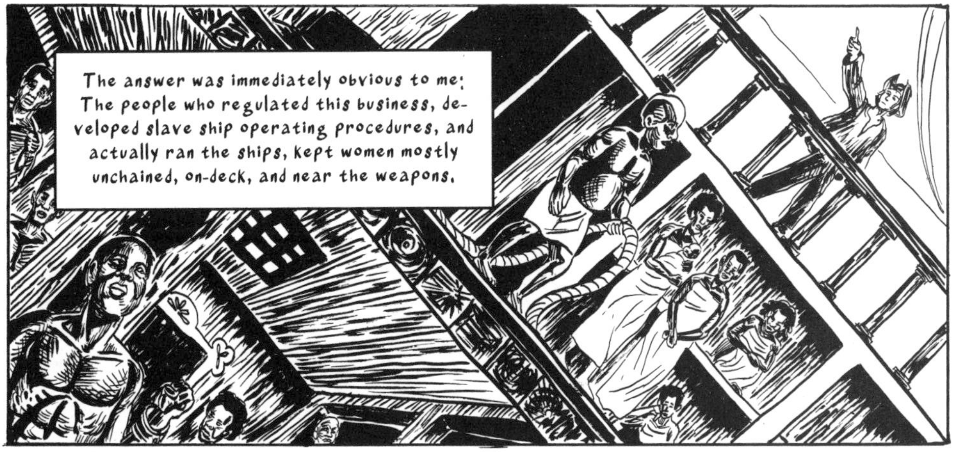
The answer was immediately obvious to me: The people who regulated this business, developed slave ship operating procedures, and actually ran the ships, kept women mostly unchained, on-deck, and near the weapons.

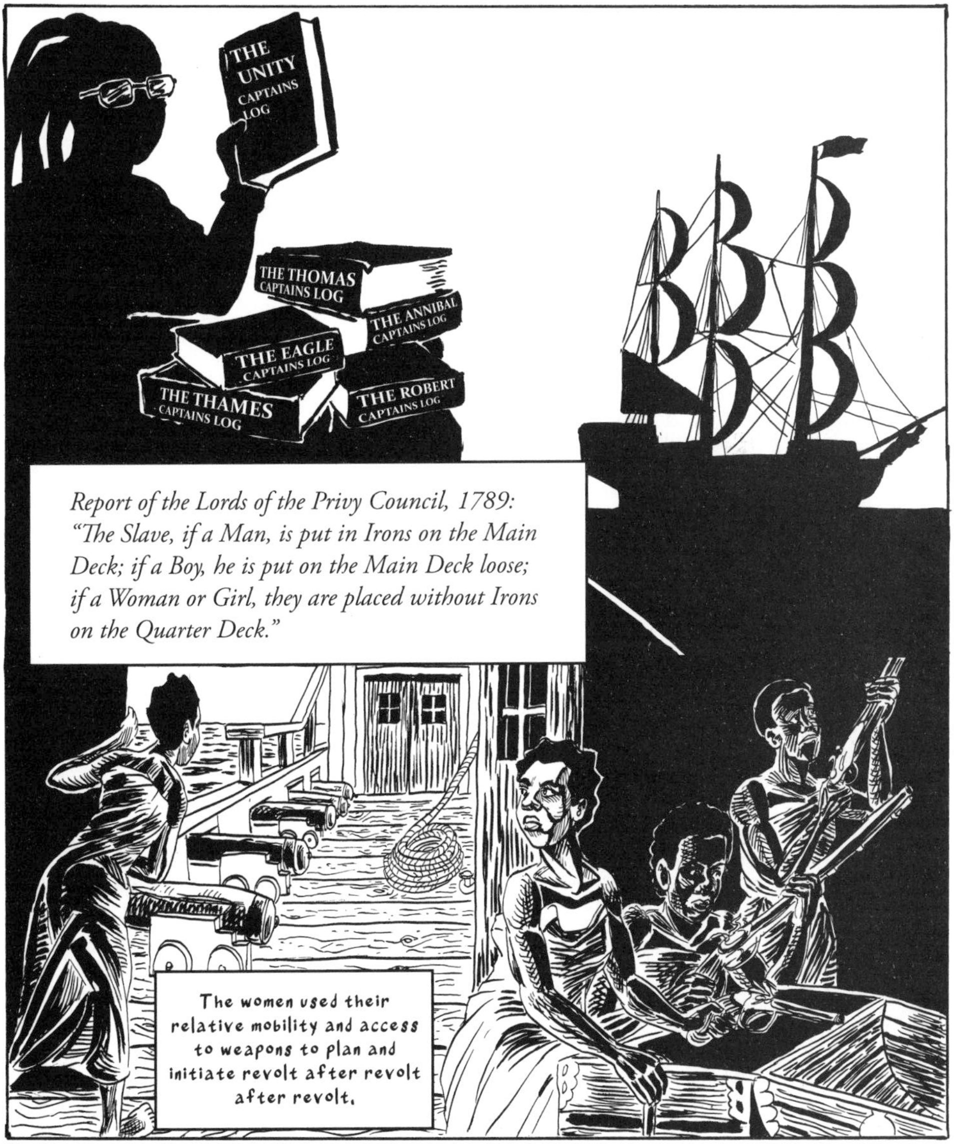
THE UNITY CAPTAINS LOG
THE THOMAS CAPTAINS LOG
THE ANNIBAL CAPTAINS LOG
THE EAGLE CAPTAINS LOG
THE THAMES CAPTAINS LOG
THE ROBERT CAPTAINS LOG
Report of the Lords of the Privy Council, 1789: "The Slave, if a Man, is put in Irons on the Main Deck; if a Boy, he is put on the Main Deck loose; if a Woman or Girl, they are placed without Irons on the Quarter Deck."
The women used their relative mobility and access to weapons to plan and initiate revolt after revolt after revolt.

The purpose of generating all of this endless documentation was to set policy, maximize profits, and avoid costly revolts.

So why would the enforcers on the ships keep making the same stupid mistake, like the one mentioned in this captain's log?

Two or three of the female slaves having discovered that the armoror had incautiously left the arms chest open . . .

conveyed all the arms which they could find through the bulkheads to the male slaves, about two hundred of whom immediately ran up the forescuttles, and put to death all the crew who came in their way.

—the *Thomas*, 1797

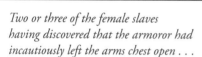

Generally, the slave ship crews remained oblivious to the agency of enslaved women.

For example, a crewman aboard the *Eagle* in 1704 wrote that the crew was so worried about a revolt that they checked the *mens'* chains day and night, and a revolt happened anyway. They had no idea how it happened.

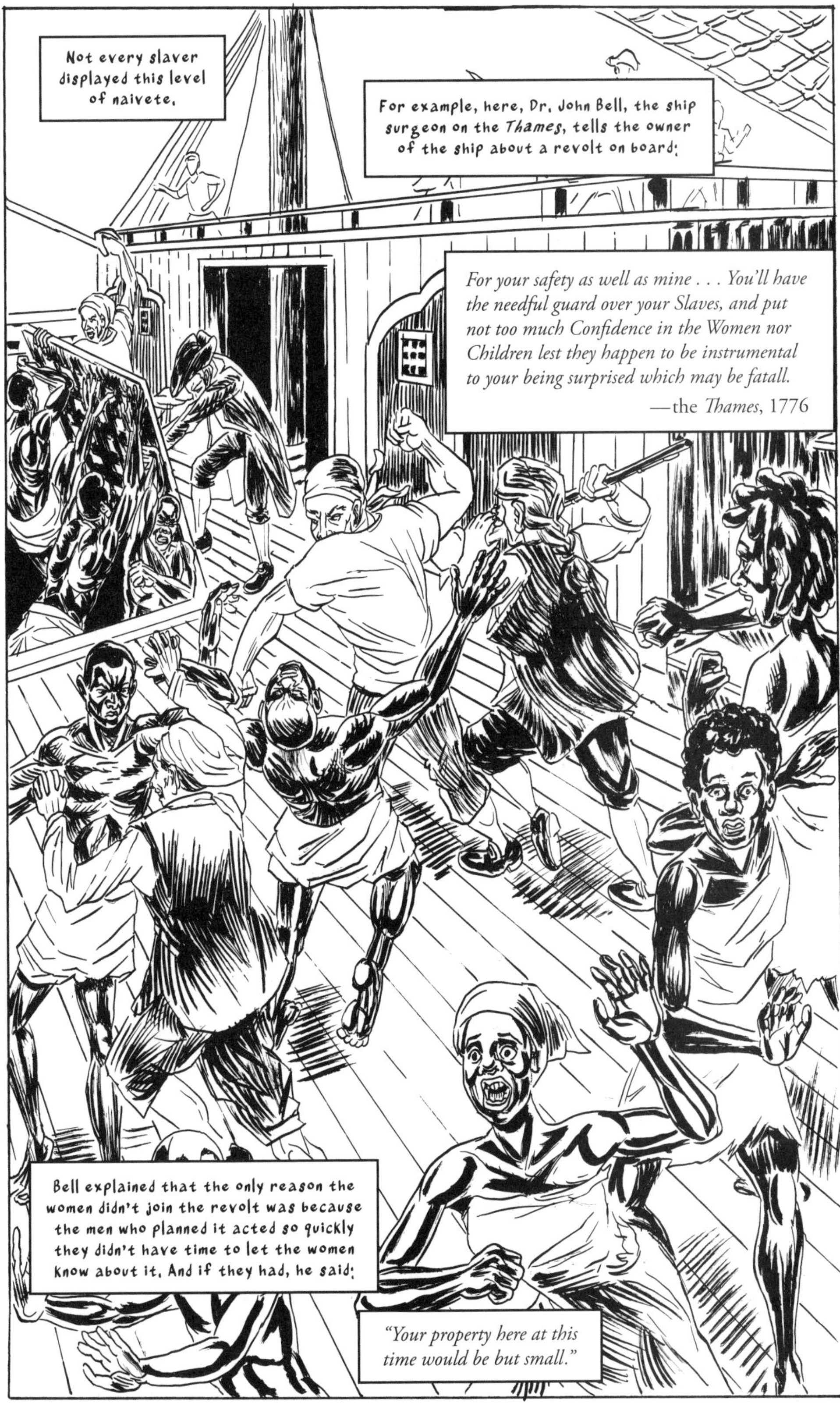

Not every slaver displayed this level of naivete.
For example, here, Dr. John Bell, the ship surgeon on the *Thames*, tells the owner of the ship about a revolt on board:
For your safety as well as mine . . . You'll have the needful guard over your Slaves, and put not too much Confidence in the Women nor Children lest they happen to be instrumental to your being surprised which may be fatall.
—the *Thames*, 1776
Bell explained that the only reason the women didn't join the revolt was because the men who planned it acted so quickly they didn't have time to let the women know about it. And if they had, he said:
"Your property here at this time would be but small."

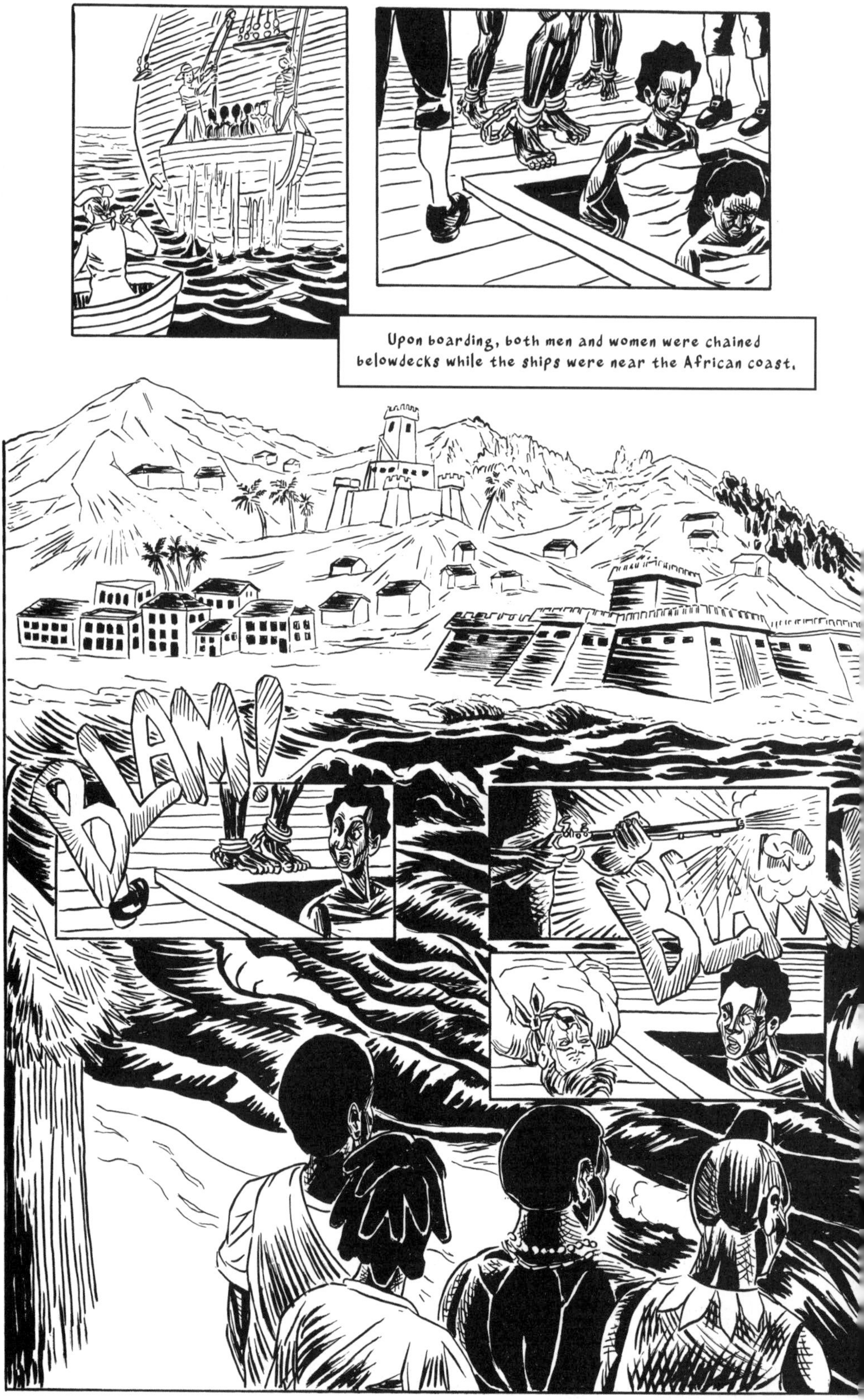
Upon boarding, both men and women were chained belowdecks while the ships were near the African coast.
BLAM!
BLAM

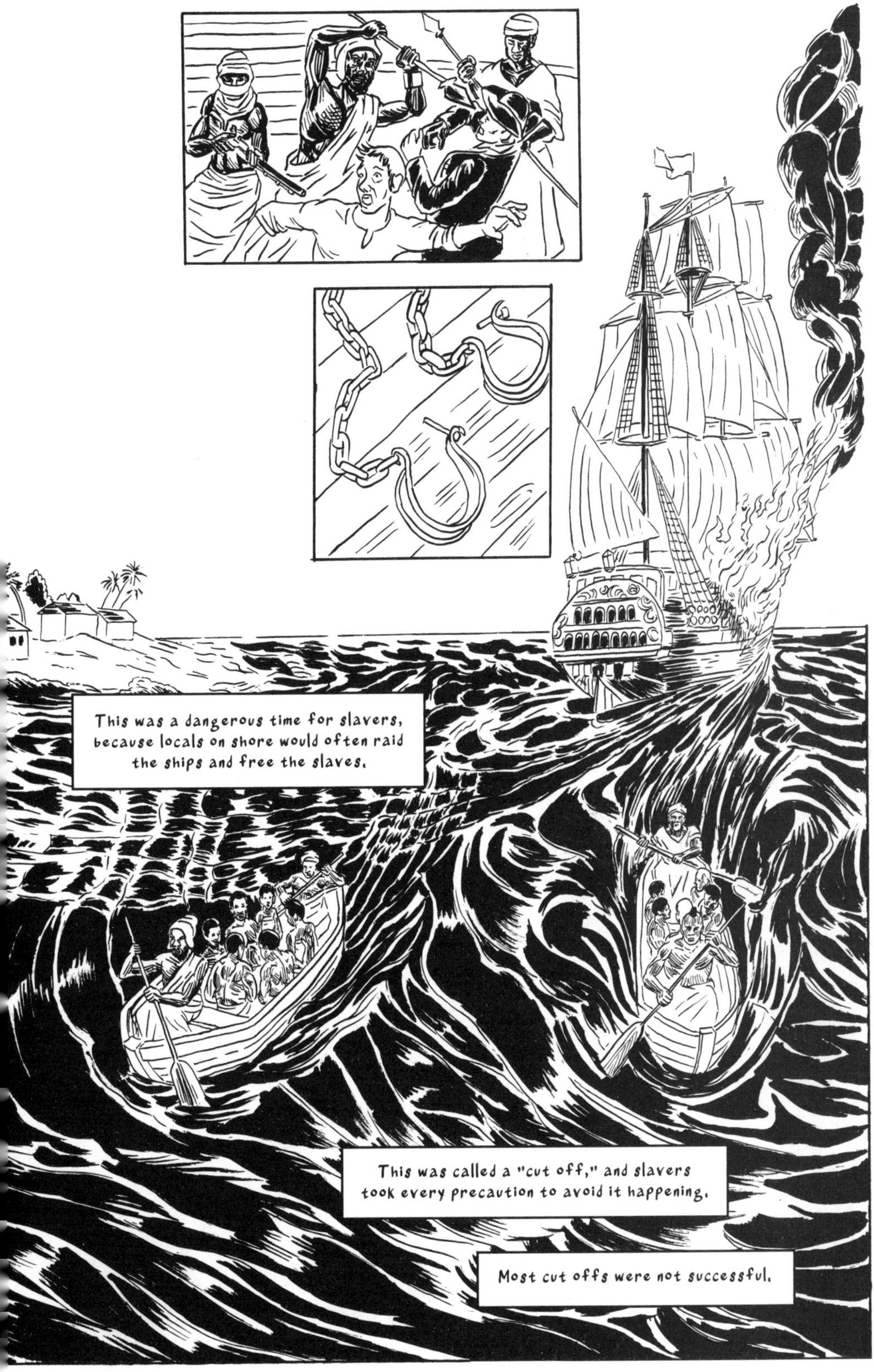
This was a dangerous time for slavers, because locals on shore would often raid the ships and free the slaves.
This was called a "cut off," and slavers took every precaution to avoid it happening.
Most cut offs were not successful.

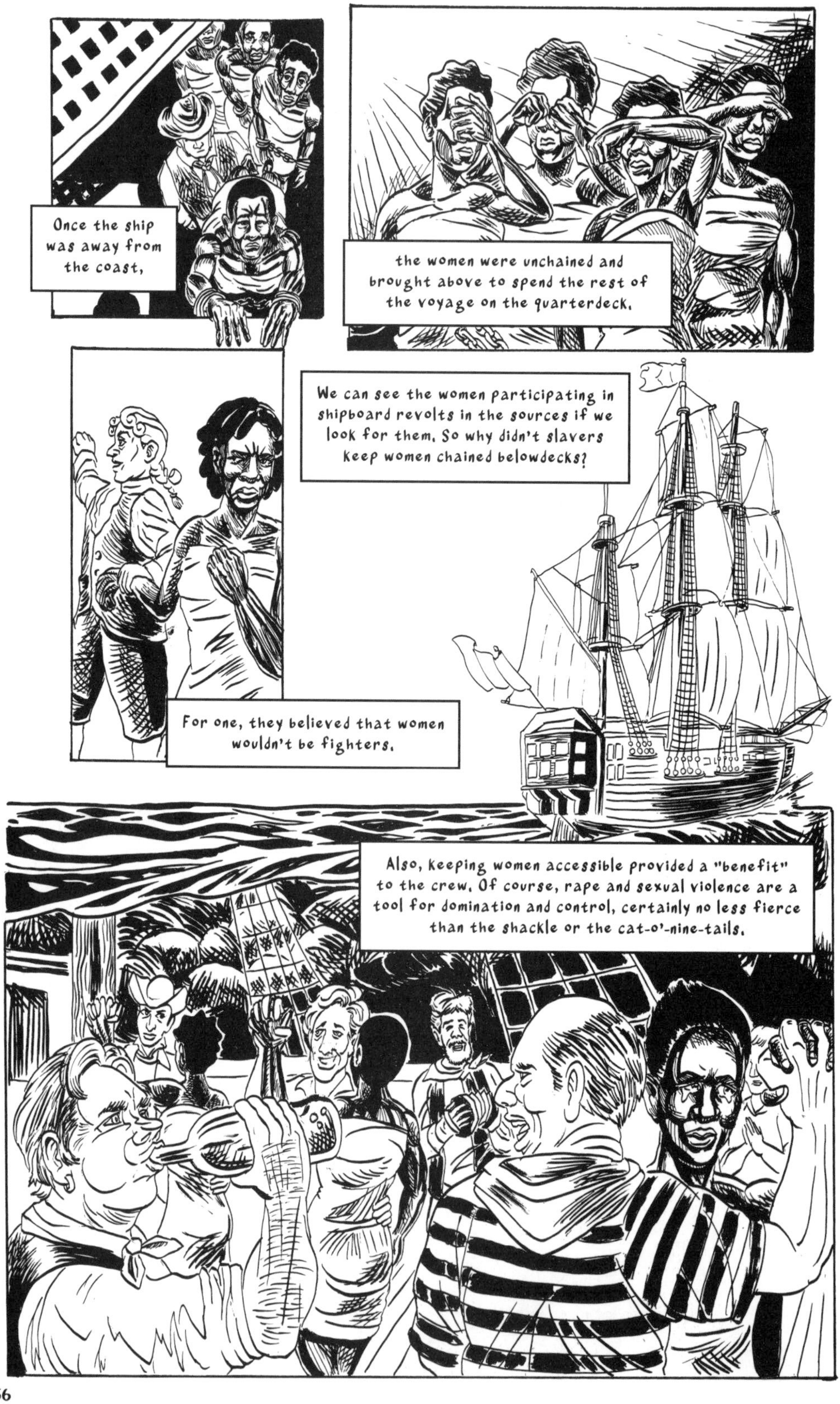
Once the ship was away from the coast,
the women were unchained and brought above to spend the rest of the voyage on the quarterdeck.
We can see the women participating in shipboard revolts in the sources if we look for them. So why didn't slavers keep women chained belowdecks?
For one, they believed that women wouldn't be fighters.
Also, keeping women accessible provided a "benefit" to the crew. Of course, rape and sexual violence are a tool for domination and control, certainly no less fierce than the shackle or the cat-o'-nine-tails.

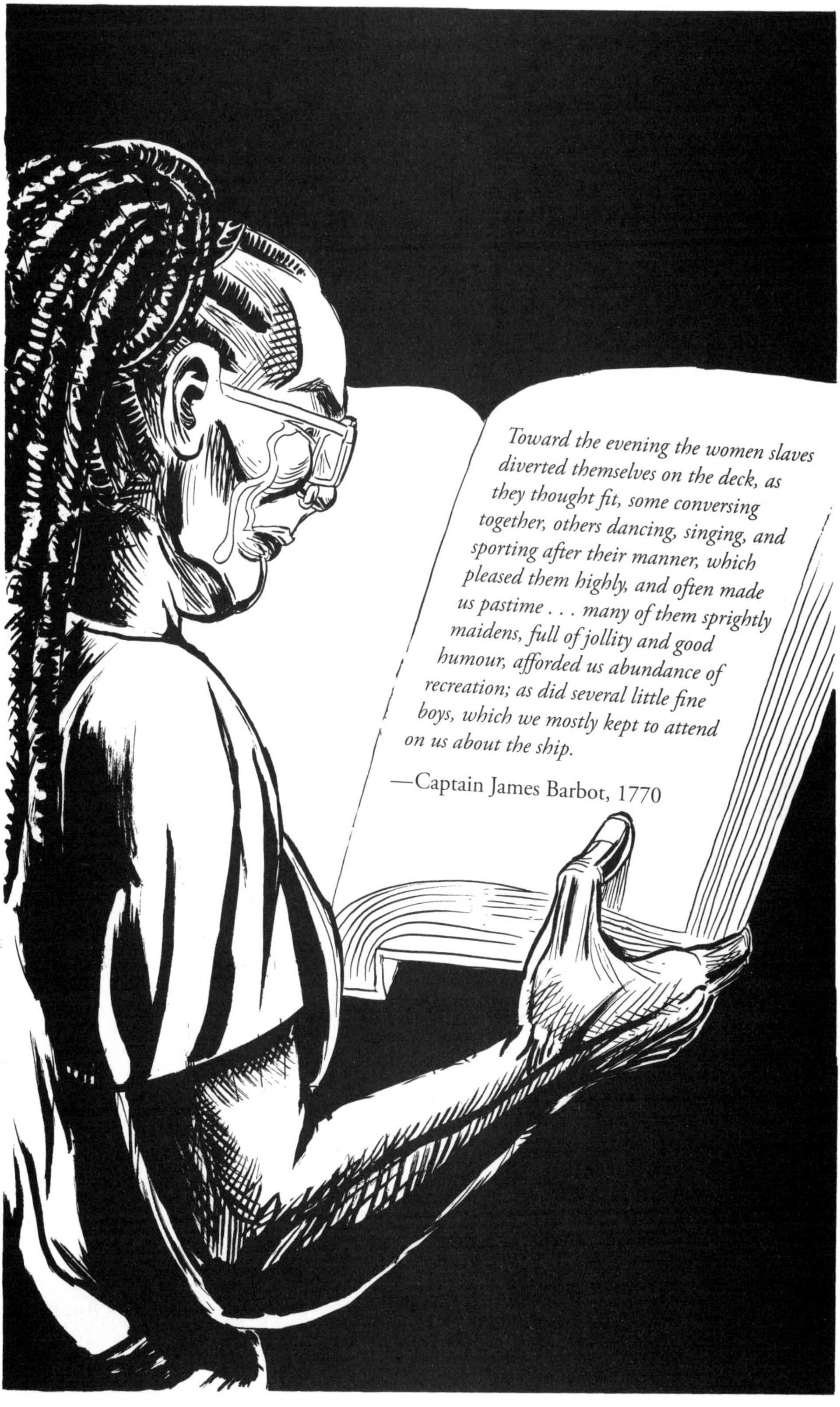
Toward the evening the women slaves diverted themselves on the deck, as they thought fit, some conversing together, others dancing, singing, and sporting after their manner, which pleased them highly, and often made us pastime . . . many of them sprightly maidens, full of jollity and good humour, afforded us abundance of recreation; as did several little fine boys, which we mostly kept to attend on us about the ship.
—Captain James Barbot, 1770

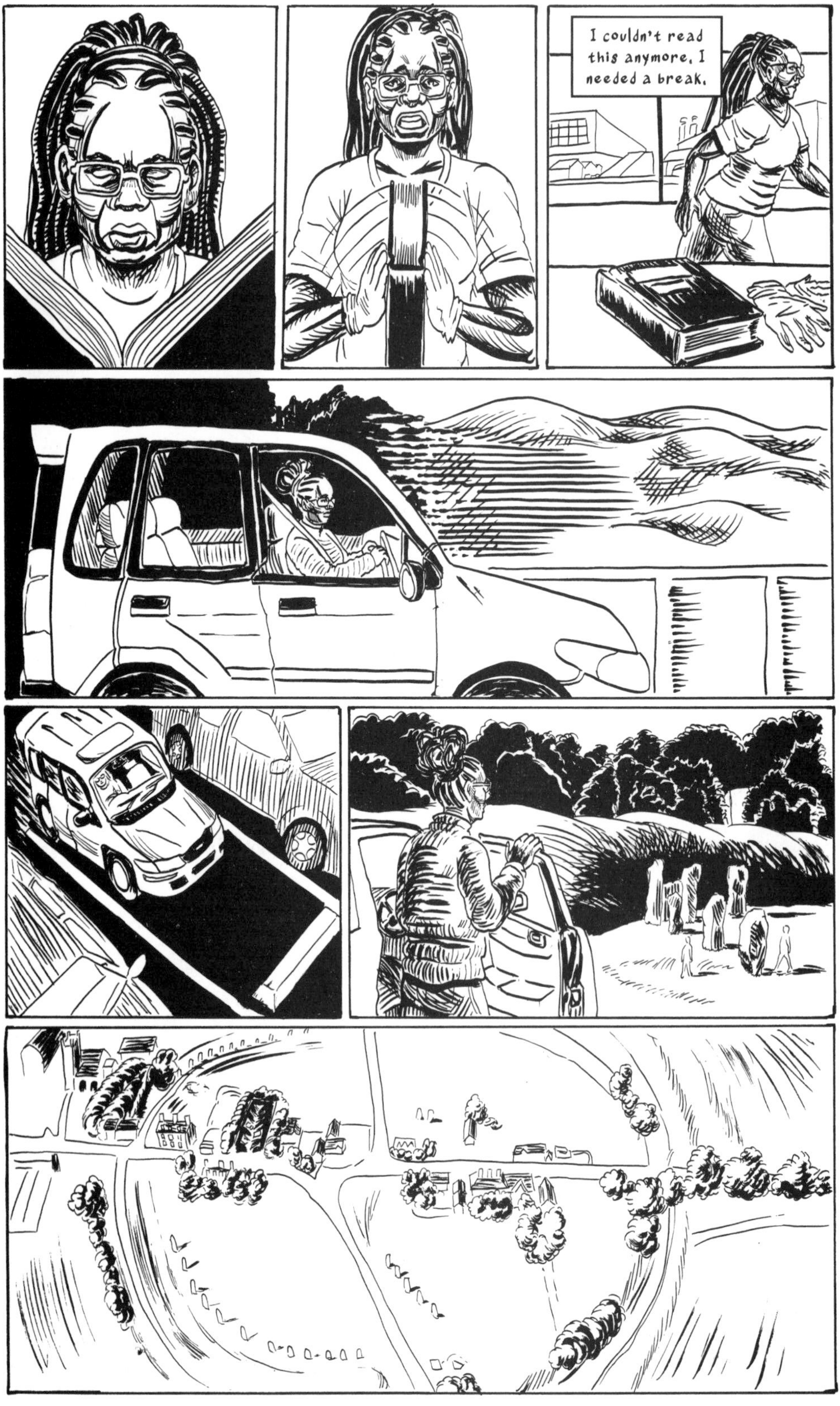
I couldn't read this anymore. I needed a break.

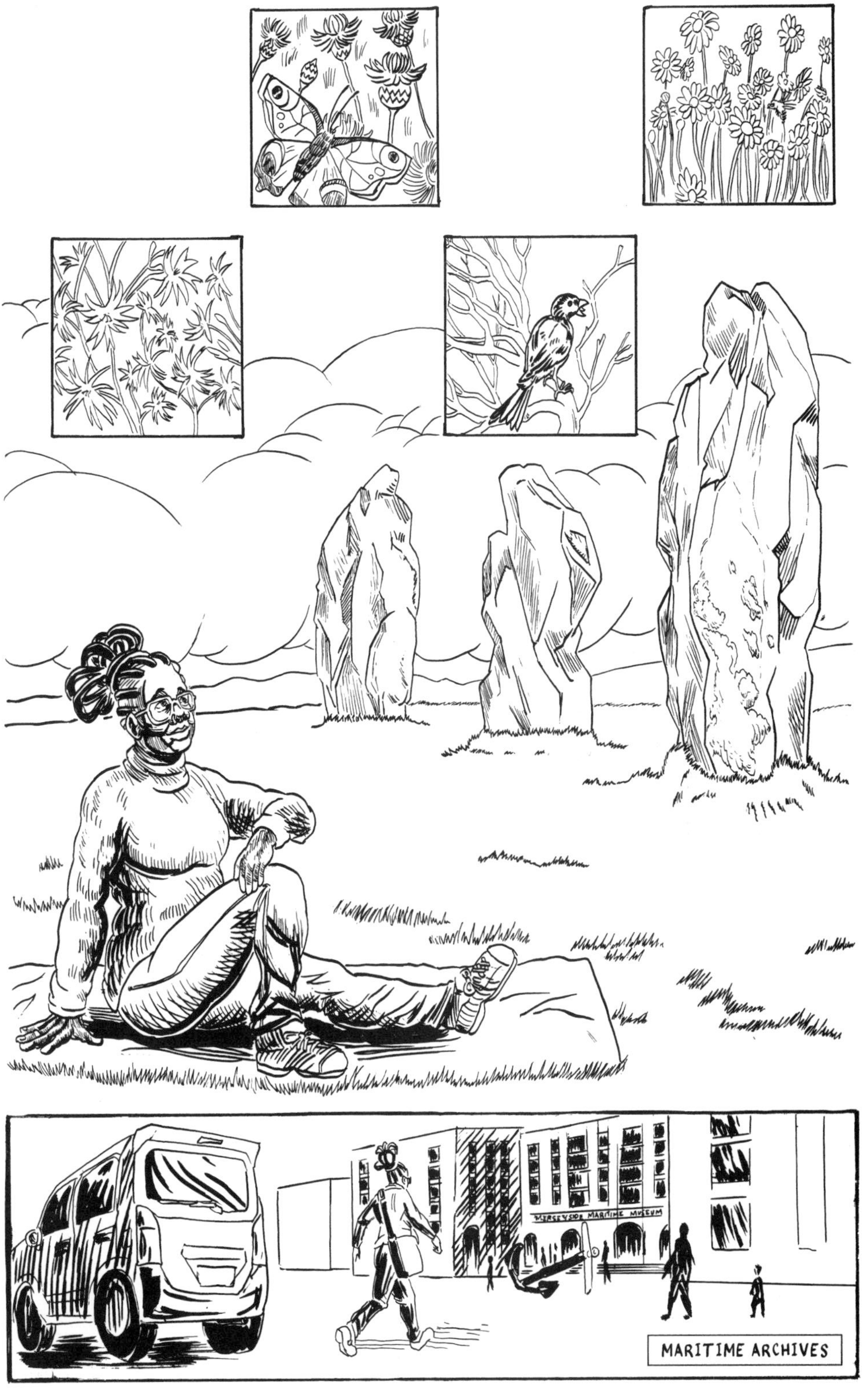
MERSEYSIDE MARITIME MUSEUM
MARITIME ARCHIVES

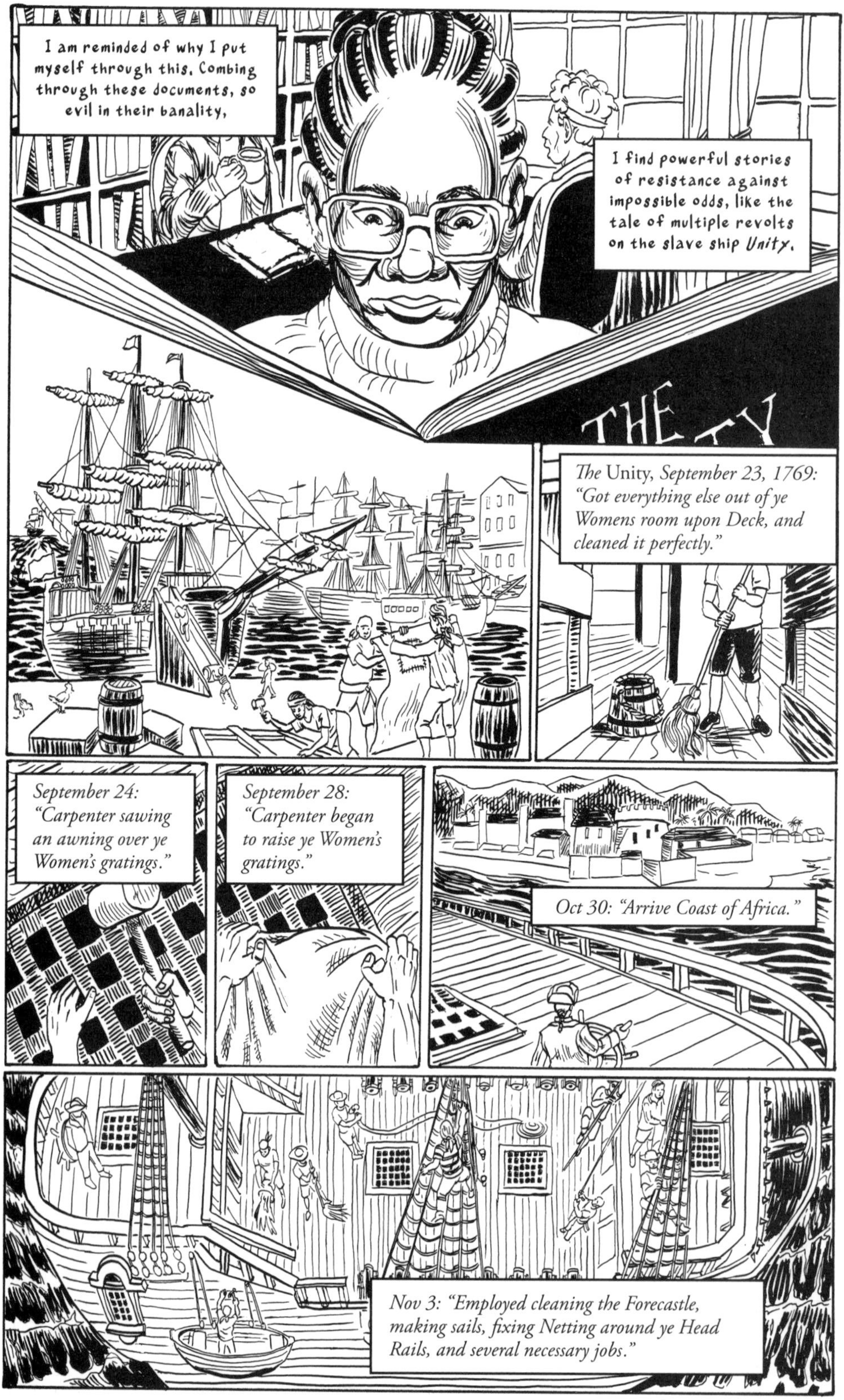
I am reminded of why I put myself through this. Combing through these documents, so evil in their banality,
I find powerful stories of resistance against impossible odds, like the tale of multiple revolts on the slave ship *Unity*.
THE TY
The Unity, *September 23, 1769: "Got everything else out of ye Womens room upon Deck, and cleaned it perfectly."*
September 24: "Carpenter sawing an awning over ye Women's gratings."
September 28: "Carpenter began to raise ye Women's gratings."
Oct 30: "Arrive Coast of Africa."
Nov 3: "Employed cleaning the Forecastle, making sails, fixing Netting around ye Head Rails, and several necessary jobs."

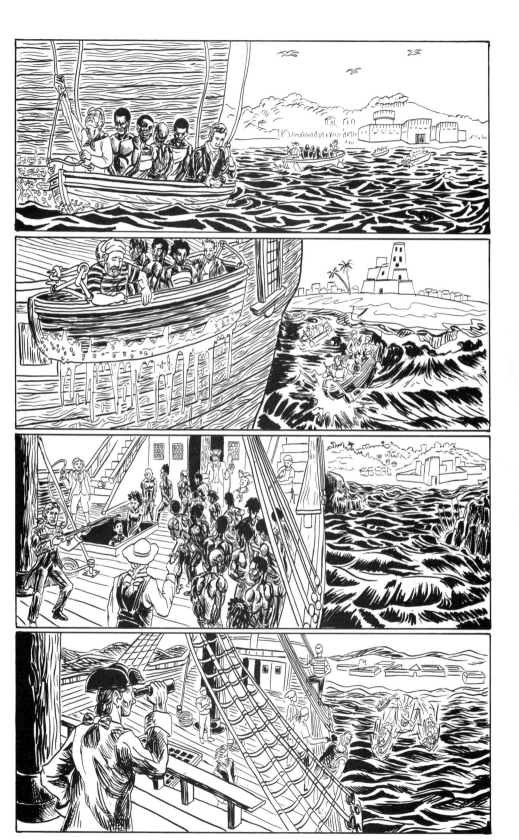

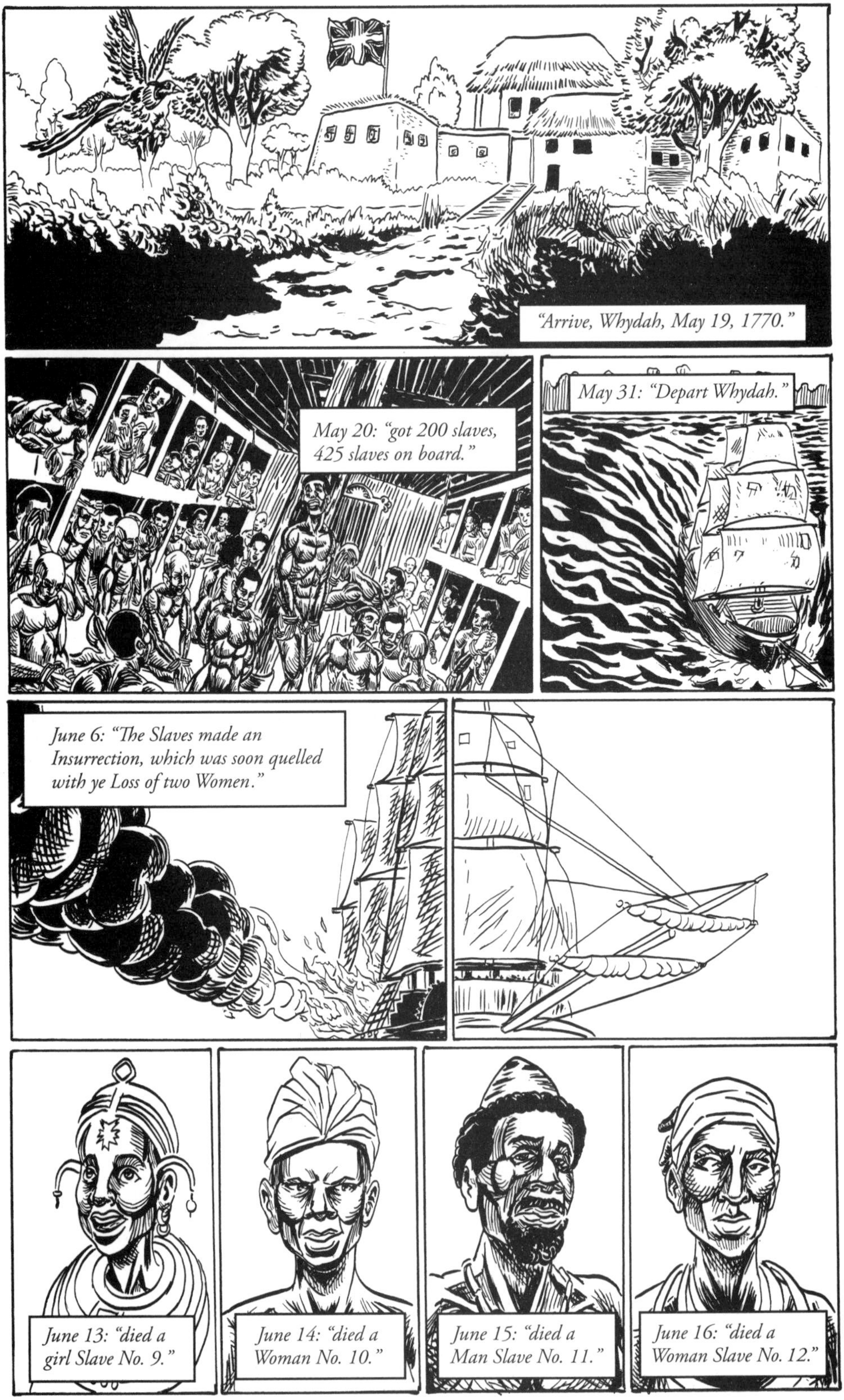
"Arrive, Whydah, May 19, 1770."
May 20: "got 200 slaves, 425 slaves on board."
May 31: "Depart Whydah."
June 6: "The Slaves made an Insurrection, which was soon quelled with ye Loss of two Women."
June 13: "died a girl Slave No. 9."
June 14: "died a Woman No. 10."
June 15: "died a Man Slave No. 11."
June 16: "died a Woman Slave No. 12."

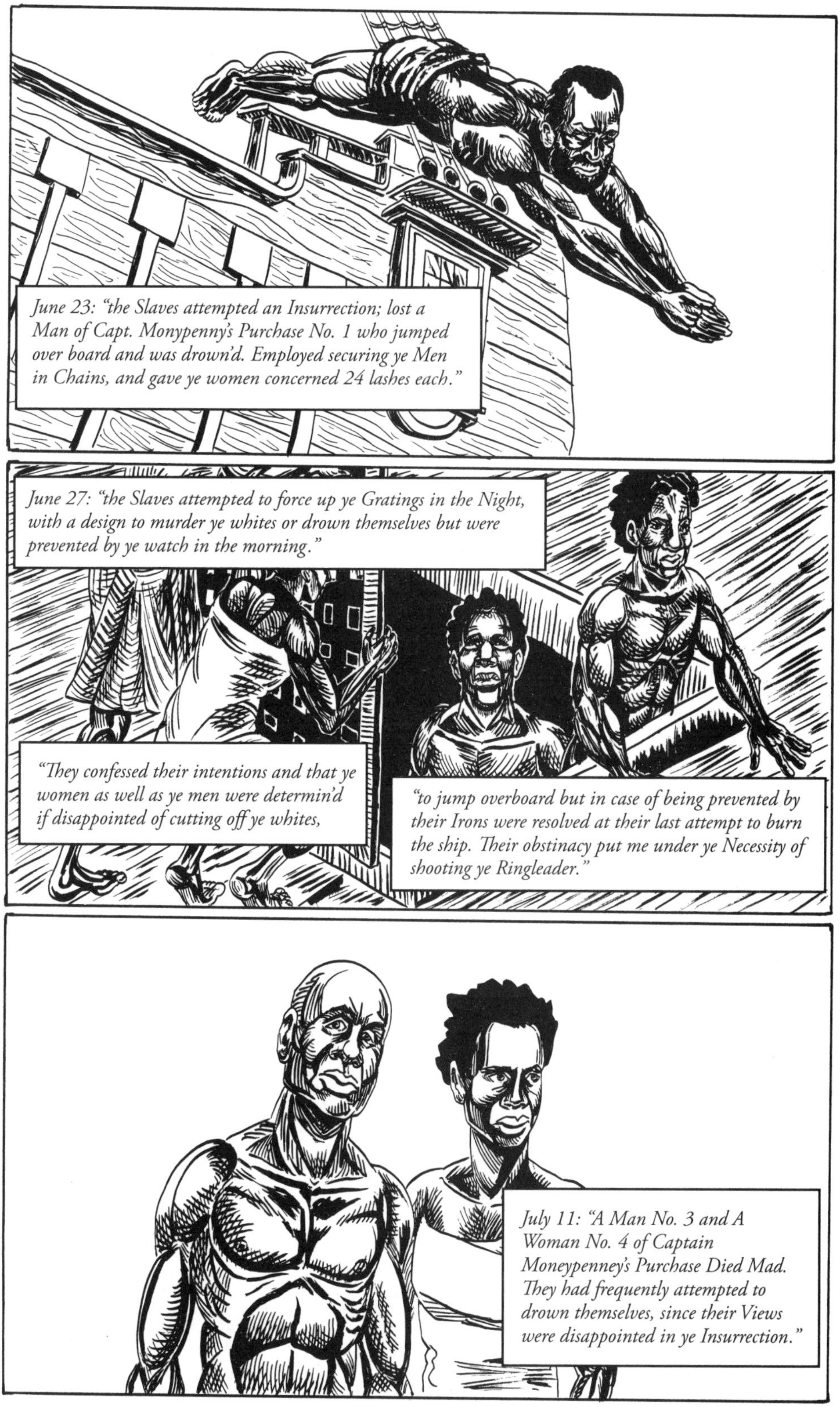
June 23: "the Slaves attempted an Insurrection; lost a Man of Capt. Monypenny's Purchase No. 1 who jumped over board and was drown'd. Employed securing ye Men in Chains, and gave ye women concerned 24 lashes each."
June 27: "the Slaves attempted to force up ye Gratings in the Night, with a design to murder ye whites or drown themselves but were prevented by ye watch in the morning."
"They confessed their intentions and that ye women as well as ye men were determin'd if disappointed of cutting off ye whites,
"to jump overboard but in case of being prevented by their Irons were resolved at their last attempt to burn the ship. Their obstinacy put me under ye Necessity of shooting ye Ringleader."
July 11: "A Man No. 3 and A Woman No. 4 of Captain Moneypenney's Purchase Died Mad. They had frequently attempted to drown themselves, since their Views were disappointed in ye Insurrection."

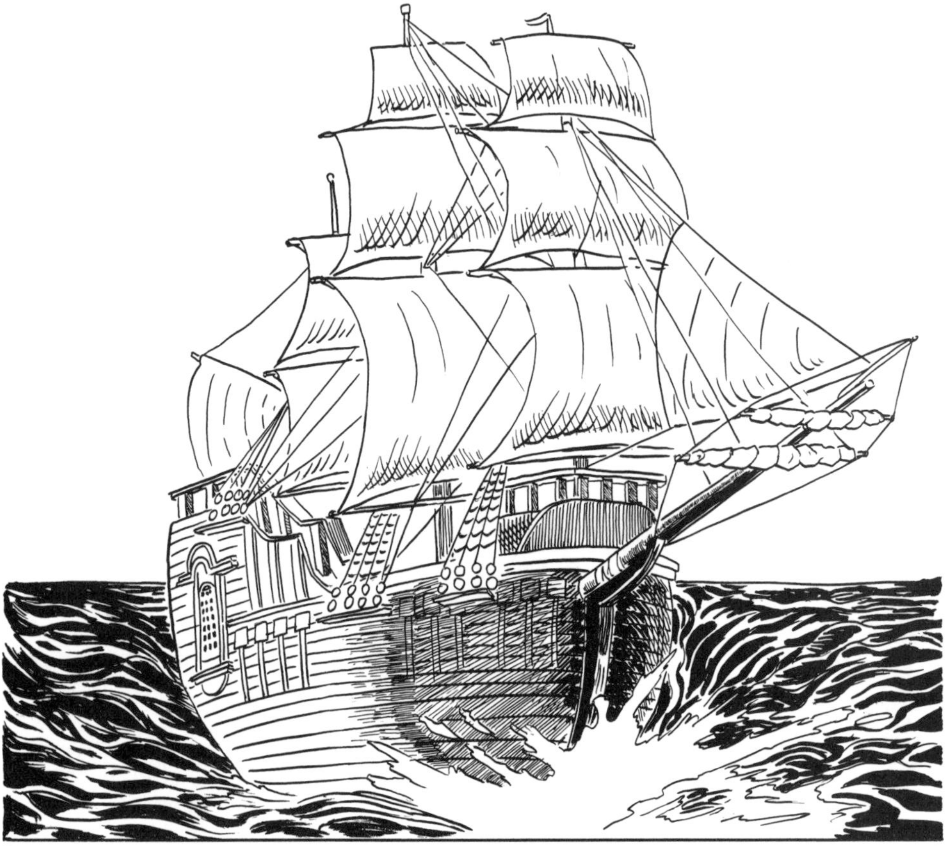

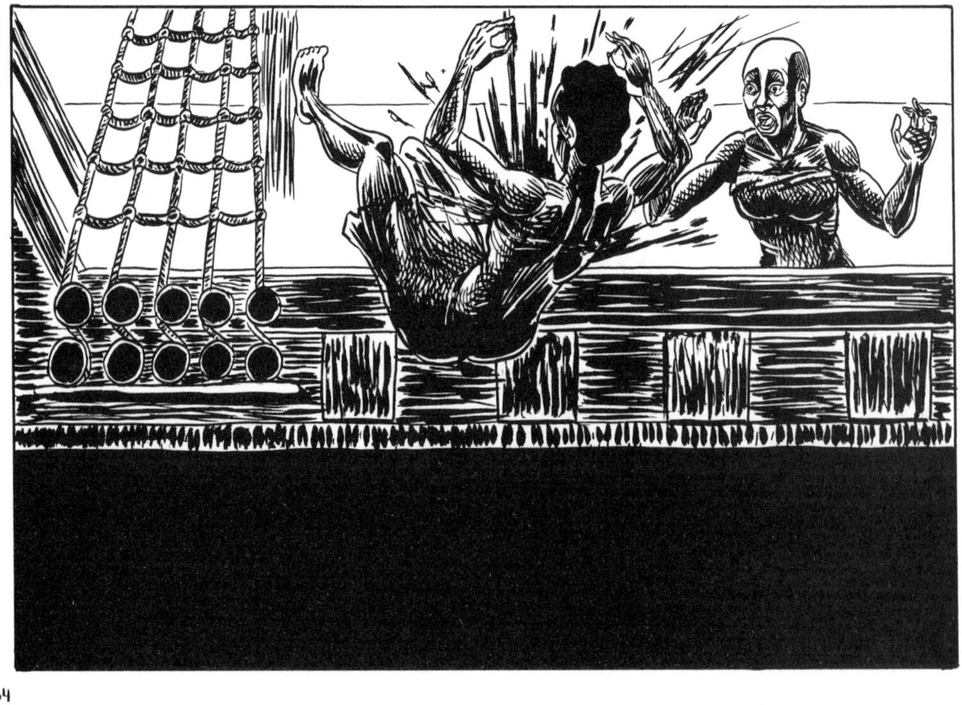

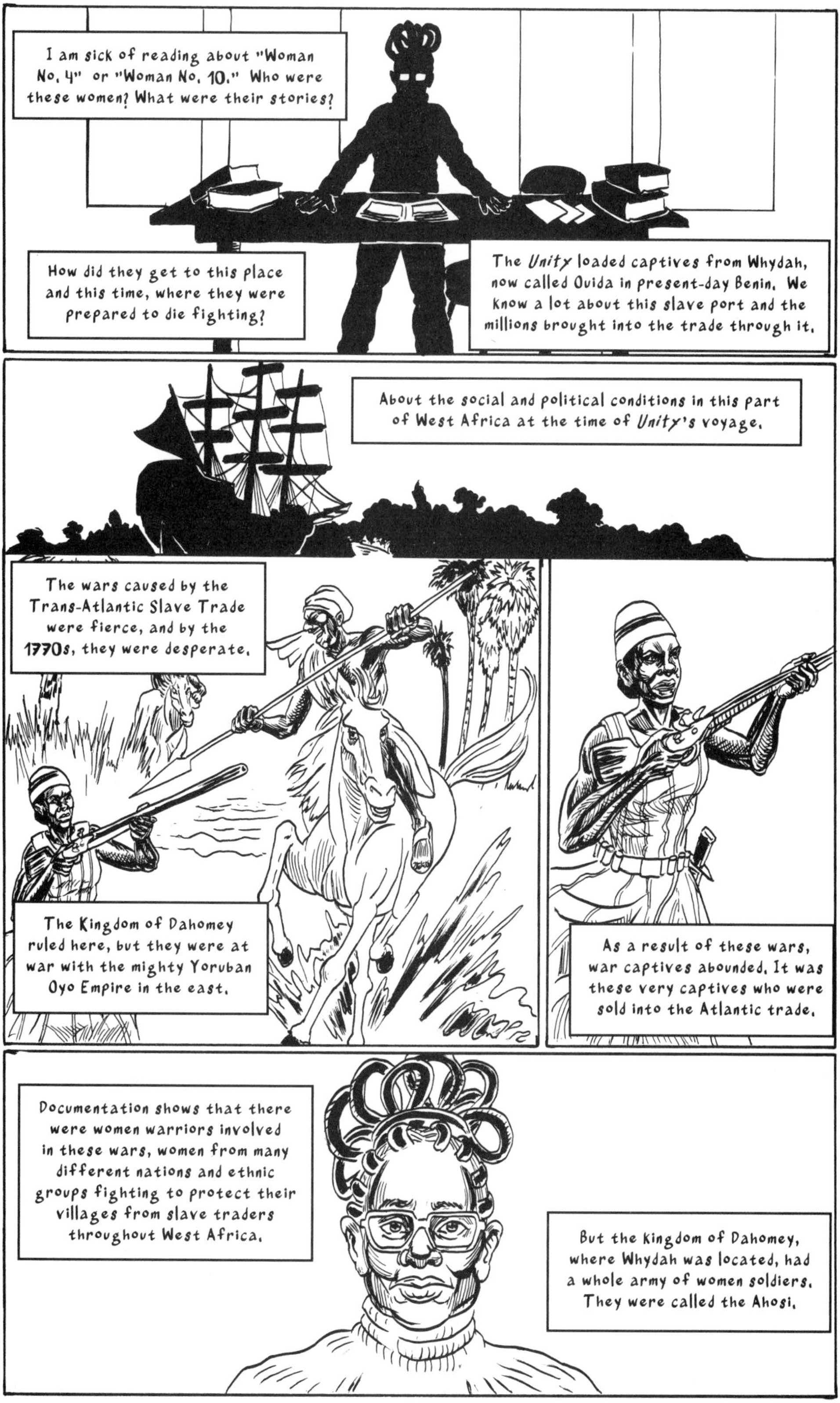

I am sick of reading about "Woman No. 4" or "Woman No. 10." Who were these women? What were their stories?
How did they get to this place and this time, where they were prepared to die fighting?
The *Unity* loaded captives from Whydah, now called Ouida in present-day Benin. We know a lot about this slave port and the millions brought into the trade through it.
About the social and political conditions in this part of West Africa at the time of *Unity*'s voyage.
The wars caused by the Trans-Atlantic Slave Trade were fierce, and by the 1770s, they were desperate.
The Kingdom of Dahomey ruled here, but they were at war with the mighty Yoruban Oyo Empire in the east.
As a result of these wars, war captives abounded. It was these very captives who were sold into the Atlantic trade.
Documentation shows that there were women warriors involved in these wars, women from many different nations and ethnic groups fighting to protect their villages from slave traders throughout West Africa.
But the kingdom of Dahomey, where Whydah was located, had a whole army of women soldiers. They were called the Ahosi.

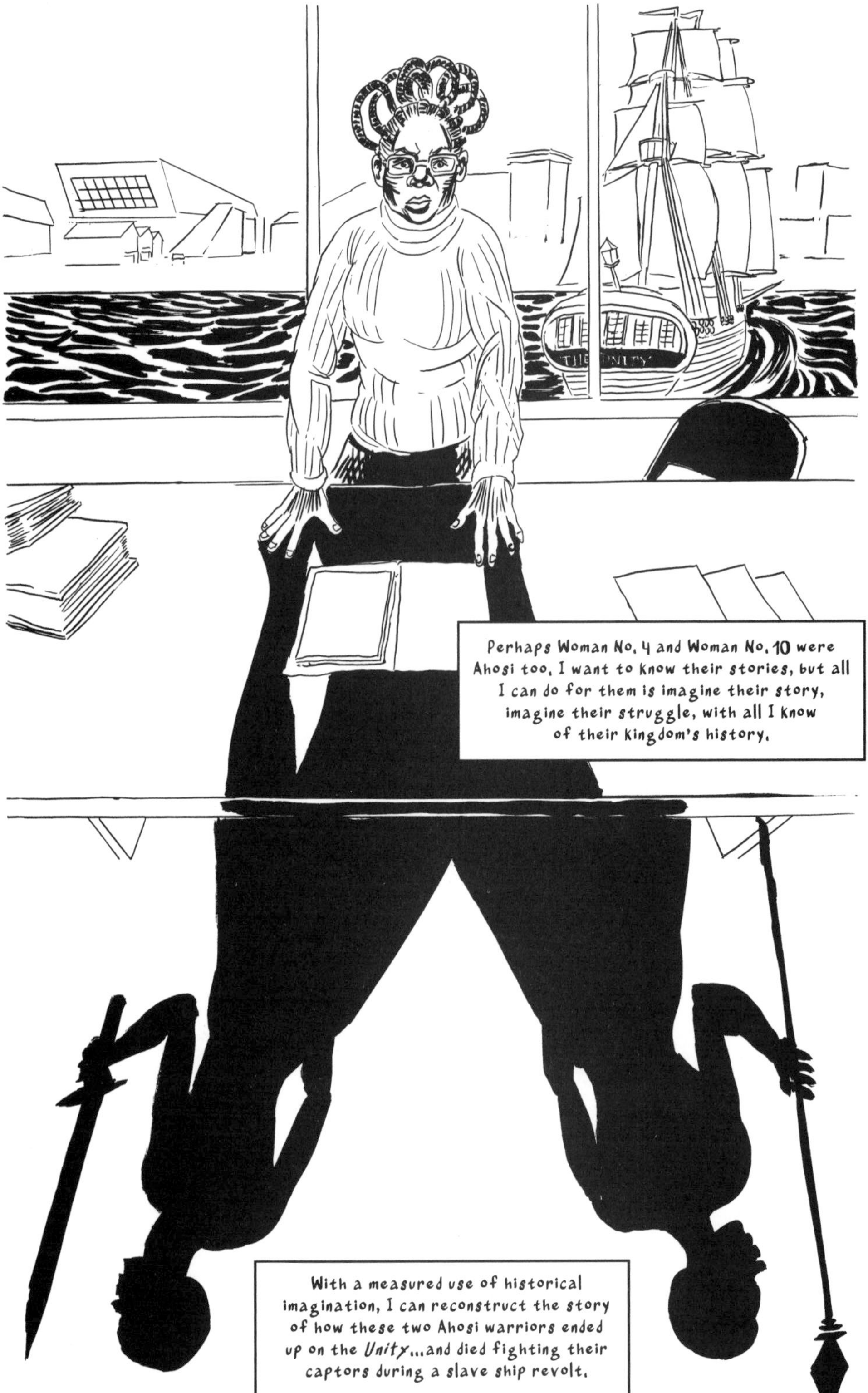
THE UNITY
Perhaps Woman No. 4 and Woman No. 10 were Ahosi too. I want to know their stories, but all I can do for them is imagine their story, imagine their struggle, with all I know of their kingdom's history.
With a measured use of historical imagination, I can reconstruct the story of how these two Ahosi warriors ended up on the *Unity*...and died fighting their captors during a slave ship revolt.

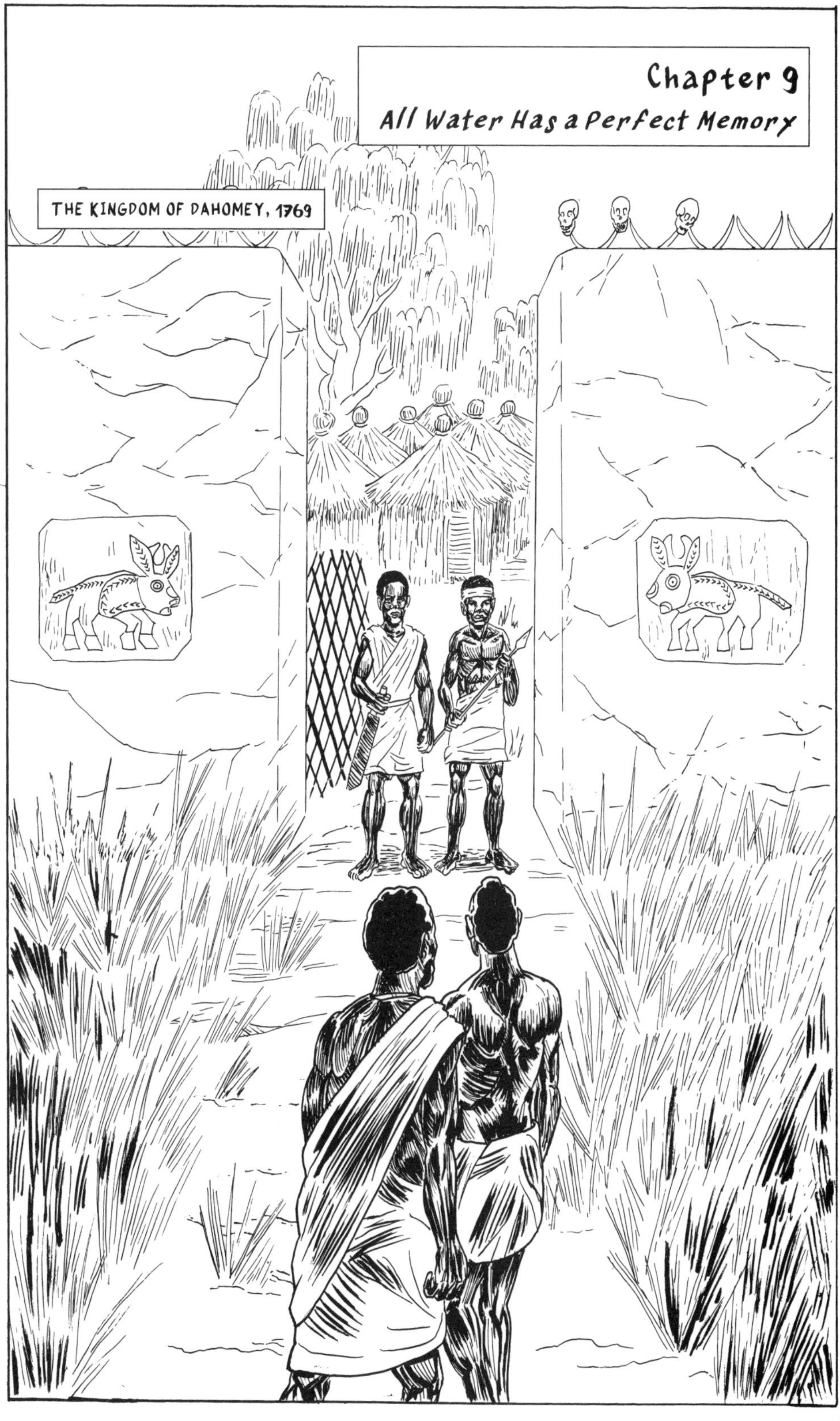
Chapter 9
All Water Has a Perfect Memory
THE KINGDOM OF DAHOMEY, 1769

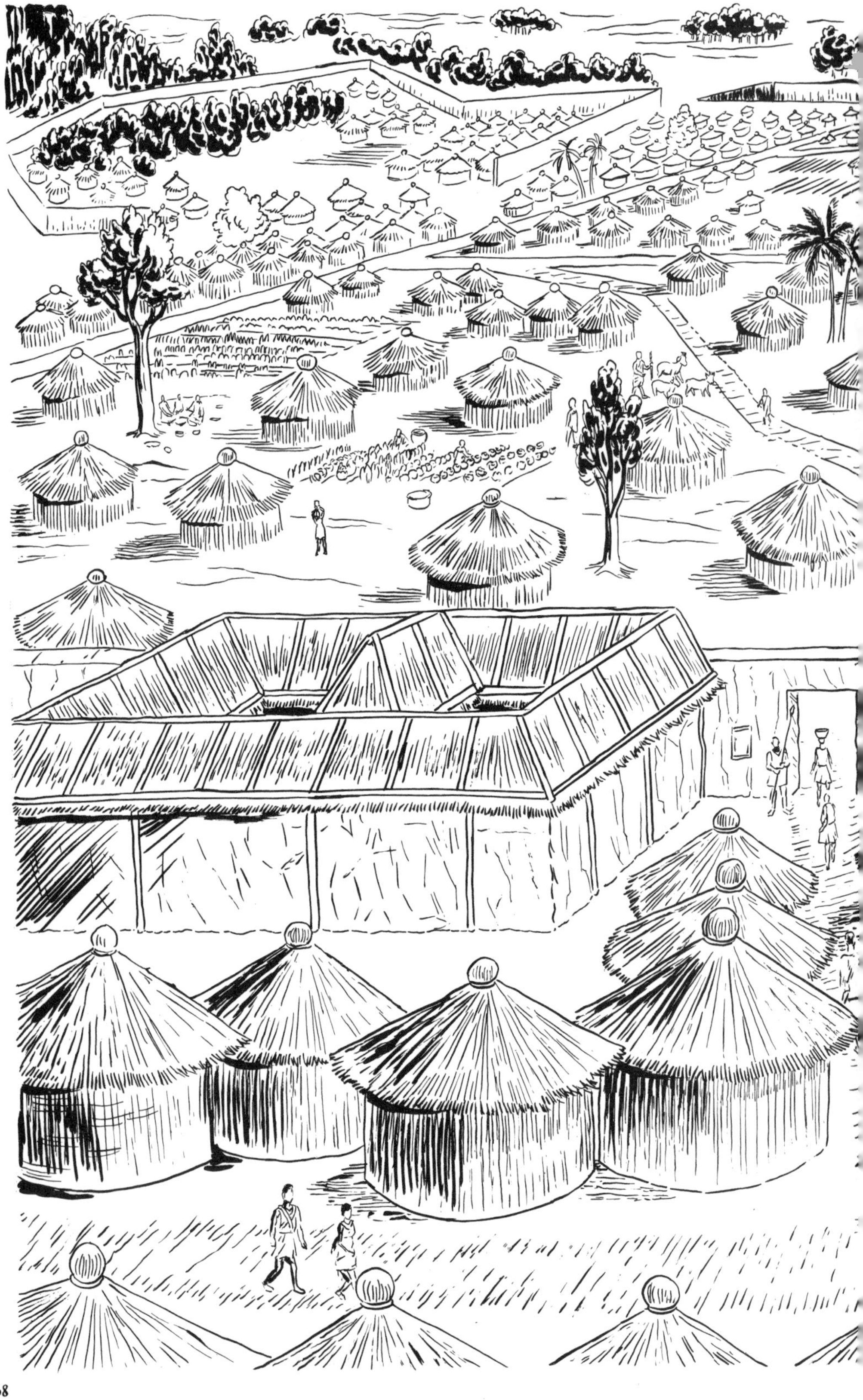

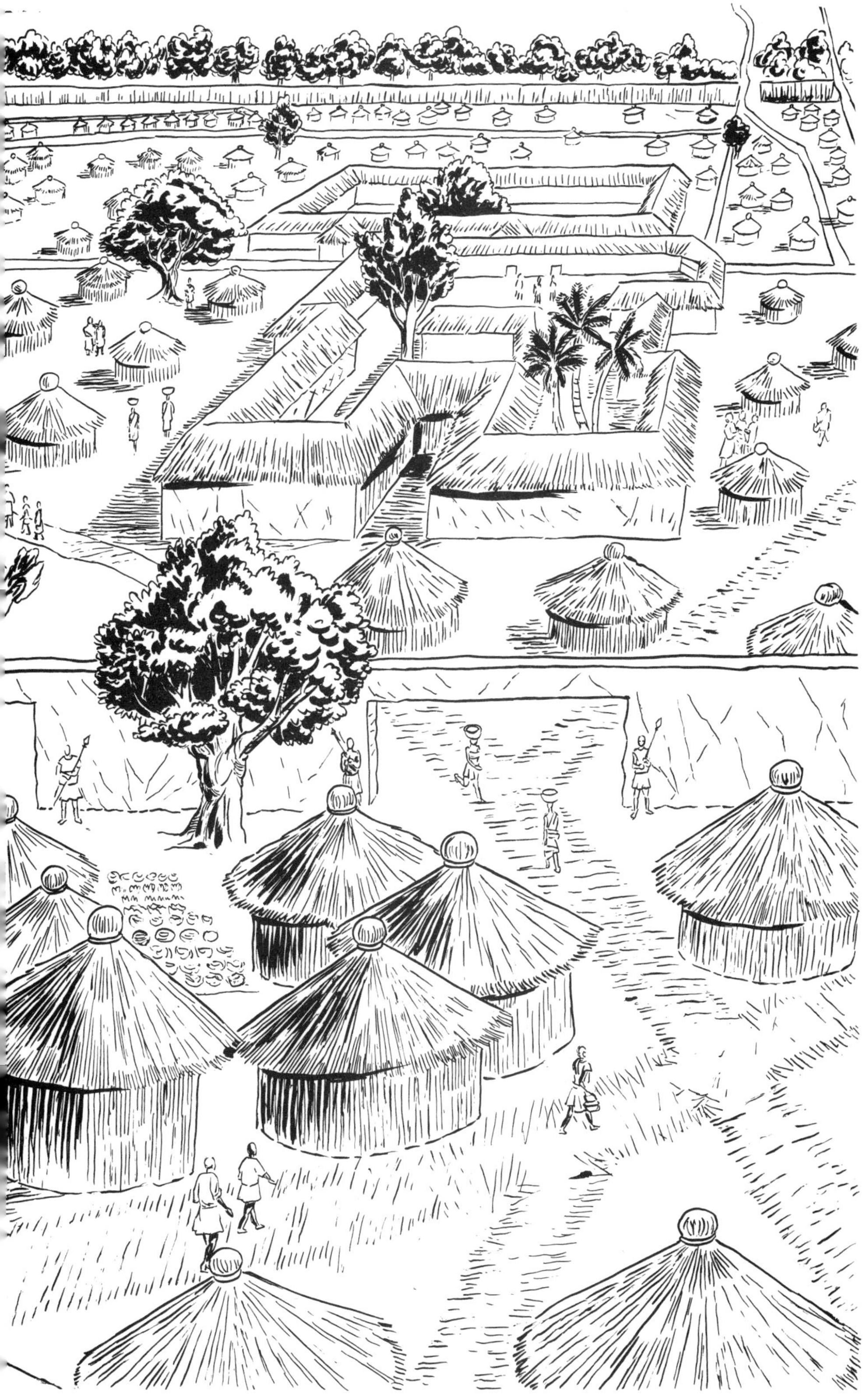

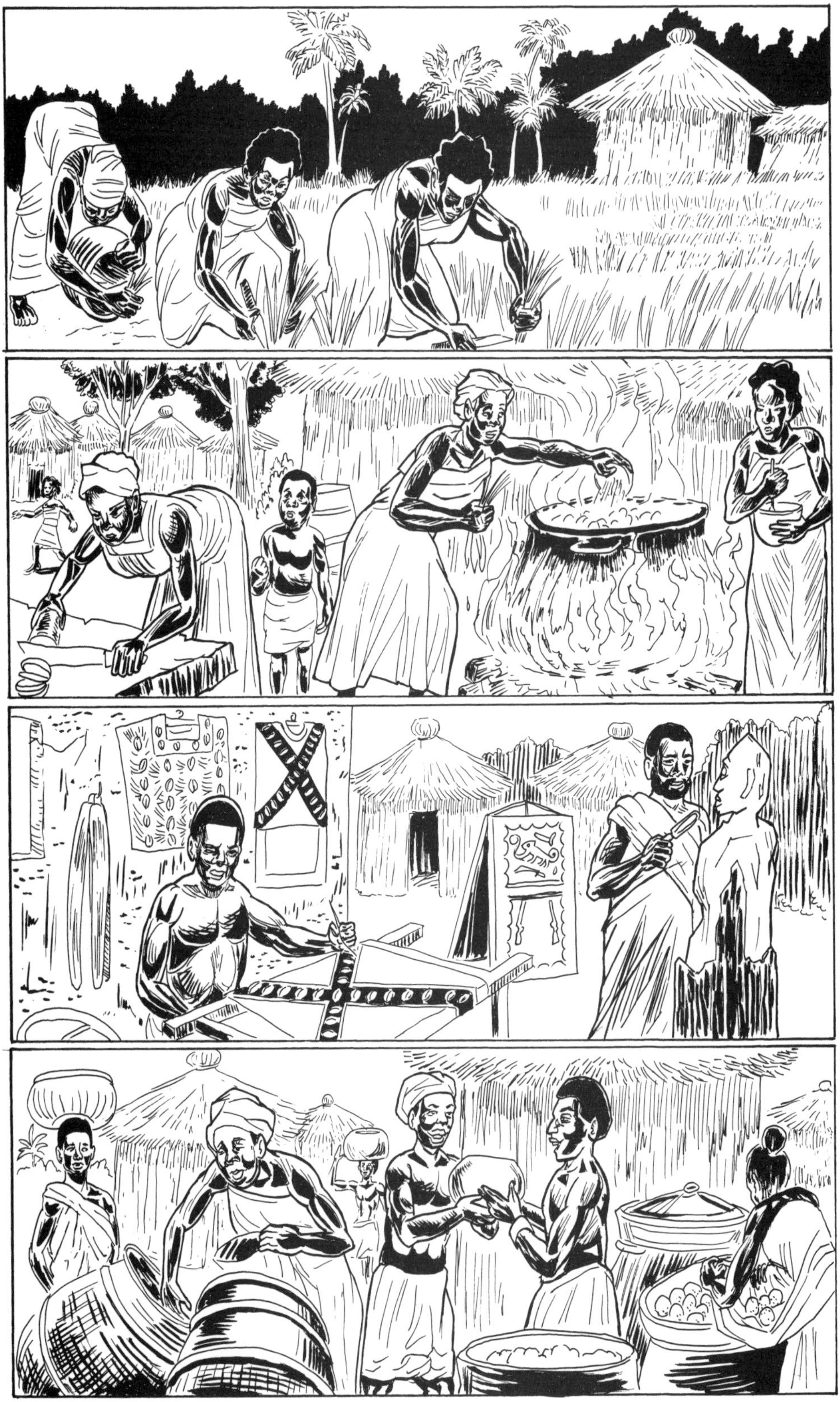

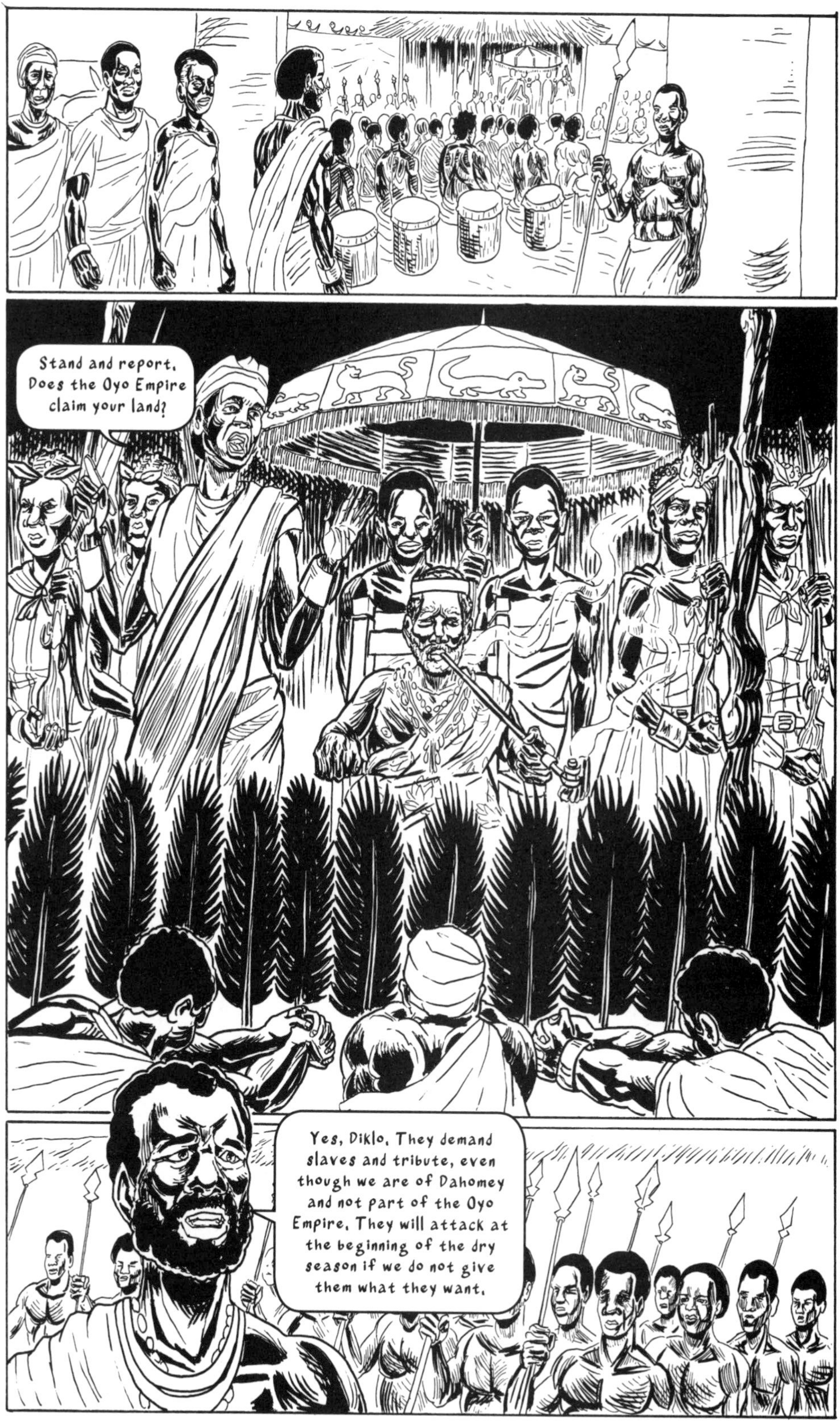
Stand and report. Does the Oyo Empire claim your land?
Yes, Diklo. They demand slaves and tribute, even though we are of Dahomey and not part of the Oyo Empire. They will attack at the beginning of the dry season if we do not give them what they want.

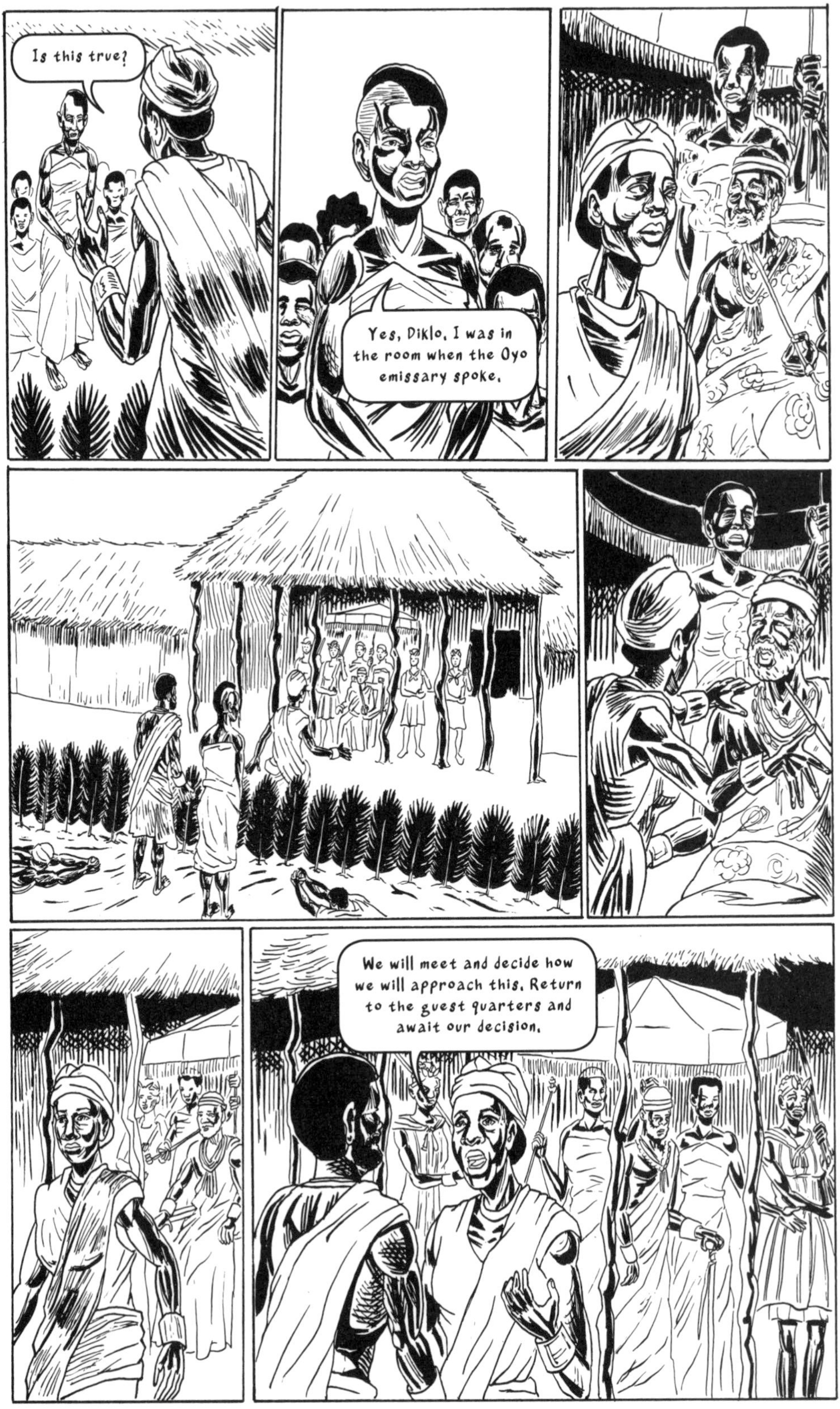
Is this true?
Yes, Diklo. I was in the room when the Oyo emissary spoke.
We will meet and decide how we will approach this. Return to the guest quarters and await our decision.

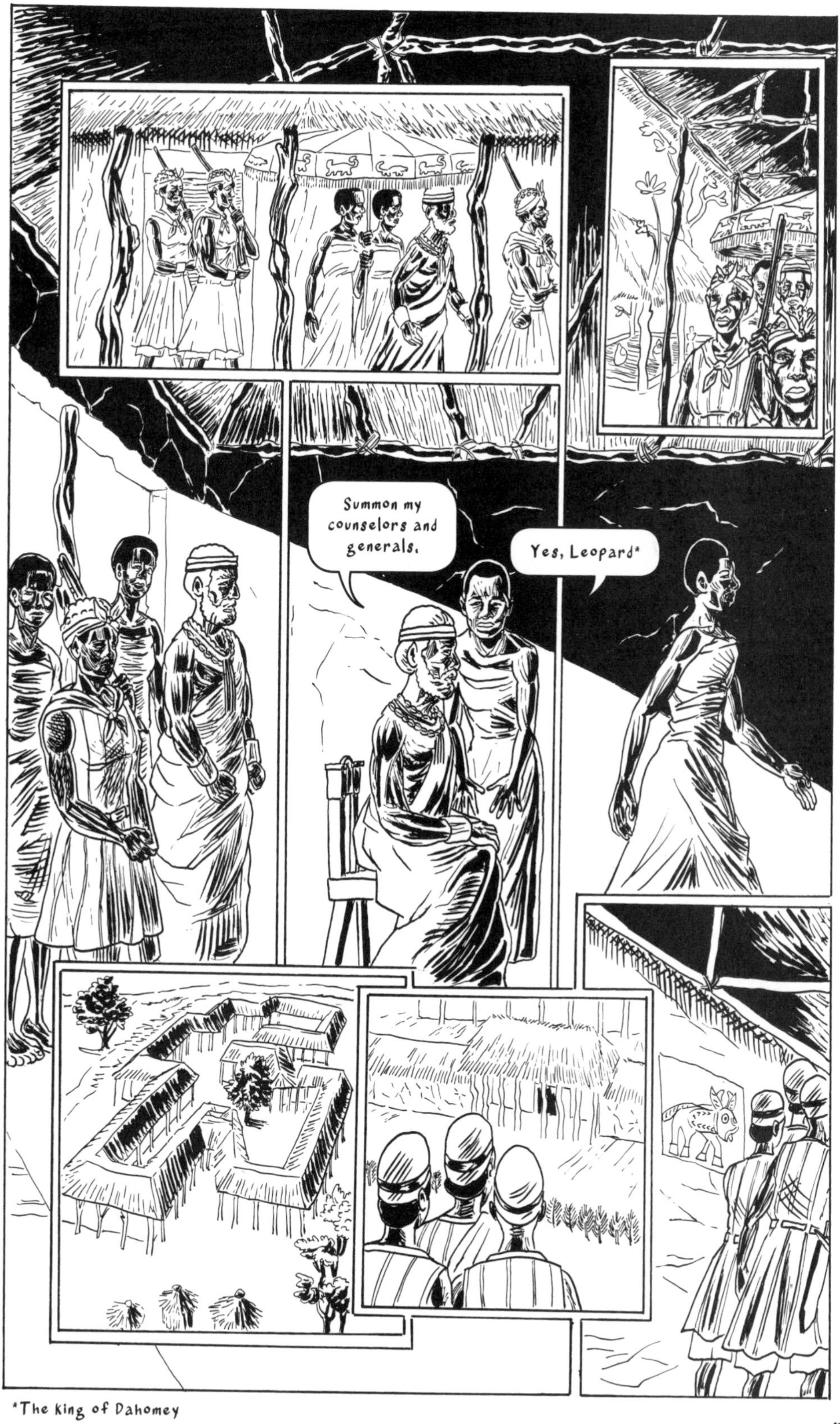
Summon my counselors and generals.
Yes, Leopard*

*The king of Dahomey

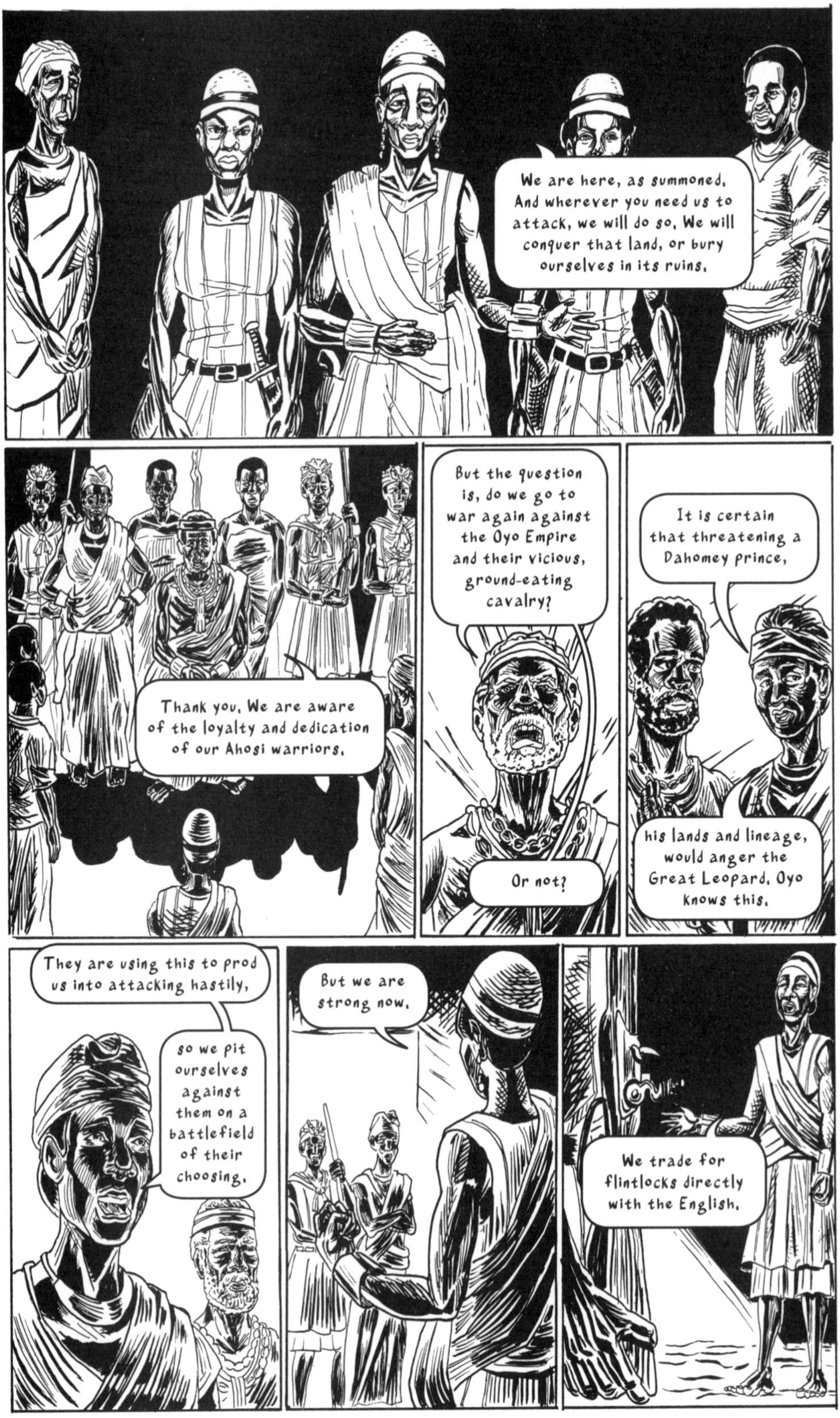
We are here, as summoned. And wherever you need us to attack, we will do so. We will conquer that land, or bury ourselves in its ruins.
Thank you. We are aware of the loyalty and dedication of our Ahosi warriors.
But the question is, do we go to war again against the Oyo Empire and their vicious, ground-eating cavalry?
Or not?
It is certain that threatening a Dahomey prince,
his lands and lineage, would anger the Great Leopard. Oyo knows this.
They are using this to prod us into attacking hastily,
so we pit ourselves against them on a battlefield of their choosing.
But we are strong now.
We trade for flintlocks directly with the English.

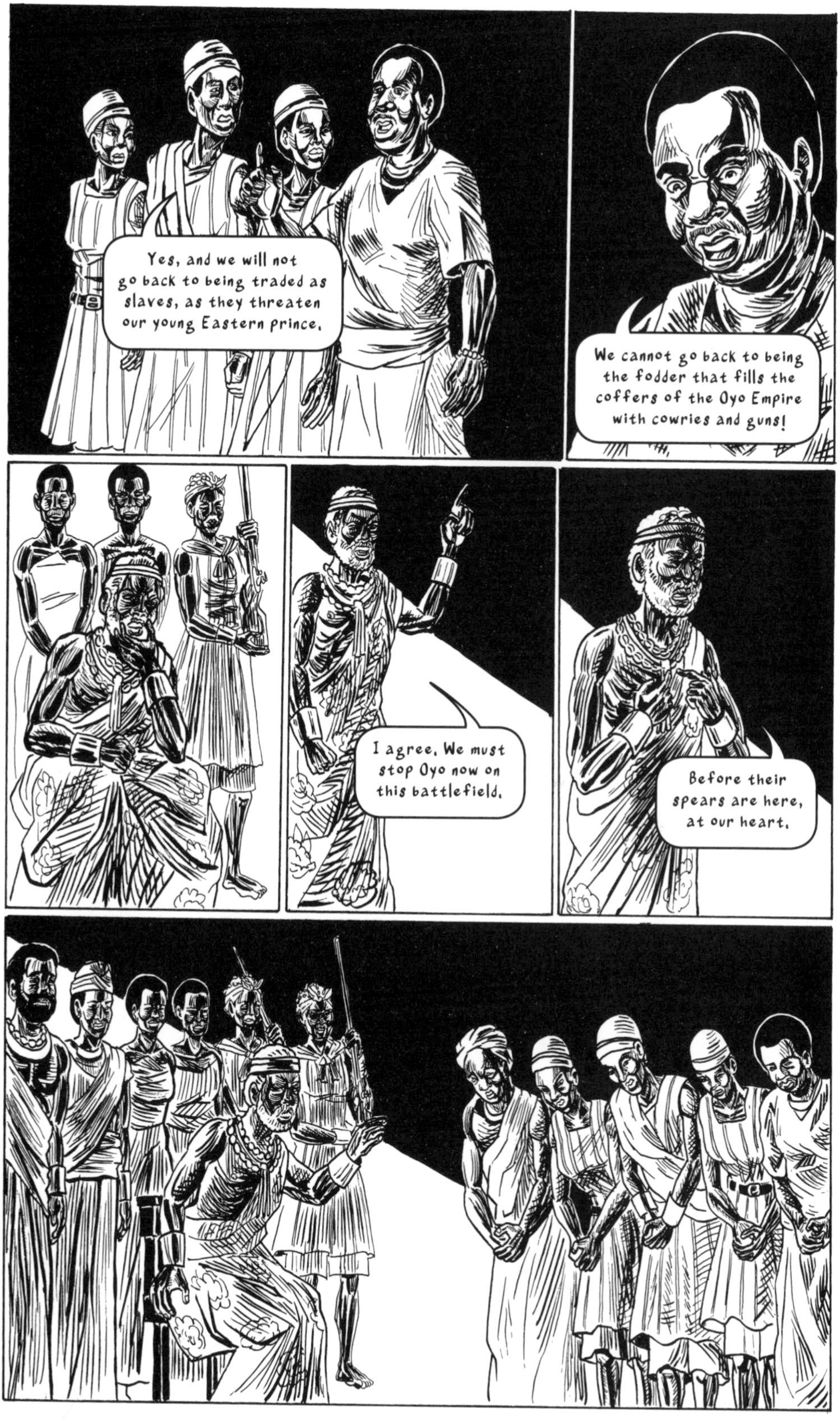
Yes, and we will not go back to being traded as slaves, as they threaten our young Eastern prince.
We cannot go back to being the fodder that fills the coffers of the Oyo Empire with cowries and guns!
I agree. We must stop Oyo now on this battlefield.
Before their spears are here, at our heart.

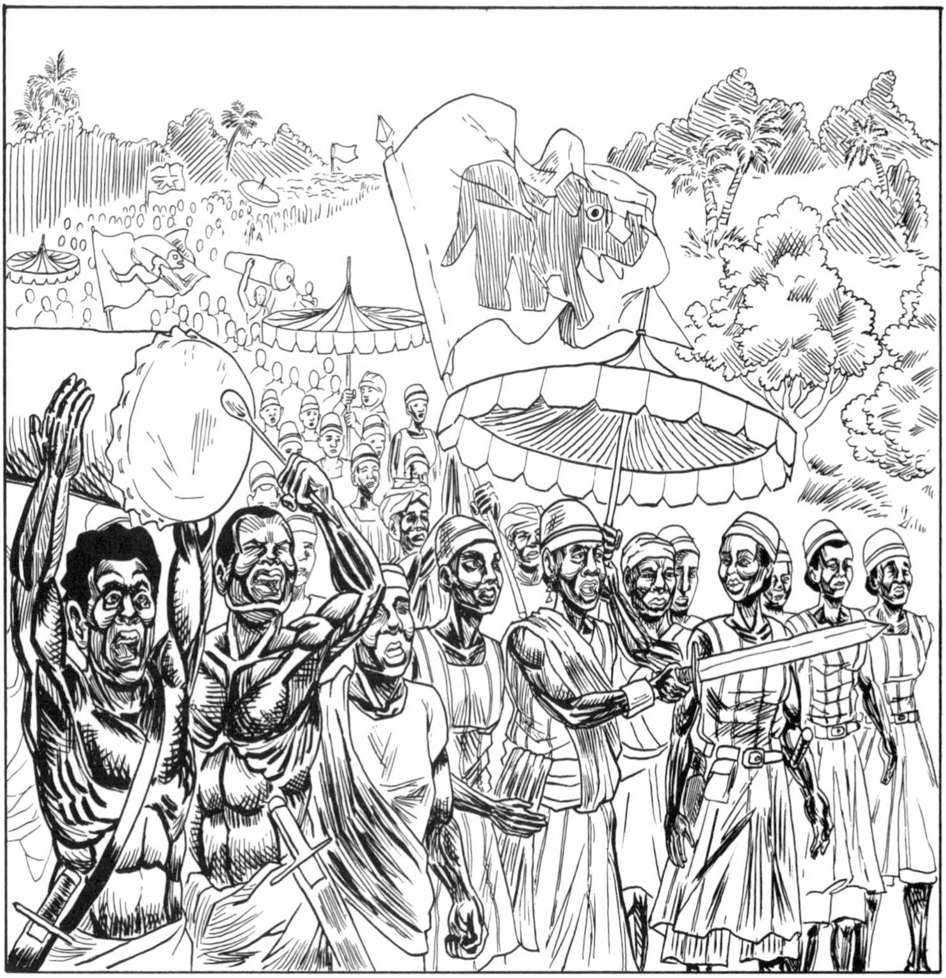

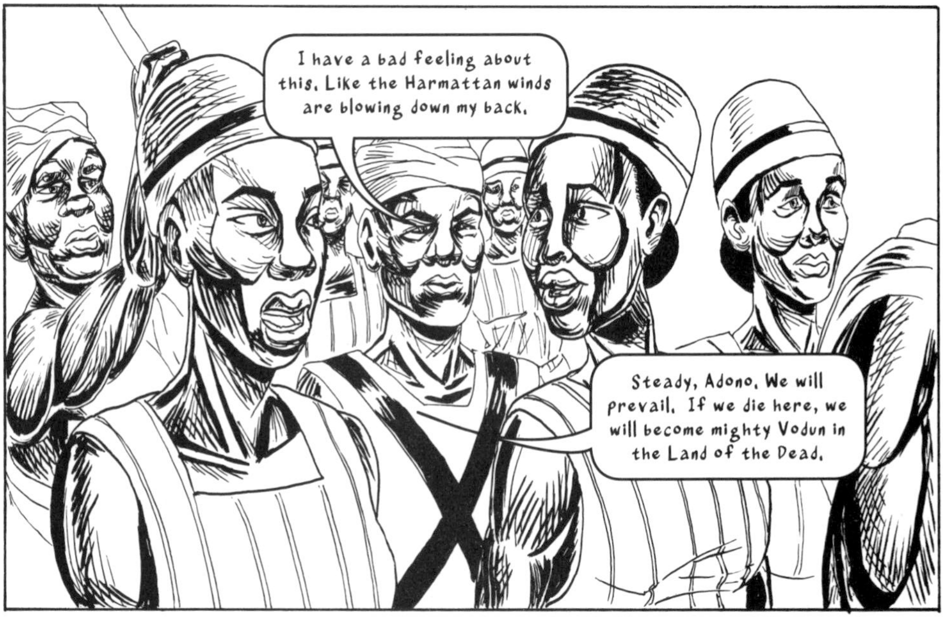
I have a bad feeling about this. Like the Harmattan winds are blowing down my back.
Steady, Adono. We will prevail. If we die here, we will become mighty Vodun in the Land of the Dead.

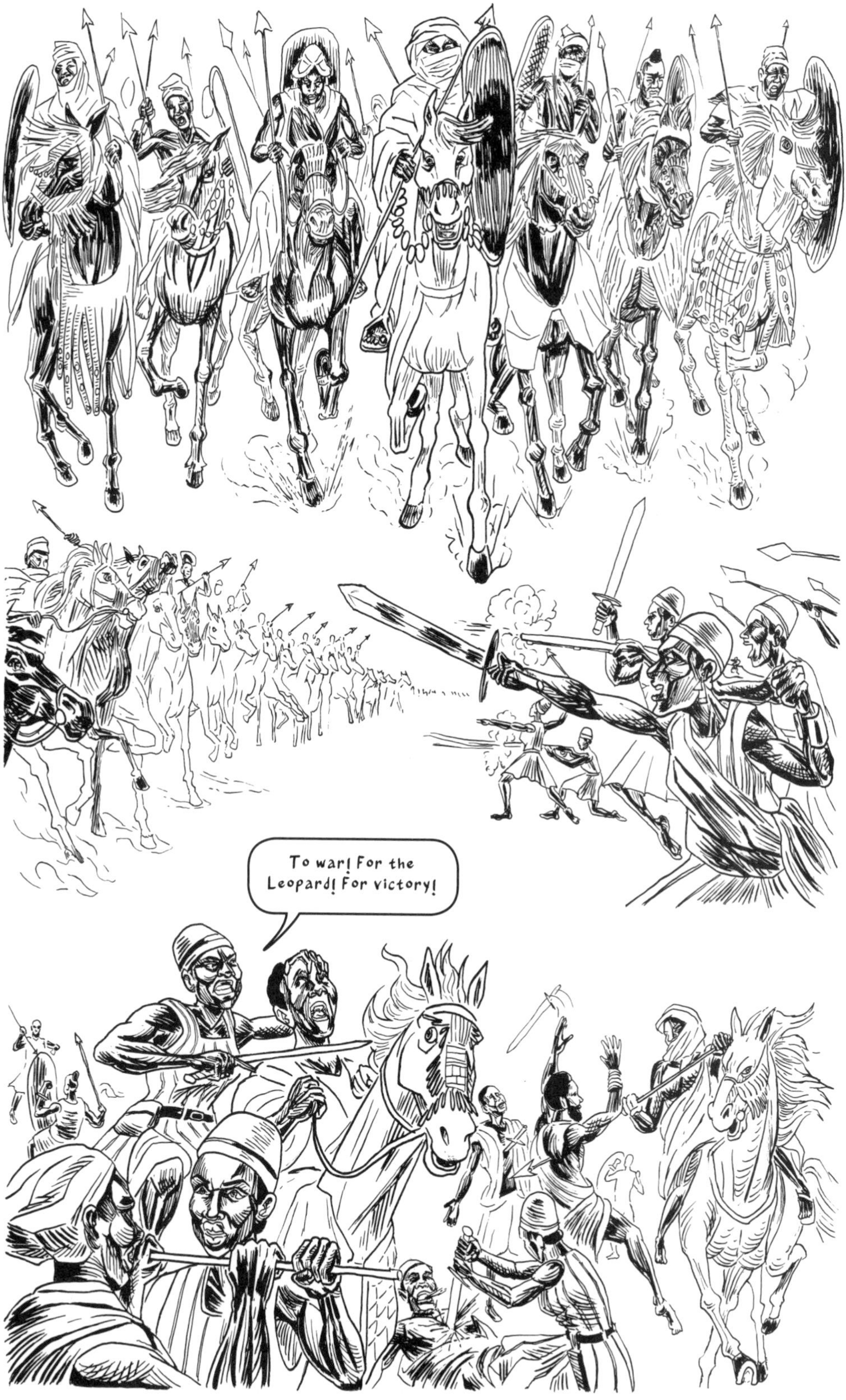
To war! For the Leopard! For victory!

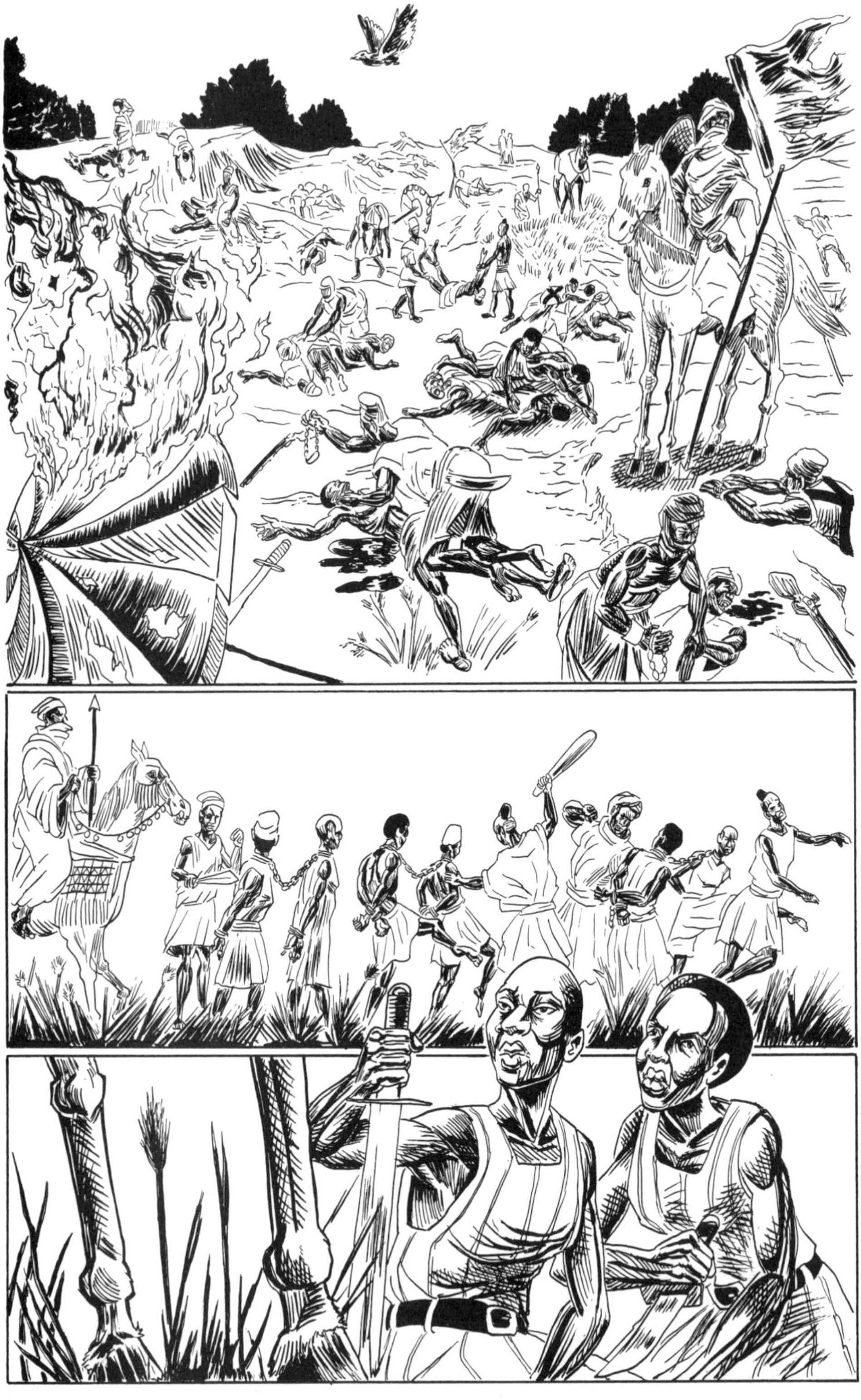

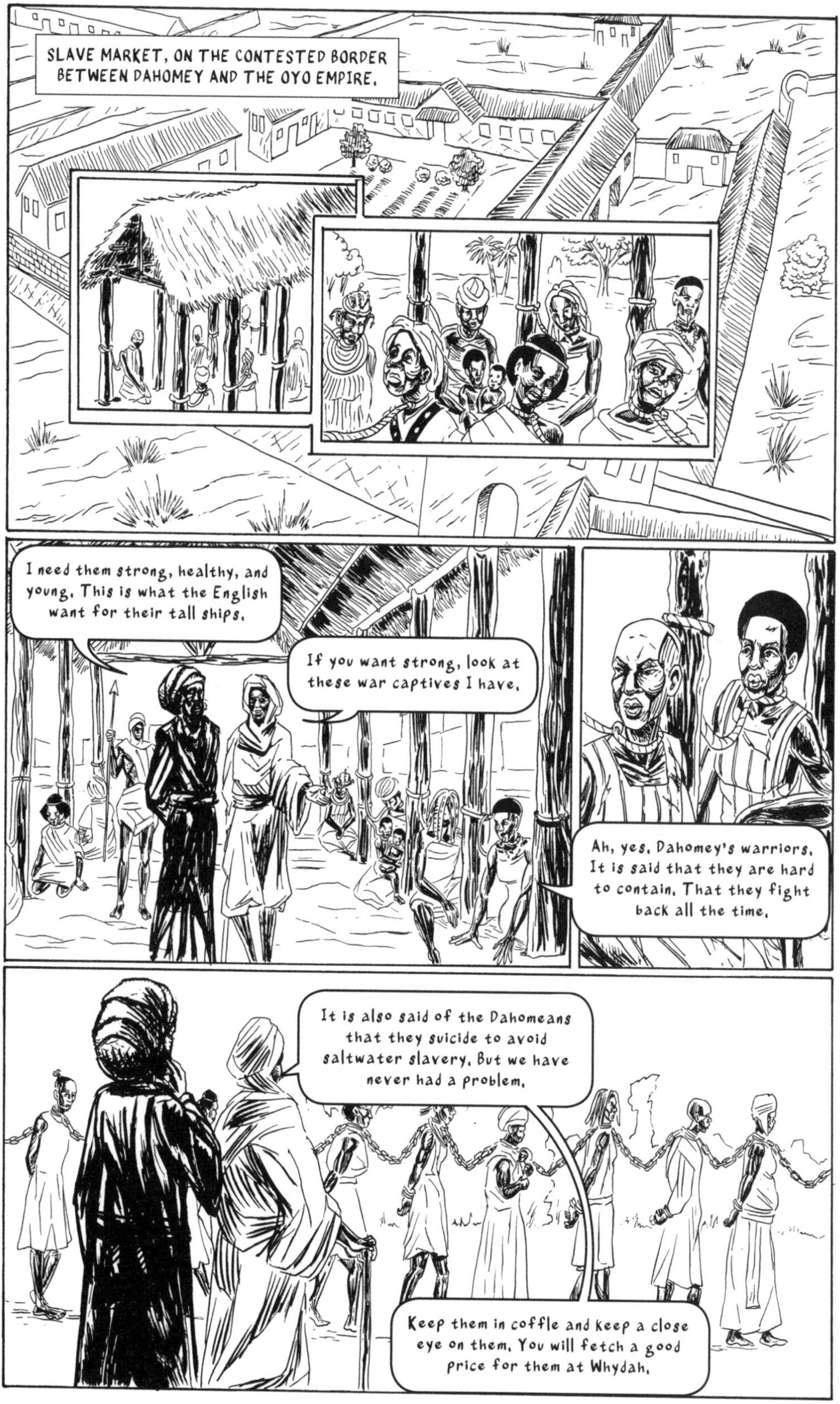

SLAVE MARKET, ON THE CONTESTED BORDER BETWEEN DAHOMEY AND THE OYO EMPIRE.
I need them strong, healthy, and young. This is what the English want for their tall ships.
If you want strong, look at these war captives I have.
Ah, yes. Dahomey's warriors. It is said that they are hard to contain. That they fight back all the time.
It is also said of the Dahomeans that they suicide to avoid saltwater slavery. But we have never had a problem.
Keep them in coffle and keep a close eye on them. You will fetch a good price for them at Whydah.

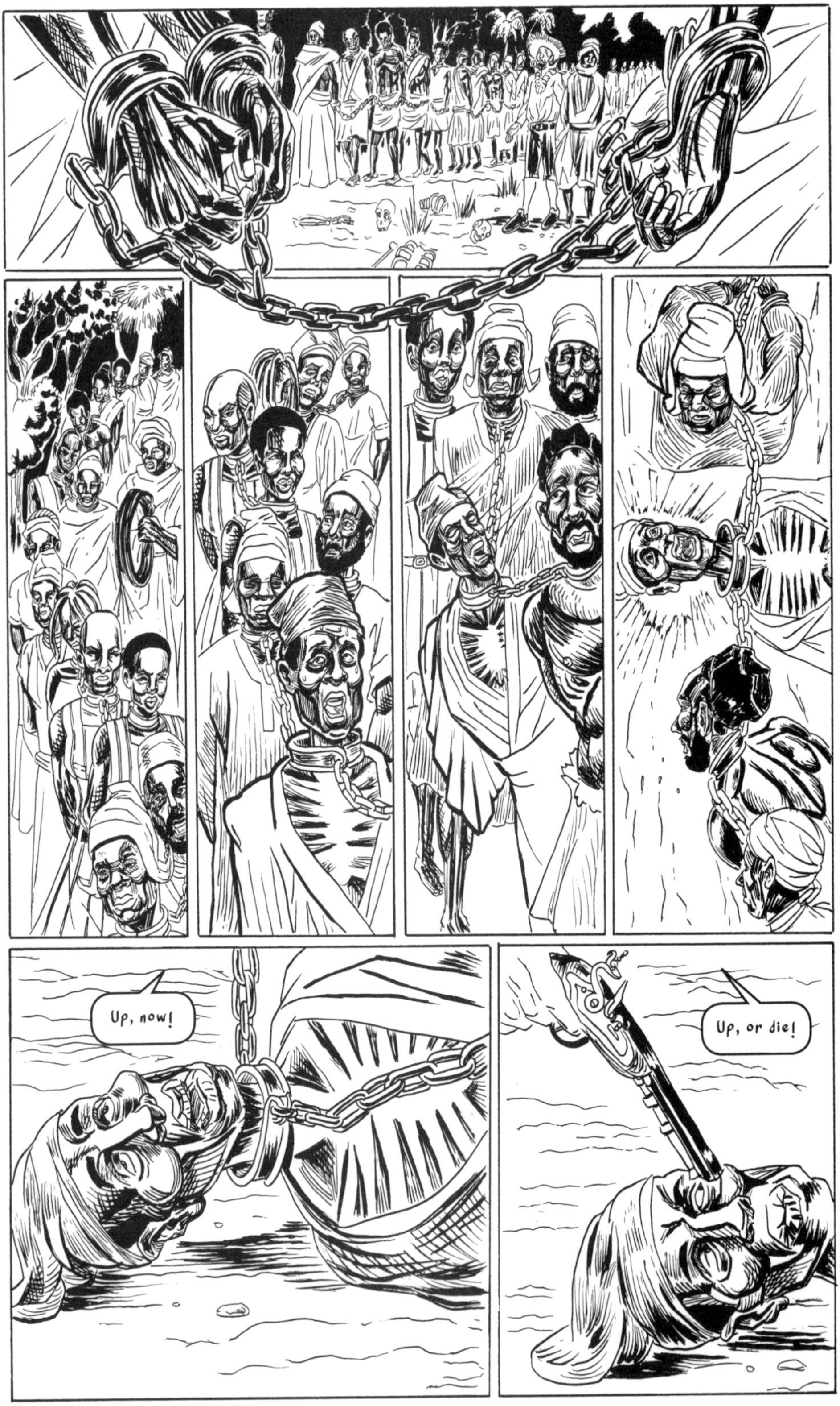
Up, now!
Up, or die!

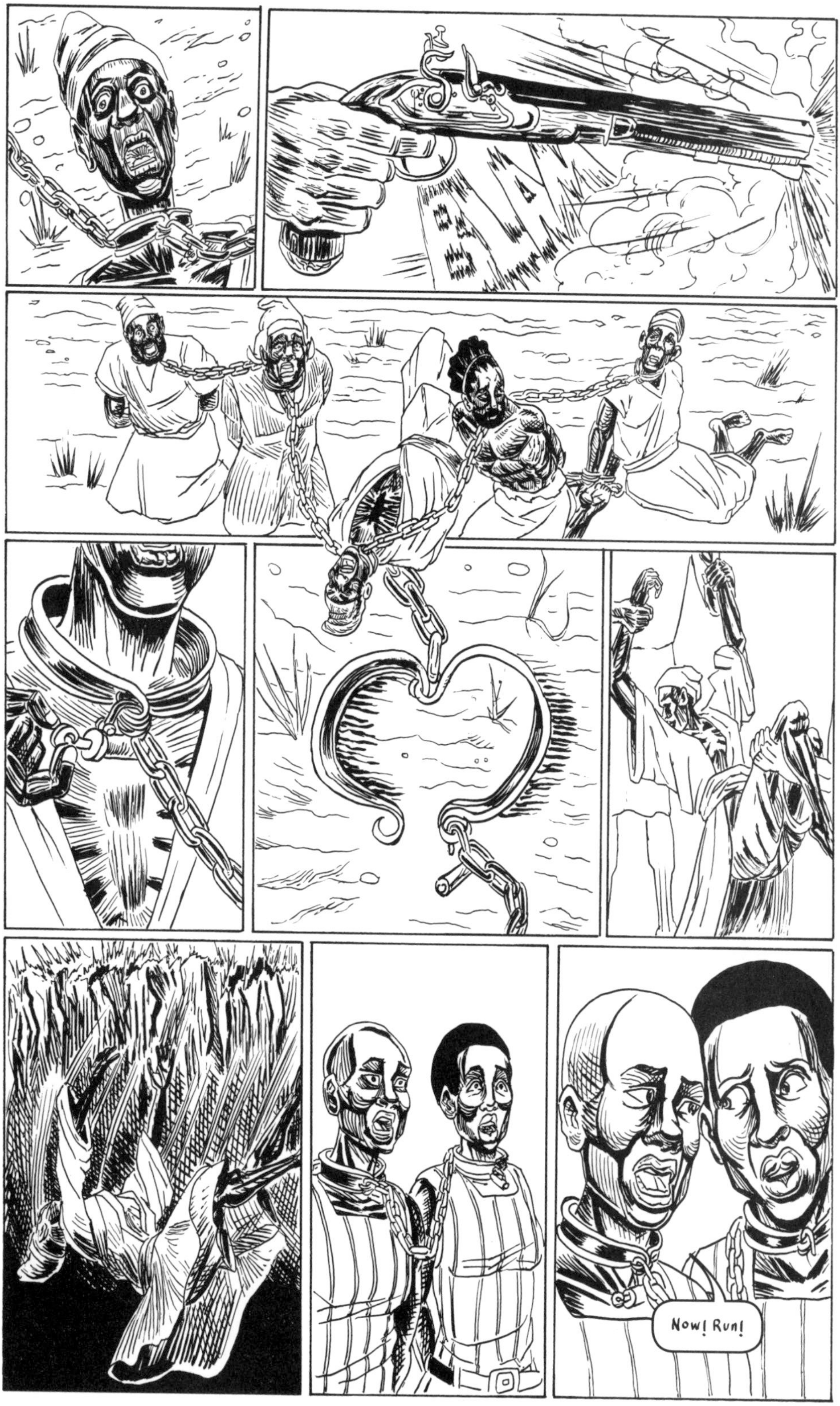
Now! Run!

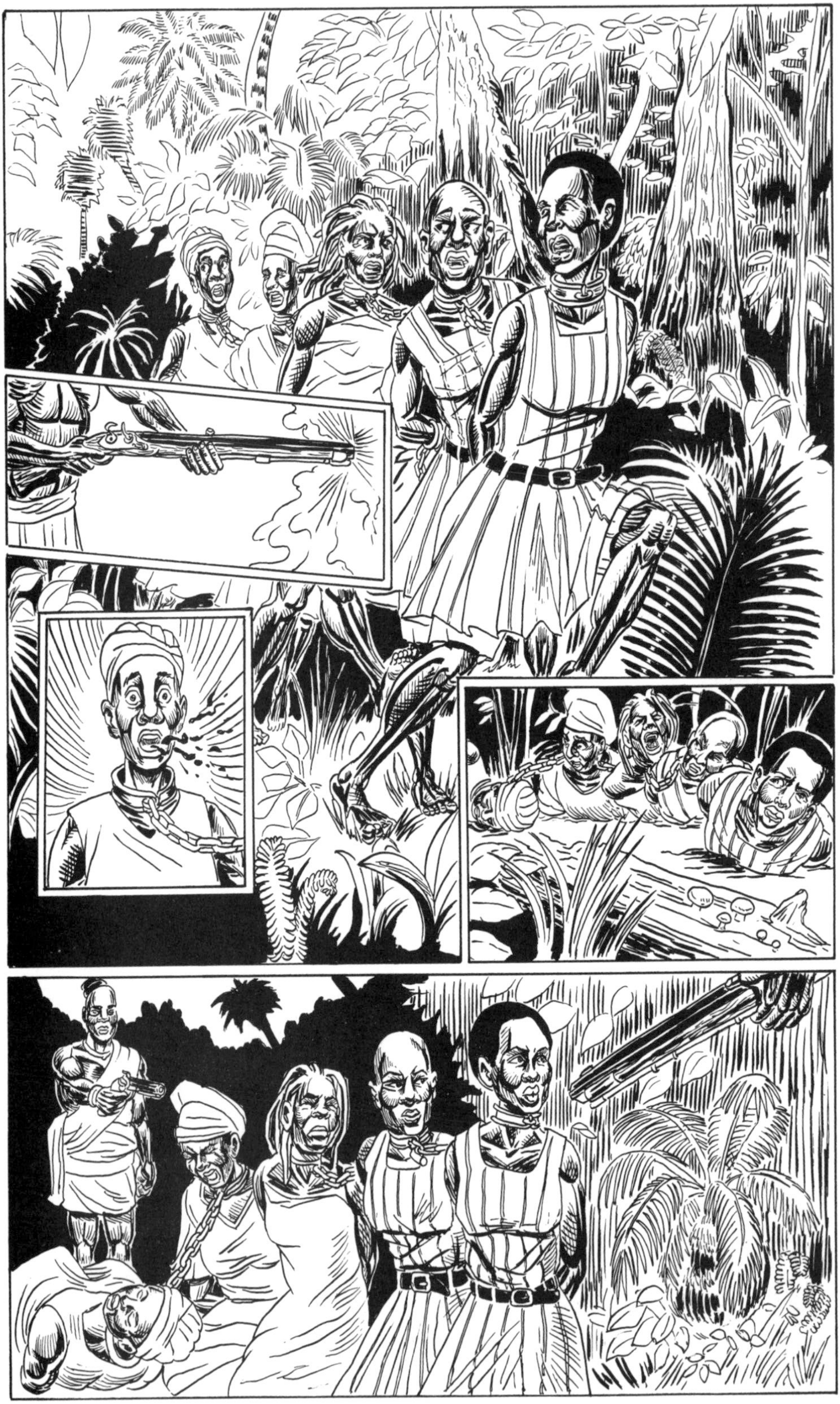

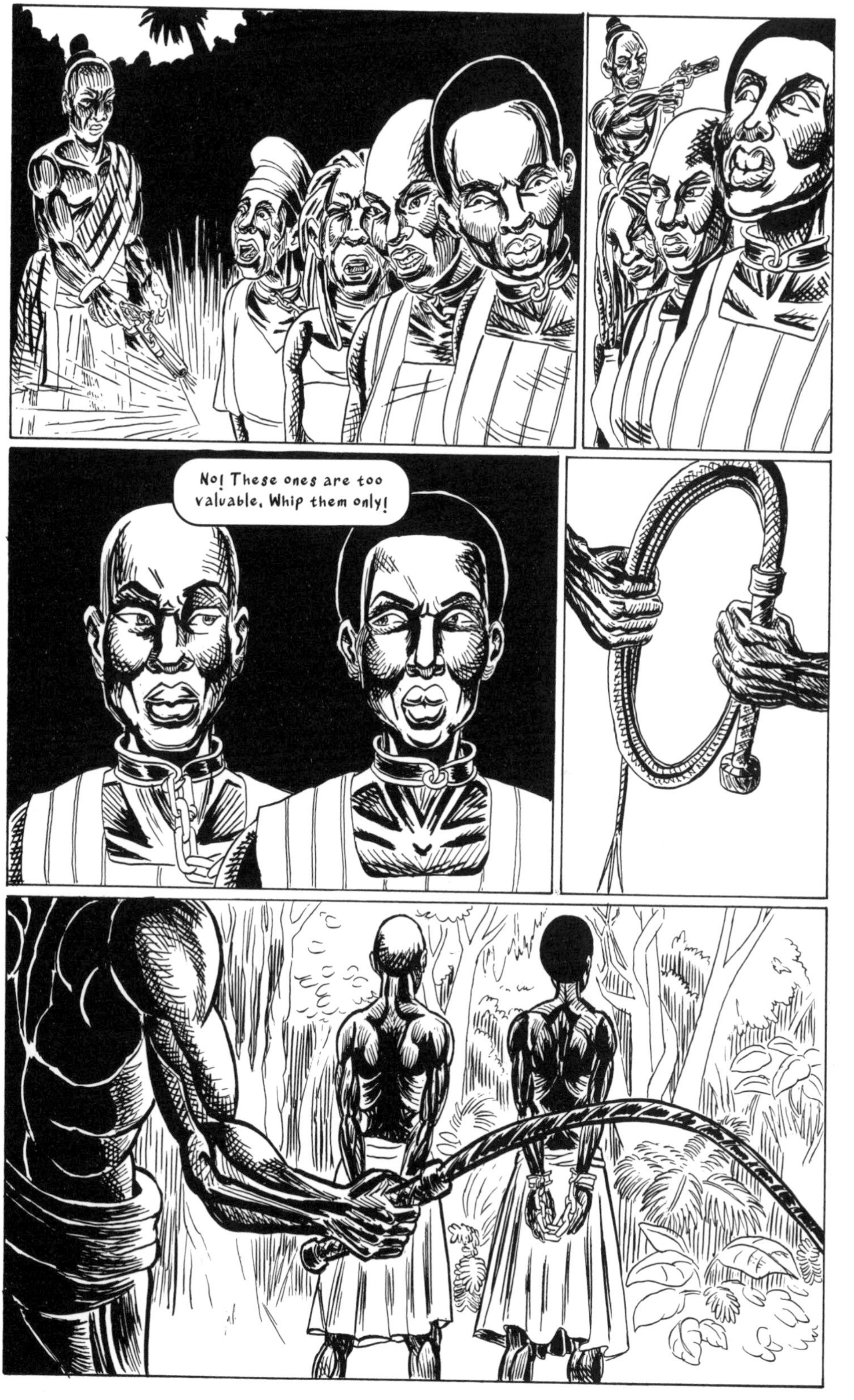
No! These ones are too valuable. Whip them only!

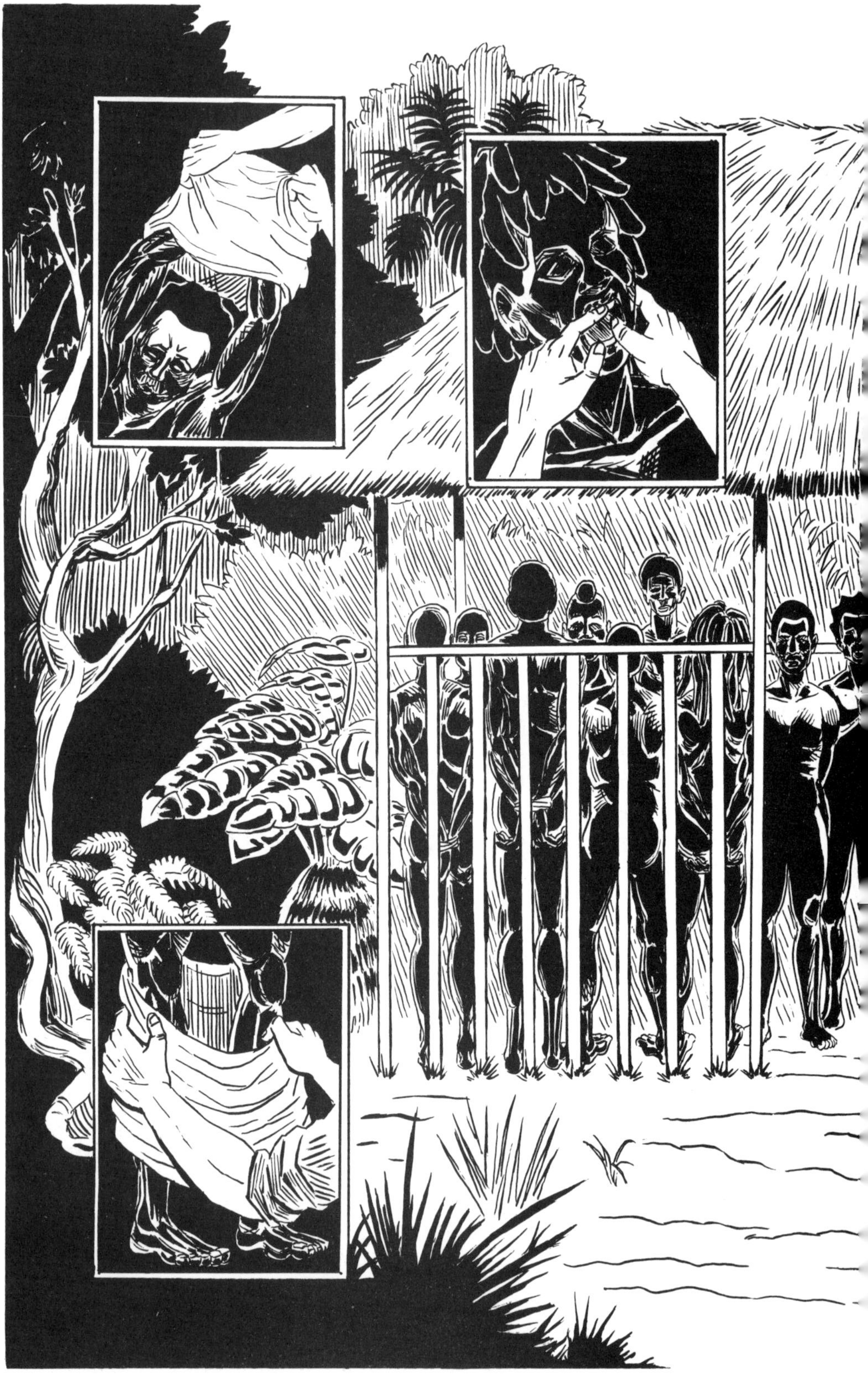

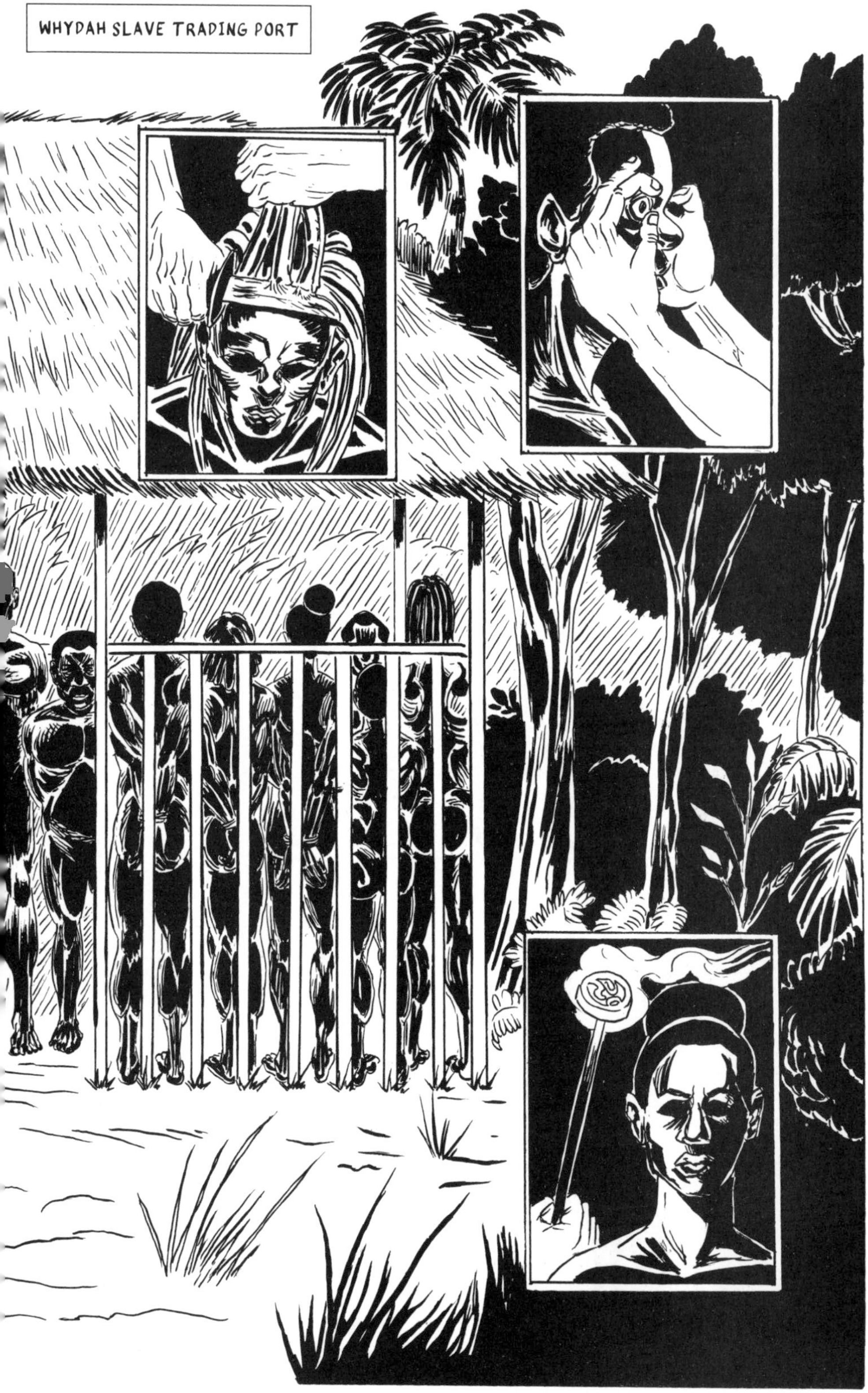
WHYDAH SLAVE TRADING PORT

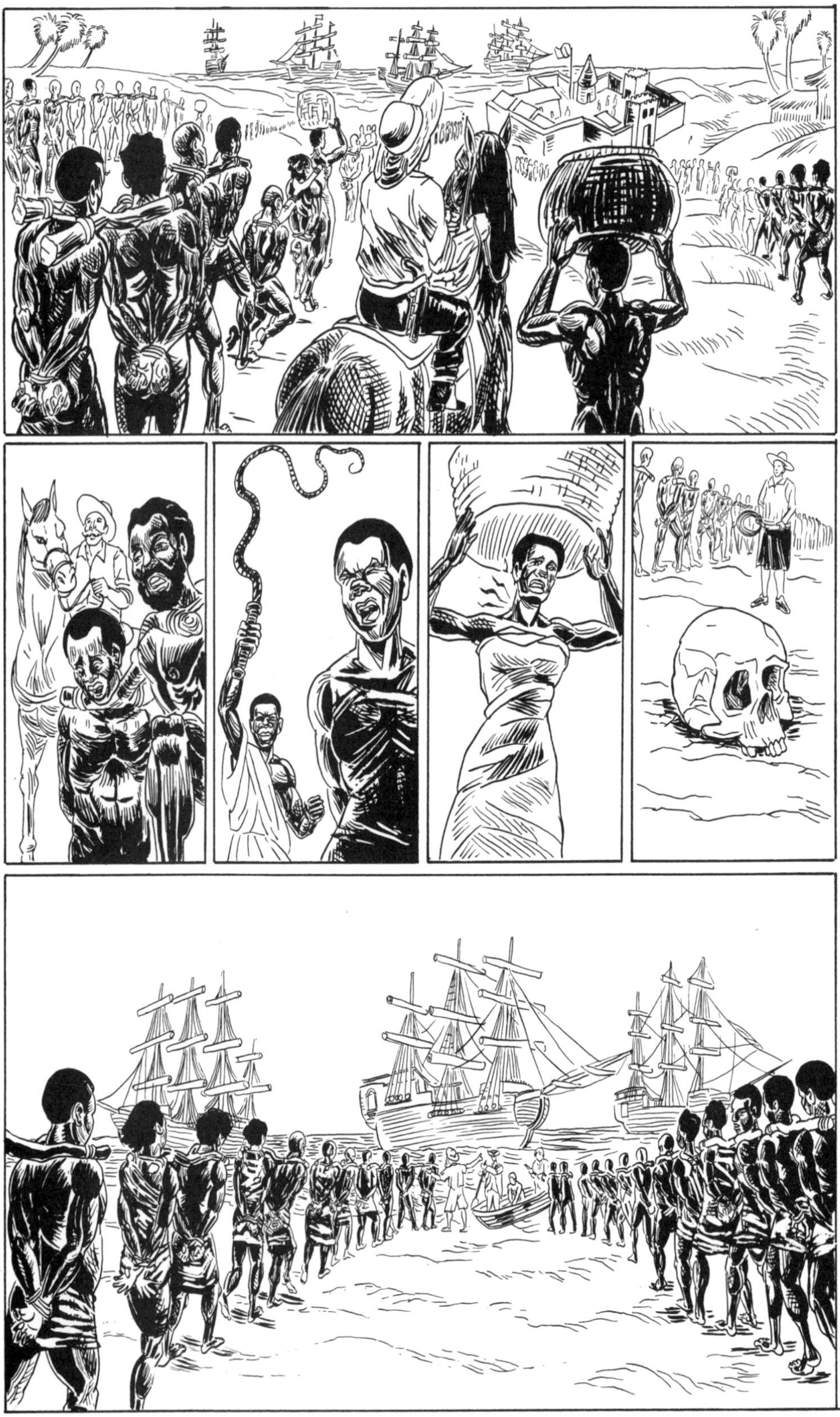

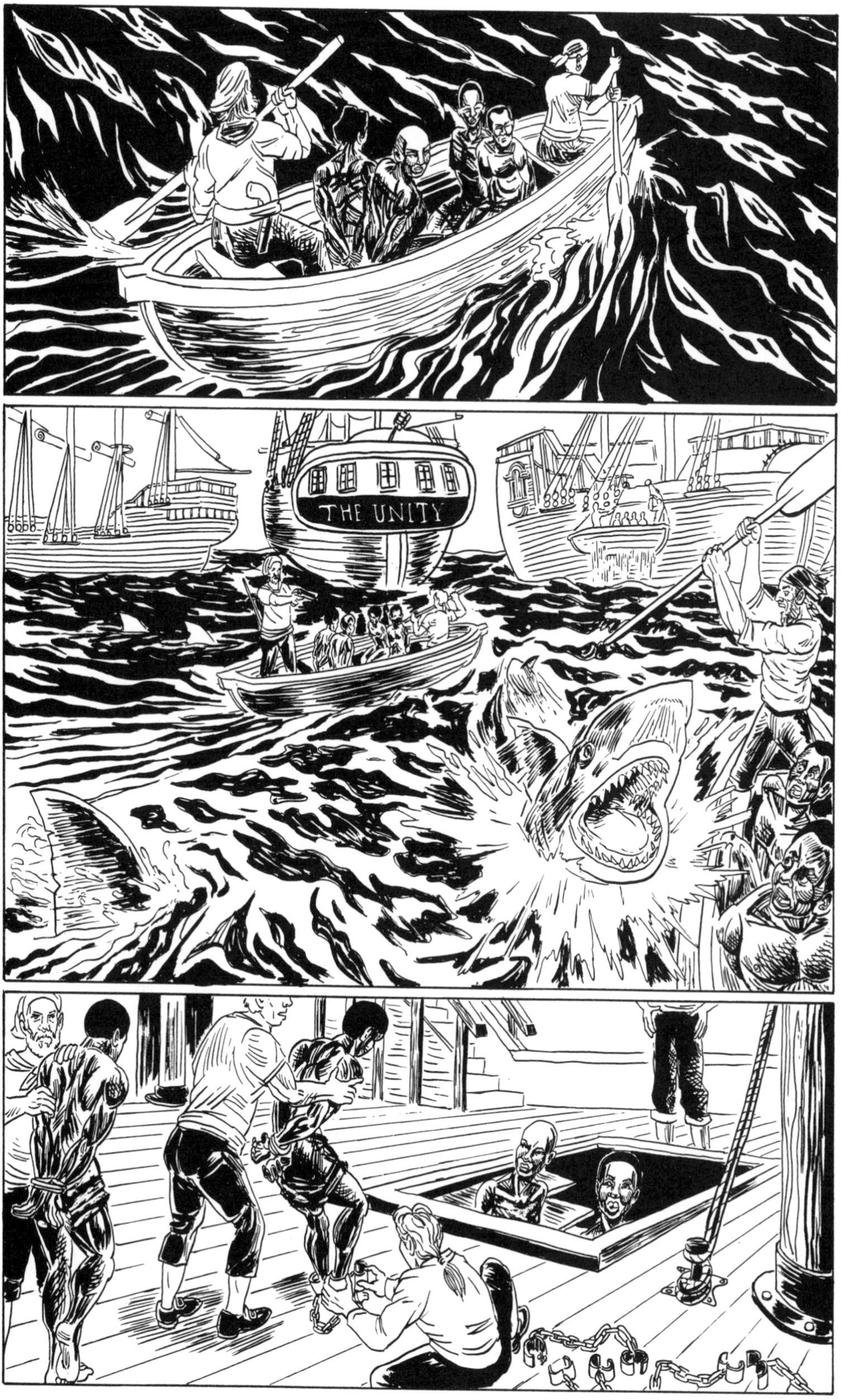
THE UNITY

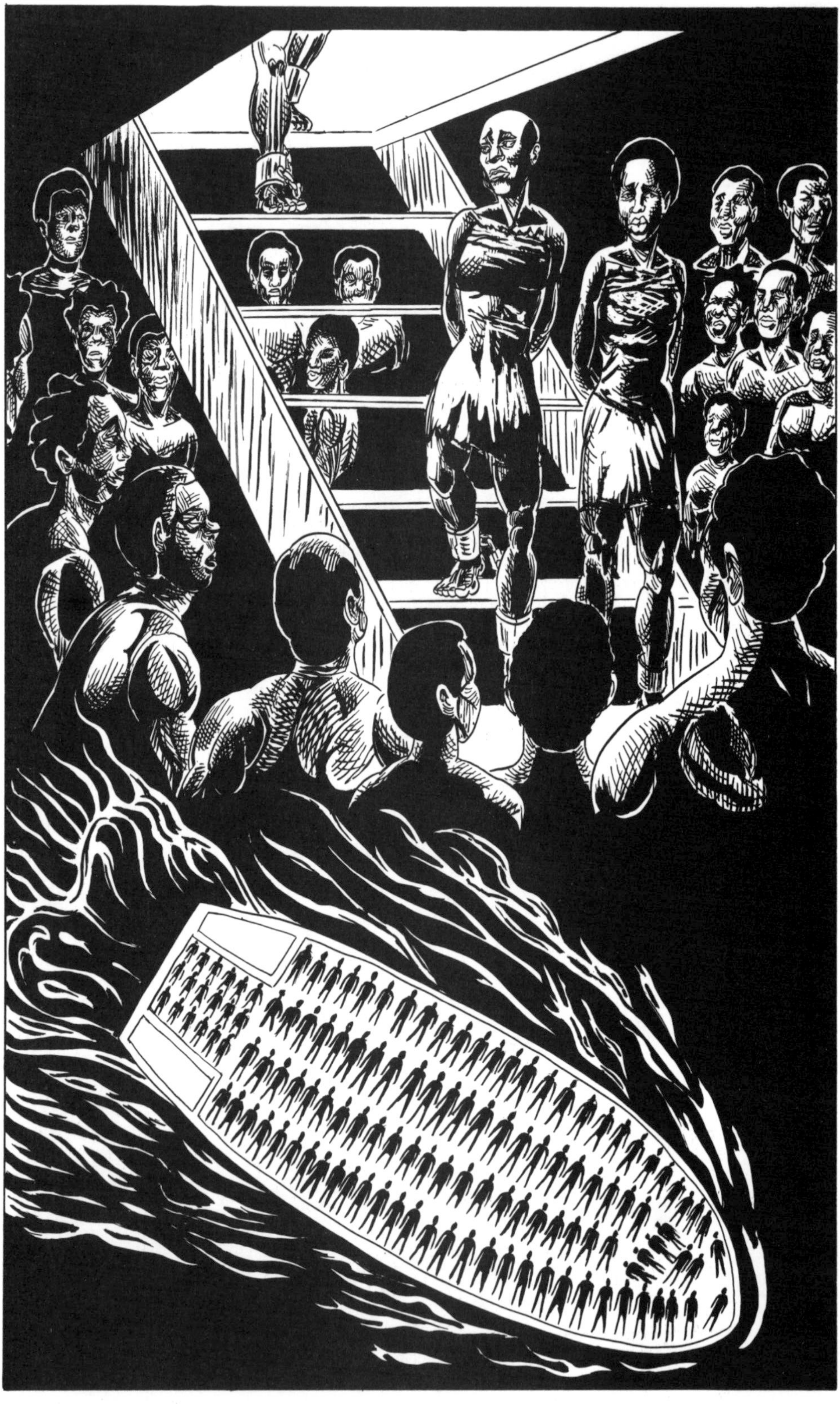

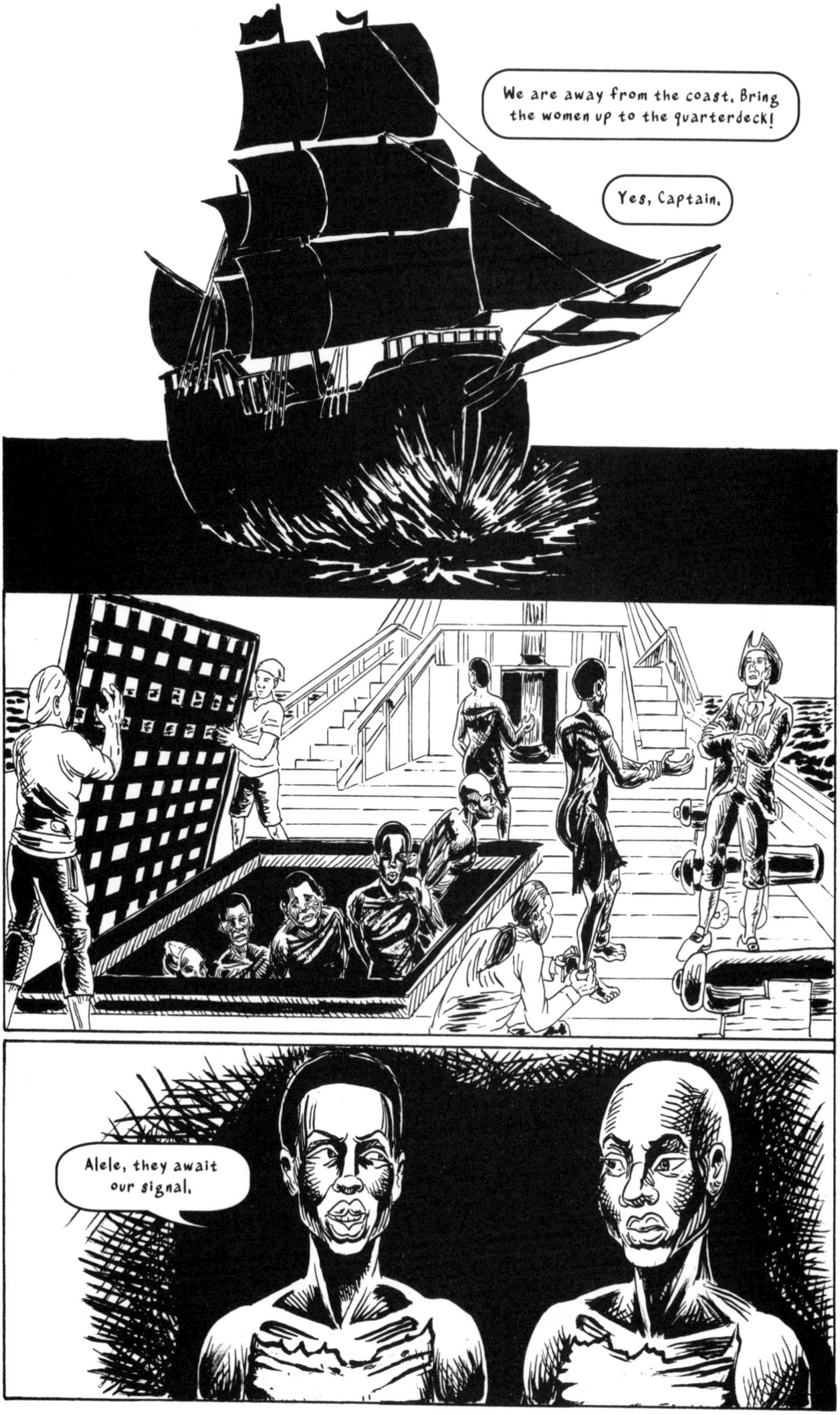
We are away from the coast. Bring the women up to the quarterdeck!
Yes, Captain.
Alele, they await our signal.

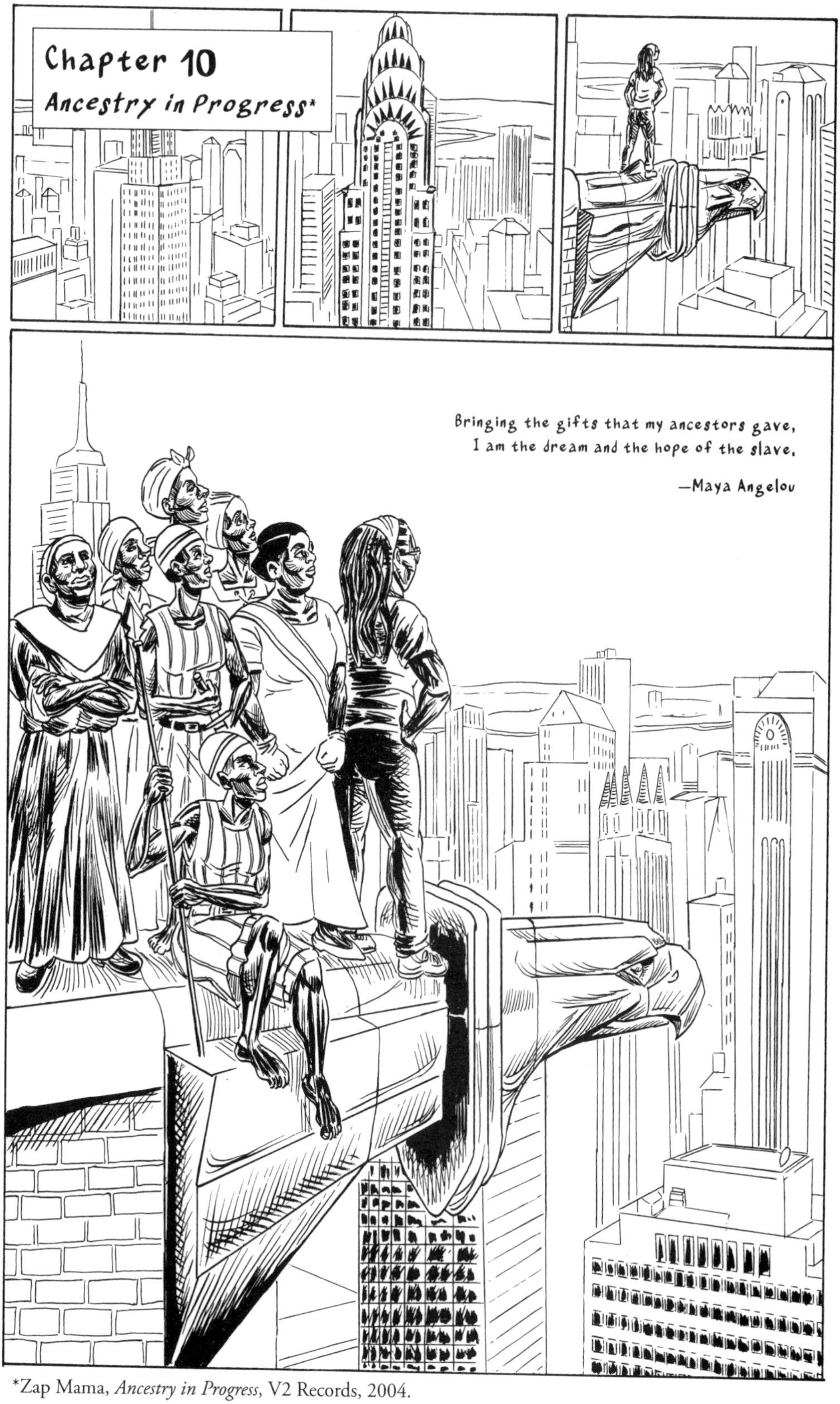
Chapter 10
Ancestry in Progress*
Bringing the gifts that my ancestors gave,
I am the dream and the hope of the slave.
—Maya Angelou

*Zap Mama, *Ancestry in Progress*, V2 Records, 2004.

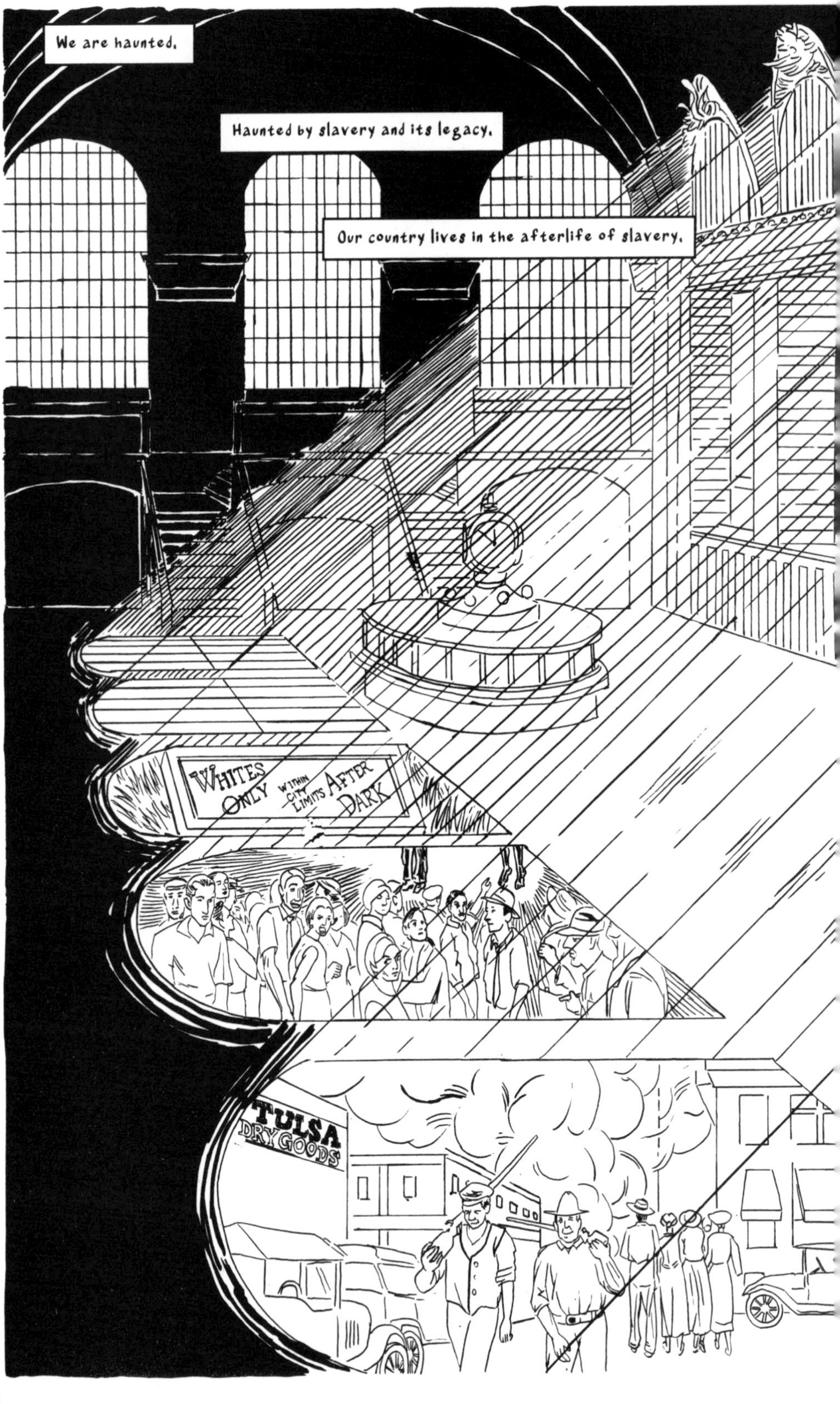
We are haunted.
Haunted by slavery and its legacy.
Our country lives in the afterlife of slavery.
WHITES ONLY WITHIN CITY LIMITS AFTER DARK
TULSA DRY GOODS

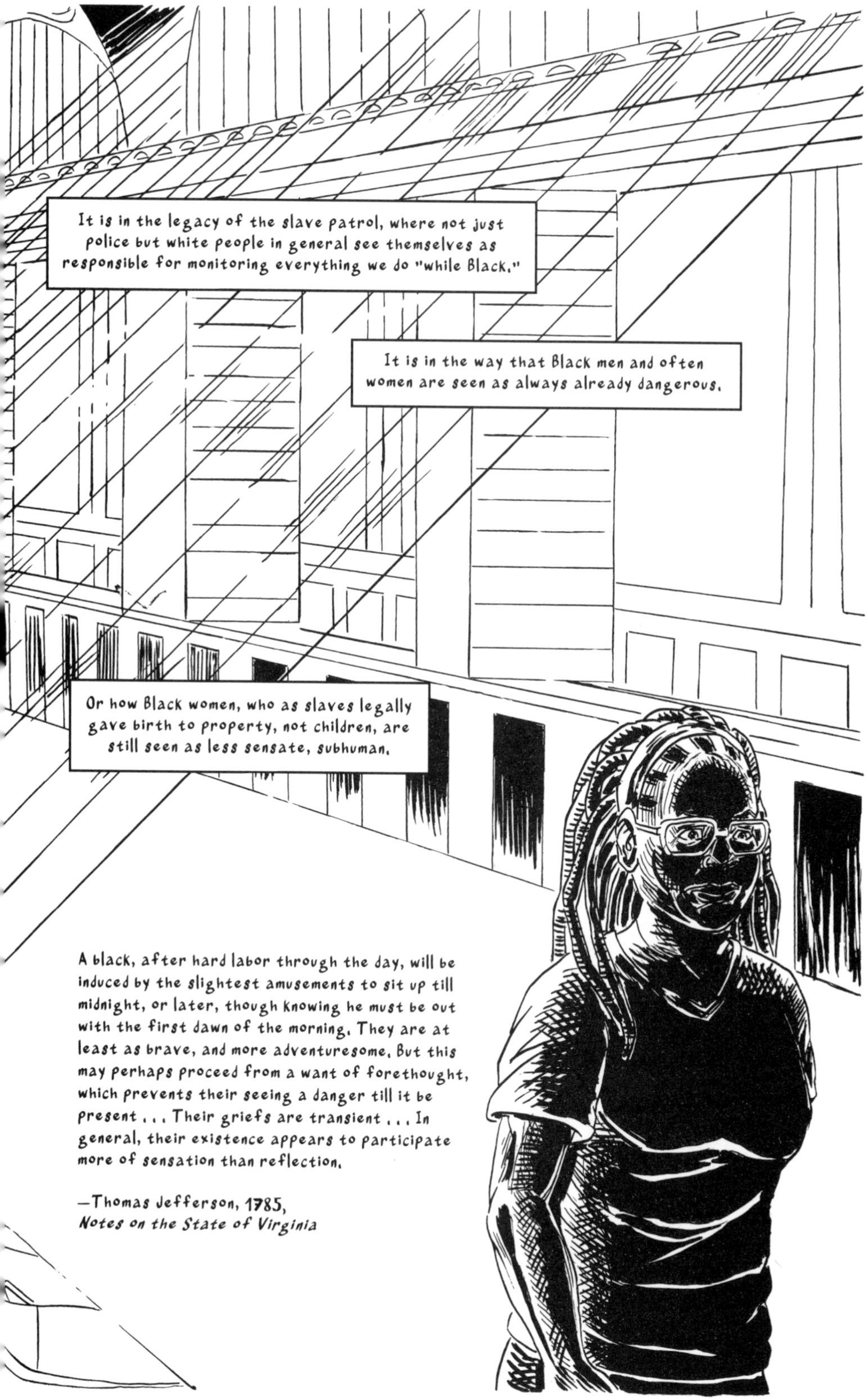
It is in the legacy of the slave patrol, where not just police but white people in general see themselves as responsible for monitoring everything we do "while Black."
It is in the way that Black men and often women are seen as always already dangerous.
Or how Black women, who as slaves legally gave birth to property, not children, are still seen as less sensate, subhuman.
A black, after hard labor through the day, will be induced by the slightest amusements to sit up till midnight, or later, though knowing he must be out with the first dawn of the morning. They are at least as brave, and more adventuresome. But this may perhaps proceed from a want of forethought, which prevents their seeing a danger till it be present . . . Their griefs are transient . . . In general, their existence appears to participate more of sensation than reflection.
—Thomas Jefferson, 1785, *Notes on the State of Virginia*

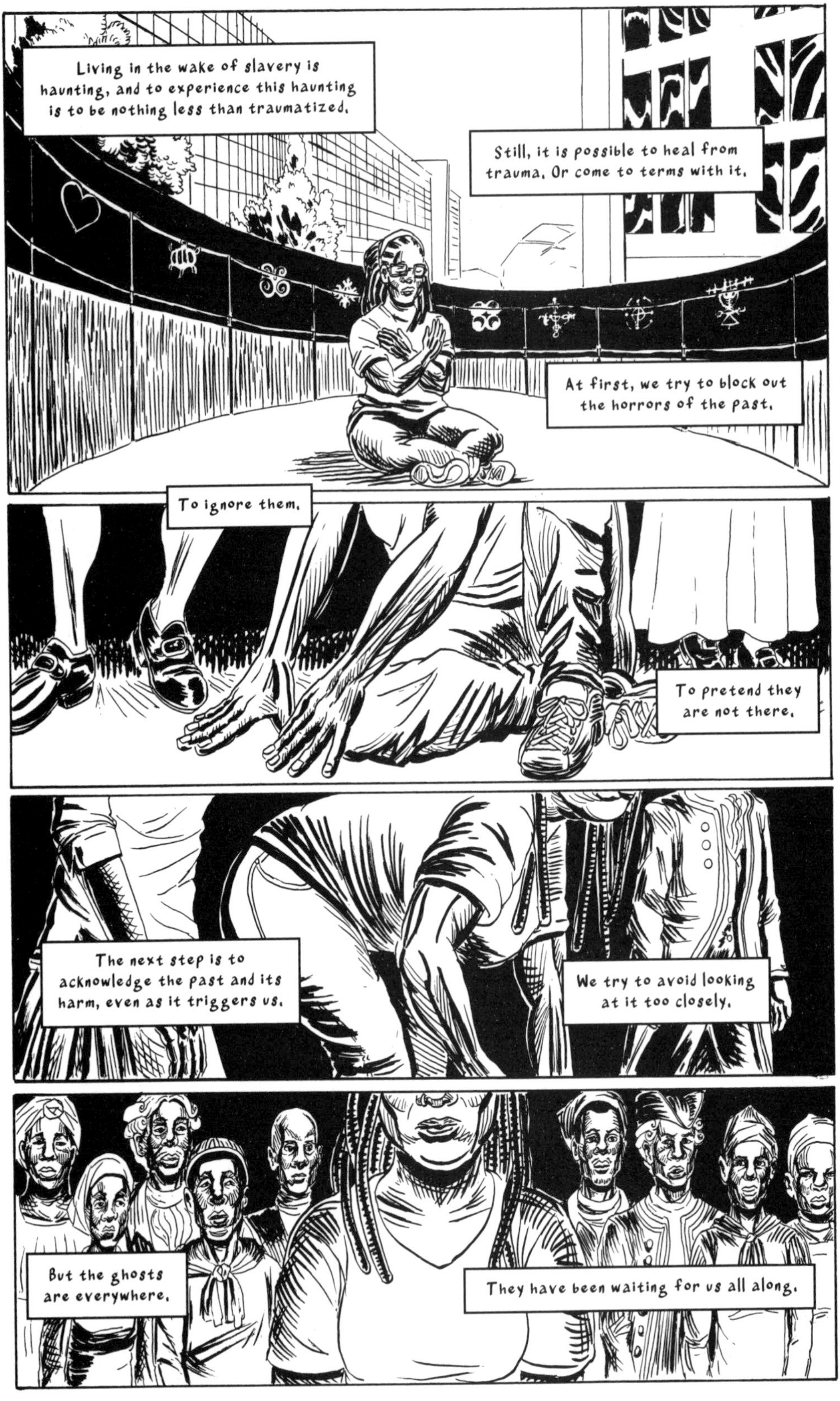
Living in the wake of slavery is haunting, and to experience this haunting is to be nothing less than traumatized.
Still, it is possible to heal from trauma. Or come to terms with it.
At first, we try to block out the horrors of the past.
To ignore them.
To pretend they are not there.
The next step is to acknowledge the past and its harm, even as it triggers us.
We try to avoid looking at it too closely.
But the ghosts are everywhere.
They have been waiting for us all along.

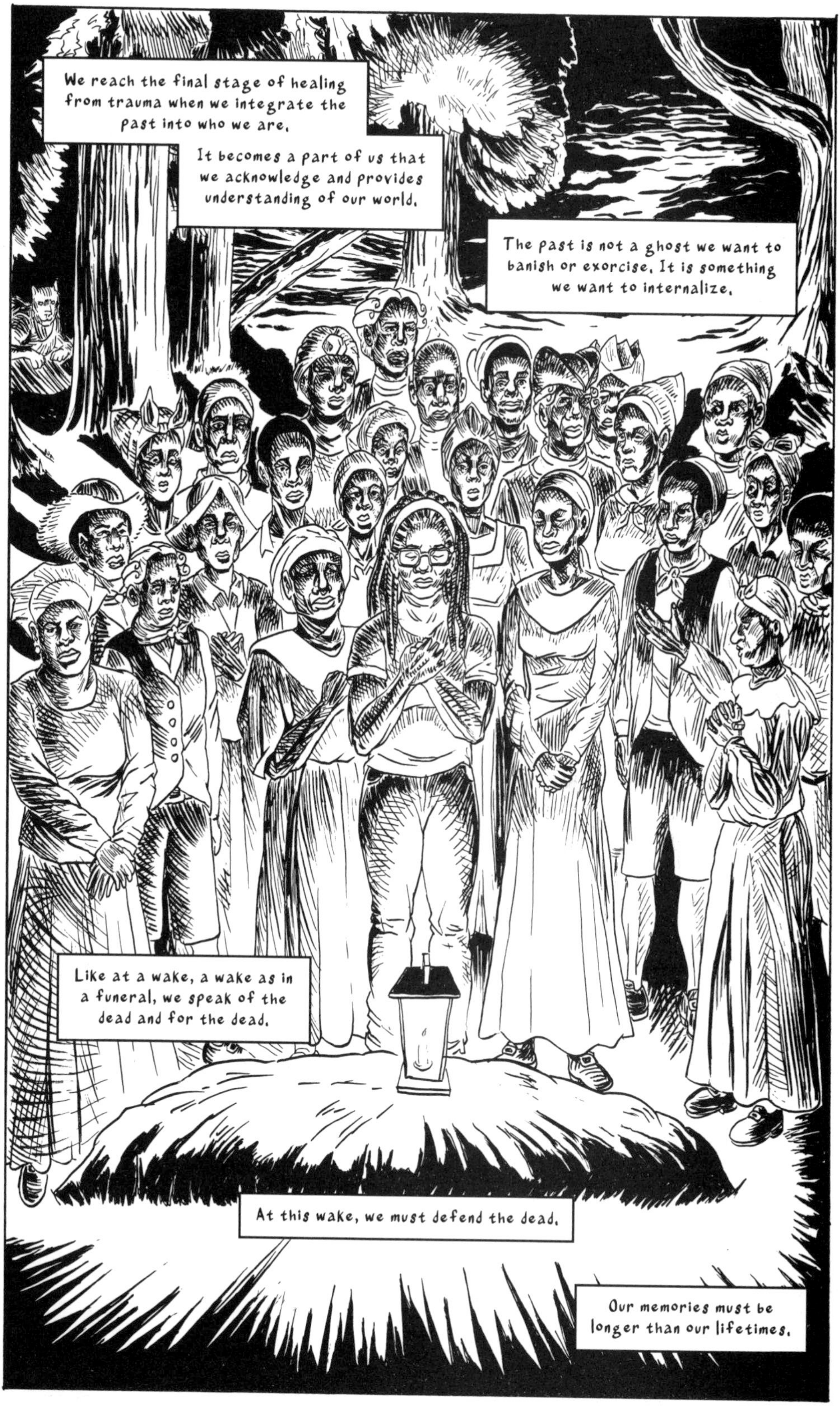

We reach the final stage of healing from trauma when we integrate the past into who we are.
It becomes a part of us that we acknowledge and provides understanding of our world.
The past is not a ghost we want to banish or exorcise. It is something we want to internalize.
Like at a wake, a wake as in a funeral, we speak of the dead and for the dead.
At this wake, we must defend the dead.
Our memories must be longer than our lifetimes.

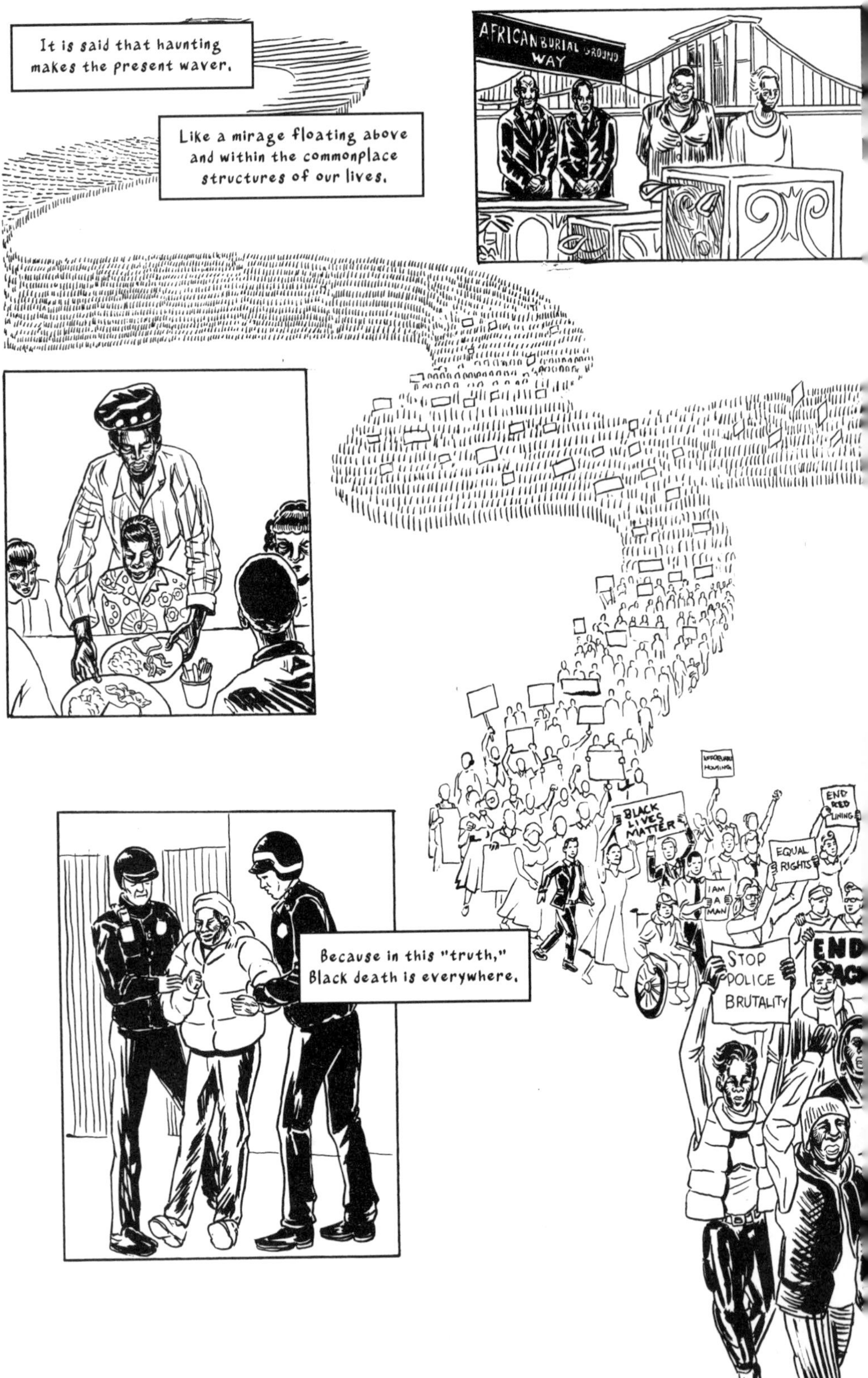
It is said that haunting makes the present waver.
AFRICAN BURIAL GROUND WAY
Like a mirage floating above and within the commonplace structures of our lives.
BLACK LIVES MATTER
END RED LINING
EQUAL RIGHTS
I AM A MAN
Because in this "truth," Black death is everywhere.
STOP POLICE BRUTALITY

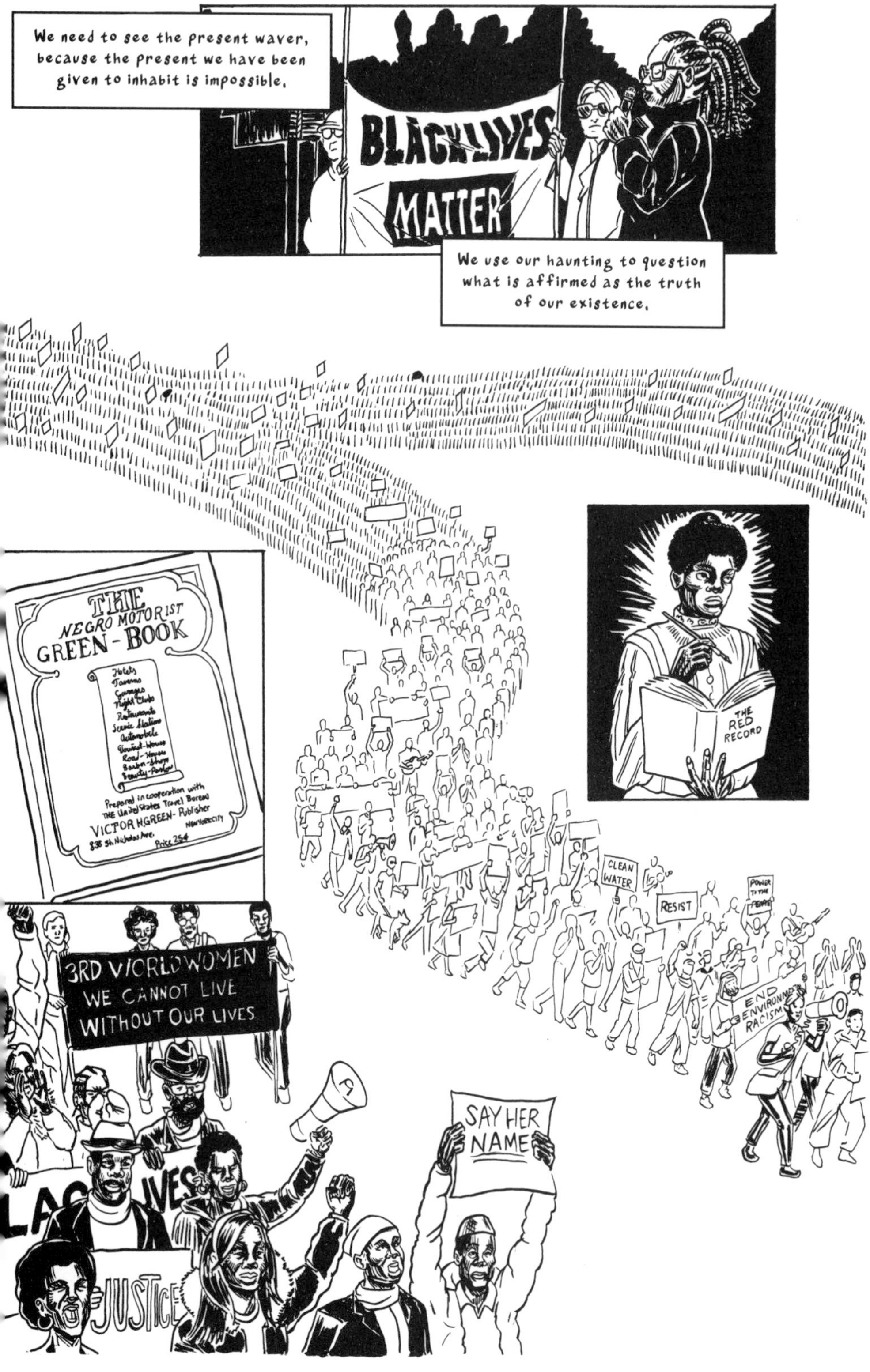

We need to see the present waver, because the present we have been given to inhabit is impossible.
BLACK LIVES MATTER
We use our haunting to question what is affirmed as the truth of our existence.
THE NEGRO MOTORIST GREEN-BOOK
Hotels
Taverns
Night Clubs
Restaurants
Service Stations
Automobile
Road-Houses
Barber-Shops
Beauty-Parlors
Prepared in cooperation with THE United States Travel Bureau
VICTOR H. GREEN - Publisher
838 St. Nicholas Ave.
NEW YORK CITY
Price 25¢
THE RED RECORD
CLEAN WATER
RESIST
POWER TO THE PEOPLE
END ENVIRONM RACISM
3RD WORLD WOMEN WE CANNOT LIVE WITHOUT OUR LIVES
SAY HER NAME
JUSTICE

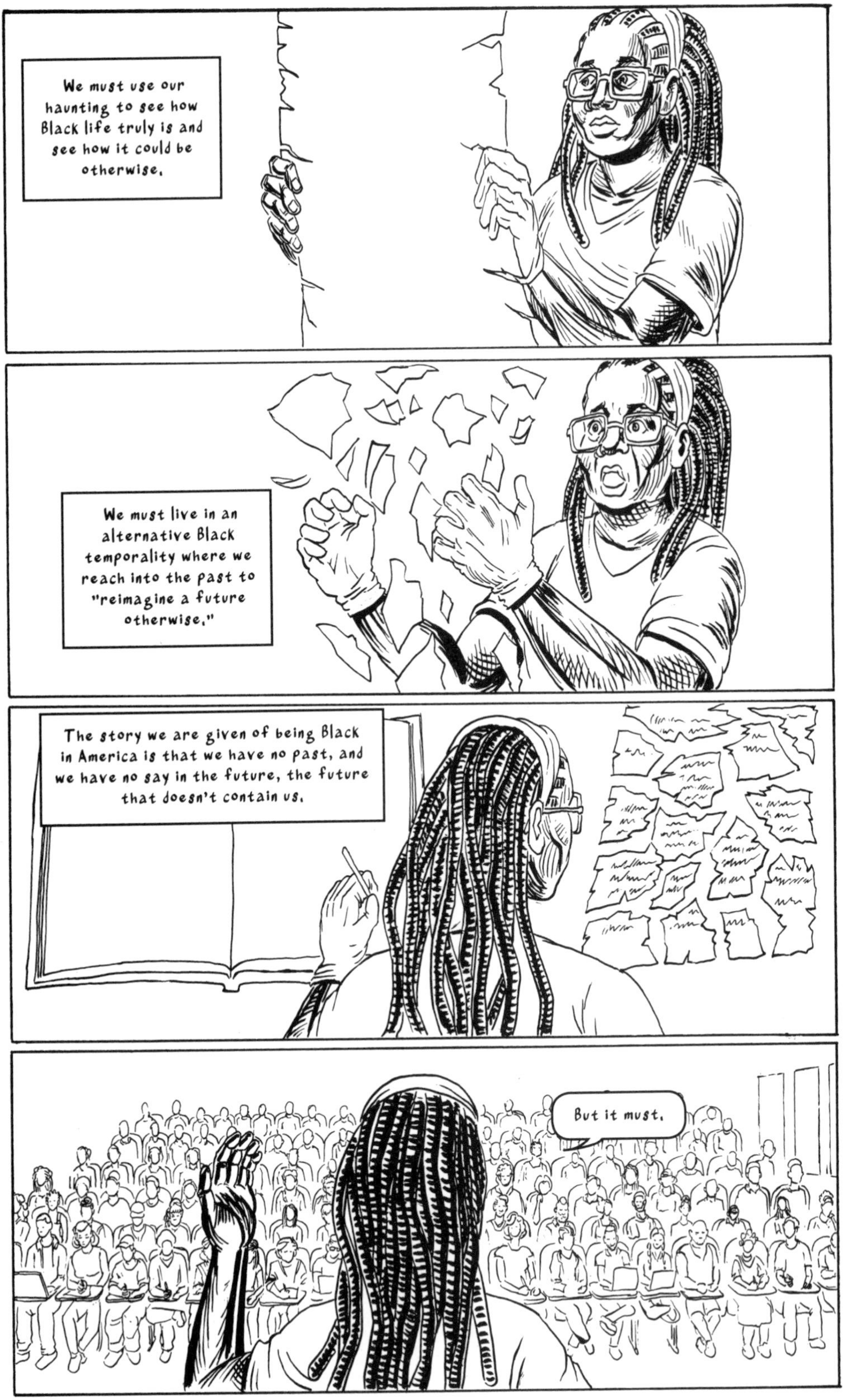
We must use our haunting to see how Black life truly is and see how it could be otherwise.
We must live in an alternative Black temporality where we reach into the past to "reimagine a future otherwise."
The story we are given of being Black in America is that we have no past, and we have no say in the future, the future that doesn't contain us.
But it must.

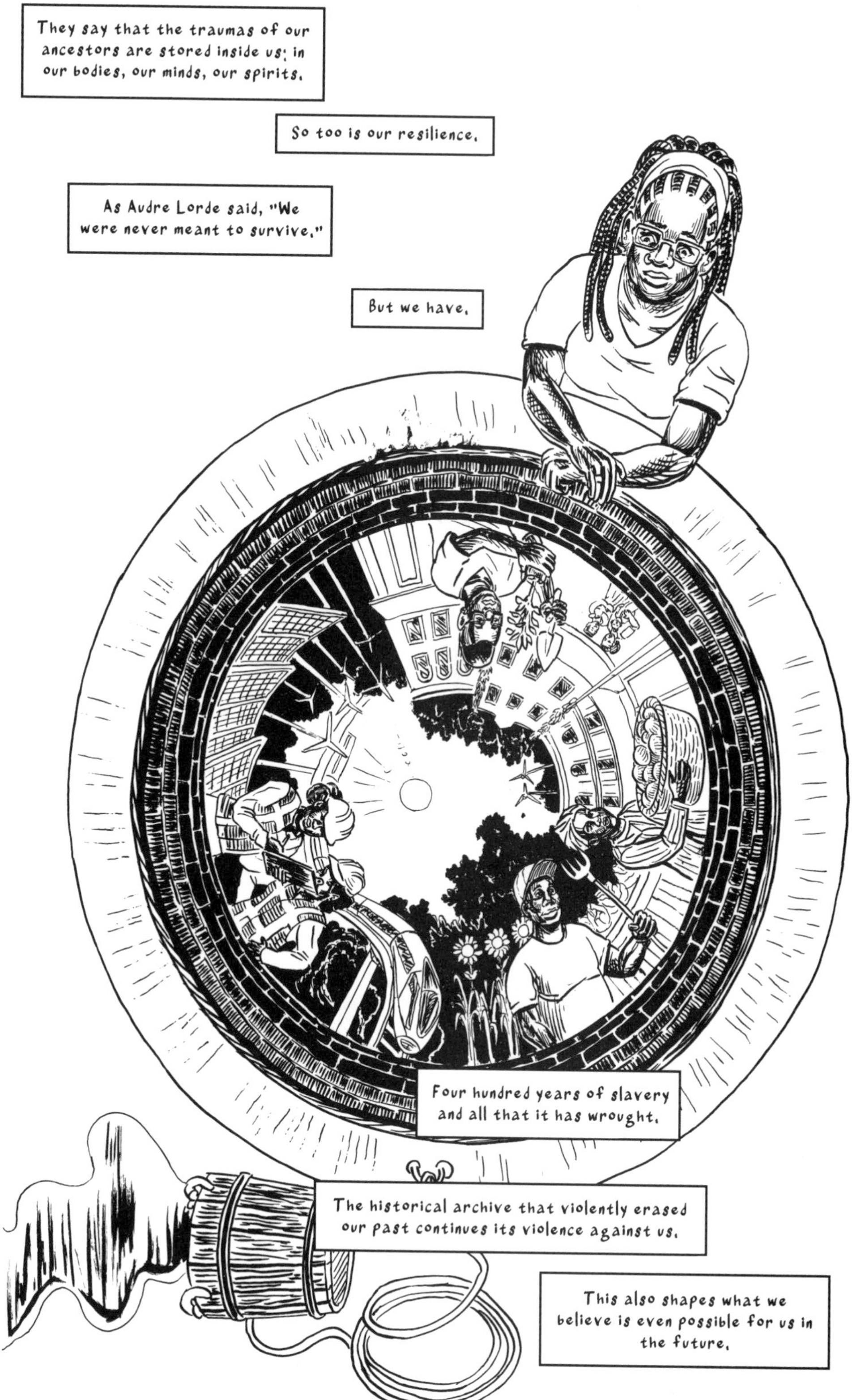
They say that the traumas of our ancestors are stored inside us: in our bodies, our minds, our spirits.
So too is our resilience.
As Audre Lorde said, "We were never meant to survive."
But we have.
Four hundred years of slavery and all that it has wrought.
The historical archive that violently erased our past continues its violence against us.
This also shapes what we believe is even possible for us in the future.

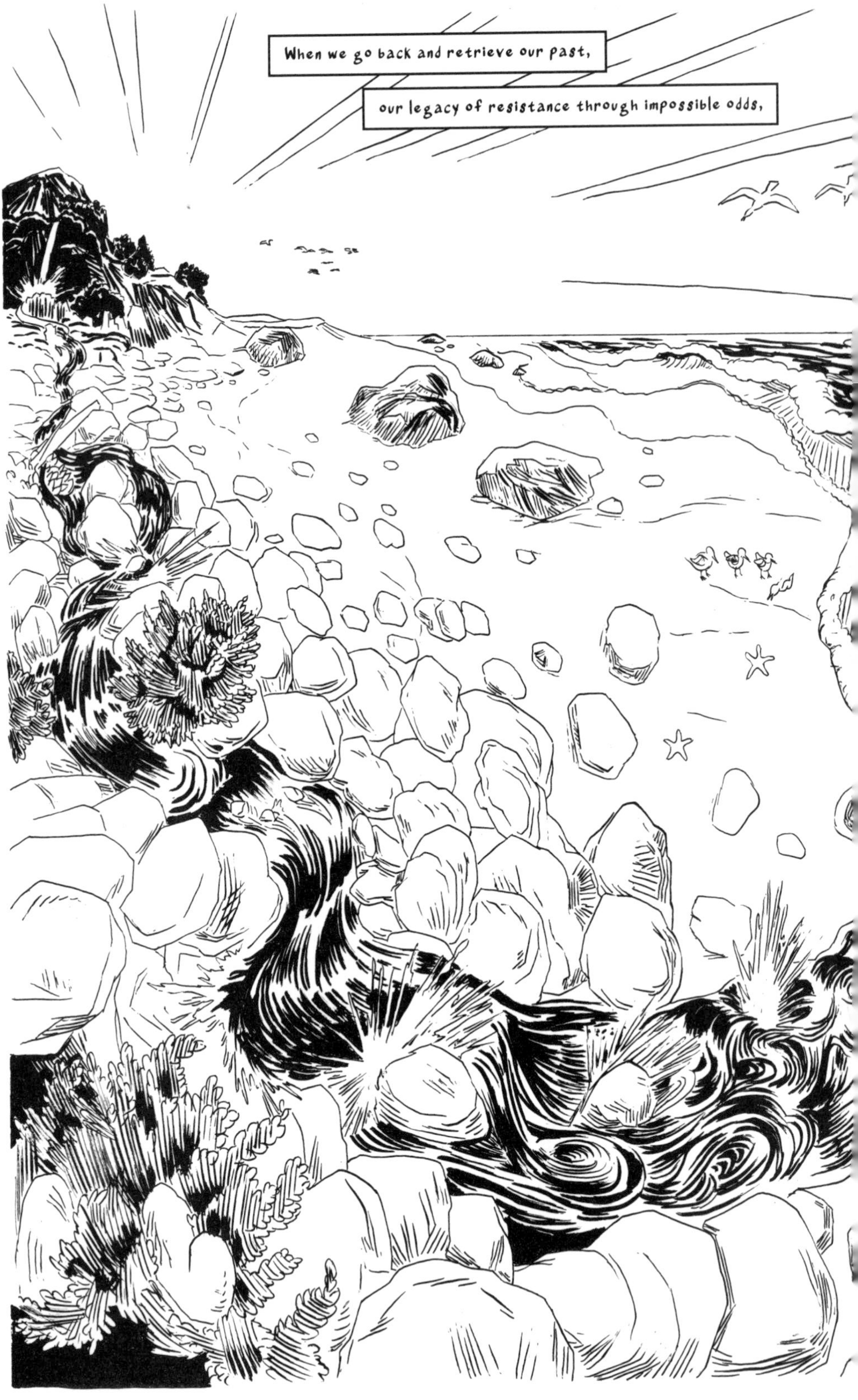
When we go back and retrieve our past,
our legacy of resistance through impossible odds,

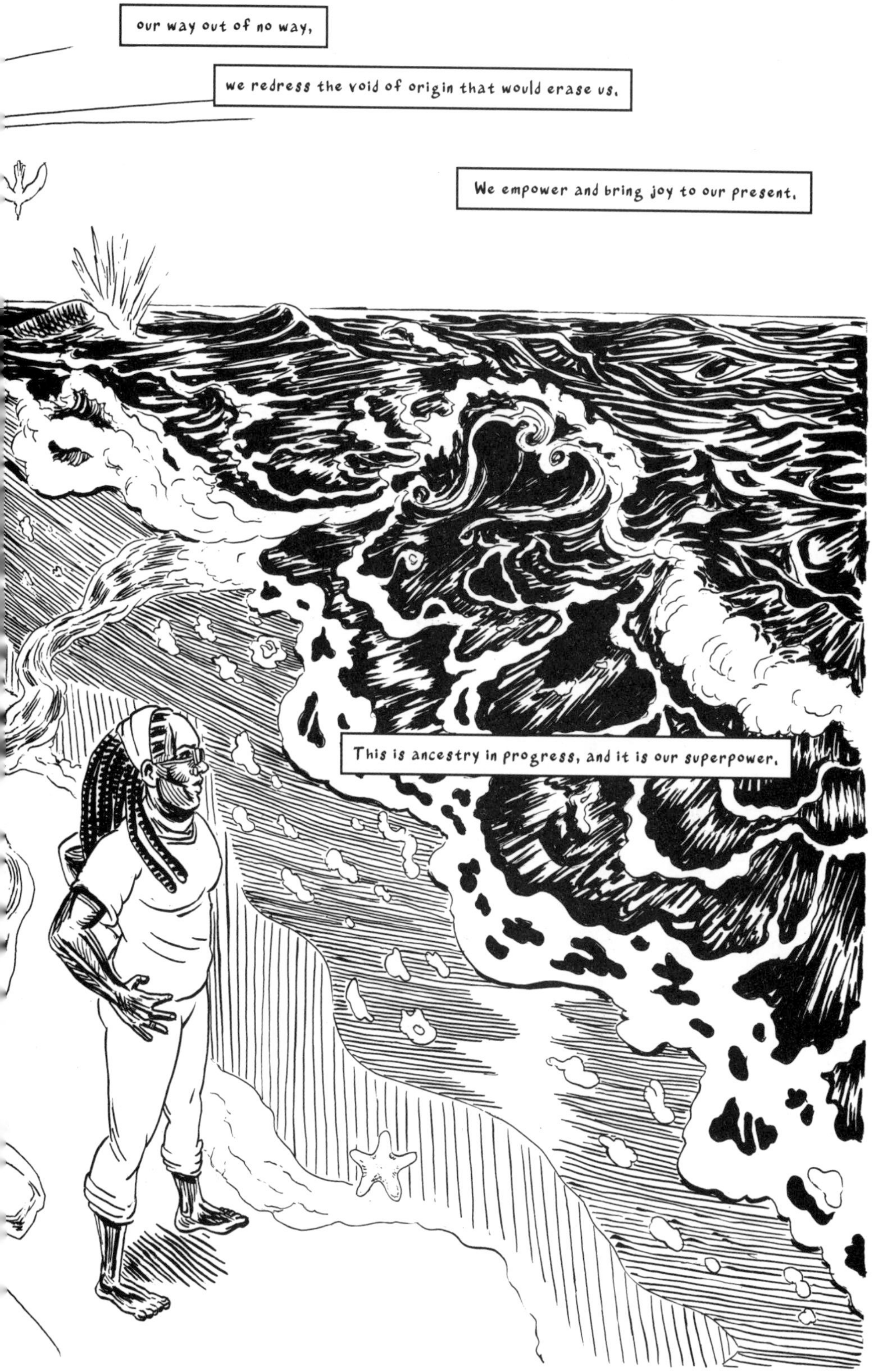
our way out of no way,
we redress the void of origin that would erase us.
We empower and bring joy to our present.
This is ancestry in progress, and it is our superpower.

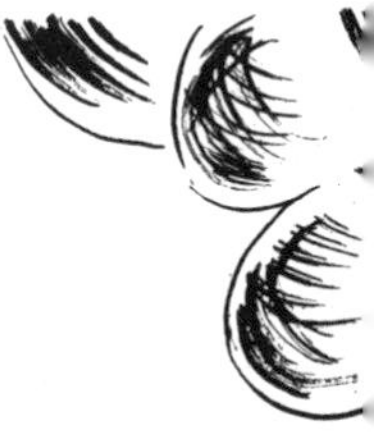

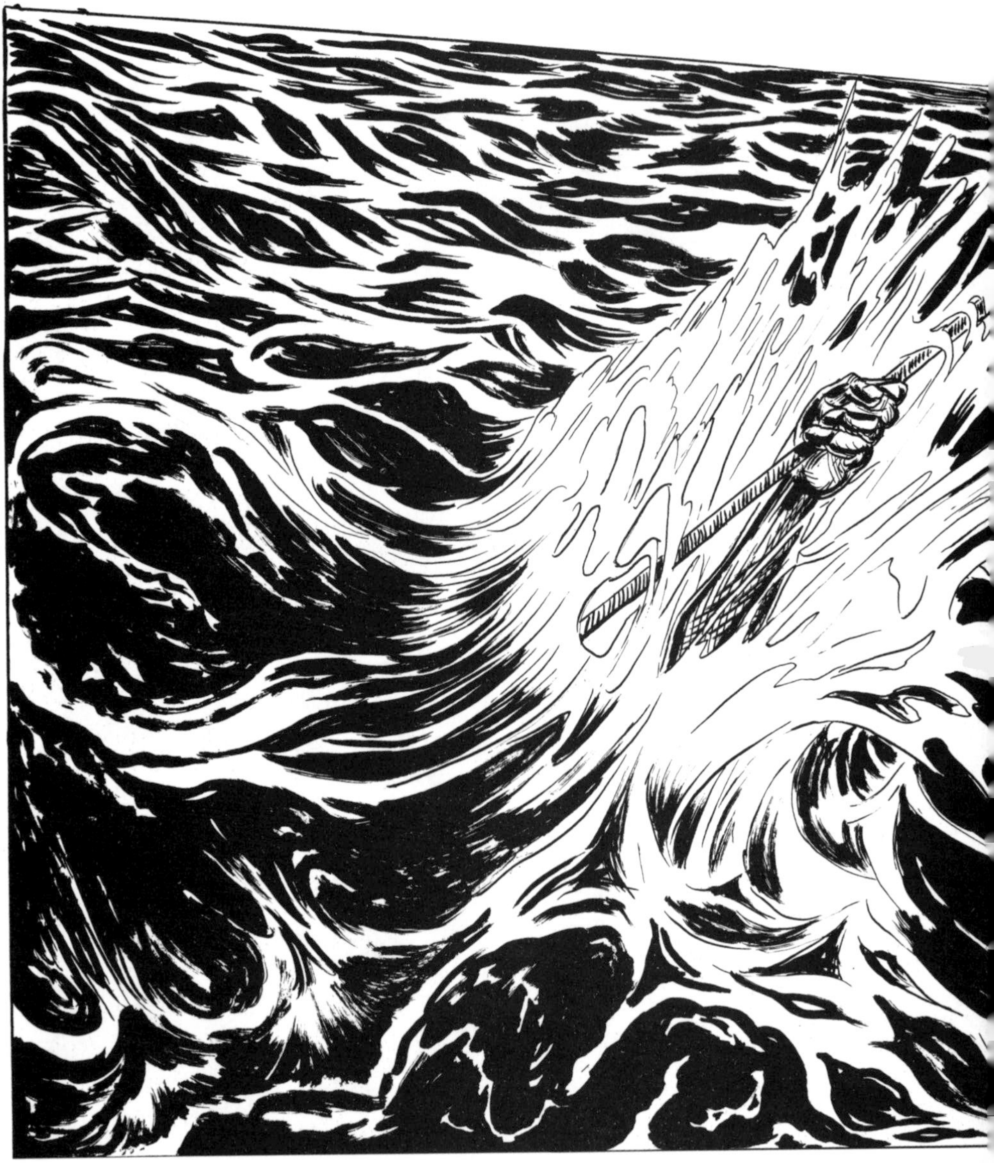

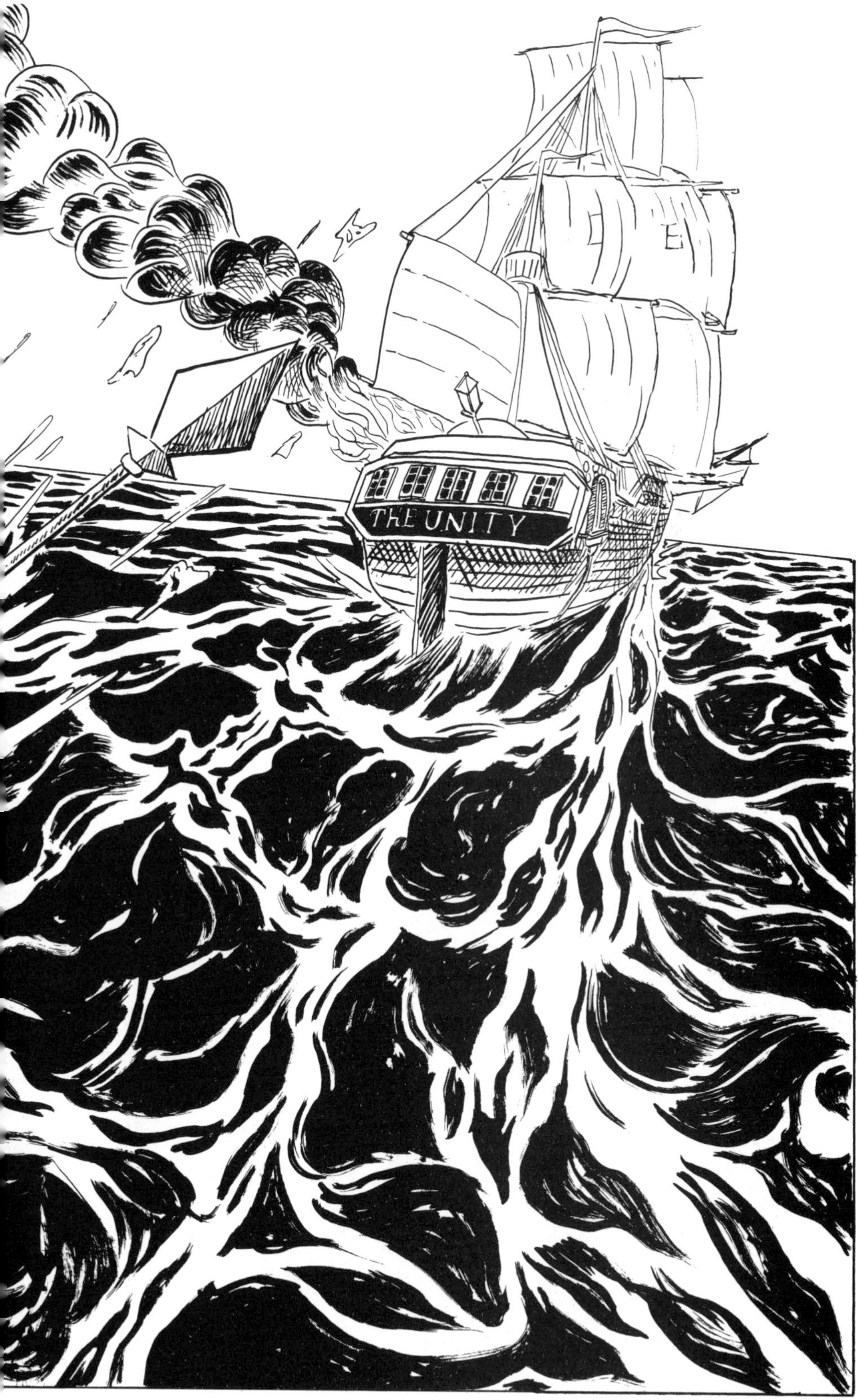
THE UNITY

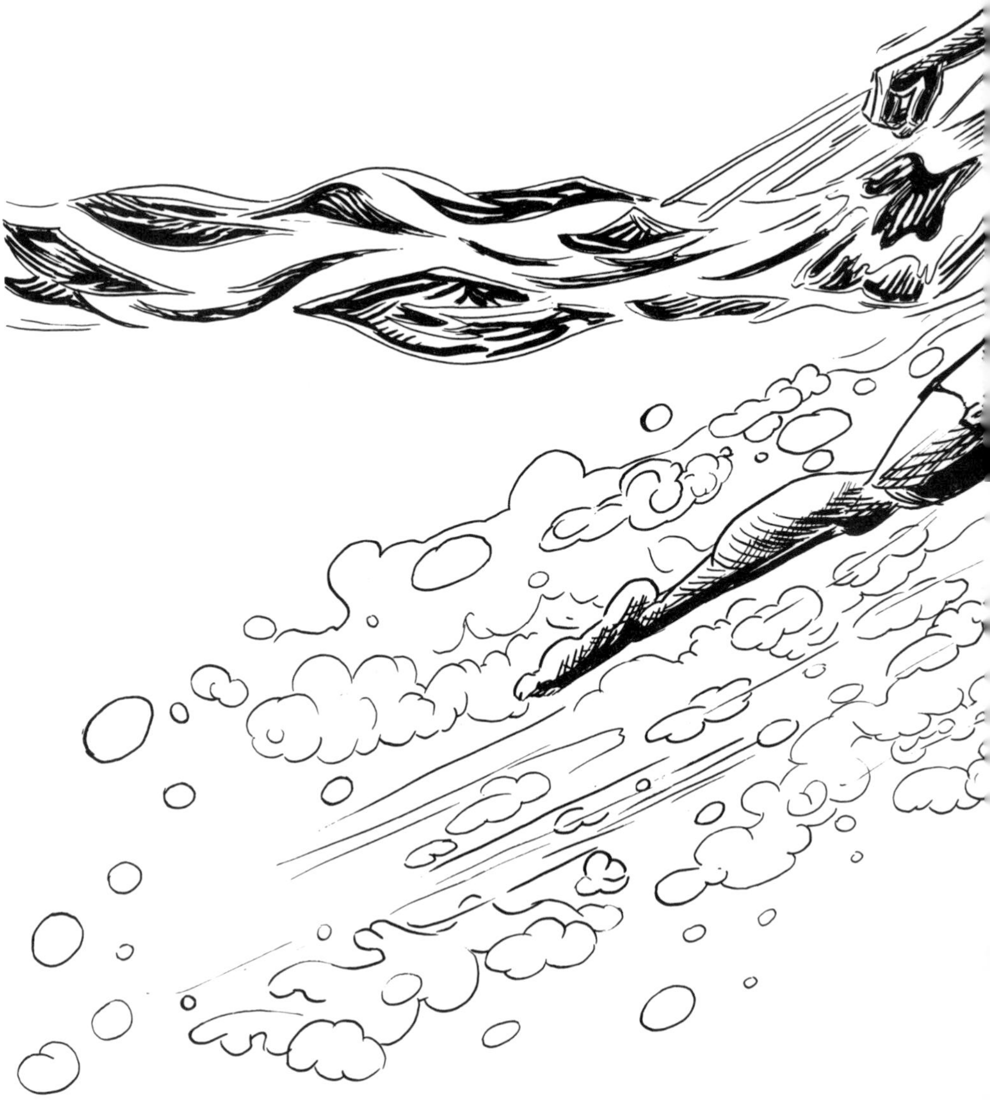

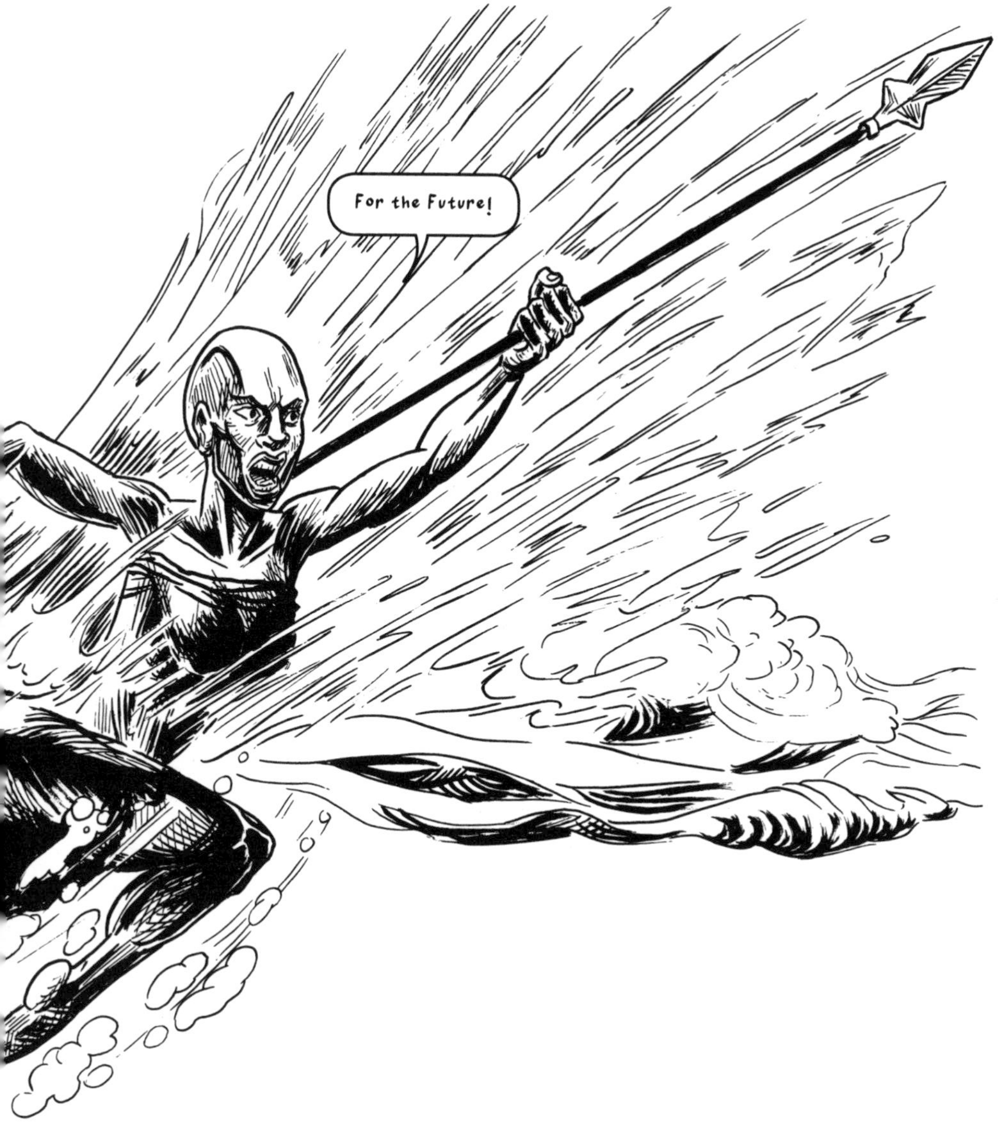
For the Future!

Acknowledgments

I wrote this book for my grandmother Harriet Thorpe Hall (1860–1927), for all the women who fought slavery, and for all of us living in its afterlife.

This book would not have happened without the support of Bea Hammond, my partner of thirty-two years. After the fourth time I was racist-fired from a professorship or teaching position, we agreed that I should step out of institutions of white supremacy, and Bea supported the family, giving me the time to figure out what was next for me. That turned out to be turning my dissertation and published articles into this graphic novel. Our son, Caleb, has helped me stay focused on what is truly important, even in the face of adversity. I also joyfully thank all of *Wake*'s supporters on Kickstarter, who gave me the resources to get a start on this book, and even more importantly, created buzz and visibility. And thanks Easton Smith for contacting the press about the Kickstarter campaign entirely on his own initiative. Special thanks here to Sara Ramirez for using their Twitter account to recommend my Kickstarter project to their gazillion followers.

Anjali Singh is my agent and my angel. Everyone thanks their agents in their acknowledgments, but Anjali picked up a somewhat abstract idea and taught me everything from how to write a book proposal to how to deal with a publishing auction. I literally knew nothing about this process and would never have thought in a million years that my passion project would be of interest to more than a handful of people. Anjali helped me see that this book was so much more than that and kept reminding me until I began to believe it. Thanks to Tananarive Due and John Jennings for connecting me to Anjali. I had the honor of Anjali calling me to say she wanted to represent me, and ever since she has fought for me and this project like a mother lion. And she even responds to my texts on weekends.

I want to thank my friend Kate Savage, who helped me think about this project in its pre-infancy, and for suggesting I be a character in this book. Kate also connected me to Hugo Martínez, who has been a diligent, thorough, and brilliant artist to work with. Hugo, your art has brought this work to life. And thanks to both Vita Ayala and Jason Little, who helped me understand how to write a graphic novel script. Deep thanks go to Sarula Bao and Caroline Brewer, who joined Team *Wake* right after it was picked up by S&S and managed pre-production. They held my hand and gave me confidence as I fumbled in the dark, trying to shift from an academic writer to a visual writer. And special thanks to Sarah Beth Hufbauer, who has been my dearest friend for over forty years, and has had my back through some very dark times. Thank you for helping me edit the final draft of this book in the midst of a pandemic over several five-hour phone calls when I had lost all sense of motivation and direction.

I also must thank Dawn Davis, the publisher and original editor of *Wake*. She believed in this project from jump and her edits made this a better book. And after Dawn left S&S, Carina Guiterman smoothly stepped in as editor, shepherding me and this book through the dizzying publishing process with the help of Chelcee Johns and Lashanda Anakwah. Thanks also to Kayley Hoffman for proofreading, Jon Evans for copyediting, and Morgan Hart, the production editor. Brianna Scharfenberg of publicity and Leila Siddiqui of marketing joined Team *Wake* with amazing enthusiasm for the work and patience with me as I kept forgetting which of them was in charge of what.

Donna Haraway, my feminist theory professor and dissertation advisor, has supported my academic work on women in slave revolts in so many ways, continuously, even fifteen years after receiving my PhD. A rare and generous advocate, her belief in the importance of this work helped me stay on course.

Finally I want to acknowledge my parents. My mother, Gwendolyn Midlo Hall, for showing me that being a historian can have a profound impact on the world. My father, Harry Haywood (1898–1985), for telling me stories of my grandmother, giving me great books to read at an early age, and showing me through lived example how to be brave and proud in the face of constant white supremacist violence—and to never give up the fight.

—Rebecca Hall

For this incredible opportunity, I thank Dr. Rebecca Hall. Also Kate Savage, our Kickstarter supporters, Leah Champagne, Jesse Moss, Dan Brawner, Gene Menerat, Brett Thompson, Luke Howard, Mike Vulpes, Bob Snead. Michael Lapinski, Sally Richardson, Kalli Padget, Erika Witt, Jonah Quinn, and Fernando Lopez.

—Hugo Martínez

Selected Primary Sources

1712 Revolt

Boston News-Letter, April 7–12, 1712.

Coroner's Inquest of William Asht, April 9, 1712. Coroner's Inquest of Augustus Grassett, April 9, 1712. Misc. MSS. NYC, Box 4, Manuscripts Collection, New-York Historical Society.

Coroner's Inquest of Adrian Hooglant, April 9, 1712. New York Public Library Manuscripts and Archives.

Governor Robert Hunter. Letters to the Lords of Trade. Public Records Office, London, CO5 1091.

Minutes of the Privy Council, 1712. Public Records Office, London, PC2/A84.

Minutes of the Common Council of the City of New York, 1675–1776. New York: Dodd, Mead, 1905.

Minutes of the Supreme Court of Judicature, 1712. Pp. 399–427. New York City Municipal Archives.

Minutes of the Quarter Sessions, 1694–1731. Pp 214–241. New York City Municipal Archives.

O'Callaghan, E. B. *The Documentary History of the State of New-York*. Albany: Weed, Parsons, 1850.

———. *Documents Relative to the Colonial History of New York*. Albany: Weed, Parsons, 1855.

———. *Calendar of New York Colonial Commissions, 1680–1770*. New York: The New-York Historical Society, 1929.

Philipse, Adolphus. Will of Adolphus Philipse. Manuscripts Division Collection, New-York Historical Society.

The Laws of His Majesties Colony of New York. London: William Bradford, 1719.

Van Dam, Rip. Inventory of the Estate of Rip Van Dam, 1749. Misc. MSS. NYC, Manuscripts Collection, New-York Historical Society.

1708 Revolt

Boston News-Letter, February 10, 1708; February 1623, 1708.

Lord Cornbury. Letter to the Board of Trade, February 10, 1708. In *Documents Relative to the Colonial History of the City of New York*, E. B. O'Callaghan, p. 39. Albany: Weed, Parsons, 1855.

Riker, James. Papers. New York Public Library, Manuscripts and Archives.

Town Minutes of Newtown. New York: Historical Records Survey, 1940.

Slave Ship Sources

Atlantic Slave Trade Database, https://www.slavevoyages.org/voyage/database.

Bandinel, James. *Some Account of the Trade in Slaves from Africa as Connected with Europe and America*. London: Longman, Brown, 1842.

Burton, Richard. *A Mission to Gelele, King of Dahomey*. New York: Praeger Publishers, 1966.

Brooke, Richard. *Liverpool as it was During the Last Quarter of the Eighteenth Century*. P. 236. Liverpool: Liverpool Publishing House, 1853.

Donnan, Elizabeth. *Documents Illustrative of the History of the Slave Trade to America*. 4 vols. New York: Octagon Books, 1965.

Hair, Paul, ed. *Barbot on Guinea: The Writings of Jean Barbot on West Africa, 1678–1712*. 2 vols. London: The Hakluyt Society, 1992.

Hastings, Hugh. *Ecclesiastical Records, State of New York, Vol. III*. Albany: J. B. Lyon Company, 1902.

House of Lords Records Office. Misc. slave ship captains' logs and surgeons' logs. London.

Snelgrave, Captain William. *A New Account of Some Parts of Guinea and the Slave-Trade, Slavery Series, No. 11*. London: James, John, and Paul Knapton, 1734.

The *Unity*, log of, 1769-1771, Earle Family Papers, Merseyside Maritime Museum, Liverpool, D/EARLE/1/4 (no pagination).

For a complete bibliography of sources see rebhallphd.org

A Conversation with the Author

Why a graphic narrative?

Graphic narrative is a powerful medium that allowed me to accomplish what I couldn't in any other format. The use of text and images in a complex back-and-forth relationship allowed me to put the past right up against the present, which was crucial for this book. It also allowed me to make this story more accessible while keeping its complexity. The sources on enslaved women are only fragments in the archive. The structure of the medium—panels with gutters (the blank space between panels)—is uniquely suited to recover and honor these stories and restore them to the historical record.

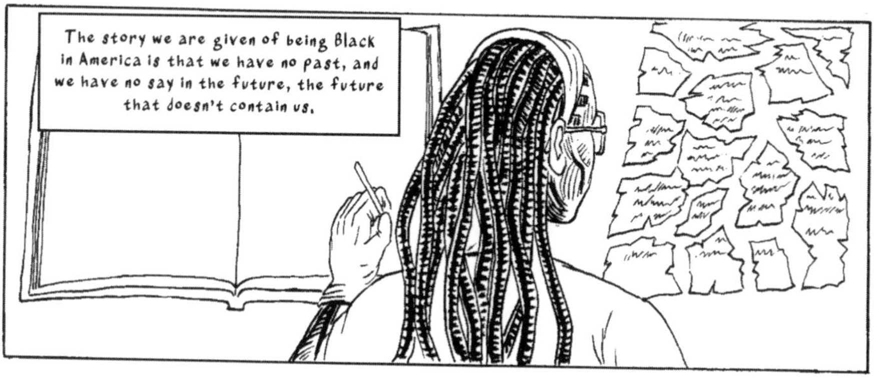
The story we are given of being Black in America is that we have no past, and we have no say in the future, the future that doesn't contain us.

The graphic narrative format is a powerful methodology for portraying what I call the "shape of absence." Hugo and I do this here, while also breaking the pacing of the panel/gutter arrangement to then push at the form's boundaries to create more emotional impact. Here, the four women prosecuted for their involvement in the New York City Slave Revolt of 1712, drawn in blank outline, push up through the gutter and pierce through the panel above where I sit, researching them.

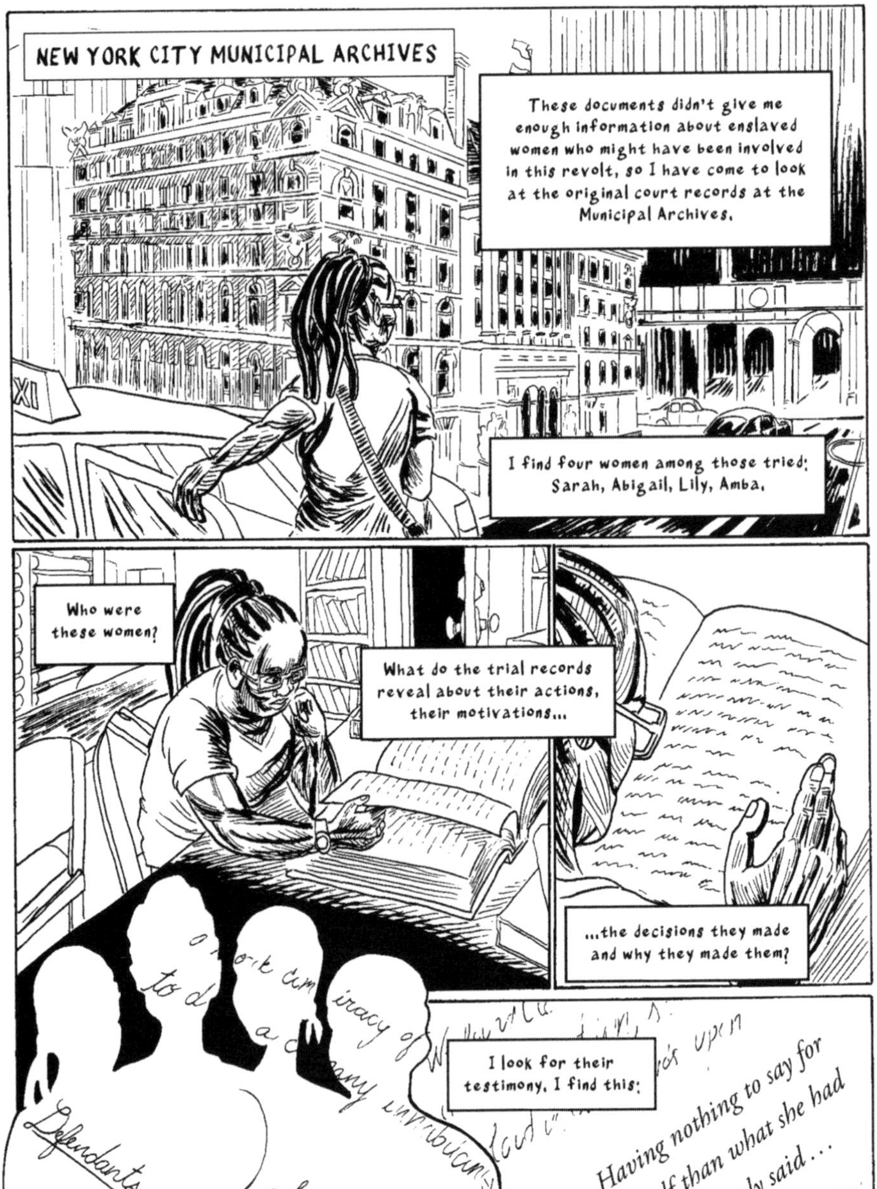
NEW YORK CITY MUNICIPAL ARCHIVES
These documents didn't give me enough information about enslaved women who might have been involved in this revolt, so I have come to look at the original court records at the Municipal Archives.
I find four women among those tried: Sarah, Abigail, Lily, Amba.
Who were these women?
What do the trial records reveal about their actions, their motivations...
...the decisions they made and why they made them?
I look for their testimony. I find this:
Defendants
Sarah
Abigail
Lily
Amba
Having nothing to say for herself than what she had previously said . . .

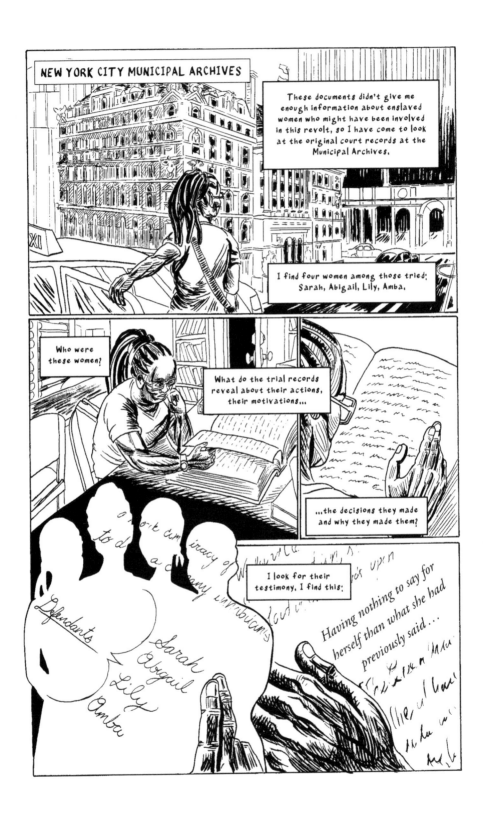

Why should we learn about slavery and slave resistance? Can't we just move on to Black joy?

I am all for Black joy! But in order to have it, we need to honor the powerful resilience and resistance of our ancestors. Otherwise, Black people become burdened with shame about our history and thus ourselves. Our joy becomes shallow, rootless. A certain hip-hop artist recently said that since slavery lasted so long, it must have been a choice. During the George Floyd uprisings, I saw a photo of a young woman wearing a T-shirt that said: "We are NOT our ancestors. We will f*ck you up!" It made me sad, because the history of slave resistance is taught so poorly, if it is taught at all. We need to know this history so we can take pride in it, so we can draw on the strength and power of our ancestors to fight for the change we need.

Unfortunately we can't "just move on." If we are going to understand our present and how to change it, we need to understand the past. The United States is plagued by the legacy of slavery. The history we are taught in high school is usually one long process of erasing resistance, and erasing how social change actually happens. Grounding our joy firmly in the power of our ancestors is ancestry in progress, and it is the path to Black joy.

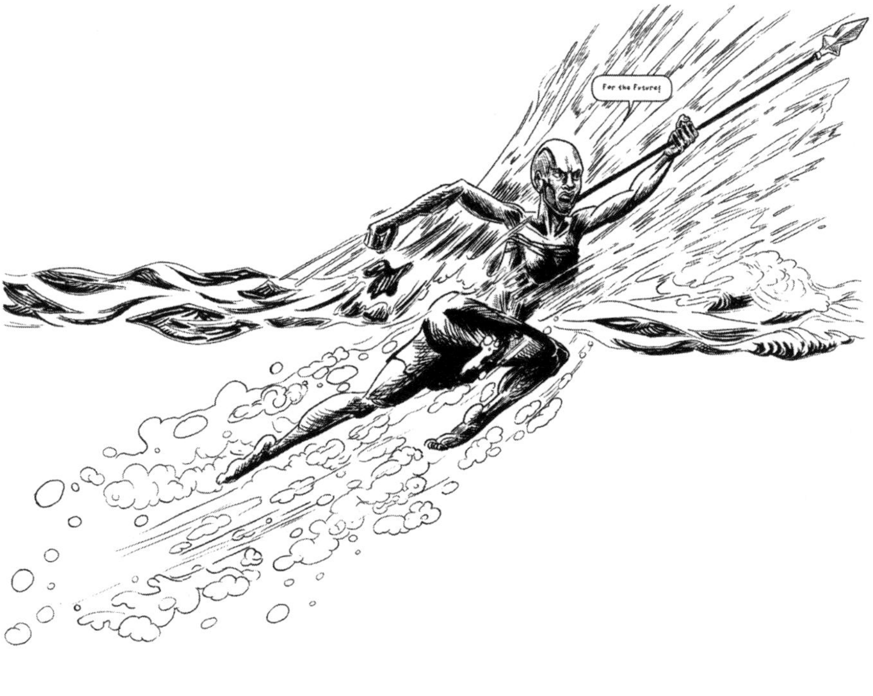
For the Future!

Why does *Wake* focus on the eighteenth century?

In *Wake*, I talk about how I left the practice of law to go back and study this history. I knew that the history of slavery was deforming the justice system and the world around us, but I didn't understand how.

I study racialized gender. I focus specifically on how concepts of race and gender were used to create the law of chattel slavery and how this still shapes our lives today. Slavery unfortunately existed in many times and in many places, but the race-based chattel slavery in the Americas was a uniquely horrible new thing introduced in the early colonial period, and it continues to structure systems of race and gender today. This form of chattel slavery, in which Black people were transformed into property and their children inherited this status, was created by law in the Americas in this early period. It takes a lot to legally turn people into property. In order to make this happen, the new laws that established chattel slavery created two genders of women: white women who gave birth to heirs of property, and Black women who gave birth to property. People who give birth to property and people who are born property are thereby constructed as subhuman.

This is what drew me to that early time period. And as I quickly found in graduate school, it is a bad mental health formula to study slavery and not study slave resistance. This is how I came to the study of slave revolt.

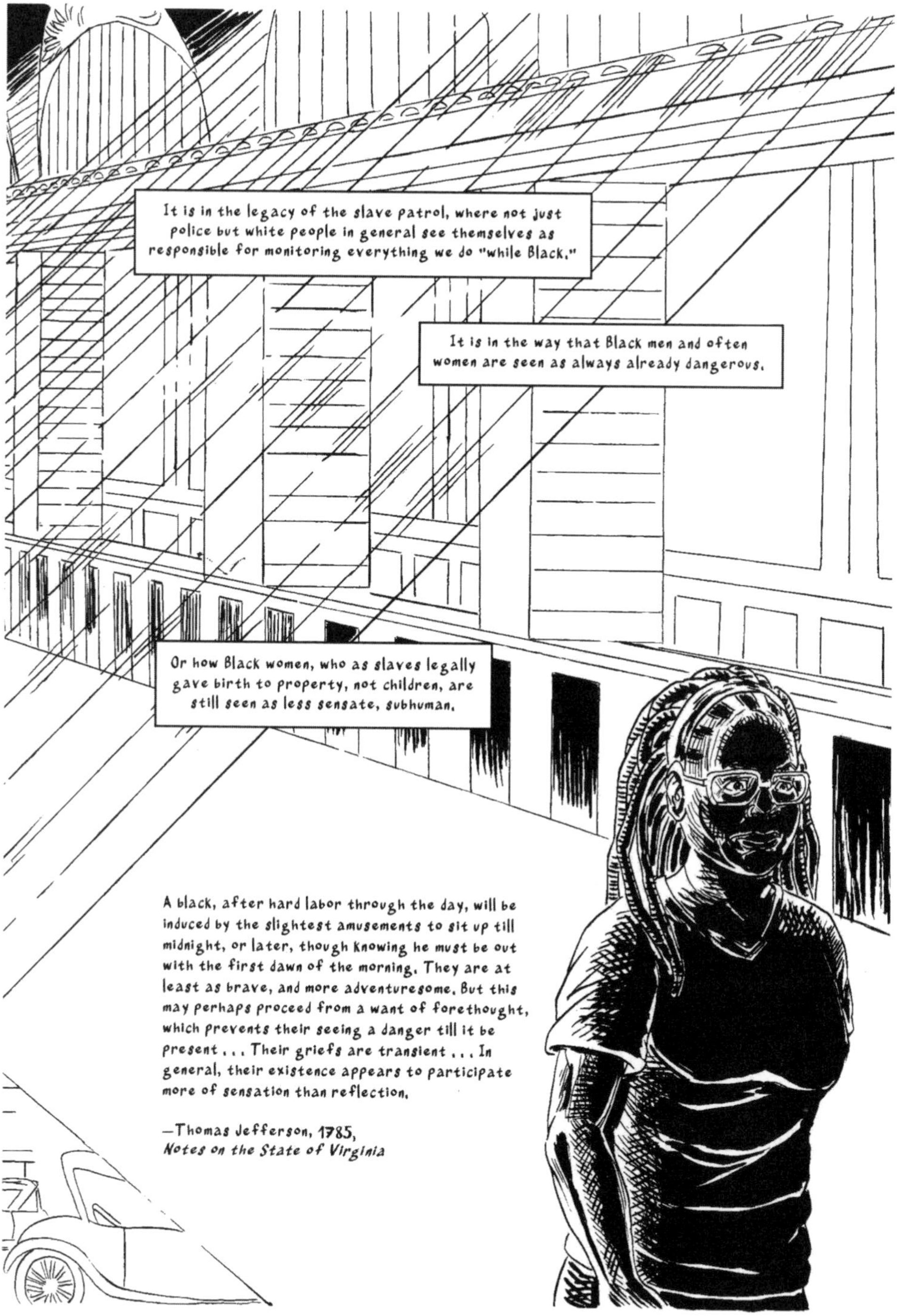
It is in the legacy of the slave patrol, where not just police but white people in general see themselves as responsible for monitoring everything we do "while Black."
It is in the way that Black men and often women are seen as always already dangerous.
Or how Black women, who as slaves legally gave birth to property, not children, are still seen as less sensate, subhuman.
A black, after hard labor through the day, will be induced by the slightest amusements to sit up till midnight, or later, though knowing he must be out with the first dawn of the morning. They are at least as brave, and more adventuresome. But this may perhaps proceed from a want of forethought, which prevents their seeing a danger till it be present . . . Their griefs are transient . . . In general, their existence appears to participate more of sensation than reflection.
—Thomas Jefferson, 1785,
Notes on the State of Virginia

Why New York City?

I'm from New York City and have always been drawn to its history. Yet I didn't learn until graduate school about just how central both the institution of slavery and the slave trade were in the creation and building of New York City as the world's financial capital.

If people are taught the history of slavery, they are taught that it was a southern, rural institution. But slavery existed everywhere in the British colonies and continued to exist in parts of the northern United States well into the nineteenth century. Enslaved labor was used to build and run urban areas as well as rural areas. Enslaved people built the infrastructure of New York City: the roads, the docks, even the wall that protected the city from Indigenous people trying to get their land back. That wall ran the length of what is now called Wall Street.

In 1700, half of the white population of New York City owned slaves. Enslaved people made up over 20 percent of the population. The only other city that had a higher population of enslaved people in 1700 was Charleston, South Carolina.

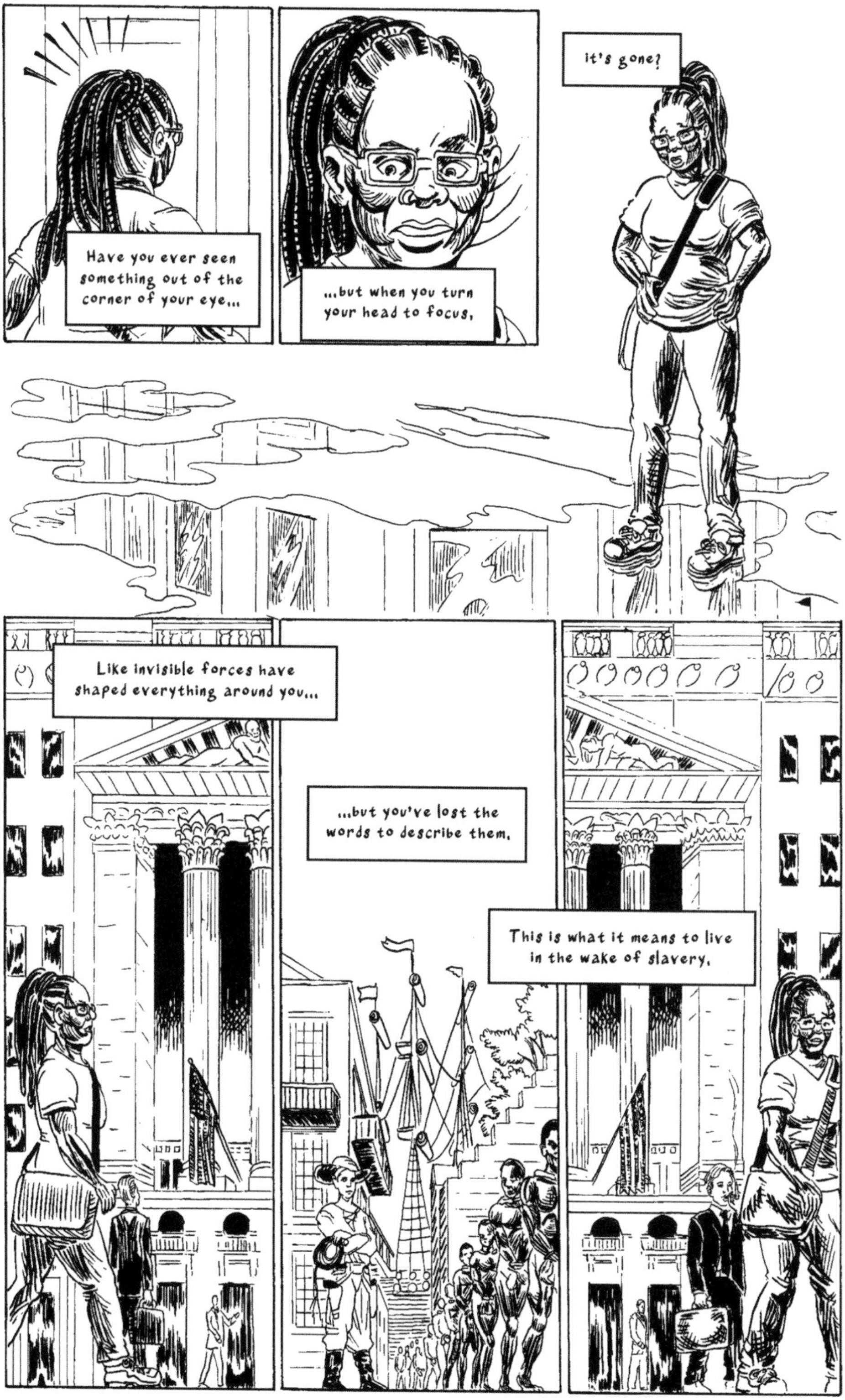
Have you ever seen something out of the corner of your eye...
...but when you turn your head to focus,
it's gone?
Like invisible forces have shaped everything around you...
...but you've lost the words to describe them.
This is what it means to live in the wake of slavery.

Why is the history of women in slave revolts "hidden"?

To understand why the role of women in slave revolts has been erased from history, it is necessary to understand something called "historiography" and how it differs from history. History is the event in the past being studied. Historiography is the study of how history is written and what factors shape the historical interpretation of the past. All historical writing is someone's perspective. Historiography traces those perspectives and what shaped them. It is the study of how those perspectives shift over time and why. This is actually really important! Historians always write in a social and political context, and this shapes how they write about the past. They also write in conversation with other historians' interpretations of the past. In *Wake*, I show how historians claimed that women didn't participate in slave revolts despite the fact that their participation was documented in the records created at the time of those events. But why did historians leave women out of the story?

The perspective of the historians who first wrote about the history of slave resistance was that there was none. Mainstream history taught that slavery was a benign institution, a civilizing force, and no one wanted to resist it. When these blatant racists were no longer part of the mainstream, other historians started focusing on recovering the story of slave revolts from the archives. When this shift happened in the late 1960s and 1970s, US culture was saturated with the idea that Black people lived in their own subculture, created during slavery, that was responsible for the poverty and disenfranchisement they faced. It was caused not by systemic racism and economic exploitation, but by this so-called defective culture, caused by having the "wrong" gender roles. Black women were matriarchs who emasculated Black men, and therefore Black people as a whole would never succeed unless they changed their gender roles. The historians who were interpreting the history of revolt insisted that this was not true. That Black people always had the "correct" gender roles. That Black women "did not undermine their men" by participating in organized violent uprisings like revolts.

No historian pushed back at this sexist interpretation, even during the later rise of feminist historiography. The study of women's history became more mainstream in the 1980s and onward, and these historians focused on recovering and honoring what they saw as more "feminine" types of resistance. This included "individual" acts of violence, like poisonings or arson, or acts that were less violent and less confrontational, like breaking tools or feigning illness. These historians wanted to honor this type of resistance, and I agree. It should be reclaimed and honored.

When I was working on my dissertation at the turn of the century, my research and interpretation rejected the original idea that women weren't involved in revolts. I received a lot of pushback. The idea is still seen by many as controversial, despite the existence of historical records proving otherwise. That is the power of historiography!

What does "the measured use of historical imagination" mean? How is it different from fiction?

All history is written by historians who use sources to then create a vision of what happened in the past. But sometimes the records fall completely silent, as they often did in my research for *Wake*. But instead of just giving up and leaving the lives of these women in complete silence, I use the same historical training to take this process one step further and try to reconstruct what *could* have happened. I call this "the measured use of historical imagination." And in the one and a half of the ten chapters in *Wake* where I do this, I clearly let the reader know when I am doing so, to keep integrity in the process.

Perhaps Woman No. 4 and Woman No. 10 were Ahosi too, I want to know their stories, but all I can do for them is imagine their story, imagine their struggle, with all I know of their kingdom's history.

With a measured use of historical imagination, I can reconstruct the story of how these two Ahosi warriors ended up on the *Unity*...and died fighting their captors during a slave ship revolt.

For example, in imagining and creating visuals for the stories of the women involved in the New York City Slave Revolt of 1712, there is not one cobblestone, not one plant, not one city layout, that wasn't carefully researched.

The oathing ceremony in chapter 3, only briefly referred to in the colonial governor's correspondence, is drawn from sources in another British colony where the enslaved people were also predominantly Akan. These documents, which described in detail how these ceremonies work, were created to prevent slave revolts. It cautioned enslavers about what to be on watch for. If they saw an enslaved person gathering graveyard dirt, it was probably for an oathing ceremony and a revolt was being planned. This allowed Hugo and me to use those detailed descriptions to visualize the oathing ceremony that occurred before the revolt.

Since there are obviously no photos of the city in the early 1700s, I used the first two decades of eighteenth-century city council meetings to get a sense of what New York City looked like. The council minutes reveal incredibly useful details in their recording of mundane disputes about things like how to light the streets and who had to pay for the candles, or passing an ordinance that a specific neighborhood had to do a better job weeding around their houses for fire prevention. This allowed us to visualize the city. I also used forensic anthropologists' analysis of the skeletons in the African Burial Ground, which showed that men and women were forced to do equally hard labor. There were even skeletons of women who had died from skull collapse from carrying heavy loads. Burial arrangements with specific grave goods showed that one woman was likely an Obeah priestess. We even know how many of those buried were originally born in Africa by analyzing nutrition patterns. Those born in Africa started with good nutrition that then deteriorated after being taken to New York City, whereas enslaved people born in New York City had poor nutrition from the start.

The measured use of historical imagination, as opposed to fiction, describes only what absolutely could have happened. For that reason, I felt comfortable using it in *Wake*.